esualdo

Marenzio

Italian Madrigal/Alfred Einstein

ove's Dictionary of Music

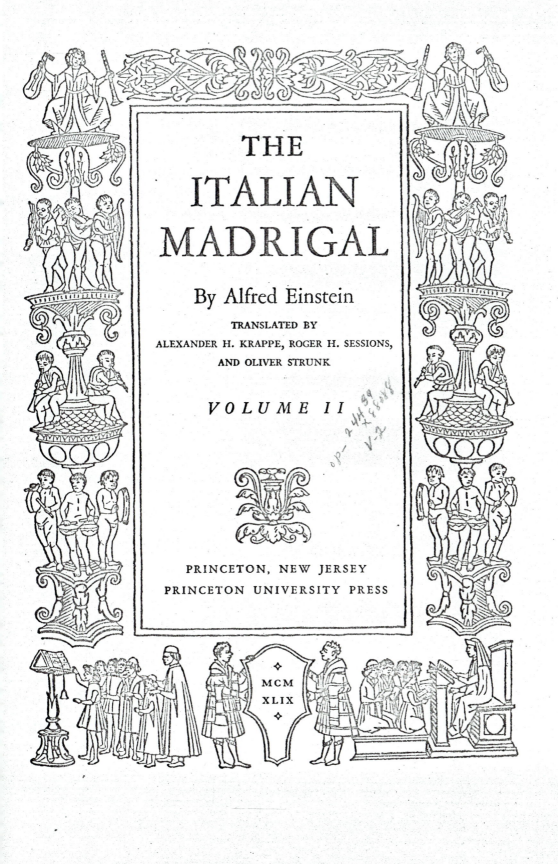

THE
ITALIAN
MADRIGAL

By Alfred Einstein

TRANSLATED BY
ALEXANDER H. KRAPPE, ROGER H. SESSIONS,
AND OLIVER STRUNK

VOLUME II

PRINCETON, NEW JERSEY
PRINCETON UNIVERSITY PRESS

MCM
XLIX

THE ITALIAN MADRIGAL

PRINTED IN THE UNITED STATES OF AMERICA BY PRINCETON
UNIVERSITY PRESS AT PRINCETON, NEW JERSEY
LONDON: GEOFFREY CUMBERLEGE
OXFORD UNIVERSITY PRESS

DESIGNED BY P. J. CONKWRIGHT

THE PUBLICATION OF THIS BOOK
HAS BEEN AIDED BY GRANTS FROM THE CARNEGIE CORPORATION OF NEW YORK
THROUGH THE AMERICAN COUNCIL OF LEARNED SOCIETIES
AND FROM THE WESLEY WEYMAN FUND

THE ITALIAN MADRIGAL

CHAPTER VI · THE THREE
GREAT OLTREMONTANI: LASSO, MONTE, WERT

ORLANDO DI LASSO

BEFORE turning to the madrigals of the most important of Rore's successors and of one of the greatest masters of all time, Orlando di Lasso, we must first draw some lines of demarcation and make some reservations. Lasso's work in the field of the madrigal is only a fraction of his enormous total production, indeed of his secular production as a whole, which besides the madrigal includes secular ceremonial pieces (the Latin motet), the chanson, and the German part-song. But the madrigal is perhaps the most important fraction. There can be no question about the national leanings of Orlando di Lasso, the international or cosmopolitan master from Mons in Hainaut; that for which he entertained the liveliest affection was the Italian. Lasso's madrigal reveals most strongly and clearly one aspect of the inner change that takes place in music during the second part of the sixteenth century: the increasing gloom, the trend away from gaiety, vitality, and artlessness toward contrition and a tormenting awareness, the transition from the Renaissance to the Counter Reformation. But at the side of this development, or rather, cutting across it, there is an increase in external means, which was bound to lead to a revolution. As a madrigalist Lasso begins with the crudity and lasciviousness of his Neapolitan villanelle; he ends with the gloom of the poet Luigi Tansillo's *Lagrime di San Pietro*, an excess of penance and regret, a tearful turning away from everything secular. It is the same change that took place in Tansillo himself: from the exuberant and lascivious stanzas of the *Vendemmiatore*, which was placed on the Index in 1559, to the exaggerated self reproach of the *Lagrime di San Pietro*, printed in 1585. It is the same change—indeed the same disease, religious scruples—that takes place in Torquato Tasso, except that it develops more rapidly in the shorter life of this poet (1544-1595): Tasso begins with the love songs to Laura Peperara and the pastoral play *Aminta* and ends with the solemn poem on the "Creation of the World," the *Mondo Creato*. Lasso clothes his villanelle in the lightest and most natural musical dress consistent with art, while for the spiritual poem he chooses the weightiest and most elaborate of textures, in seven real voices.

For Lasso, the composer of madrigals and villanelle, the material is almost completely accessible in the collected edition of his works, carefully prepared and annotated by Adolf Sandberger. To his commentary we should be able to add little that is new, were our task not a quite different one: that of placing Lasso's Italian secular work in its proper relation to the history of the madrigal. When we have done this, it will appear that his historical importance is relatively insignificant and that it becomes steadily less significant in the second part of his life. Unlike Verdelot, Willaert, or Rore, he invents nothing; he never seizes control of the development; he uses an already existing store of formulas. With increasing age he loses his immediate contact with Italian intellectual life, with the homeland, despite his frequent journeys through the Brenner Pass. His later madrigal publications are no longer as successful as his earlier ones; the composer of church music gradually crowds out the composer of secular music. His contemporaries felt this quite clearly, and he himself seems not to have been unaware of it. His fourth book of madrigals for five voices (1567), the last to appear in Italy, is described on the title-page as "da lui novamente in Germania composto," and in the dedication to Duke Alfonso of Ferrara a remark escapes him that is perhaps not wholly free from resentment: the world will learn, he says, that the Muses are also nourished and protected in Germany ("potrà anche il mondo conoscere che le Muse di Germania non sono punto aliene d'ogni sorte di virtù, anzi le nutriscono e conservano, secondo le qualità delli amatori et cultori suoi"). At the end of his life Lasso is a reactionary, and in a conversation with the Imperial choirmaster, Filippo di Monte, his contemporary and fellow sufferer, he complains of the change that has taken place in the musical world about him.

Yet one cannot overestimate the greatness and force of his personality. If the madrigalist Lasso was no longer fully appreciated by the world about him, despite all the honors and eulogies he received, he was the more "actual," and precisely as a madrigalist, to posterity. In his relation to his Italian contemporaries, Lasso fared much as Mozart did later: to those about him the great ultramontane Italian or Italianate *Oltremontano* was never wholly accessible. The Italian contemporaries of Palestrina and Boccherini grasped them fully, although to say this is to pass judgment only on the specifically Italian qualities in Palestrina and Boccherini and not on their importance; Mozart and Lasso they do not fully grasp.

By artistic training Lasso is an Italian through and through. At the same time he is a typically "international" composer who in later life inclined strongly toward settling at the French court, and a polyglot—except for German, which he never spoke or cared to speak correctly. Tradition has it that as a choir boy at the church of St. Nicolas in his native Mons, he was thrice kidnaped because of his beautiful voice and twice returned to his parents. But the third attempt, when he was a boy of twelve—we assume that he was born in 1532—carried him to the camp of Ferrante Gonzaga, the younger son of Isabella d'Este and the Marquis Francesco of Mantua. Ferrante, viceroy of Sicily, was then besieging St. Didier as the "gran capitano" (supreme commander) of Charles V. On the whole an unattractive figure—"a brave and capable general, but miserly beyond all measure," says Zedler's *Universal-*

Lexikon—Ferrante was a music lover and in this a true son of the famous marchioness, as we learn from a letter of the celebrated Nicolas Gombert, the Imperial choirmaster, who dedicates a motet to him on June 3, 1547, "sachant que vostre noble esprit se delecte en la musique" (cf. J. Schmidt-Görg, *Nicolas Gombert*, 1938, p. 107). Later on (before 1554) Ferrante took the musician L'Hoste da Reggio into his service as "maestro della musica," which must mean that he had his own private chapel. In three madrigal prints Hoste styles himself the holder of this office and dedicates the first to his patron, while another is dedicated to Cristoforo Fornari, the paymaster of the imperial armies in the Piedmont. Ferrante, the founder of the dynasty of Gonzaga-Guastalla, presumably picked the bright, witty, amiable boy as a companion for his daughter Ippolita to divert and encourage her in her music lessons; this sort of thing was by no means unusual in the education of princesses. (Subsequently, at the Bavarian court, Lasso occasionally resumes this office of court merrymaker.) Ippolita, who married Fabrizio Colonna, Duke of Tagliacozzo, in Milan in 1548 and Antonio Carafa di Mandragone in 1554, seems to have done honor to her musical training: Hoste and Rufilo dedicated madrigals to her.

In the summer of 1544 Ferrante takes the young Orlando with him to Fontainebleau where the peace negotiations with the gay King Francis I are in progress; after a longer stop on the way, either in Milan or Mantua, he proceeds with him to Sicily: they land at Palermo on November 1, 1545, having embarked at Genoa. But at the beginning of 1546 Ferrante is also appointed governor of Milan, and Lasso remains in the Lombard capital until 1548, when he loses his voice; from thence Constantino Castrioto, cavaliere di Malta, takes him to Naples. Naples was at this time a Spanish province, with Spanish musicians holding the highest musical offices; but it was also the home of a very flourishing native art, the scene of the activity of Gio. Domenico del Giovane da Nola, and if we may credit the *Dialoghi della Musica* of Luigi Dentice (Napoli, 1552) a center of attraction for foreign musicians: Gianleonardo dell'Arpa, Perino da Firenze, Battista Siciliano, Giaches di Ferrara. Here Lasso enters the service of the highly cultivated Giovanni Battista d'Azzia, Marchese della Terra, one of the most prominent members of the Accademia dei Sereni. Here, too, he makes the acquaintance of Giulio Cesare Brancaccio, an actor, singer, and adventurer from an old Neapolitan family, who will reappear in Lasso's life a little later on.

In 1551 the twenty-year old Lasso comes to Rome. At first he is the guest of Antonio Altoviti, Archbishop of Florence, who had good reason to reside in Rome, since as the son of the wealthy Bindo Altoviti, the most violent opponent of the Medici and especially of Duke Cosimo, he was unable to take up his ecclesiastical duties in Florence until 1567. But later on he is appointed choirmaster at S. Giovanni in Laterano, one of the highest musical offices in Rome, and as Palestrina's predecessor he occupies this post for about two years. News of the illness of his parents calls him back to his home in Flanders in 1553 or 1554. There he fails to arrive until after the death of both parents. From Flanders he is supposed to have gone to England in the company of Giulio Cesare Brancaccio, the instrument of that fantastic attempt in the summer of 1554 to win the hand of Mary Tudor, the new Queen of England, for Philip II of Spain. But there is no evidence for this English journey. All that is certain is that on May 13, 1555, Lasso published his Opus I at Antwerp, the *Primo libro dove si contengono Madrigali, Villanesche, Canzoni francesi, e Motetti a quattro voci* and that in this connection he too says nothing in his dedication about an excursion to England, for he refers to the characteristically miscellaneous contents of the print as a "part of the labors accomplished in Antwerp after his return from Rome." (Of course he may have been in Rome a second time between England and Antwerp, but this is a most unlikely conjecture.) About the same time his first book of five-voiced madrigals is published by Gardano in Venice, apparently without his knowledge.

With this Lasso's wanderings are at an end. Toward the end of 1556 he goes from Antwerp to Duke Albrecht V of Bavaria in Munich, first as a tenor in the court chapel whose director he becomes in 1563, and there he dies in 1594.

We repeat: the musician Lasso, who spent his most impressionable years—his twelfth to twenty-second—in Italy, may with justice be called an Italian artist, and it is almost superfluous for him to say of the motets as well as of the madrigals of his Opus I, in its French title: "faictz a la nouvelle composition d'aulcuns d'Italie"—"made in the new style of certain Italian masters."

There can be no question as to what this style was or who these Italian masters were. Lasso's Opus I contains among its five motets the chromatic *Alma nemes*, whose counterpart, Rore's *Calami sonum ferentes* is also included. And we have from Lasso's youthful period a half secular or humanistically sacred motet cycle, the *Prophetiae Sibyllarum*, a sort of musical companion piece to Michelangelo's representations of the Sibyls on the Sistine ceiling—a cycle for four voices whose "chromatic" inclination would be quite unthinkable without Rore's preparatory work, more exactly, without certain of Rore's four-voiced madrigals. It may be said without fear of contradiction that this work cannot have been composed later than 1560 or earlier than 1555, the date Rore's *Madrigali a quattro* appeared in print. As he grew older Lasso turned more and more away from experimental chromaticism, and it is most significant that King Charles IX of France, when parts of the *Prophetiae Sibyllarum* were sung to him, could scarcely bring himself to believe that Lasso was their author. Yet Lasso began as Rore's spiritual pupil. Surely it will not be unprofitable to trace the immediate influences to which the young Lasso was subject in Milan, Naples, and Rome; it would be difficult to overestimate the importance of his years in Naples and Rome. In Naples he becomes a composer of villanelle, in Rome of madrigals. But after Petrucci's invention, personal influences and the direct relation of master to pupil no longer have quite the same importance as in the Trecento and Quattrocento. As a composer of church music Lasso was profoundly influenced by Nicolas Gombert, the great Imperial choirmaster, whom he may perhaps have met in his youth as a canon at Tournai though he was never an actual pupil of his. To Gombert, the first great master of close-woven imitation and of a fuller and more organic way of writing, Lasso owed the conciseness of his ecclesiastical style. In choosing three chansons by Gombert as models for masses, Lasso was simply repaying a debt. But it is Cipriano de Rore who is reflected in Lasso's secular writing. In the decisive years between 1544 (when he arrives in Italy) and 1552 (when, as choirmaster at S. Giovanni in Laterano, he is a mature master), the decisive works of Rore had already made their appearance and their impression. It is absurd to suppose that Lasso did not know them or that his precocious genius did not at once assimilate them. His point of departure is no longer Verdelot or Arcadelt; it is already Willaert, Rore, and their circle. Significant, too, is his personal relation to Antonio Altoviti (1521-1573), the son of the Bindo Altoviti to whom Hubert Naich had dedicated his madrigals. For Naich belonged to Rore's immediate circle. Lasso's physical starting points as a madrigalist are Naples and Rome; his spiritual one is Rore's work. If one were to name another of his models, it would be Alfonso della Viola. Nothing whatever is known about the possible relation of Lasso to the older Ferrarese master; it seems to me, however, that their common love of color and of the close-woven texture points to an affinity between them. Lasso's reputation as a madrigalist begins in Rome. Here his scattered pieces are collected, and here Antonio Barre publishes the third book of his five-voiced madrigals (1563). Some of his texts point also to Rome.

Lasso lived until 1594. A few days before his death he signed the dedication of a madrigal print—and of one that a dying man could fittingly acknowledge: it was the *Lagrime di San Pietro* and it was dedicated to a Pope. Even after he had found a permanent home in Munich, he returned to Italy again and again—in 1562, 1567, 1574, 1578, 1585, and 1587—and strove to make himself familiar there with the new trends in musical life. Yet even at this point it is already possible to evaluate his total output as a madrigalist. Even in his later production, despite a noticeable stylistic division at the beginning of the 'eighties, he no longer departs in any inwardly significant way from the standpoint of the 'fifties and 'sixties; it is simply that his mastery is constantly increasing and that the profile of his motifs becomes more chiseled and more arresting, his harmonic style smoother and less effective in an external sense. (As a harmonist he is perhaps just as bold as are his "experimenting" contemporaries, except that he makes his effects within the half-light of the given tonal limits.) He was a man of character and no longer cared to understand that side of the spirit of the times that went beyond the spiritual and lost itself in the sensuous. This is perhaps connected with the spells of depression whose visitations become more and more frequent after 1574 and which led in the end to complete melancholia. The melancholy man knows as an antithesis the coarseness and gaiety of Lasso's villanelle, but not the lasciviousness and over-refinement of pastoral sensuality. Between Lasso's *napoletane* and his madrigals there can be no middle ground. In the work of Filippo di Monte, his contemporary and colleague at the imperial court, there is a noticeable break: Monte is aware that in the isolation of provincial Prague he has as it were lost contact; thus he hastens to turn to the lighter, more sensuous, pastoral form of madrigal—a sad spectacle in an older master. But with very few exceptions, there existed for Lasso within the limits of the genus only the noble and serious madrigal, and even this he regarded as a lighter species than the motet. In the madrigal Lasso avoids any rigid relation of the voices. Only in the madrigal book of 1585, dedicated to a connoisseur, Count Bevilacqua of Verona, does he conclude with a composition for six voices in a canon in which the second cantus follows the first at the unison—like an echo. From the 'seventies on, the favorite poet of the madrigalists, apart from Torquato Tasso, is Giambattista Guarini. For Lasso, Guarini does not exist at all, and Tasso seems to exist only in connection with a text set to order or in competition. Lasso is the composer of Petrarch—whom he explores from many sides, though not from all. He avoids the setting of sonnets previously set by Rore—a further proof, it seems to me, that Rore was his point of departure and that he wished to avoid entering into competition with him. In his choice of texts he is guided by musical, not literary, considerations. He has no scruples about mutilating single sonnets and does not hesitate to link the tercets of a sonnet with a sestina stanza

Ov'è condotto il mio amoroso stile

whenever he thinks this justified for musical or poetic reasons. Much that seems to reflect a "literary" choice is actually occasional composition, thus for example the sequence of Ariosto's five stanzas in praise of Alcina, in the mixed print of 1573, which is simply vocal banquet music for a wedding in the Fugger family. For the same occasion and as a special joke, Lasso sets to music for these "economic royalists" of the sixteenth century the Praise of Poverty from the *Orlando furioso*:

> Spesso in poveri alberghi e in picciol tetti
> Nelle calamitadi e nei disagi
> Meglio s'aggiungon d'amicizia i petti,
> Che fra ricchezze invidiosi ed agi

Delle piéne d'insidie e di sospetti
Corti regali e splendidi palagi,
Ove la caritate è in tutto estinta,
Ne si vede amicizia se non finta.

Lasso is likewise writing for an occasion when in his madrigals of 1585 for Count Bevilacqua he sets to music the following strange text from Petrarch's *Trionfo della fama* (III, 1-6), one that the Florentine composer Bernardo Giacomini had already set, with a similar intention, as early as 1563:

Io non sapea da tal vista levarme;
Quand'io udii: "Pon mente all'altro lato;
Che s'acquista ben pregio altro che d'arme."
Volsimi da man manca, e vidi Plato,
Che'n quella schiera andò più presso al segno
Al qual aggiunge a chi [cui?] dal cielo è dato.

This pays homage to the art-loving count in Verona and to his musical *ridotto*, which is compared to Plato's academy. And Lasso sets it to music accordingly, in the elaborately representative style. That Lasso remained throughout his life a reactionary composer in a certain external sense is also reflected in his attitude toward rhythm. He uses the *misura di breve* almost exclusively—the exceptions are to be counted—and in the one or two instances where he actually indicates four-four time instead of four-two, he seems to do so without any particular intention. I need only compare his two settings (1560 and 1562) of the quatrains from Petrarch's sonnet

In dubbio di mio stato.

One is in *note bianche*, the other in *note nere* (VIII, 1, 13 and 1, 16): the difference is purely external. (The comparison also shows the exact and rigid workings of Lasso's imagination: in either case the sixth line is for three voices, while the two settings of the seventh line use exactly the same motif.) One or two of his pieces, floating uniformly in their movement and written throughout in the *misura di breve*, do not differ in appearance from madrigals by Festa or Verdelot.

But for the rest it is Lasso himself who is one of the greatest masters of rhythmic flexibility. In earlier madrigals from the 'fifties and 'sixties whose chronology is not established in individual cases—for it seems that most of the contents of his second book for five voices (1559), already published two years earlier in the *Secondo libro delle Muse*, must antedate the contents of his first book (1555)—the underlying rhythm is the *misura di breve* or four-two time, but it is always susceptible to acceleration and, having once accelerated, to a return to its former animated calm or calm animation. The extreme limits of this flexibility, this heightened rhythmic resourcefulness, is reached in the last decade of Lasso's life. Between the fourth madrigal book of 1567 and the fifth of 1585 there is a division, a reversal of the rhythmic premise, a reversal which is at the same time austere and audacious in its harmonies, already foreshadowed as early as 1565 in a sestina

Si come al chiaro giorno.

Lasso holds fast to his usual notation (¢), but the unit is no longer the half note but the quarter, and the rhythm no longer flows from andante to animato and back but from animato to ritardando and largo. And since Lasso now goes on to subdivide the quarter note into eighths, his flexible tempo has at its disposal three possibilities of contrast which flow constantly from one into another. The change to triple time is rarely used: Lasso does not need this stimulus. How deliberately he makes use of these possibilities may be seen in an early example, in which by way of exception he passes from accelerato to andante, to represent the "quiet nights" of a Petrarch sestina stanza:

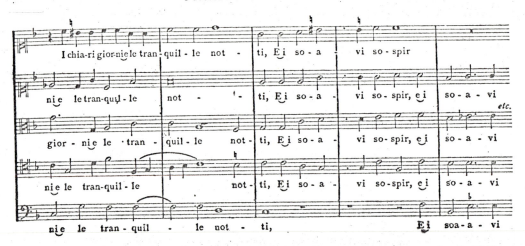

The quieter flow which begins at this point is again accelerated at the half line

Volti *subitamente*

and then brought to a definite stop at its continuation

in doglia e pianto.

At another time, in *Occhi piangete, accompagnate il core,* the first quatrain of a Petrarch sonnet from the Antwerp Opus I (1555), a dialogue *en miniature,* he sets the question to music in a broad tempo, the answer in a more animated one; that he opens this answer with paired voices, with "duality," is one of those archaic, naïvely symbolic features which he is sometimes unwilling to do without. When he sets the Petrarch canzone that turns on the flight of time:

Il tempo passa e l'hore son si pronte . . .

it is only natural that he should resort to the combination or simultaneity of the two *misure.* Two contrasted voices symbolize the brevity of human existence:

Lasso is serious in his treatment of the poet's oxymora, the immediate juxtaposition of contrasted images. This is the *musica riservata*, the "new style" defined as follows by Samuel Quickelberg, the commentator on Lasso's penitential psalms in the illuminated codex at Munich: ". . . ad res et verba accomodando, singulorum affectuum vim exprimendo, rem quasi actam ante oculos ponendo . . ." (Sandberger, *Beiträge*, 1, 56, note 2).

As we know, Lasso is not the inventor of this style; on the contrary, for every possible symbol of expression he has at his disposal a ready-made formula, and he has only to utilize it. What distinguishes him is the plasticity and forcefulness with which he uses them. And essential to forcefulness is brevity. Compared with Willaert or Rore, Lasso is, as it were, impatient: he aims to exhaust the musical possibilities of a text quickly and energetically. To resort to the measuring-rod: for the musical setting of Petrarch's sonnet *Mentre che'l cor* Willaert requires 118 measures, Lasso only 81. And the artistic means for attaining the most concise effect is not the line, which expands or is spun out, but the chord, the harmonic factor. In this, however, Lasso avoids the extreme, and avoids it more and more as time goes on. His tonality is fundamentally "neutral," and his harmonic pendulum swings in either direction. A "colorful," "chromatic" line, as in the sonnet

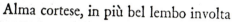

Alma cortese, in più bel lembo involta

where he passes from G minor to B major through the harmonic semicircle: g C F D G C E a A D B, is just as rare as the literal imitation of a genuinely chromatic motif, as seen in the first example on next page. But as the following opening shows, Lasso knew from the start how to interpret Petrarch's oxymora through the use of purely harmonic symbols, and he did this with astonishing conciseness and concentration (see second example on next page).

Each voice expresses the contrast in a different way, and each expresses it with the

same force. Willaert's music for the same opening (cf. above, p. 337) is by comparison old-fashioned and awkward. Or to take another example, we need only compare

the beginning of a sonnet by Petrarch as set by Lodovico Fogliano and Lasso to see
reflected in the two beginnings, which are thematically identical, the change in style
that has taken place within eight years and the discrepancy, not only between two
representatives of different generations, but also between two personalities, one
contemplative, the other active:

To get over the ground quickly, Lasso deprives the bass of its first line instead of
repeating the line with five voices or with another combination of four; he has
developed an entirely new sense for harmonic conciseness in homophonic writing.
The passage may serve to refute the familiar assertion that "harmony," two-dimensional art, and the vertical point of view are indigenous to the "South" and that
"polyphony" and the linear point of view are indigenous to the "North," an assertion
which, in its broad formulation, is as erroneous as all other "racial" generalizations.
Lasso, the Fleming, is no more "polyphonic" than Giovanni Luigi from Palestrina
in the Sabine hills or Andrea Gabrieli from Canareggio. He is capable of purely

homophonic declamation or purely chordal progression, as in the tercet from one of Petrarch's sonnets (1562, VIII, I, 14):

> Ben veggio di lontan'il dolce lume

where only the concept "sospiri" gives rise to the usual naturalistic pauses and the usual play on motives; or in the dedicatory madrigal addressed to a noble lady (1564; VIII, I, 17)

> Alma real, dignissima d'impero,
> Chi vede, quant'in voi natura ascose . . .

where there is only a single line in imitation with a motif running through all the voices. The difference between Palestrina and Lasso is not a difference of race or style but a difference of personal temperament; in a similar way, Johann Sebastian Bach is not the supreme master of polyphony because he is a German, a Thuringian, or (as some would have it) a "Gothic" master, but simply because he is Bach—this follows sufficiently from the homophonic, two-dimensional motets of other Thuringian members of the Bach family.

This does not mean that Lasso did not sometimes abandon his harmonic incisiveness to spin out a motif or round out the form. Lasso is also a universal master in that he has at his disposal *all* means and *all* forms. One of the five-part madrigals of 1557, Fortunio Spira's sonnet

> Volgi cor mio, la tua speranza homai

contains in its *prima parte* an outstanding example of contrapuntal freedom: the soprano illumines the other parts like a ray of sunlight:

But in the *seconda parte* there occurs an interweaving of motifs which when repeated extends over sixteen measures:

It is this sort of motival work that Monteverdi carries to the point of exaggeration and that recurs in a similar form in the last quartets of Beethoven.

Most characteristic for Lasso are the pieces and passages in which "graphic" and "harmonic" symbolism are combined. Such a combination occurs, for example, in the following four measures from a setting (printed in 1563) of Petrarch's sonnet

Amor che vedi ogni pensier aperto.

Three voices—soprano, alto, and bass—are "graphic"; the two inner voices fill in and have a purely harmonic function. Lasso feels altogether too great a need for expression to declaim his text homophonically in the manner of Arcadelt, and is at the same time far too impatient to carry the music of a single line through all the voices in the motivically expansive manner of Willaert. He thus arrives at a solution that is wholly personal.

Although Lasso composed a hundred pieces in one and two sections, he is preeminently a composer of sestine and canzoni. Indeed one might say that the sestina stanza is particularly suited to his musical requirements, as is the ottava with its brevity and its inevitable trick of inverting the expressive word. Some of his cycles are occasional compositions, thus for example the early sestina that opens the Antwerp print of 1555

> Del freddo Rheno a la sinistra riva . . .

a song for a betrothal or wedding; there may be an allusion to the bride's name in the lines

> Dir volsi 'o nume' e sorrise ella e'l sole
> Ch'io dissi 'o neme' . . .

Another occasional piece is the sestina presented to Duke Alfonso d'Este on his visit to Munich, printed in 1565:

> Qual nemica fortuna oltra quest'alpe.

Other cycles are music for the academies, chamber music for connoisseurs, thus for example the canzone by Gabriele Fiamma that closes the madrigal print of 1585, dedicated to Conte Mario Bevilacqua in Verona and to his famous *ridotto*.

In all this Lasso nearly always holds fast to an unchanging number of voices; the only exceptions are the above-mentioned sestina for Duke Alfonso and *Non ha tante animali* in the *Terzo libro a cinque*. Here too he follows Rore's example rather than Vincenzo Ruffo's. But strangely enough he never strives for thematic unity. In the sestina, with its progressive permutations of the six key-words, like combinations turned up by mechanical dice, one might expect to find repetitions of particular motifs. Nothing of the sort occurs in Lasso or in any of his contemporaries. Only in the late "Mermann madrigals" of 1587, which are already under the influence of Marenzio, does Lasso consistently bring out the key-words "venti" and "corso" in G. Fiamma's sestina *Per aspro mar*, varying his treatment of them for illustrative reasons. Impulsive and direct, Lasso shows remarkably little feeling for the intertwining of motifs and for any formal "rounding out." In a bipartite wedding song (1565) for Alessandro Farnese and Maria of Portugal (VIII, 1, 24), *Vieni, dolc'Imeneo, vieni e infiamma*, he ends by literally repeating the first ten measures of the opening, but this is a festal piece, in spite of its modest four-voiced texture. (Quite familiar in tone is the *lontananza* in which the speaker is presumably this same Maria: *Quando fia mai quel giorno*.) The "academic" cycles are chamber music, and Giulio Bonagionta, who edited a collection of them (1568[1]), names their chief characteristic when he speaks of "a kind of music in which the harmonies correspond closely to the 'points' of the poem"—"una Musica, che rende concenti molti proprij alli concetti delle parole." It is not a question of well-balanced form, but of truth and plasticity in expression.

One of Lasso's earliest canzoni is at the same time one of his best; printed by Antonio Barre and published by Gio. Batt. Bruno in Rome in 1557, though presumably written in 1553, it was later reprinted as the first number of the *Secondo libro a cinque* (1559). It is a setting of Petrarch's canzone of the "six visions," on the transience of the beautiful:

> Standomi un giorno, solo, alla finestra

a work that may well have been intended for the edification during Holy Week of some devout but also humanistically minded circle in Rome. The poet has six visions: the hind which is torn to pieces by two hounds, the ship with the silken sails, driven against a reef by the east wind; the celestial laurel tree which is shattered by lightning; the clear spring at which the nymphs and muses tarry and which is swallowed up by a chasm; the phoenix which, seemingly deathless, takes its own life; and the woman in the bloom of youth who, like Euridice, is killed by a snake-bite:

> "... ogni cosa al fin vola ...
> ... ahi null'altro che pianto al mondo dura!"

Each of the stanzas arranges its content in the same way: first the idyllic narrative, then the transition to gloom and the catastrophe. Following this plan, Lasso begins as a rule with the rhythm of the narrator or of the anecdotal French chanson, which he has known since early childhood: ♢ · ♦ ♢ or ♦ ♦ ♦ ♦ ♦ ♦; following the thread of the poem, he then passes on in an almost imperceptible sweep from the narrative to the dramatic description, from repose to animation. This canzone is the artistic justification of the flexible tempo and of the highly artificial form of the madrigal in general. One has only to imagine Petrarch's poem in any other musical dress, perhaps disguised as a cantata for solo voice with instrumental accompaniment with every incident realistically described, to realize that the form of the madrigal is the one intrinsically possible and intrinsically adequate embodiment of the poem in music. A passage from the fifth stanza (*Una strania fenice*) will show how description, illustration, and subjective feeling merge with one another:

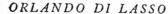

This hurrying forward toward an outburst, with the ensuing pause for all the voices and the entrance in a new tempo, quasi largo—of such a contrast the first generation of madrigalists had not yet dreamed; it is a testimony to the dramatic power with which Lasso was imbued. Had he been born forty or fifty years later, he would have been one of Monteverdi's fellow revolutionaries.

Lasso's dramatic instinct prevents his carrying the hunt for metaphors too far. Compared with most of his contemporaries, he is sparing in his use of symbolism; he seems still more so when compared with the generation that followed. Together with the canzone just discussed, the collection of 1557 also contains Lasso's music for Bernardo Tasso's fine stanza

Vostro fui, vostro son, e sarò vostro . . .

This was often set to music and one such setting appeared three years later in a madrigal book of the Bolognese Gio. Tom. Lambertini. This artist can scarcely control his excitement and his tendency to paint details. For the line

Negri e ardenti fian le nevi e'l gelo

he uses the black notation; in the line

> Per *cangiar* clima e *variar* di pelo

he changes the tonality to A-flat and the time to three-four; and at the line

> Anzi *crescerà* sempr'il mio bel foco

he changes the time to three-one. Scholars who believe in a "spirit of the age" will certainly class this composition as "baroque." Nothing of the kind occurs in Lasso. He does not paint; he sets the ethos of the poem to music: the repose and stability have their roots in inner animation.

As he grows older, Lasso becomes the specific master of the Counter Reformation —even in his secular work. He now confines himself to religious madrigals—*madrigali spirituali*—and his "newly composed" (*nuovamente composti*) madrigals of 1585, dedicated to Count Mario Bevilacqua, are exclusively devoted to two ascetic poets: the Petrarch who has definitely renounced this world, and Gabriele Fiamma, canon at the Lateran and bishop of Chioggia, whose *rime spirituali*, which first appeared in 1568, were expressly meant to "lead Italian poetry back to virtue and to God" (*ritornata . . . la poesia toscana alla virtù ed a Dio*). Fiamma's first sonnet, which opens this madrigal print of 1585, is a manifesto:

> De l'eterne tue sante alme faville
> Tal foco in me, sommo Signor, s'accende,
> Che pur non dentro l'alm'accesa rende,
> Ma fuori ancor convien ch'ard'e sfaville.
>
> E tanto l'hore mie liete e tranquille
> Fa questo ardor, mentre mi strugge e'ncende,
> Che di lui bramo, ovunque il sol risplende,
> Poter l'alm'infiammar a mille a mille.
>
> Per questo alti misteri, occulti sensi
> Vorrei scoprir de le sacrate carte
> Con affetto, e con stil purgato e mondo.
>
> Tu, che le gratie, almo Signor, dispensi,
> Giungi a sì bel desio l'ingegno e l'arte,
> Perch'arda meco del tuo amore il mondo!

"Con affetto, e con stil purgato e mondo" — "with passionate zeal, and purified and cleansed in style"! But also in a style of extreme plasticity. There is a marvelous symbolism in the progression of the middle voice, resolute and unperturbed, amid the crowding and pushing of the outer pairs:

Lasso feels himself an old man and, taking a text from Petrarch's *Trionfi* (*Trionfo del Tempo*, vv. 70-78) which he had already set somewhat playfully for six voices the year before (1584), he assumes the role of an ironic exhorter of the young:

> Hor vi riconfortate in vostre fole,
> Giovani, e misurate il tempo largo;
> Chè piaga anteveduta assai men duole.
> Forse ch'indarno mie parole spargo;
> Ma io v'annunzio che voi sete offesi
> Di un grave e mortifero letargo:
> Che volan l'ore, i giorni e gli anni e i mesi;
> E insieme, col brevissimo intervallo
> Tutti havemo a cercar altri paesi.

It is in keeping with Lasso's mature and final mastery of the treatment of the "flexible tempo" and with the gloomy view he takes of human life and eternity that in so many pieces of this madrigal book the theme is time and its relativity. Among the four-, five-, and six-voiced madrigals, dedicated in 1587 to his Munich friend, Thomas Mermann, physician in ordinary to the Duke, one finds an occasional "secular" piece: dramatic ottave from the *Orlando furioso*, for example the wounded Zerbino's halting address to Isabella (XXIV, 78), Sacripante's love lament (I, 41), even thoroughly amusing pastoral things that show that Lasso could not yet quite withdraw himself from his social obligations. (The very year of Lasso's death saw his most frivolous contribution to the literature of the pastoral madrigal: a composition half in dialogue form: *Silen di rose ha'l volto*, from a collection entitled *Il bon bacio. . . .*) But the *madrigali spirituali* predominate, and the poet Fiamma occupies a prominent place; for sheer length (though not for inner worth) the chief number in the print is a paraphrase of Psalm VI by Antonio Beccuti, detto

Coppetta, an anticipation of the psalm-settings in Benedetto Marcello's *Estro poetico-armonico*. As previously mentioned, Lasso concludes his life work with the enormous cycle of the *Lagrime di S. Pietro*; it is in twenty sections, half narrative, half lyric expansion, a spiritual counterpart to the cycles from the great epics of Ariosto and Tasso, an old man's work, comparable in its artistry, its dimensions, its asceticism only to the "Musical Offering" and the "Art of the Fugue." An anticipation of this work—and more than an anticipation in spirit and treatment —is the ten-voiced setting of three tercets from Petrarch's *Trionfo del Tempo* (112-115), printed in 1584:

> Passan vostri trionfi e vostre pompe,
> Passan le signorie, passano i regni;
> Ogni cosa mortal tempo interrompe ...

a composition of terrifying vividness and power, only to be measured by the standards of a Michelangelo.

It is strange that this tired old man, afflicted in his last years by psychic disturbances and religious mania, should still have published a *Libro de Villanelle, Moresche, et altre Canzoni, a 4, 5, 6 et 8 voci*—not in Italy but in Paris—even though he did so at a time (1581) when he could still enjoy himself in the company of his patron Duke William V, to whom the print is dedicated. Lasso's letters to his prince faithfully reflect his personality, both in their polyglot mixture of German, Italian, French, Spanish, and Latin, and in their alternate scurrility and seriousness: from this soil grew the apocalyptic tercets and the lascivious chansons and *villanelle alla napoletana*. In his dedication Lasso excuses the late date of the publication: "Sarebbe stato più conveniente che io havessi publicato queste mie villanelle in mia gioventù, nel qual tempo io le feci, che publicarle in questa età grave, nella quale io mi truovo ..." —"it would have been more fitting had I published these villanelle in my youth, when I wrote them, than in this my mature age...." To be sure, Lasso is not quite candid in this observation. He may have written these sixteen four-voiced compositions in his youth, but it is obvious that he must have revised them about 1580. He has given us a means of comparison himself. For the six *villanesche* among the madrigals, chansons, and motets of his first Antwerp print of 1555 are also written for four voices, wholly in the manner of Willaert's *Canzoni villanesche* of 1544: in all six he uses the upper voice of older three-voiced *napoletane* as tenor and, by adding a fourth voice, he ennobles them, "Italianizes" them, and elevates them into the realm of art. Four of these melodies we were able to identify in Fontana, the other two (*Tu traditora* and *Sto core mio*) in a previously mentioned (p. 369) collection (*Il primo libro delle Villotte*, 1560[3], No. 9). Those who know Willaert's canzoni know those of Lasso also: both have the same liveliness in maintaining the folk tone and the same seemingly unpretentious method of arrangement.

In the six pieces of 1555 Lasso follows his model faithfully: in 1581 he does so no longer. Here too it is possible to identify every one of the three-voiced models that Lasso has followed: four are by Gio. Domenico da Nola (*Ecco la Ninf'ebraica, Ad altre le voi dare, O belle fusa, S'io ti vedessi*); the others are anonymous. But he is much more independent now; he aims at comical rhythmic and contrapuntal effects; everything is much more personal and original. In one case (*Tutto lo di*) he reduced his own four-part version to the level of mere material, treating it for eight voices, for two choirs, and in dialogue form, and making it even richer rhythmically. The six- or eight-voiced writing in such pieces is in itself a joke and the ostentation is in itself absurd, since Lasso's listeners of course recalled the three-part originals. This comic intention is particularly clear in the *moresche*. We have already (p. 373) questioned the authenticity of the *moresca* (*O Lucia miau miau*) printed under the designation "d'Orlando" in the *Terzo libro delle Villotte* (1560). Lasso did not invent pieces of this sort; he simply reworked them. (It is to be presumed that the *Villanelle d'Orlando di Lassus ed altri eccellenti Musici libro secondo*, Rome, Dorico, 1555, a print unknown to Vogel and Sandberger, use Lasso's name only as an advertisement.) These elaborations of his are the crowning glory of this class of music: nothing is destroyed, everything is heightened and more vivid. But they are "salon pieces" (if we may call them so) written to amuse court society, the academies, and the Venetian patricians, the only public then able to appreciate the wit and artistry of such works.

Along with the villanelle, the Paris print of 1581 also contains a few pieces known the world over, all of which show unmistakable signs of their late date and of their "derivative" or "relative" character. Two of them, the *Echo* and the excruciatingly comic dialogue between the old Pantalone and the intoxicated Zanni in the wine cellar, will be discussed in another connection. The famous serenade of the German mercenary

Matonna mia cara

and the appearance of the fat baker

Mi me chiamere mistre righe

(the text already mentioned in Calmo's comedy *La Travaglia*, written in 1545 and performed in 1548) can no more be regarded as genuine *mascherate* than Lasso's *moresche* as genuine Neapolitan *moresche*. No longer do three or four disguised maskers appear; an "ideal" person is described in music: the honest German, thirsting for love and strumming his lute (for four voices); the lascivious baker who in older prints (cf. Ghisi, p. 127) already has a German father, "Mistre" Gal (for five voices). These have the form of the French chanson, not of the *mascherata*; it is a part of Lasso's cosmopolitan superiority that he oversteps the boundaries of national styles and exchanges the landmarks.

FILIPPO DI MONTE

IF THERE have been attempts to interpret Lasso and Palestrina as musical antipodes, and there is some justification for so doing, then Lasso and Monte are certainly musical brothers, almost musical twins, and they considered themselves as such. To an astounding degree their lives run a parallel course. Monte was born at Malines in 1521; he is therefore somewhat younger than Rore and somewhat older than Lasso. He doubtless owed his first musical training to one of the choir schools of his native town. Like Lasso he goes to Italy in his early youth—whether at first to Venice or to Rome, we do not know: the character of his early production points to both places. But about 1540 we find him as music teacher and music master in the service of Cosimo Pinelli, a noble of Genoese descent residing in Naples. He tells us this himself, dedicating his nineteenth madrigal book (1598) to a scion of this family, Don Geronimo di Ghevara. Here he recalls his long, happy years as a member of the Pinelli household: "ov'io ho passato in dolcissimi servitij molti anni della mia gioventù appresso l'Illustrissimo et Eccellentissimo Signor [Galeazzo] Duca di Cirenza, et il virtuosissimo et honoratissimo Signor Giovan Vincenzo Pinelli fratelli della Signora Madre di V. S. Illustrissima. . . ." "Many years of my youth"—this must mean at least ten—so that Monte was probably still in Naples when the young Orlando Lasso came there, and it is hardly to be supposed that the two compatriots should not have become intimately acquainted. Like Lasso he goes to Rome shortly after 1550, where in 1554 his first madrigal book was published by Giovanni Battista Bruno, the same Bruno who, three years later, will also publish the madrigals of Lasso's *Secondo libro delle Muse*. But before the end of the year he had left Rome, presumably because he had not succeeded in obtaining an appointment there, and had gone on to Antwerp, where he enjoyed the patronage of Johann Fugger: "La molta humanità mostratami da Vostra Sig. molto Illustre, et in Anversa gli anni 1554 et 55 et ultimamente l'anno passato in Augusta. . . ." So begins the dedication of his first book of *madrigali spirituali* for six voices (1583) to the wealthy baron and merchant prince. In the course of the year 1555 he must have been in London as a member of the private chapel of Philip II of Spain, then betrothed to Mary Tudor; we learn this from a noteworthy letter of the Bavarian agent and imperial vice-chancellor, Dr. Seld of Brussels (September 22, 1555), who recommends Monte to Duke Albert V as a composer: "If furthermore Your Highness should wish for a good composer, it seems to me that I should try to find you one in some other place [than Ghent, where Seld had been negotiating with Cornelius Canis]. Thus there is a suitable man in England now, in the King's chapel, Philippe de Monte by name, a native of Malines whom I know very well. He is a quiet reticent man, as modest as a girl, who has spent the greater part of his life in Italy, speaks Italian like a native, and also Latin, French, and Flemish. For the rest he is unquestionably the best composer in the whole country, especially in the field of modern music and the *musica reservata.* I now observe that he has no wish to remain in the Royal Chapel, because the other singers are all Spaniards and he the only Fleming. . . . Thus I should have for Your Highness the certainty of providing you with a better composer than His Imperial Majesty, the King of England, the King of France, or any other prince in Germany. . . ." (During these months in London Monte made the acquaintance of the very young William Byrd, and later on, in 1583 and 1584, they began a friendly exchange of compositions.)

In spite of their urgency and warmth, Seld's recommendations led to no result. Before the end of 1555 Monte had left England to return to Antwerp. From thence he soon returned to Italy where he must have made his living as a singer and occasional composer, for he seems not to have found a permanent post: neither in Naples, where he signed the dedication of his *Primo libro a 4* on September 20, 1562; nor in Florence, where he practiced music with the younger members of the grand-ducal family in 1566 (dedication of the *Secondo libro a 7*, 1600); nor in Genoa, where he may have lived for some time as the teacher of Giovanni Battista della Gostena. His longest stay was presumably in Rome, as is suggested by the appearance of some compositions of his in the collections of Antonio Barre, for example in the *Terzo libro delle Muse a 4* of 1562 (unknown to Vogel), in which Barre publishes certain "belli parti, che quasi per negligentia de i padri perivano" which he could have obtained only from the authors themselves. With the Roman house of Orsini, Monte is certain to have cultivated friendly relations. Thus in 1558 he composed a festive madrigal for the wedding of Paolo Giordano Orsini, Duke of Bracciano, and Isabella Medici, born in 1542 as the second daughter of Duke Cosimo I and Eleonora of Toledo, a piece reprinted in the first book of his six-voiced madrigals:

> Il più forte di Roma,
> La più saggia di Flora e la più bella,
> Paolo ed Isabella,
> Gionse qui in terra il Cielo hor questa chioma;
> Chi puote ornare quella,
> Se perle, oro e diamanti
> Già non son tanti—al gemino valore,
> Che vince ogn'altro honore.

(This same festive event was also celebrated by Bernardo Giacomini, *gentilhuomo fiorentino*, in a sonnet-setting printed in a madrigal book of 1563: *Nobil coppia gradita in cui risplende*.) Even in Vienna and Prague, Monte remained in touch with Isabella, the most beautiful and most charming lady of her time, a poetess, a singer, and a musician. When he referred to the Duke as the "strongest Roman" and to Isabella as the "wisest daughter of Florence," he did not dream that in 1576 the couple would play the chief parts in the most notorious tragedy of the century: the Duke, for the sake of the beautiful Vittoria Accoramboni, was to strangle his wife in the Castello Cerreto Guidi near Empoli, thereby bringing the proud house of Orsini to ruin. (Another musician who stood close to Isabella was Stefano Rossetto from Nizza in Florence, who in 1566 and 1567 dedicated two madrigal books to her; of these the second is particularly interesting in that it presents the entire *Lamento di Olimpia* [Ariosto, *Orlando furioso*, x, 19-34] in the form of a great canzone for four, five, and six voices.) In 1568 Monte was again in Rome, in the service or under the patronage of Cardinal Flavio Orsini, when at forty-seven he received a summons from the Emperor Maximilian II to come to Vienna as Imperial choirmaster to succeed the Fleming Jacobus Vaet, who had died on January 8, 1568. Doubtless it was Count Arco, the Imperial ambassador in Rome, who approached Monte after his similar advances to Palestrina had led to nothing (cf. Pastor, *Geschichte der Päpste*, VIII, 152, note 7). On May 1, 1568, Monte entered upon his duties in Vienna.

From now on his life flows in a quiet channel, indeed much quieter than that of Lasso, who travels and is fond of traveling. Monte directs his choir under two emperors, under Maximilian II in Vienna and under Rudolf II in Prague (after 1576); he looks after the church service and writes church music; he trains pupils and tirelessly publishes one madrigal book after another. In 1570 he is sent to the Netherlands to recruit new members for the chapel, and from his native town he brings back a girl "who plays right well on the virginals and who is also in other respects a good singer and player." He seems never to have returned to Italy, though the dedications of a number of his madrigal books are dated from Venice; one is actually dated from Naples on March 1, 1569, at a time when he was again in Vienna. The dedication of his ninth book of five-voiced madrigals is signed in Prague, that of his fourth book of six-voiced madrigals in Venice, both on one and the same day, September 20, 1580. Yet it is clear that at this time Monte was in Prague and not in Venice. He remains in touch with Lasso. Not only is there an exchange of masses and motets between the two masters in Munich and Vienna, but they sometimes worked together on secular assignments also. Thus the *Second libre des Chansons a Quatre et cinq Parties* ... (Louvain, Phalèse, and Antwerp, Bellère, 1570) contains a wedding song, the tercets from Petrarch's sonnet *Per divina bellezza indarno mira*, followed by two pieces by Lasso, *Vieni dolc'Hymeneo* and *Indi gl'acuti strali*. The three songs be-

Beginning of Rore's Composition of Horace's "Donec gratus eram tibi,"
for Eight Parts. *Hans Müelich*

Miniature in Mus. Ms. B, Munich, State Library, fol. 35

Portrait of Giovanni Nasco. (In the background the Members of the
Veronese Accademia Filarmonica.) *Domenico Brusasorzi*
Verona, Museum

long together, for all three were intended for the wedding of Alessandro Farnese and Maria of Portugal (1565). At the Diet of Ratisbonne (1593) the two old masters meet again, the one in his seventy-third year, the other in his sixty-second; here they commiserate with one another on the decline in musical taste and shake their heads over eccentricities in musical notation (and doubtless over other artistic misdemeanors) committed by a younger colleague, then only forty—surely it is Luca Marenzio (cf. Lodovico Zacconi, *Prattica di musica*, II, cap. 12). Monte died on July 4, 1603. Seld's characterization seems applicable to his life as a whole: he was a refined and quiet man, an ecclesiastic by profession and a bachelor by inclination, well educated and interested in all the arts and sciences then cultivated at the court in Prague. He was thoroughly at home in the Italian, Latin, and French languages, which he spoke with the same ease as his mother tongue; that he preferred Italian or was at least most used to it, is evident from the letters now in Leyden, addressed to his fellow countryman, the botanist Charles de l'Ecluse (Clusius), who lived near him in Vienna from 1573 to 1587 (cf. *Quatorze lettres inédites du compositeur Ph. de Monte*, ed. Paul Bergmans, *Académie Royale de Belgique, Classe des Beaux-Arts. Mémoires*, I, fasc. II, Bruxelles, 1921). They also show his tolerance, for Clusius was a Protestant, and bear witness to his many-sided interests, his modesty and love of truth, his loyalty in support of his friends, and his quiet sense of humor: in 1590, when he is visited at seventy by that scourge of old age, the gout, he makes little account of it: "Sono entrato nella compagnia de podagrosi. . . ." Sadeler's engraved portraits bear out this impression; at first sight they seem only to be the features of a trade-master, say a goldsmith or carver in wood; but on looking more closely one discovers the finer features of the artist.

Yet it would be a mistake to conclude from the parallelism of their lives that their secular work runs parallel also. Of the two, Lasso is by far the more adaptable and many-sided. We do not know a single German song by Monte, and to balance Lasso's rich chanson production we can produce only a single book by Monte, his settings of the *Sonetz de Pierre de Ronsard* . . . (Louvain and Antwerp, 1575), an important work, containing twenty-nine numbers for five to seven voices. Add to this that Monte, as an ecclesiastic, flatly refused to touch the canzonetta and the villanella. In this respect, his youthful ten years in Naples and his later stay in Naples in the 'sixties left no mark on his work. He leaves it to his subordinates to satisfy the demands of the Viennese court and the world outside for cheap trash of this sort.

Monte makes up for this lack of versatility by his enormous productivity in the field of the madrigal. Of all madrigal composers he is by far the most prolific. Between 1554, when he published his first book of five-voiced madrigals, and the year of his death, 1603, we know of three books of madrigals for seven voices, nine for six voices, nineteen for five voices, four for four voices, and one for three voices, to which must be added five books of *madrigali spirituali* and a large number of single pieces in collections. This makes a total of about 1,150 madrigals and far outweighs the collected secular output of any of his rivals—Lasso, Marenzio, Striggio, Wert, Andrea Gabrieli, or Monteverdi.

If Lasso is by training an Italian master, this is still more true of Monte. And if Vice Chancellor Seld says of Monte the man, that he speaks Italian like a native, he could have said this with even greater truth of Monte the musician, who lived in Italy for at least forty of his first fifty years and who had published five of his madrigal books in Italy before the time of his summons to Vienna. And even after this time, it is not to be supposed that he considered himself exclusively at the service of the imperial house and that he now produced his madrigals only for the special requirements of the courts of Vienna and Prague—far from it. It is rather that he feels himself a free artist and addresses the world at large. It is extremely significant that in dedicating his eighth book of five-voiced madrigals to the Emperor, Rudolf II, he thanks his past and present imperial masters for having generously enabled him to dedicate himself freely to his art—"che posso comodissimamente attender ancora a questo studio." Always mindful of this obligation, he dedicated a large number of his madrigal books to his two imperial masters and to other members of the imperial court and household. But it would be fruitless to search among the contents of these books for specific personal applications to Vienna and Prague. On the contrary, it is precisely the sixth book of five-part madrigals, dedicated to Duchess Isabella Medici Orsini, which contains a few (Latin) dedicatory pieces for Archduke Ernst. Monte invariably addresses himself primarily to the international world of the friends of the madrigal. To show this we need scarcely name those many other dedications of his that point to the south and to the Italian home of this kind of music: to the Levantine merchant, poet, and musician Antonio Molino, the most original music-patron in Venice (*Terzo libro a 5*, 1570), a work for which the poet Leandro Mira is unlikely to have written the dedication without Monte's approval; to Mario Bevilacqua in Verona (*Undicesimo libro a 5*, 1586), the patron of the most famous Accademia of all Italy; to Duke Alfonso II of Ferrara, the patron of Torquato Tasso and of the musician Luzzasco Luzzaschi (*Quattordicesimo libro a 5*, 1590); or to the Grand Duke Ferdinando Medici (*Secondo libro a 7*, 1600).

At this point, it is not possible to evaluate Monte's madrigal work as a whole, as was still possible to some degree in Lasso's case. It is not only that Monte's life exceeded Lasso's in length by nearly ten very productive years, but there is also a break in his work which does not admit of our treating its last third together with the first two. For Monte's extensive production must certainly be divided into three parts. The first extends from his beginnings to his summons to Vienna; in this period he is purely an Italian composer, as much or perhaps even more so than Willaert, Rore, or Nasco. The second period extends to the year 1586 or, more exactly, to his eleventh book of five-voiced madrigals, in which he became aware of a crisis in his style and tried to overcome it. The last period extends to his death; in it the crisis seems to have found a personal solution of a sort, though one that is no longer important historically.

The first period comprises two books of madrigals for five voices and two for four, also the first book of six-voiced madrigals; all of these fall into Monte's Italian years, although the second book for four voices, dedicated to a Neapolitan, did not appear until the spring of 1569. He begins in 1554, relatively late and at about the same time as Lasso, almost twelve years his junior. One ought always to bear in mind that the composer of these many madrigals was already mature and soon to be well advanced in years. In his first works Monte belongs among the leaders, even to the vanguard, of modernity. If we consider his first work of 1554 as a special case (and this is necessary, since the next, for four voices, does not follow for fully eight years), we are struck at once by his original choice of texts; apart from a dedicatory madrigal addressed to a member of the house of Colonna, it presents a very independent selection from Petrarch's *Canzoniere*: eight sonnets and the quatrains of a ninth; further, a sonnet of Lorenzo de' Medici and a descriptive stanza from the *Orlando furioso* (x, 96), the representation of Angelica, bound naked to the cliff so that she seems to Ruggiero a statue:

"... Se non vedea la lacrima distinta
Tra fresche rose e candidi ligustri
Far rugiadose le crudette pome,
E l'aura sventolar l'aurate chiome ..."

a choice that can scarcely be otherwise interpreted than as the order of a noble lover desirous of complimenting his fair one. And of course the setting of the quatrains of Petrarch's *I vid'in terra angelici costumi* was also written in praise of a lady.

As compared with Rore, from whom both he and Lasso derive, the musician Monte begins with great animation, freely and colorfully; Naples and Rome seem to have made him articulate. His temperament has already a definite stamp; it is an unusual yet highly harmonious combination of the expressive and artistic, of the animated and at the same time subdued. The contrast to Lasso—the concise, the hurried, the impatient master—reveals itself in the great melodic breadth and fullness, in the frequently long drawn-out melismatic writing. How poetic and calm and perfectly in keeping with Monte's human personality is the beginning of Petrarch's sonnet:

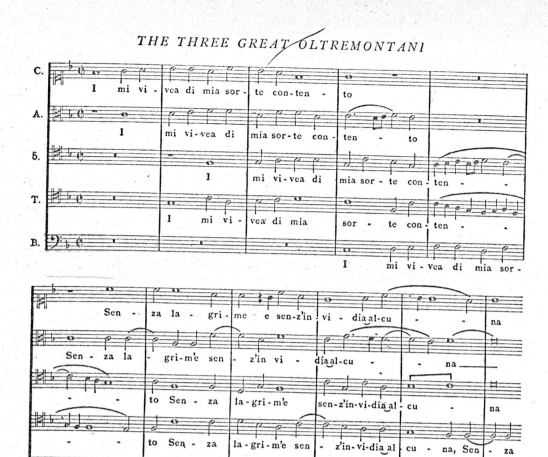

That the tenor takes no part in the strict imitation of the opening is wholly in accord with the madrigal's informal style. Yet ten years earlier Rore had painted the same opening in somber colors, for five men's voices and in a low register (*Secondo libro*, No. 16):

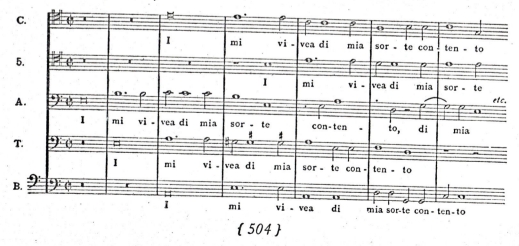

At most, Monte's Netherlandish origin reveals itself in the tender, delicate, song-like quality of his melody, which adds a touch of feeling to the style of the native Italians, who tend rather to declaim:

In this, his first work, Monte already renounces almost completely the naïve bits of tone-painting with which the average lovers of the madrigal were so infatuated; the "eye-music" in connection with allusions to darkness and light (in his vast madrigal production as a whole there is only one example of this); the *suspirium* for sighs; the puns on the solmization-syllables. The deliberate pace of his madrigal is already enlivened by the use of *note nere*, though these are always motivated by the text, and by spirited meter and rhythm; none the less, the basis of the conception is always the equality of the moving voices, as melody and as declamation—homophonic details are infrequent.

All at once, in the first two books of four-voiced madrigals and the book of six-voiced madrigals (all of which appeared in Venice and not, as heretofore, in Rome), Monte becomes very modern (1562, 1569, and presumably 1564). They form a group by themselves. In any case, the combination of voices is not a normal one, for in this period of five-part writing, four voices are as much a deviation from the norm as six. In the meantime Monte has studied the two books of four-voiced madrigals by Cipriano Rore. In his first book he sets two entire sestine of Petrarch's, *Mia benigna fortuna* and *L'aer gravato*, just as Rore had set one, *Alla dolc'ombra*. Composed *a notte negre* and in the style of chamber music, the two cyclic pieces are astonishingly bold in their harmonies, although relatively little use is made of "chromaticisms" (Monte goes only as far as the B major triad) and of genuine chromatic writing. The general impression is thoroughly homophonic and declamatory, and since Monte is a less violent, less ruthless musician than Rore, his style already looks forward to a period of greater serenity. Other compositions, such as the madrigal *Voi volete ch'io moia*, one would ascribe to Marenzio's circle if one did not know their real author. And the second book of four-voiced madrigals, filled with texts from Petrarch and Bembo, carries this tendency still further. Again there are a few cyclic pieces, almost wholly homophonic, which move rapidly along and whose declamation, harmony, and chromaticism do little more than give the emotional content of the poetry its expressive accents and a sonorous dress. They belong among the landmarks pointing the way from the analogous four- and five-voice pieces of Rore to Marenzio and to monody. It is strange that one and the same setting of Petrarch's sonnet *Quando mi viene innanzi il tempo e'l loco* is found in both books—Monte has repeated it at the end of the second, as though to give expression to his love for his abandoned Italy. (Or is it supposed that personal human traits like these are foreign to the madrigal?)

Likewise progressive, though in another sense, is the first book for six voices, whose first edition—now lost—appeared about 1564, presumably with a dedication to Duke Paolo Orsini da Bracciano, for—as already mentioned—it contains a piece written for his marriage to Isabella Medici in 1558, together with a number of other "Roman" pieces written to order. Also "Roman" in this work is the use of the technique of choral division that we note and admire in Palestrina's *Missa Papae Marcelli* and to which we have given the name "alternazione." By "alternazione" we mean the alternating and combining of three-, four-, and five-part half-choirs within the general framework of the six-part texture, a much finer technique than the cruder, echo-like writing for two and more choruses, which is simply more obvious to the eye and ear. After Willaert and Rore, Monte is among the first to make use of this style, and he does so without yielding anything of the artistry and inner animation of his voice-leading. With this sort of "alternazione," rhythmic animation goes hand in hand. Monte knows only the *misura comune*, but within its limits he often pushes the animation to the point of great vivacity. In one of the sonnets, a Roman gallant informs the nymphs and *amoretti* that he has attained the goal of his desires:

Leggiadre Ninfe e pargoletti Amori
Che tra i colli di Marte v'ascondete . . .

The passage works itself up to a tempest of feeling and imagery rare in Monte and in the madrigal:

At the same time it gives in miniature a partial picture of what we have called "alternazione."

Likewise "Roman" in content is Monte's second book of five-voiced madrigals (1567). It contains the lament of a Roman or of Rome herself on the departure for

Florence of a lady, presumably Isabella Medici-Orsini at the time of her separation from her husband:

> Porta sì lieti giorni un'altr'aurora
> E sì dolce e sì lieta tramontana
> A la bella Toscana,
> Che ben dimostra apertamente il cielo
> Di rallegrarsi alla sua amica Flora
> Nella cui ricca valle
> Più non si teme gielo
> Ma vi produce il verno l'herb'e i fiori
> E le Ninfe e i Pastori
> Tesson nobil corona alle sue palle.
> L'Istro di tanta gioia ha'l'Arno pieno
> Ch'arena d'oro port' al mar Thirreno—
> Io sol sempr'ho di pianto gl'occhi molli,
> Perche più non m'appoggio
> A quel gradito poggio
> Ch'alza la cima sopra i sette colli.

For the rest, insofar as it was possible for Monte to make it so, the book is the five-voiced counterpart to Rore's chromatic and recitative-like madrigals, as shown, for example, by the opening of the tercets of one of Petrarch's sonnets:

Insofar as it was possible for Monte to make it so: we say this advisedly, for he is far less "programmatic" than Rore; since as a true master he cannot repudiate his instinct, which loves the polyphonic liveliness that consists in the artful intertwining of the voices, he seizes every opportunity to work with motifs. Yet in this very book he again betrays his direct dependence upon Rore. At the end of the print there is a dirge on the death of a certain Carlo, evidently the little son of a patron:

> Carlo che in tenerella e acerba etade . . .

(Reprinted in *Denkmäler der Tonkunst in Oesterreich*, LXXVII.) It is modeled on one of Rore's madrigals, *Tu piangi e quella*: it shows precisely the same poetic motif, the same use of dark, low voices, and the same unusual combination of clefs—two altos, tenor, and two basses.

The summons to the Imperial court in Vienna also meant a decisive change in Monte's work as a madrigalist, little inclined as he was to break off his connections with Italy. His productivity increases; his recognized importance receives, as it were, added weight and a sort of official stamp as a result of his activity in so prominent a post. In 1570 he publishes his chansons for four and five voices, in which (and this proves the esteem in which he is held) he is associated with Rore and Lasso; the collection also contains a madrigal. From now on scarcely a year passes without some publication of his: in 1580 alone there appeared three books of madrigals. To begin with, Monte attains his full stature as a master of a madrigal style that one may even call classic. Some pieces in the first books of this period—the second book *a sei* and the third and fourth *a cinque* must still have been written in Italy: the last named contains a sonnet by Battista Guarini which Monte can only have obtained from the author himself, for Giulio Fiesco had set an altogether different version of the poem in his *Musica nuova* of the previous year (1569, *Hor che'l mio vivo sole*). And how much more free, more clear, more smooth—in a word, more Italian—than Fiesco is Monte! These first Vienna madrigal books contain a few exceptional pieces: a Petrarch sonnet (*I piansi, or canto*) with a signature of two flats which extends harmonically from the region of D major to an inclination toward D-flat, yet without seeming forced; a dialogue *a sette* (della Casa's *Stolto mio core*) without any concession to conventional or schematic choral writing; Petrarch sonnets such as the rarely set *Amor mi sprona*, new in tempo, bold in harmony, full of contrasting images. But Monte is at his best in those pieces of this period that are "normal" (if I may call them so), with their light and artistic structure, their balance of choral "alternazione" and melodic animation, and their taste.

In the fifth book *a cinque* he even manages a "world success"—what we should call a "hit." It is a madrigal on a text of G. Guidiccioni's, *Veramente in amore*, a lachrymose affair that is actually beneath his *niveau* and that is copied from older models. But in general he is beginning to lose touch with the beneficent native soil of the madrigal and with the changes in Italian taste or, if one prefers, of Italian fashion. The contents of his sixth book for five voices (1575) is a strange mixture of occasional compositions and pieces of the highest literary quality. From the choice of texts one can see that Monte is working in exile—as it were, *in partibus infidelium*. There are exceptions; but in general he knows only the bipartite sonnet and the ottava, favors canzoni and sestine, and remains faithful to his favorite poets: Petrarch, Bembo (for whom he has an unfortunate predilection), and Sannazaro. A certain lyric anthology, edited by Lodovico Dolci, is his vade mecum. He continues on a high level, but he remains on that level, headed in an unfashionable direction; this is why the contemporary consumers gradually forsook him. His madrigal books are now infrequently reprinted, and beginning with the ninth book for five voices (1580), the first edition we know is often also the last. By nature a sober-minded artist, he is undoubtedly becoming more conservative again; even in his last two books of four-part madrigals, in other respects quite "modern," he distinctly draws the line at the canzonetta, which had by that time (about 1580) already exerted a strong influence on the style and attitude of the madrigal.

He is of course aware of his growing isolation. The dedication of his eighth book for five voices already reveals to the Emperor Rudolf II how preoccupied he is with differences in taste: "Se fin qui, Sacra Cesarea Maestà, si è visto che quanto ogn'uno può, va cercando di ridur la Musica con nuovo stile a maggior perfettione; necessariamente ne segue, ch'ella non è ancor giunta a quella eccellenza, che potrebbe arrivare. Essendo io dunque uno di quelli, che della Musica fanno professione, se ben quanto più ho cercato di trovare strada da poter più dilettare a quelli che d'essa debbono, et possono dar giuditio, tanto più forse me ne sia discostato, nientedimanco, facendo quant'io posso.... Se io non meritasse lode dell'effetto, non però merito biasmo della mia intentione...."—"Imperial Majesty, when we see that up to now everyone is doing his best to lead music to greater perfection by means of a new style, it necessarily follows that it has not yet attained the perfection that it might. Since I am one of those whose profession is music, I have done all I could to find a way to give more pleasure to those who should and can form a judgment on it, but it is perhaps true that the more I try the less I succeed. None the less, I do what I can ... and if I deserve no praise for what I have accomplished, I at least deserve no blame for my intention...." This is a painful and historically remarkable self-confession. A year later (1581), in dedicating another madrigal book (his tenth) to the Emperor, he speaks frankly of attempts to change his style, with a view to pleasing even those who have been dissatisfied with his earlier works: "Ho cercato, et cerco tuttavia col variar stile dare qualche contento a quelli a chi havessero poco piaciute l'altre mie compositioni...." He begins to experiment and tries here and there a lighter and more facile way of writing, characterized by greater transparency and the use of smaller motifs. It is only in the field of harmony that he never experiments, not even in this period of his production. The Italians' voyages of discovery do not attract him; on the contrary, his harmony becomes more and more economical, more and more reserved. He can do anything, but he is not sure what to do. He writes masterpieces that are at once didactic and artistic, artful and poetic, like his first and only book of three-voiced madrigals (1582), commissioned by the publisher Angelo Gardano, who dedicated it to Maddalena Casulana, herself a composer. His thematic material becomes more melismatic. Each book shows new aspects that reveal his mastery but at the same time a certain bewilderment, and with every book he falls further behind the times. With the year 1586 and his eleventh book of five-voiced madrigals, he brings to a close the great change in style that had introduced the last period of his work as a madrigalist. In dedicating this book to Count Mario Bevilacqua in Verona, the great musical Maecenas and the patron of the most famous of the *accademie*, he makes it very clear that he wishes this latest work of his may give the singers as much pleasure as it has given him amusement to write it in as animated and gay a style as possible: "... si come ho havuto grandissimo gusto in compor questi madrigali in quello più vivace et allegro stile che a me sia stato lecito di poter ritrovare; acciò che porghino altrui materia d'esser allegramente cantate. ...." In the end he entirely abandons the *misura di breve* for the *misura cromatica*; he forsakes the lofty muse of Petrarch, Bembo, Bernardo Tasso, and Luigi Tansillo in favor of Guarini and Celiano. He is now sixty-five, and it is little short of tragicomic to see the old man become an Arcadian—like Don Quixote at the end of his life, after the collapse of his knightly ambitions. It is this sort of madrigal that Cerone (*Melopeo*, I, 33) has in mind when he inappropriately associates the elderly Monte with the youthful Marenzio: "Philippo de Monte y Lucas Marenzio tienen muy lindos y muy suaves passos chromáticos, o per dezirlo más propriamente, passos moles, lacivos, y affeminados. ...."—"Filippo di Monte and Luca Marenzio delight in using very pleasant and very sweet chromatic progressions, or to put it more exactly, very soft, sensuous, and effeminate ones." We repeat: all this is little short of tragicomic, for this gesture toward modernity and toward the latest fashion was made in vain. The actual change was due to the great Venetian who succeeded Willaert and Rore and gave new direction to the madrigal —Andrea Gabrieli, the cultivator of the sensuous, elegant, epigrammatic, pastoral tendency that reflects the reverse side of the Counter Reformation. It was due also to the new canzonetta, in which this new tendency appears in its purest form. It is thus as an imitator that Monte begins his third period as a madrigalist; its characterization must be left for a later chapter.

GIACHES DE WERT

TOGETHER with Lasso and Monte the third great Italian composer of madrigals of Flemish birth is Jachet Wert or, as he preferred to style himself, Giaches de Wert. If he pleases, the reader may begin by questioning the justice of placing Wert on an equal footing with his two compatriots, for until now he has been disposed of in the lexicons with a line or two, just as the art-historical texts and reference books of thirty years ago used to dispose of Tintoretto and El Greco in comparison with Titian. But as a musical personality Wert can hold his own in comparison not only with

Monte, but also (or very nearly) with Lasso; aside from this his later influence was far greater than theirs, for he was one of the real intermediaries between Rore and Monteverdi and his role was by no means limited to that of a mere intermediary.

It is amazing that no attention has ever been paid to his "romantic" life, a life which for sheer interest is hardly surpassed by that of the Principe di Venosa, the "musician and murderer," and which was thoroughly explored years ago by A. Ramazzini ("I musici fiamminghi alla corte di Ferrara—Giaches de Wert e Tarquinia Molza," *Archivio storico lombardo*, vi [1879], 116-133) and Pietro Canal ("Della musica in Mantova," *Memorie del Reale Istituto di scienze, lettere ed arti*, xxi, 704f.). Like Lasso and Monte, Wert comes to Italy from Flanders in early youth —it is possible that he was born in the county of Horn in 1536—but unlike them he never returned home, and in 1566 when he accompanied his employer, Duke Guglielmo Gonzaga, to Augsburg, where his mastery in improvised counterpoint aroused general admiration, he is said to have declined an invitation to enter the service of the Emperor. (Zacconi too is still praising Wert's unusual mastery or "singolarità" in counterpoint in the second volume of his *Prattica* [2da parte, libro iii], where Wert appears in the company of Porta, his colleague Baccusi, and Massaino.) He begins as a choir boy (*ragazzo da cantare*) in the employ of Maria di Cardona, Marchesa della Padulla, and thus in the kingdom of Naples, or, more precisely, in the region of Salerno or what is now called Campania. Yet he must have filled more than one place in this part of Italy, for he dedicates his third madrigal book (1563) to Consalvo Fernandes di Cordova, Duke of Sessa, pointing out in this connection that the Duke had entrusted him with the "governo di sua Capella." Leaving Naples, he is for many years in the service of the counts of Nuvolara —Francesco II, Camillo I, and Alfonso I Gonzaga—Francesco and Camillo warriors seldom seen in their own territories, Alfonso a prince of the church (in his youth) and Wert's actual benefactor; it is to him that Wert dedicates his first work in 1558 (and 1564), and he seems to have shown some understanding for the grandeur and audacity of Wert's vocal chamber music. Today Novellara is a shabby little place with hardly more than 2,000 inhabitants, but in those days the Count's castle was the scene not only of an intimate artistic practice but also of dramatic performances. Thus in 1567 Alfonso builds a theater and entrusts his former choirmaster with the composition of intermezzi for a *commedia* (1568).

For in the meantime Wert had entered the service of the musical and music-loving Guglielmo, Duke of Mantua, who had become acquainted with his abilities as a composer for festive occasions at the time of the wedding of Count Alfonso (who had given up his ecclesiastical career) and Donna Vittoria da Capua. About 1565, or shortly before, Wert is appointed choirmaster at Saint Barbara's, the private chapel of the Gonzaga family. He was the declared musical favorite of the Duke and as such seems to have been responsible for the prompt removal of Giovanni Contino, the former choirmaster. From the first he meets with the outspoken hostility of the choir members, who know how to strike at his most vulnerable spot. His wife, the daughter of a well-to-do family in Novellara and herself well-to-do, becomes the mistress of a certain Agostino Buonvicini, one of her husband's subordinates; the cuckold husband is thus exposed to the ridicule of the rabble and of the whole choir and forced to break off relations with his partner, who returns to Novellara about 1570. It was probably but small consolation to him that she came to a disgraceful end. She was involved in the intrigues of a certain Claudio, the bastard son of Count Francesco of Novellara, who laid claim to the succession in Novellara on the death of his father (1577) and even sought to have his uncle Alfonso done away with. The conspiracy failed and, though Claudio escaped, the woman was caught with other accomplices and died in prison a few years later. For some years Wert wrangled with the Count over her confiscated estate; in the end he was lucky to get a third of it. The three children naturally interested him less, for it is scarcely to be presumed that they were all of them his.

Not less unfortunate for Wert was the outcome of his great passion for Tarquinia Molza, the most famous poetess and singer of the day. Born on November 1, 1542, at Modena, and a widow after 1578 (her husband's name was Paolo Porrino), Tarquinia entered the service of Lucrezia Duchess of Ferrara in April 1583 as a *dama d'onore* and became at once the center of musical life at the court of the Este— we shall hear more about this later on. Wert, a frequent guest in Ferrara, conceived a deep passion for this maturely beautiful woman, a passion that she returned with equal intensity. He was now oftener in Ferrara than in Mantua, and on December 22, 1584, Guglielmo had to demand, in the sharpest possible language, the immediate return of his choirmaster. The lovers did not know that they were beset by spies and that their letters were secretly opened and copied. In October 1589 Tarquinia was forced to leave the court to return to Modena under the close surveillance of the ducal *governatore* and to forego all further communication with Wert. Thus the tragedy of Torquato Tasso, who dedicated one of his dialogues to Tarquinia ("On Love") and was well acquainted with Wert, was not the only one to take place at the court of the Este. Mantua and Ferrara were then so closely related, politically and culturally, that the musical history of the two courts can be followed only if both places are considered simultaneously. Ferrarese musicians came to Mantua, and Mantuan musicians went even more frequently to Ferrara. It goes without saying that during the carnival of 1579 the Mantuan musicians accompanied Guglielmo's heir, Vincenzo, to the marriage of his sister, Margherita Gonzaga, and Alfonso II, a marriage that was once more to disappoint the Estes in their hopes for an heir. There were any number of splendid feasts, tournaments, balls, and banquets, and these provoked the unfortunate Tasso, who had just returned from Turin, to that fit of rage that was to lead him to the cage at the hospital of Sant' Anna. Was Wert present at this scene? It is certain that he had made Tasso's acquaintance earlier, at the time of the poet's visits to Mantua in 1565 and 1578.

Tasso's regard for Wert is attested by the madrigal stanza which, in the edition of 1724 (II, 542), bears the heading "Ad un Musico, che avea posto in musica alcuni madrigali":

> Queste mie rime sparte
> Sotto dolci misure
> Raccolte hai tu nelle vergate carte:
> E co'tuoi dolci modi
> Purghi le voglie impure,
> Ove il mio stil talora
> Nella tua voce, e nell'altrui s'onora:
> E più, quando le lodi
> Del bel Vincenzo, e i pregj
> Canti degli avi gloriosi egregj.

The allusion to Vincenzo Gonzaga as patron makes it certain that the poem is addressed to Wert; incidentally, the stanza is more than a compliment to an individual musician—it is also an eloquent testimony to the refining effect that Tasso ascribed to music itself. When was the poem written? Wert's first settings of texts by Tasso are printed in his seventh madrigal book (1581): a sonnet (*Donna se ben le chiome*) and what is presumably the earliest setting of a fragment from the *Gerusalemme liberata*, the first of a long series which will end only with Monteverdi and Mazzocchi. But Tasso's stanza refers rather to the eighth book (1586), which contains virtually nothing but pieces from the *Gerusalemme liberata*, unless by *raccolta* he means some MS collection.

When added to Mantua's unhealthy climate, these blows of fate evidently took their toll. In the summer of 1582 Wert fell seriously ill and was obliged to turn over his duties at St. Barbara's to G. G. Gastoldi, though he continued to compose for the chapel and in 1587 wrote the festive mass for the coronation of Duke Vincenzo. In 1585 and 1586 he was ill again, and in May 1596 (on the 6th or 23d—the date is not certain) he died, two years after Palestrina and Lasso, at the age of sixty. Tarquinia survived him by more than twenty years; in 1600 she was made a Roman citizen, an unusual honor, and on August 8, 1617, she also died, at the age of seventy-five. But her relations with Wert have left a lasting trace.

Even though he died soon after Palestrina and Lasso, as a representative of a somewhat younger generation, active at two courts that were the centers of a sumptuous and progressive musical life, Wert looks forward in his later work to a new time. He is not only a forerunner of Luzzasco Luzzaschi and thus of the concerted vocal music of Ferrara—this we shall see later; he is also active as a composer for the *favola boschereccia*, the pastoral drama.

He began with a work for five voices in 1558 as a pupil of Rore, more precisely of the Rore of the 'fifties who had just discovered the free, homophonic style of declamation. He enters into direct competition with Rore by setting della Casa's sonnet *O sonno, o della quet'umid'ombrosa* and follows this with another sonnet by the same poet, *Cura che di timor*. His procedure is quite different from Rore's: he lays more stress upon the polyphonic interweaving of the voices and is at the same time more reserved in his harmonic style. But he resembles Rore in his indifference toward everything merely formal and in his striving for the most intense expression. In the *Canzon seconda* of this print, a symphonic lament for voices on the death of a lady, presumably a Gonzaga, we are puzzled when we find an excess of mere "eye-music"; on the other hand, we can understand Wert's being satisfied with an artfully decorative music in the wedding song that opens the edition of 1564. He shows his youth by giving the contents of this book the greatest possible variety: a *madrigale spirituale* for six voices, a dialogue for eight on one of Bembo's sonnets, a few of the more impassioned and gloomy sonnets of Petrarch, among them the one inveighing against the corruption of the papal court at Avignon, in an extraordinarily vivid setting (cf. p. 240). The basis of his style is homophony. In setting Petrarch's sonnet (1560, *Primo libro a cinque*, 11)

> Pien d'un vago pensier, che mi desvia
> Da tutti gli altri, e fammi al mondo ir solo,
> Ad or ad or a me stesso m'involo,
> Pur lei cercando, che fuggir devria . . .

he uses homophony for the first three lines, but not without stressing the word *solo* at the end of the second, to pass over to polyphony in the fourth for the sake of *fuggir*. This is perhaps the first use of polyphony as such—of polyphony as a specific means of poetic expression and not as a neutral instrument for musical development. Aside from this, the book already reveals another of Wert's characteristics—his fondness for high voices, to which he will later give a special stamp.

In the *Secondo libro a cinque* (1561, 1564, and later reprinted, with a change in contents and a dedication to Ottavio Farnese, Rore's patron) his choice of texts is more uniform than in the first, but the contrasts of musical structure are more pronounced. Apart from a sonnet by G. Guidiccioni (*Superbi colli*) all the identifiable poems in the book (and there are only three I cannot identify) are from Petrarch and from Ariosto's *Orlando furioso*. Wert now sometimes frees himself not only from all consideration for the poetic form but also from the constraint of well-ordered imitation:

Indifference to the intelligibility of the text and independence of the voices could not be carried much further, particularly if one recalls the meticulous observance of the poetic form and the subordination of the accompaniment to the vocal melody that the frottolists imposed on themselves in setting such a canzone by Petrarch. And if the members of the Florentine *Camerata* of 1600 had sought a classic example of the "laceramento della poesia" (the "laceration of poetry"), they could not have found a better one than this opening. But opposed to this are pieces like Petrarch's *Trionfo d'Amore*:

Nel tempo che rinnova i miei sospiri . . .

whose whole Capitolo I (omitting lines 94-156) Wert sets to music for seven voices and in two sections as a straightforward homophonic choral declamation, broken up by the use of divided choirs. How is such a work to be explained? It can only have been the accompanying music for a *Trionfo*, a *tableau vivant* come to life and culminating in the entrance of Caesar as Cleopatra's slave: Mantegna's famous triumphal procession, now at Hampton Court, shows that the Mantuans have always taken special pleasure in such spectacles. An extreme contrast to this sort of homophony is again presented in a piece like Petrarch's sonnet *Amor io fallo*, whose opening, a Monteverdian inspiration, depends on the expressive power of the seventh leap (see example on next page).

Other such contrasts occur in Petrarch's *Quand'io mi volgo indietro*, when Wert brings the motif in inversion, or in *Cantai or piango*, a text often set to music, when he endeavors to reproduce the oxymora as plastically as possible. For an apotheosis of homophony we have only to turn to Wert's first (and only) book of four-part madrigals (1561), dedicated to the Marquis of Pescara, then governor of Naples.

Portrait of Filippo di Monte. Engraving. *N. L'Armessin*

BASSO

DI LVCA MARENZIO
IL QVARTO LIBRO DE
MADRIGALI A CINQVE VOCI
Nouamente compofi, & dati in luce.

IN VENETIA
Appreffo Giacomo Vincenci, & Ricciardo Amadino, compagni.

M D LXXXIIII.

M

Title Page of Luca Marenzio's Fourth Book of Madrigals for Five Parts, Venice, 1584

To be sure, there are still some reminiscences of the early madrigal with its freely animated voices. Thus when Wert chances upon an old-fashioned text in the style of Cassola, such as *Madonna, poi ch'uccidermi volete* (No. 20), he sets it archaistically in the style of Arcadelt or Verdelot. But in general he is already prematurely writing monodies. It is significant that he again sets to music, in R. Gualtieri's translation, Dido's last words from the *Aeneid* (*Dolci spoglie felici—Dulces exuviae*), a favorite text with the frottolists. It is again significant that he begins to apply this same style to the lyric climaxes of the *Orlando furioso*, for example Bradamante's jealous outburst at the sight of Ruggiero (XXXVI, 32 and 33):

> Dunque baciar sì belle e dolci labbia
> Deve altra, se baciar non le poss'io? . . .

(Wert won special fame with his music for another stanza from the *Orlando furioso* —*Chi salirà per me, Madonna, in cielo* [XXXV, 1], set to music after minor textual changes in a lively, humorous style. It speaks for W. Barclay Squire's fine taste that he included it in his published collection.) Still closer to the "aria" and to the lyric-dramatic soliloquy is a piece like *Chi mi fura il ben mio* (No. 11), which might almost have been taken from a pastoral drama in the style of Torquato Tasso's *Aminta*. Such pieces make it quite clear that even for the most expert masters polyphony had become an anachronism and that monody was some day bound to appear. One is almost tempted to view such pieces as monodies, the more so since in the printed part-books Wert always chooses the simplest cadence-formulas, even for the upper voice, thus leaving the details to the improvisation of the singers. Yet it would be a mistake to view them in this light. For although Wert makes it a principle to declaim rapidly and to do justice to the individual word and line, he also seizes every opportunity for expressive, madrigalesque tone-painting, whether emotional or realistic, whether *imitazione dell' affetto* or *imitazione della natura*. The stock of formulas for this purpose had by 1560 become so enormous that the slightest hint was enough, and so adaptable that the expression no longer interfered with the flow of the declamation.

The change that takes place in Wert's next madrigal prints may be described both from the biographic and the artistic point of view as a change from Petrarch and Ariosto to Guarini and Torquato Tasso; musically, from the madrigal *à la* Rore to the madrigal of the later Venetians and of Andrea Gabrieli. The third book (1563), dedicated to his former benefactor in Southern Italy, Consalvo Fernandes di Cordova, Duke of Sessa, contains, along with a number of dedicatory pieces, three great cyclic compositions: two of Petrarch's canzoni and a capitolo by Ariosto. The fourth book (1567) stands under the special patronage of Duke Guglielmo of Mantua inasmuch as it is not only dedicated to him but is also opened by one of his compositions—different from the piece with the same words which opens the Duke's (anonymously published) madrigal book of 1583. It contains settings of a series of ottave attributed to Luigi Tansillo:

> A caso un giorno mi guidò la sorte . . .

one of the earliest examples of the pastoral cantata connecting narrative and dialogue, a musical variety to which we shall later return (p. 547). Wert still sets it in the old style, as a narrative in the manner of the *canzon francese*. In the fifth and sixth books (1571 and 1577) Petrarch and Ariosto still predominate, and with them, in ever-growing measure, Luigi Tansillo; the sixth already contains a sonnet by Torquato Tasso:

> Tolse Barbara gente il pregio a Roma
> Dell'imperio, e dell'armi, e serva fella.
> Oh nome a lei fatale! ecco novella
> Barbara vincitrice anco la doma.
>
> E a quale in lei più per beltà si noma
> Tolto lo scettro, e'l titolo di bella,
> Spiega sue squadre in Campidoglio, e quella
> De'suoi prigioni incatenata, e doma.
>
> Sono i guerrieri suoi molle rigore
> Con pudica beltà, sdegno cortese,
> Che quanto sfida più, tanto più piace.
>
> I vinti un sesso, e l'altro: e l'un d'amore,
> L'altro d'invidia: e colla stessa face
> Agghiaccia or l'uno, onde già l'altro accese.

It is a sonnet written in Rome in 1573 in praise of the beautiful Barbara Sanseverino, Countess of Sala, who at that time was living there with her step-daughter Leonora Sanvitale (cf. A. Solerti, *Vita di Torquato Tasso*, I, 180); it can hardly have been much later that Wert set it to music. The seventh book (1581) contains a setting of Battista Guarini's *Tirsi morir volea*, the favorite "cantata" before the birth of the cantata itself, the music in a wholly novel declamatory style (cf. infra, p. 541), and in addition to this what are probably the earliest compositions to texts from Torquato Tasso's *Gerusalemme liberata*—incidentally, these were published four months before the first authorized edition of the poem in June—one is a lyric description (*Vaghi boschetti*, VI, 21), another a half-dramatic narrative (*Giunto alla tomba*, XII, 96 and 97). With the eighth book (1586) the change is complete; the work belongs to Tasso and at the same time to a new concerted style. The later Wert is no longer Rore's successor; he is the contemporary of Marenzio, Gesualdo, and the young Monteverdi and one of the forerunners and founders of the music of the seventeenth century.

CHAPTER VII · THE RISE OF VIRTUOSITY IN THE PASTORAL AND THE DRAMATIC MADRIGAL

ANDREA GABRIELI

THE advent of a lighter, more fanciful, socially more adaptable variety of the madrigal had been long preparing, particularly in the work of Vincenzo Ruffo and within the Veronese Accademia Filarmonica. But it could only be brought to pass by a greater master and in a culturally more decisive and more cosmopolitan city: by Andrea Gabrieli in Venice.

Andrea Gabrieli was a pupil of Willaert's. Rore he passed by, though he had studied him thoroughly. Rore is too one-sided in his greatness: a master of high art, but of high art alone. Gabrieli is many-sided like Willaert, even more so, for he already knows several varieties of madrigal and adds to his master's *canzoni villanesche alla napoletana* his own *giustiniane* and *greghesche*, his pseudo-antique dramatic music, and his state cantatas. The year after his death his nephew and pupil, Giovanni Gabrieli, pronounced this eulogy in his memory: "Se Messer Andrea Gabrieli (felice memoria) non fosse stato mio Zio, ardirei di dire (senza timore d'esserne biasimato) che, si come pochi Illustri Pittori, et Scultori insieme sono stati al mondo, così pochissimi fossero stati gli eccellenti Compositori, et Organisti, com'egli fù. Ma perchè di consanguinità le sono poco meno che figliuolo, non mi si conviene dir di lui liberamente quello, che l'affettione dettata dal vero mi ministrarebbe: perchè, chi può negare, che non sia stato mirabile, et quasi Divino in tutti i generi Armonici? potrei lodarlo nell'arte, nelle rare inventioni, nelle maniere nove, nel dilettevole stile, non solamente, perchè sia stato grave, et dotto nelle sue compositioni, ma per esser insieme comparso tanto vago, et leggiadro, che chi hà gustato il suono de'suoi concenti, et l'Armonia de suoi contrapunti (e vaglia dir il vero), può dire d'haver provato, che cosa siano i veri movimenti d'affetti: et che cosa sia goder dalla Musica, vera, et inusitata dolcezza. Potrei dire, che da suoi componimenti si vede apertamente quanto egli sia stato singulare nell'imitatione in ritrovar suoni esprimenti l'Energia delle parole, e de'concetti. Ma per non parer trabocchevole nel colmo dell'affettione, essendogli io Nipote, lasciarò il farne giuditio à gli intendenti, che l'hanno conosciuto fin nell'interno ricetto de suoi pensieri. Piacque al sommo voler di Dio l'anno passato di trasferirlo di terra in Paradiso, in età matura sì, et assai colma d'anni, ma in tempo, che più che mai i spiriti erano nella Musica vivaci, et pieni di leggiadrissime inventioni. Haveva esso ridotto à compita perfettione varij bellissimi Concerti, Dialoghi, et altre Musiche proportionate à voci, et stromenti, come hoggidì s'usa nelle principal Chiese de Principi, et nelle Academie Illustri;

de quali egli (bona memoria) havea deliberato farne dono à V.S. Illustriss. per scoprirle un vivo segno dell'osservanza et devotione che le portava. . . ." — "If Messer Andrea Gabrieli (of blessed memory) had not been my uncle, I should venture to say (without fear of being blamed for it) that, just as there are at one time few illustrious painters and sculptors in the world, so there have been very few such distinguished composers and organists as he. But since by reason of consanguinity I am to him little less than a son, it is not fitting for me to say frankly of him those things that affection guided by truth might suggest to me: for who can deny that he has been admirable and as it were divine in every harmonic variety? I might praise him for his skill, his rare inventions, his new means of expression, and his pleasant style, not simply because he was dignified and learned in his compositions, but because he seemed at the same time to be so beautiful and graceful that he who has reveled in the sound of his harmonies and his counterpoints (to speak frankly) may say that he has learned what the true movements of the affections are and what it is to enjoy true music and unheard-of sweetness. I might say that it can clearly be seen from his compositions how unique an imitator he was in finding sounds to express the force of words and of ideas. But in order not to seem overzealous in the excess of my affections, being his nephew, I shall leave the judgment of him to those connoisseurs who had followed him even into the secret recesses of his thoughts. It pleased the supreme will of God to take him, last year, from this earth into His Paradise, at a mature age and rich in years, yet at a time when his musical spirits were more than ever alive and filled with the most delightful inventions. He had fully perfected various most beautiful concertos, dialogues, and other pieces of music adapted to voices and instruments, such as are used today in the principal churches of the nobility and in the illustrious academies; these the departed (of blessed memory) planned to offer as a gift to Your Excellency to discover to you a lively sign of the reverence and devotion he bore you. . . ."

Great master though he was, conspicuous as was the scene of his activity, the life of Andrea Gabrieli is veiled in an obscurity difficult to understand. We do not know exactly when he was born or when he died; no monument marks his last resting place. What we do know is that he was born in the quarter known as Canareggio, supposedly about 1510, though more probably about 1520—for it would otherwise be difficult to understand his late appearance in 1550, and he can in no case be older than Rore. Since his earliest madrigal appears in a print of Vincenzo Ruffo's, he was perhaps a singer under Ruffo at the cathedral of Verona. Perhaps he also sang for the members of the Accademia Filarmonica, for the Petrarch sestina, first published by Bonagionta in 1568, then reprinted as the opening number of his posthumous *Madrigali e Ricercari* for four voices (1589), can have been intended only as chamber music and for such a purpose. To judge from its style, it can only have been written about 1555: in it we see a young talent struggling to release itself from restrictions. In 1558 he is mentioned as organist at San Geremia in Venice (Canareggio). In the same year he becomes a member of the Accademia della Fama founded by Federigo Badoer, an academy that was promptly suppressed by the Council of Ten. In 1566 he is called to the second organ at San Marco as Claudio Merulo's successor: "...D. Andreas de canal regio se contulit Venetias ad inserviendam Ecclesiam," the documents record in July of that year, and Andrea is given fifteen ducats to cover the expenses of his journey. He came from abroad, then, presumably from Munich, where in 1562 he is recorded as Lasso's traveling companion in Bohemia and on the Rhine. This tallies with the fact that he dedicated a book of his motets to Duke Albrecht of Bavaria in 1565 and that even later he was in close touch with the court of Munich and with Archduke Charles of Graz (who was himself connected with the ducal house of Bavaria) as well as with the house of Fugger at Augsburg. He never became choirmaster, but continued for the rest of his life as Gioseffo Zarlino's subordinate. It was only in 1584, when Merulo left his post to go to Parma, that he was given the first organ, while the second went to his nephew Giovanni, who for some time had been replacing Merulo at the first. He was married but seems to have had no children. Toward the end of 1586 he died, and Vincenzo Bell'Haver was named to succeed him. He appears to have been a quiet, likable man and to have disliked publicity. His place in musical history may be briefly defined by saying that, if Zarlino was Willaert's official successor, it was Andrea, as the greatest Venetian master of the day, who succeeded him in spirit. In tendency, he is Lasso's direct opposite. Lasso, despite certain exceptions, never deviated in principle from the austere, sublime conception of the madrigal: the poet about whom his work is centered is Petrarch, "the sensual, supersensual lover." Andrea Gabrieli continued to worship at Petrarch's shrine, but his texts are already dominated by the sensuality of Torquato Tasso and Giambattista Guarini, and his music is in keeping with them.

Andrea Gabrieli's position was clearly a central one, for in his day one would scarcely have thought of bringing out an anthology without applying to him for one or more contributions. His earliest madrigal is thoroughly conventional, but already in the *misura cromatica*:

> Piangete, occhi miei lassi,
> Piangete il vostro errore,
> Et con voi pianga il misero mio core ...

Significantly enough, it appeared in the *Scielta seconda*, the third book of five-voiced madrigals by Vincenzo Ruffo (1554). Some years later, Rore (or his printer) included a sonnet-setting by Gabrieli in the fifth book of Rore's five-voiced madrigals (1566); in the meantime, the chain of single pieces had grown longer and longer, and from henceforward it continued to grow. But Andrea was somewhat lazy about bringing out whole books: he might have published three times as many as he did. There are only six in all: two books of madrigals for five voices (1566 and 1570), two for six (1574 and 1580), one for three (1575), and a book of *greghesche* and *giustiniane* (1571). But there is a rich posthumous gleaning: the music written for a performance of *Edipo tiranno* (1588), written three years earlier (1585) for the opening of Palladio's Teatro Olimpico in Vicenza; the *Concerti* edited by Giovanni Gabrieli (1587); a third book of five-voiced madrigals (1589) which is merely a collection of scattered pieces; and the *Madrigali e Ricercari a quattro* of the same year. Finally, in 1601, came a gleaning of *mascherate*, most of them already known and previously printed.

There is no master whose work so completely and faithfully reflects the Venetian life of the third quarter of the Cinquecento as does Andrea Gabrieli's, unless it be, in another field, the work of Paolo Veronese. It was a gay, exuberant, sumptuous life: the troubles that were to beset the Republic were still far off or yet unborn. The most urgent of these, the fear of the Grand Turk, was allayed by Don Juan of Austria's naval victory at Lepanto (1571), which filled all Europe and especially Venice (the point directly threatened), with tumultuous joy and brought the city's love of life and of pleasure to a sort of climax. (The victory gave rise to a whole literature, or rather to a deluge of poesy, enough to fill half a reading room.) During the carnival of the following year (1572) the craving for pleasure found an outlet in organized celebration. We still have, in a report printed by the Venetian publisher Giorgio Angelieri, the *Ordine, et Dechiaratione di tutta la mascherata, Fatta nella Città di Venetia la Domenica di Carnevale*, M.D. LXXI (according to the Venetian division of the year, in reality 1572) *Per la Gloriosa Vittoria contra Turchi*. There were seven "Musiche di più sorte," i.e., variously constituted bands of singers and players, and a total of more than 180 musicians were engaged. After a number of *carri* and *mascherate* "there followed the three continents, singing, that is, four persons who sang, dressed as Turkish women and representing Asia" — "Le tre parti del Mondo poi seguivano cantando; cioè, Quattro vestiti da donna alla Turchesca figurati per l'Asia, che cantavano":

> Asia felice ben poss'io chiamarmi
> Ch'è vinto in mar di me l'empio tiranno;
> Ma più sarò, quando de Christo l'armi
> In terra anchor de lui Vittoria havranno.

Gabrieli's music is preserved in the posthumous print of 1589. What sort of music did he give to liberated Asia, so intensely desirous of completing the naval victory by one on land?

Africa and Europe also sing in this same harmonically animated and sonorous style, which is calculated to make a simple acoustic effect, Africa being represented by a lower combination of voices, Europe beginning almost exactly as Asia had. Then the three choirs join in a conclusion for twelve voices whose music is unfortunately not preserved:

> Cantiam dunque, cantiamo; e in ogni parte
> Gratie si renda al sommo Re del Cielo,
> Et sol a lui si dia con puro zelo
> Lode, e gloria del ben che a noi comparte!

We do not know whether Gabrieli also wrote the music for the *mascherate* that come next: "Four peasants singing villotte to the accompaniment of a lira," "music for lute, viola da gamba, and flautino," " music for four voices to be sung by aged patricians (*magnifici*) dressed in velvet and red damask:

> Se ben semo cosi quattro vecchietti . . ."

"for four peasants, singing in dialogue as follows:

> Ceccon, cantemo frello . . ."

"for four German drunkards with bottles of malmsey and goblets in their hands, singing as follows:

> Viva, viva, Bacco, Bacco
> Che di vino ha colmo il sacco,
> Ne di bere alcun'è stracco . . ."

"a music for *putti* [boys] dressed in silk in a courtly [Castilian?] fashion, singing:

> Putti siamo, o gentildonne. . . ."

We only know the itinerary of the festive procession: from the Chiesa della Madonna dell'Orto through the Merceria to San Marco, Santo Stefano, and San Samuele.

But all these types or typical groups haunt Gabrieli's villanelle, some of which he collected and published in his *Greghesche e Giustiniane* of 1571. It is of these villanelle that Giovanni Gabrieli is thinking when he refers to Andrea's "pleasant style." The "old people," the *vecchietti*, the enamored but impotent, sniffling, thin-legged old gentlemen, play a special part in all this, are indeed the exclusive subjects of the *canzoni alla villanesca*, or *giustiniane*, as they are called by Andrea Gabrieli and his Venetian colleagues Baldisserra Donato, Giuseppe Policreti of Treviso, Domenico Micheli, Claudio Merulo, Gaspare Vinciguerra, and Vincenzo Bell'Haver. With the old *giustiniana* this new variety has nothing whatever in common: the name of the old patrician family was presumably chosen simply because it best characterized the genteel senility held up to ridicule.

The musical and extra-musical characteristic of the elderly lover is his stuttering. The age must have found the representation and misrepresentation of this speech defect irresistibly comic; we too are still diverted when Don Curzio in the *Nozze di Figaro* and Wenzel, the befuddled bridegroom in the *Bartered Bride*, struggle in vain to master their unruly tongues. We have already seen (p. 374), in Andrea's parody of Cipriano Rore's most famous madrigal, how easily musical parody can be combined with coarse humor. Sometimes the three oldsters appear as beggars:

> Per chè madonna darne cambiananananao
> A nu che semo tre fideli amanti

I anni e'l tenenenencmpo havemo consumanananananao
E deventai poveri mendicananananti!
Cusi intravien chi senenenerve donne ingrate
Che spand'el bruo e rompe le pignananate!

sometimes (*Chinde dara la bose*) solmization puns provide dubious allusions; sometimes the old man, personified by the three voices, recites his experiences in love as a warning to a stranger.[1]

The old man's warning is a simple little ditty, and the imitated stuttering sounds rather more good-natured than realistic. It is a *gondoliera*, the first example of the form that the Venetian serenade had inevitably to assume; the refrain in particular, with the gentle rocking of its sixths, has all the local color one could ask. Formally, the little piece is still—or perhaps again—a frottola, but other numbers of the collection take on the form of the *canzone alla villanesca*—the strambotto with a refrain after each couplet—while still others are short iambic quatrains with *sdruccioli* at the ends of the lines, a form in special favor with Vincenzo Bell'Haver, Gabrieli's imitator and successor:

Tutto'l dì ti te spampoli
Che mi son un petegolo
E che paro un coruogolo
Con la coa tutta toccoli!

etc.

From these *giustiniane* a straight line leads to the madrigal-comedies of the Modenese Orazio Vecchi and the Bolognese Adriano Banchieri. When Banchieri limits himself to three voices in his madrigal-comedies *La Pazzia senile* (1598) or *Saviezza giovenile* (before 1628), the implication is that they are simply canzonette or *giustiniane*, and we have only to look at the dialogue between Graziano and Pantalone in his *Saviezza*:

Msier Piatelon, scarissimo piastron . . .

to recognize in Pantalone the old man of the *giustiniana*:

In la malora, tanto voio andar
Dal mio barbier. . . .

I need scarcely go on to prove that it is in these canzoni, which one might call "character-canzoni," that the immortal types of the *commedia dell'arte* are formed: Pantalone, Pulcinella, Graziano, Zanni Bergamasco, Pedrolino, the Spanish captain, etc. Here they existed long before they made their appearance on the stage, and though the poet and comedian Andrea Calmo (1510-1571) is generally credited with having created the figure of Pantalone, this figure in turn is only a Venetian variety of the *senex* of ancient comedy. As Benedetto Croce once shrewdly pointed out ("Pulcinella e le relazioni della commedia dell'arte con la commedia popolare romana," *Arch. stor. per le provincie napolitane*, xxiii [1891], reprinted in his *Saggi sulla letteratura italiana del seicento*, iv, 197ff.), Pulcinella as a person defies definition: he is a "collezione di personaggi," a number of persons in one. Such a type, created by the imagination of the folk—or shall we discreetly question this view of its origin?—has the capacity to add one new trait after another to the core of its character, and in the hands of the poet it then becomes a characteristic type of monumental grandeur, embodying a national peculiarity with overwhelming expressive vigor. The first to place the figure of Pulcinella upon the stage was the Neapolitan actor Silvio Fiorillo (from about 1570 to 1620). But had not Pulcinella, or at least certain aspects of his character—his naïveté, his absurdity as a lover, and his awkwardness—existed all along in the villanella, from Nola on? From the beginning, Pulcinella is celebrated for his cleverness in imitating the cries of animals. Does this not recall Baldisserra Donato's *Canzon della gallina* (cf. page 449)? The creators of the figure of Pantalone are Andrea Gabrieli and Antonio Molino—these two at least gave the figure its decisive traits.

The *greghesche* differ from the *giustiniane* chiefly in their dialect. This is the creation of an individual—Antonio Molino, known in Italian literary history as Burchiella, a man with whom Andrea was undoubtedly well acquainted and to whom he dedicated the second book of his *Madrigali a cinque* in 1570. (In his *Origini*, ii, 112, A. d'Ancona has assembled some biographical details about Molino, and of these it can at least be said that they are all correct, whereas the reference books and bibliographies in general, under Molino alias Manoli Blessi alias Burchiella, offer only the most misleading information.) The one forerunner of Molino seems to have been a certain Giandominico La Martoretta of Calabria, a *dottore in musica* and apparently an ecclesiastic, who had visited the Holy Land in 1554 and brought back from Cyprus a Greek text, which he set to music for four voices in his third book of madrigals. Antonio Molino was poet, patron, merchant, reciter, and comedian all in one; his travels had taken him to the Levant, whence he had brought back not only riches but also that dialect which is a comical mixture of Venetian, Dalmatian, Istrian, and Greek. It is a linguistic creation comparable to the macaronic Latin of Teofilo Folengo, called Merlino Coccaio, whose acquaintance we made in connection with Vincenzo Ruffo. Just as Folengo entrusts his jargon to Baldus, the hero of his poem, Molino invents a speaker for his dialect, Manoli Blessi ("Manoli" is doubtless an anagram of Molino), makes him the hero of a mock epic in the style of the *Orlando* (*I Fatti, e le prodezze di Manoli Blessi*, Venice, 1561), and ends by identifying himself with the character he has created. (Lodovico Dolce, in dedicating this mock epic to Giacomo Contarini, praises Molino as follows: ". . . when in his later life he dedicated himself to trade, he traveled in various parts of the Levant without forgetting a single one of his talents [dancing, jumping, playing, and singing]. Thus it happened that, not wishing to remain idle, he began in Corfu and Candia [Crete] to practice the recitation of comedies. Having returned home, he founded a musical academy with Frate Armonio and his companions which was a source of pleasure for the whole city. To establish this academy still more firmly, he endeavored to show how talented he was himself in the performance of comedies, and he was the first to introduce parts in more than one language. . . .") And in his character as the music-patron Manoli Blessi, he printed in 1564 one of the quaintest works in all musical literature: *Di Manoli Blessi il primo libro delle Greghesche Con la Musica disopra, composta da diversi autori, a 4, a 5, a 6, a 7, et a 8 voci*, dedicated to the "Eccellenti musici" Messer Paulo Vergeli (i.e., Vergelli), M. Claudio de Currezo (i.e., Claudio Merulo da Correggio) and M. Francesco Bunaldi (i.e., Bonaldi). To give an idea of his prose style, we reproduce the dedication:

"Essendo sta sembre mai chesta costumanza del vecchi andighi e del muderni scrivauri servao, Affendimu misser Paulo, m. Claudio, e m. Francesco, infra tutti candi li altri amisi a mi carissimi, de mandari sul pumblico le fantige de li sui frognimi inzegni, sutto la favur e prottetiun del Principi, del Re, e del Imperaduri, overamente de calche Megallos, grando persunazo, a fin chie'l valur el grandezza de chesti; da la invidia, e da le false calunnie del cativi reprensuri, li habbia à defenderi e far restar seguri. Mi, mo, no seghitando li costumi de chesti; hò pinsao, de prucederi aldramende, in mandar fora in luse per la mundo, cheste mie fantighe, perchie mi la stimo se habbiano à indrizzari, e dedicari le opere a chelli chie siano iteligenti de chella materia chie esse trattano; Parendo a mi chesti chie intitulano nel primo modo, frutti del inzegni soi tìpota gnende dessumegiai da colù chie vulesse dari a vederi, a fari giuditio de l'arte de un statua del fidia, del Policletto ò della Sansovin, a una fauro, ò à chalche aldro artesano del varia e diversa professiun dal desegno, talmende chie costui no sel truvasse atto a decerniri e cognusseri l'arte del scoltura, gnanghe del pittura à intenderi la bellezza de un figura del man del Rafael ò del Tician; cusi anga mi fra mi cun la mio cervello inseme, havemo deliberao de cavar fora e pumblicari al mundo chesta musica per mi fada cumponere da multi Eccellendi Autturi del Musica sora li mie Versi e Rime della Rumeca linga nostra, hò giudicao chesta esser dunatiun multo cunveniende alla vostra professiun, esendo l'uno, è l'aldro de vui cussi eccellende e perfetto Musico, como chie sèu: E chesto xe canto al vostro valori del Musica, alla chal se azunze puo l'andiga amicitia, e conversatiun e fradellenza chie mi havèn con tuttitre vui, unde, mi essendo sta spento, è cazzào dal'meriti del vostre Virtue, mel par rasunevolmende esser mosso à farve che sta dedicatiun la challe, paracollósso vel prego, no alla umellezza del dùno, mo alla gligora presta, e prunda vulundae del donaùro resgardando, vel piasa cun piasevule allegro viso de accettari. E alla vostra buna gratia mi medemo cun l'opera recumando.

Vostro Manoli Blessi."

The work shows Molino in the center of a circle of twenty musicians, among them such immortal names as Willaert, Rore, Wert, and above all Andrea Gabrieli himself, who is represented by more numbers than any of the others, namely six, among them a threnody on Willaert's death. Together with the Abruzzese Giovanni Armonico, likewise a comedian, Molino founded a musical academy: we now know its members.

In the end Molino-Burchiella's fanaticism for music seems to have led him to become a musician himself; for who else can the Antonio Molino be who, in 1568, published over the imprint of Claudio Merulo a book of "dilettevoli madrigali" for four voices, dedicated to the composer Maddalena Casulana of Vicenza? The dedication speaks a clear language: the gay Venetian or Levantine, in his advanced age (*in questa grave mia età*), has been carried away by the art of the young woman from Vicenza and this has led him to engage in experiments of his own ("dalla virtù vostra, atta ad accendere ogni fredda mente a desiderio di gloria [sono] stati in me sparsi li primi ammaestramenti di questa scientia"). A year later, in 1569, Maddalena herself collects a number of her friend's madrigals, dedicating them to Francesco Pesaro, the *capitano* of her native town (". . . perchè il Magnifico Messer Antonio Molino, hoggimai di grande età, e dotato de la virtù della musica, mi ha fatto dono d'alcuni suoi madrigali composti novamente . . ."). Several of the texts, in dialect, are presumably his own; unfortunately, the two works have not come down to us complete. But the very fact of their existence completes the anacreontic picture of the versatile old man.

Antonio Molino is also the author of the texts of the *greghesche* that Gabrieli published in 1571 with a dedication to the Provveditore delle Gambarare, Girolamo Orio. The dedication is not without interest: ". . . Essendomi M. Antonio Molino, cognominato Burchiela, stato sempre, come padre, e signore, per le soe singulari virtù, et havendo io già questi anni adietro composta la Musica sovra alcuni suoi Madrigali Grechi . . . ha paruto al presente al detto M. Antonio di donarmi alcuni suoi libretti di Terzi, per me composti, et alcuni appresso per lui fatti alla Greca piacevoli. . . ." "Since Messer Antonio Molino, called Burchiella, has always been a father and patron to me by virtue of his unique qualities; and since some years ago I set to music some of his madrigals in the Greek dialect . . . , it has recently pleased the said Messer Antonio to present to me some tercets, written for me, among them some especially prepared by him 'in the Greek manner' which are [very] gay. . . ." *Terzi*—this word sufficiently indicates the poetical form of the *greghesche*. They are strambotti, with a third line after each rhymed couplet serving as a refrain. Unfortunately, we do not have the complete music of a single one of these pieces: the genre was appreciated only in Venice, and thus neither the madrigal collection of 1564 nor this *Libro primo* of Gabrieli's went into a second edition. Of the *Libro primo*, only a single part has been preserved (in the British Museum), namely the tenor. Thus we must be satisfied with a few quotations from the text, the comic effect of which is based not only on the gibberish, the mixture of tongues, doubtless copied from life, but also upon the seemingly unintentional ambiguities:

(Mascherata):

> "Zentil donn'e segnuri
> Ben vedeu la nostra cumbania
> Chie se greghi vegnui del gregaria—
> Mi prottomastro son mezo divin"
> "Digo'l vendura fina'l fanduglin
> E mi dendro'l clissia—
> Canto cul mio papa dulce armolia"
> "Mo mi cun la mio lanza—
> Non fallo culpo e dago sembr'in panza"
> "Pero nui no pulemo
> Gratia truvar Chyrazze [pulcelle] in vostri petti
> Giathi no mai l'havemo
> Pola [molti] dinari, o greghi puveretti."

Or another, more typical in form and on a well-known theme:

> O mia canzun va in man de chy saveu
> Allegramente e no l'haver spavendo
> E cantaghe sul solfa el mio lamendo.
> E dighe anchor, chie mi me la consumo,
> Co fa'l candella, ch'arde in la gran vendo,
> E cantaghe . . .
> Faghe anghe mo sendir el gran martello,
> Chie mio cor batte gramo descundendo,

E cantaghe . . .
Se no me vol aidar in chesti affanni,
Mel vedera stu in sir del vita fora:
Ti canda un po' sul solfa, traditora.

The "lyric" of the *mascherata* and the comic alternate in the eleven pieces, and there is also a dialogue (*Manoli chie faremo*). The droll effect of the text must have been heightened by the music, which will have made use of comic babbling, flourishes, dramatic animation, and solos. None the less the words are the primary and original element, and we thus understand Andrea's gratitude as expressed in the second book of his five-voiced madrigals, which opens with a gracious and informative sonnet to Molino that is musically enchanting:

Molino, a le virtù tante e sì rare,
Onde come celeste arco v'ornate,
E già scherzando hor poetando fate
Egual il Greco al Fiorentin vulgare—
N'havete un'altr'illustre e singulare
Ch'ardend'ogn'hor di viva caritate
Spesso qual nuov'Augusto solevate
Ciascuno in cui chiara virtut'appare.
Felice Antonio, almo ricetto e pieno
Di quella cortesia ch'a giorni nostri
Scaccian li scettri e le real corone:
Mostrissi dunque il ciel chiar'e sereno
A voi Molino e siano gli anni vostri
Più che non versa arene Arno e Mugnone.

This sonnet, with its malicious allusion to the literary purists of Florence, is of interest also to the historian of Italian literature.

It is significant that Gabrieli himself brought out no book of four-voiced madrigals, and that his few pieces in this form were mostly not collected and published until after his death. He lives in a new world of sonority, a world which from the beginning stands in need of richer means, and the means at his disposal is the five- and six-voiced texture. Connected with the new sonority is a new harmonic idiom, quite different in character from Rore's, a composer with whom Gabrieli has little in common. Rore belongs to a generation of conquerors: he is bold and violent, pushing forward into an unknown and yet unmastered realm of expression. Andrea, too, knows this realm; witness his six-voiced setting of Petrarch's Good Friday sonnet:

I vo piangendo i miei passati tempi

published in the *Concerti* of 1587. Andrea had already set this poem for five voices in Scotto's collection *I dolci e harmoniosi concenti . . . Libro Secondo,* 1562 (p. 4). This five-voiced setting is a dignified piece in minor, full of character, distinguished by its rich, deep sonority and its grandiose invocation of the *Re del ciel,* an outcry in major; on the harmonic side, however, it remains wholly within traditional bounds. In contrast to this, the later six-voiced version is as uncontrolled harmonically as anything of Rore's; the chordal range extends from F-sharp major to D-flat major; there are frequent chromatic thrusts; the structure is polychoral and declamatory; and the harmonic exuberance betrays a turmoil and an inner unrest that is already completely "baroque." Such excursions into Rore's territory, the land of expression, are however by no means the rule with Andrea Gabrieli. For in this land he is already at home; he is not a discoverer but an heir; he extends the natural frontiers of harmony simply by overstepping them. His points of departure are Verdelot, Willaert, and Parabosco, not Rore. Even where he deports himself archaistically, he is at once recognizable by the way he lights up the harmony with major triads; witness, for example, the opening of a madrigal (1, 8) whose text had already been set to music by Claudio Veggio (in Doni's *Dialogo* of 1544). Veggio begins:

How deceptively similar, and yet how dissimilar, is Andrea's setting, written twenty years later!

Claudio Veggio's harmony still breathes the sentimental conception of the minor mode, typical of the early madrigal, and struggles toward the plagal cadence, with its downward drive and downward pull. Gabrieli, too, begins in minor, but in his third measure the bright Venetian colors begin to shine. An opening such as the following, in a resplendent C major, is something quite new and must have seemed to his contemporaries like the revelation of an unheard-of vocal sonority (*Secondo libro a cinque*, No. 9):

Andrea's madrigal is, as it were, weighted in the direction of sonority; in the eternal struggle between melody and harmony, between line and color, color has once again obtained the victory. To this corresponds a new conciseness and brevity in the madrigal, one altogether different from the conciseness of Orlando Lasso. With rare exceptions (*Secondo libro a cinque*, No. 17: *Angel del terzo ciel sceso fra noi*, an epithalamium), diffuseness in the exposition and interweaving of the motifs has disappeared. Close imitation is now essential (*Secondo libro a cinque*, No. 10):

Above all, Andrea aims to symbolize every concept that occurs in his text; he does so with complete mastery of every rhythmic and harmonic resource, and with consummate ease. In this he is the real precursor of Marenzio. Nor ought we to be astonished at his making occasional use of "eye-music," unlike Lasso or Monte, but just as Marenzio did: for "eye-music" was the most striking and convenient means of symbolization. A good illustration of his facile workmanship is the madrigal *O beltà rara* (1, 7; 1566), which we include in our volume of examples.[2]

The text is in no way out of the ordinary; it seems not to have been taken from a "literary" source and is aside from this quite corrupt:

> O beltà rara, o santi
> Modi adorni, luci beate piene
> Di dolcezz' e di spene —
> Ah sì tost'in oblio me post'havete!
> Ma sia pur quel che può voi non farete
> Ch'io non sia quel che'l primo giorno volli
> Fin che quest'occhi molli
> Finiran per mai sempre il longo pianto
>   [presumably: *i lunghi pianti*].

The two first lines rely for their effect upon "sonority," upon the division into two pseudo-choirs of four voices each which blend in the full "orchestration" of the third line with its low bass. Then follows a changing play of tones, characterized by light declamation, harmonic emphasis, and melismatic animation; the transitions are artless yet most artfully managed, tasteful and full of feeling. Andrea Gabrieli was a balanced, "harmonious" soul, "harmonious" also in the higher sense of the word.

Even when he turns to literary texts, to Petrarch, for example, as he does five

[2] See Vol. III, No. 61.

times in his first book and once in his second (in which his favorite poet is still Cassola), Gabrieli does not aspire to a more elevated style. For him, Petrarch's sonnet *Due rose fresche* is simply a wedding madrigal which he transforms into a masterpiece of easy grace.[3] The dedicatory ottava of this book, addressed to the "nobilissimo e reverendissimo [Abbate] Signor Dominico Paruta" and declaring him worthy not only of the cardinal's hat but even of the triple crown, is in spite of this high-flown compliment wholly unpretentious and lightly handled. The concluding sestina, a dedicatory piece in the form of a pastoral dialogue (presumably a greeting to be sung on the arrival of a papal prelate in Bergamo), is a model in its combination of a sonorous dignity and a delicacy reminiscent of chamber-music. The limits of his harmonic boldness, as they then were, are reached in the following passage, which shows that Andrea was quite aware of the meaning of "transposition":

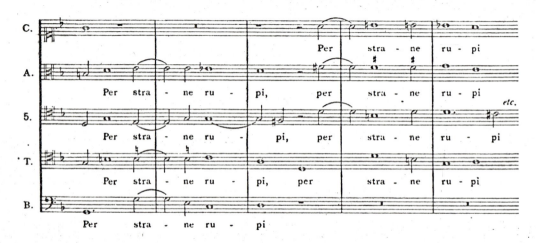

The exploitation of every sonorous possibility is carried even further in Andrea's two books of six-voiced madrigals. A rich, festive sonority predominates in the first book (1574), which opens with a musical dedication (*Rendete al Saracini Muse*) to the Magnifico S. Giovanni Saracini Bolognese, contains as its most extended piece a compliment to a lady—a canzone in short stanzas (*Da le Cimerie grotte*), and closes with a wedding madrigal that can only have been written for the wedding of Duke Francesco Maria della Rovere of Urbino and Lucrezia, the sister of Alfonso II d'Este (January 2, 1571)—a madrigal whose prophecy of a brilliant future and an "illustrious progeny" remained unfulfilled, for Francesco Maria's marriage to the princess, his senior by thirteen years, was childless and unhappy:

Goda hor beato il *Pò*, goda il *Metauro*,
Sparga l'arene d'or, d'argento l'onde,

3 See Vol. III, No. 62.

Ridan tra l'herbe i fiori, e per le sponde
Cresc'in premij d'honor la palm'e l'auro!
    Ecco l'alma *Lucretia,* ecco il thesauro
D'ogni virtù che'l ciel più larg'infonde
Che col gran sposo suo luce diffonde
Tal che per lor già torna il secol'd'oro.
    Questi come del Ciel la Lun'e'l Sole
Saran del mond'i più splendenti lumi
Cari non men per opre altere e sole
    Poi che tutti gli antichi e bei costumi
Fiorir faranno, et fia lor chiara prole
Felice coppia di terrestri numi.

As an "extra" Andrea then added an elaboration of the same *moresca* that was also published seven years later in an elaboration by Lasso. The opening will show that the two versions of the three-voiced model are almost identical:

How powerful a force convention was in the sixteenth century—a force as powerful in music as it was powerful in the fine arts and in poetry! The impulse to follow the beaten path and to repeat steps made before is an irresistible impulse that can assert itself at the same moment as the impulse toward the new, toward originality, toward progress.

The second book of Gabrieli's six-voiced madrigals (1580) is a manifesto. The madrigal has surrendered to hedonism. Andrea's first book still contained three sonnets from Petrarch; in the second there are only two bipartite pieces in sonnet form and Torquato Tasso's first madrigal. And accordingly there are only a few numbers with the old time-signature—pathos-laden, sentimental pieces like the threnody (No. 11) *Quel dolce suono e quel soave canto* (*Denkmäler der Tonkunst in Oesterreich,* LXXVII, No. 5); the rest are all in the *misura cromatica.* The prevailing tone is epigrammatic and anacreontic throughout. The possibilities of choral combination are exploited to the utmost: sometimes two sopranos give additional brightness to a combination that is already bright; sometimes two tenors, sometimes two basses vie with one another, while the remaining voices continually change their relationship to these pairs. The urge to symbolize the concepts of the text as clearly as possible sometimes assumes extreme forms, even in the work of the reserved and fastidious Andrea—as for example, when he assigns this familiar warning to a lover dressed as a shepherd:

> **Non ti** sdegnar, o Filli, ch'io ti segua
> **Perche la tua** bellezza
> **In un** momento fugge e si dilegua,
> **E se pria che** ti giunga aspra vecchiezza,
> **Non cogli il** frutto de la tua beltate,
> **Potrai** forse pentirti in altra etate!

The madrigal has at length assumed an attitude so light and pleasing that the line separating it from the polyphonic canzonetta (canzone) has become blurred. Consider, for example, No. 7 of the second book:

> Se vuoi ch'io muoia, o nuovo Basilisco,
> Fissa in me'l guardo tuo fiero e mortale
> E finirà il mio male
> E io lieto morrò quando mi tocchi
> Haver la morte mia da tuoi begli occhi.

In content and form, with its repetitions of the first and last lines, this might even be mistaken for a canzonetta, and the six-voiced canzoni of Giovanni Ferretti, the chief master of the type, present a very similar appearance. The same could also be said, and with greater truth, of the number that follows, *Dolcissimo ben mio*. A strange mixture arises: the pastoral scene is enlivened by reminiscences of the *canzon francese*, a genre with which Andrea Gabrieli, as a master organist, was sufficiently familiar (No. 12):

> "Hor ch'a noi torna la stagion novella
> Gl'augei, le fiere, e tutti gli animali
> Senton d'amor i dolci acuti strali,
> Te sola Amor non punge, o d'ogni fiera
> Più cruda in ciascun tempo e più superba"
> Così dicea Damon tra fiori e l'herba
> Dolcemente cantando a primavera.

The opening is in the typical narrative style of the *canzon francese*:

Hand in hand with the pastoral masquerade goes the tendency to treat the madrigal as a dialogue. No longer does Damon or Cloris appear on the scene alone; they appear together (II, 4):

> Clori a Damon dicea: "Dolce ben mio
> Fia mai ch'un tant'amor vada in oblio!"
> Et ei: "Nò, che'l tuo nod'è in me sì forte
> Che non si sciorrà mai se non per morte."
> Così detto stringea l'un l'altro tanto
> Che non più stringe ò l'edera ò l'acanto.

Long foreshadowed and prepared in the capitolo and sonnet, these dialogues in shepherd costume now become a sign of the madrigal's inner decay: the lyric utterance becomes more and more untrue, and its claims to a mise-en-scène lead it inevitably to the stage itself and thus to self-destruction. The several characteristics of the genre—its pastoral mise-en-scène, its sensuous action, half veiled, half unveiled, its epigrammatic formal concentration—are given their most typical expression in a piece more often set to music than any other of its kind, a madrigal by the poet Battista Guarini:

> Tirsi morir volea.

Guarini (1538-1612), Torquato Tasso's more fortunate rival at the court of Ferrara (where he, too, was sometimes the victim of intrigues), is the author of the most celebrated dramatic poem of the time, *Il Pastor Fido*, a "tragicommedia" begun after 1580 and completed in 1583 or thereabouts, printed first toward the end of 1589 and in its definitive form in 1602. We shall have to speak of it again more than once. Besides this poem, which not only requires music for its intermezzi, but is itself a premature opera, an "opera before the opera," Guarini wrote a considerable number of madrigals which were set to music long before their publication in 1598 (together with his sonnets and canzoni) and which musicians must thus have passed from hand to hand. Through the outward circumstances of his life, Guarini was almost continuously under the spell of music, a spell from which he could not escape. His sister-in-law was Lucrezia Bendidio; as the wife of the Count Paolo Macchiavelli, she was at the same time his aunt by marriage. "Dotata di una bellissima voce, esperta nell'arte musicale, ella, insieme con la sorella Isabella, aveva sempre la parte principale nei grandiosi concerti, che dal 1571 al 1584 rallegrarono il castello di Ferrara sotto la direzione del celebre Luzzasco Luzzaschi e di Tarquinia Molza. Le due sorelle Bendidio ed Anna Guarini, figlia del cavaliere, entrata più tardi nella corte, servivano alla duchessa per la musica segreta e facevano stupire tutti cantando improvvisamente qualunque *motto* o composizione si fosse loro presentata." — "Gifted with a most beautiful voice and an expert in the art of music, she and her sister Isabella always had the main part in the grandiose concerts which, from 1571 to 1584, under the direction of the famous Luzzasco Luzzaschi and of Tarquinia Molza, delighted the court of Ferrara. The two sisters Bendidio and Anna Guarini, a cavalier's daughter who later joined the court, served the duchess as chamber musicians and amazed everyone by their improvised singing of any *motto* or composition that was suggested to them." (Valdrighi, *Atti e mem.*, serie III, vol. II, parte II.) Guarini becomes the chief poet for the two musically most "progressive" courts of the second half of the sixteenth century, Ferrara and Mantua, and Duke Alfonso II d'Este and Duke Vincenzo Gonzaga turn to him more and more for texts suited to music. In 1599, the year after the surrender of Ferrara to the papal Curia and the cultural death of the brilliant city, Guarini enters the service of the Grand Duke of Florence, in which service he remains until July 1602, that is, long enough to be an eye-witness of the festivities of 1600 and of the beginnings of the opera—the end of the genre which he had supplied with texts of consummate virtuosity. But these texts survive the genre: as late as 1668 G. B. Mazzaferrata is still setting Guarini's madrigals to music (*Altro non è il mio amore, Cor mio deh non languire*), and the last of these two was even set by Al. Scarlatti (Padre Martini, *Esemplare*, II, 207). Guarini's madrigals are parodied, just as Petrarch's sonnets and Cassola's madrigals had been in the first half of the century; they called forth hundreds of imitations. A simple comparison may help to define Guarini's individuality: he can hardly be said to have invented a new motif—older ones he simply recasts in a more concise and pointed form. In Cassola's heyday, the anonymous author of a poem set to music by Alfonso della Viola (1539) sings as follows:

> Donna, del mio cor donna,
> Sgombrisi del cor vostro un tant'errore,
> Ch'in me fusse mai spent'il vostro ardore.
> Mai foco alcun più caldo
> Del foco vostro non m'acces'il petto
> Ne laccio alcun più saldo
> Del vostro laccio mai mi tenne stretto.
> Per voi sola ardo e a voi sola suggetto
> Son pur come già fui
> Ne mai sembianza altrui
> L'imagin vostra mi levò dal core
> Così lieto mi face il sant'amore.

Here is Guarini's version:

> Io d'altrui? S'io volessi io non potrei,
> Ne potendo vorrei.

Se'l mio cor tutto quanto
Possedete, se tanto
Son trasformato in voi che non son'io,
Come sarò d'altrui, se non son mio?

Epigrammatic conciseness has replaced the diffuseness of the older poet: the antitheses are as closely crowded together as possible; "imagery" has given place to
incisive declamation that demands of the musician a new and, as it were, epigrammatic technique. If we add to this epigrammatic formulation the pastoral setting
and the dialogue, we have the ideal of the late madrigal text. Here, too, Guarini
merely gives epigrammatic "point" to older models larger in scale and more diffuse.
The connecting link between the pastoral capitolo and Guarini's madrigal, the
"scenic" pastoral, is the canzone. A characteristic example occurs in the third part
of Girolamo Parabosco's collected tales, *I Diporti* (1550):

"Per que'bei crin," comincia Aminta—"giuro . . ."

This is a regular strophic canzone with *congé* and it is expressly called a *canzone
pastorale*. It seems never to have been set to music, indeed it would have proved
impossible to set it. But by crowding it into a narrower compass Guarini makes of
it a scene that can be set:

Tirsi morir volea,
Gli occhi mirando di colei ch'adora,
Ond 'ella che di lui non meno ardea,
Gli disse: "Ohimè ben mio,
Deh non morir ancora,
Che teco bramo di morir anch'io."
Frenò Tirsi il desio
Ch'avea di pur sua vita all'hor finire
E sentia morte e non potea morire,
E mentre fisso il guardo pur tenea
Ne begli occhi divini
E nettare amoroso indi bevea,
La bella Ninfa sua che già vicini
Sentia i messi d'amore,
Disse con occhi languidi e tremanti:
"Mori cor mio ch'io moro."
Le rispose il Pastore:
"Et io mia vita moro."
Cosi moriro i fortunati amanti

Di morte sì soave e sì gradita,
Che per anco morir tornaro in vita.

Nothing could better illustrate the taste of the late sixteenth century than this text. It is more obscene than the coarsest *mascherata*, the most suggestive *canto carnascialesco*, or the most impertinent chanson. It could not be further removed from true poetry, and yet it is the madrigal text most frequently composed during the so-called Golden Age of the genre. If I attempt to list the masters who chose this text, in the order of their publications, I shall probably be guilty of many omissions: Meldert (1578), Marenzio (1580), Gabucci (1580), Pallavicino (1581), Wert (1581), Vicomanni (1582), Malvezzi (1584), Milleville (1584), Caimo (1584), dal Pozzo (1585), Nicoletti (1585), Monte (1586), Heremita (1586), Trombetti (1586), Zanotti (1587), Perabovi (1588), Gabella (1588), A. Gabrieli (1589), de Castro (1589), Croce (1590), an anonymous (1591), Billi (1602), Gesualdo (1603), Luzzaschi (1604), Fornaci (1617), and Sances (1633). Among the famous names of the time only Monteverdi's is absent. But if for no other reason, my list is incomplete because the text was often varied. Andrea Rota (*Secondo libro a cinque*, 1589) sets it in the following form:

Nel dolce seno della bella Clori
Tirsi che del suo fine
Già languendo sentia l'hore vicine,
Tirsi levando gl'occhi
Ne' languidetti rai del suo desio:
"Anima disse homai beata mori."
    Quand'ella: "ahime ben mio
Aspetta," sospirò dolc'anhelando.
"Ahi crudo, ir dunque a morte
Senza me pensi? Io teco e non men pento
Morir promissi e già moro e già sento
Le mortali mie scorte."
Perche l'una e l'altr'alm'insieme scocchi
Si stringe coli soave e sol risponde
Con meste voci alle voci gioconde.
    O fortunati l'un entro spirando
Nella bocca del'altr'una dolc'ombra
Di morte gl'occhi lor tremanti ingombra
E si sentian mancand'i rotti accenti
Agghiacciar tra le labra i baci ardenti.

Orazio Vecchi (*Madrigali a cinque, primo libro*, 1589) varies the motif itself:

Tremolavan le frondi e la marina
Aure dolci spiranti
Increspava la sua fald'azzurina,
E gl'augelletti gai
Co'i garriti e co'canti
Givan sfogand'amorosetti lai,
Quando ecco il mio bel sole
Con tacite parole
Piene d'affetto, di ferventi ardori,
Disse: Ben mio, deh mori oime ch'io moro.
Ond'all'hor io languendo
Con luci tremolanti
Anheland'e morendo
Nova vita immortal dolce riprendo.

He even uses it, as does Giovanni Croce (*Canzonette, libro primo*, reprinted 1598), for a canzonetta (1585):

Con voce dai sospiri
Interrotta dicea un Pastor dolente,
"L'alma vicin'a mort'homai si sente."
Disse la Ninfa allhor con gran desio:
"Non posso più tardar, i' moro anch'io."
Il Pastor sospirando
Si la strinse, che più forte non stringe
Olmo novella vite che lo cinge
Et ella disse: "ò che felice sorte,
Se non sopravenisse a noi la morte."

It is difficult to say precisely what qualities of this worthless, indeed contemptible, text of Guarini's are responsible for its enormous vogue. No doubt it was the pastoral setting, the disease that had attacked the taste of the time, but it was also the cantata-like presentation and the latent dramatic element. When an art form decays and is about to die, it grasps at intoxicants and stimulants like a hopeless invalid and, again like him, at stronger and stronger ones until the end.

It was presumably toward the end of his life that Andrea Gabrieli set this text for seven voices—not for eight, since he wished to avoid any temptation to group the voices rigidly or schematically. The changing choral sonorities are in keeping with the flexibility of the tempo, which fluctuates between four-two ($\mathvarphi$) and four-four time (c). To be sure, Andrea assigns the narrative to the second chorus (alto, two tenors, and bass) and the role of the shepherdess to the first (soprano, mezzo soprano, and tenor), but he colors as he pleases, builds up the "recitative" to five and even to seven voices, and concludes of course with the full choir. The whole is masterly in its perfect balance and in its avoidance of the obviously dramatic; it is a dramatically animated madrigal but it is still a madrigal. And it is still chamber music, though its richer "instrumentation" brings it very close to the dividing line.[4]

The print of 1587 contains another similar dialogue, *Vorrei di vita uscire*, conceived for a bright combination of high voices, and still another, *Dunque fia vero*, in which a love lament is simply cast in dialogue form, though with such taste and so organically that the decorative presentation is not felt as external.

A series of compositions, mostly for eight or more voices, presents a different picture and seems to have been written for special occasions. They are display pieces, comparable to Tintoretto's and Veronese's great frescoes, in whose paintings this type of music has, as it were, become visible. One is a dialogue between a nymph and Cupid (*Arte musicale in Italia*, ii, 129):

Ninfa. "A le guancie di rose
Ai crin di fila d'oro,
Ohimè che non mi fido
Ch'esser non possi tu l'empio Cupido!"

Amor. Son del più nobil coro
Un semplic'Angioletto,
A riso e gioc' eletto!

Ninfa. "Ma in quest'herbette ascose
Di cui tant'arme sono?
Ahi, ahi, arco e strali,
Cagion di tanti mali?"

Amor. Miei no!

Ninfa. "Che no? son tuoi,
Ch'or ti conosco poi che ti rimiro,
E sei stratio e furore,
Benche ti chiami il sciocco volgo *Amore*."

It can be recognized at once as a wedding composition. There is also a *mascherata*, the *battaglia*

Sento un rumor

[4] See Vol. III, No. 63.

(the 2nd part only, *ibid.*, II, 139), which has many predecessors in the chanson and the instrumental music of the time, a rather regrettable illustration of the sixteenth-century enthusiasm for naïve tone-painting.

In complete contrast to these great representative and decorative compositions on the one hand and to the *greghesche, giustiniane,* and other *villanesche* for three voices on the other, is Andrea's book of three-voiced madrigals of 1575 (first edition?) which, by 1607, had gone through three further editions. Their character is wholly different from the character of his many-voiced display pieces. Unlike many other madrigal prints for two and three voices, it does not belong to pedagogical literature and is not an exercise in counterpoint or solfeggio. To recognize its individuality we shall need to look first at the texts. Only one of them (*Il dolce sonno*, an ottava also set to music by other masters—Palestrina, for example) is of unknown authorship. The others, all ottave, come from the *Orlando furioso*, from Tansillo, and from Bembo. Ariosto is the chief poet. With one exception

La verginella è simile alla rosa

every text drawn from his epic is a multipartite scene: Bradamante's displeasure (XXXVI, 32-33)

"Dunque basciar sì bell'e dolci labbia"

set by Giaches Wert as early as 1561; the narrative of Zerbino's death in Isabella's arms (XXIV, 77-81, 83, 85-86)

"Ella non sà, se non invan dolersi";

Orlando's lament over Angelica (VIII, 76-78)

"Deh dove senza me, dolce mia vita";

Olimpia's story of the girl abandoned on a lonely island (x, 25-27)

"E dove non potea la debil voce";

Bradamante's love lament over Ruggiero (XXXII, 18-21)

"Dunque fia ver, dicea, che mi convegna."

We know that the setting of such excerpts from the heroic-comic epic was nothing new. Twenty years earlier Antonio Barre had set the cycle last mentioned to music for four voices (Vogel, 1555[3]; cf. p. 208), and since the 'forties Zerbino's last words had been a favorite subject of musicians (cf., for example, Vogel, 1549[2]). Perhaps the most ambitious attempt of this kind was made by the Florentine composer Stefano Rossetto da Nizza, who in 1567 set to music the entire *Lamento d'Olimpia* (x, 19-34), not simply Gabrieli's three stanzas. But Andrea, acting perhaps on a suggestion of Zarlino's (p. 208), does not merely sum up the work of his predecessors; he prepares the ground for the ideals of opera and cantata that are to come.

He narrates, and while so doing seems to be using the folksong-like melody of the Venetian *cantastòrie*, together with motifs from the anecdotal French chanson:

It is as though a narrator were to use three languages in order to declaim more impressively, and were to strike lower, or at least broader, tones in passages more profoundly felt:

Echoes of the ottava setting, with its venerable tradition and its "popular" tone, combine with anticipations of the cantata and—at least in subject—of the opera. I need not point out that the scene of Olimpia abandoned on her island corresponds exactly to the scene of Ariadne abandoned on Naxos. It is only necessary to dramatize all these episodes and high points, to fill them with the new pathos, and the threshold of opera will have been crossed. Later on we shall make the acquaintance of those who accomplished this; one of the most important is Claudio Merulo (1580).

Andrea leads us into other regions in the two cycles with which he begins and ends his madrigal book. He ends with four (42-44, 47) of Pietro Bembo's stanzas, "recitate per giuoco da lui e dal S. Ottaviano Fregoso, mascherati a guisa di due ambasciatori della Dea Venere, mandati a Mad. Lisabetta Gonzaga duchessa d'Urbino e Mad. Emilia Pia sedenti tra molte nobili donne e signori, che nel bel

palagio della detta città danzando festeggiavano la sera del carnasciale M.D.VII,"
a duet in the form of a gigantic *canto carnascialesco*, whose fifty stanzas Giaches
de Ponte had once (1545) set to music in their entirety. This is epigram, not narrative; the motifs are more delicately chiseled and the style is not unlike that com-
monly used in setting Ariosto's stanzas of worldly wisdom. An even stranger mixture
of disparate elements is the cycle which begins the print: it is a "canzonetta" in
ottave, a "popular" version of Guarini's lascivious pastoral scene:

> A caso un giorno mi guidò la sorte
> In un bosco di querci ombroso, & spesso;
> Ove giacea un Pastor ferito a morte,
> Che la sua Ninfa in sen se l'havea messo:
> La giovane gentil piangea sì forte
> Sovra' l suo amante, che l'amante stesso,
> Se ben la piaga sua era mortale,
> Piangea'l pianto di lei più che'l suo male.

> Vaga d'udir, come ogni donna suole,
> Et di veder che fine habbia la cosa,
> In un cespuglio, ove appena entra il sole,
> Da gli occhi d'ambi due mi stetti ascosa;
> Il Pastor nel formar delle parole,
> E'l pianto della Ninfa dolorosa,
> Parea, che l'aria intorno, & le contrade,
> Facesser lagrimar per la pietate.

> Con quel poco di spirto, che gli avanza,
> "Non mi duole il morir," dicea'l Pastore;
> "Pur che dopo la morte habbia speranza,
> Di vivere alcun tempo nel tuo cuore":
> Dicea la Ninfa, "hor come havrà possanza
> Di viver l'un de due, se l'altro muore?
> S' io vivo nel tuo petto, e tu nel mio,
> Come morendo tu, viver poss' io?"

> Et mentre ella le piaghe và sciugando;
> Et quel de' suoi begli occhi il pianto beve:
> Oh caso troppo lagrimoso, quando
> Il ferito Pastor morir pur deve
> Veggio la bella Ninfa andar mancando,
> Et cader morta, e per finirla in breve,
> Si restorno amendue morti in quel suolo,
> Che l'uno uccise il ferro, et l'altra il duolo.

These verses are attributed to the Neapolitan poet Luigi Tansillo of Venosa (1510-1568), some of whose sonnets and madrigals enjoyed special favor with musicians; in the popular and pseudo-popular poetry of the time they were frequently imitated, expanded, and turned into dialect (cf. Guido Vitaletti, "Intorno alla Canzonetta *A caso un giorno mi guidò la sorte* e ad altri documenti di letteratura popolare," in *La Bibliofilia*, xxvi [1924-1925], p. 179). The earliest known print seems to be that in an ottava collection by Agostino Ferentilli (*Prima parte della scielta di stanze di diversi autori toscani raccolte da M.A.F.*, Venezia, 1571, Sessa). But Lodovico Frati (*La Bibliofilia*, xxvi, 357), whose list of settings is far from complete, has already pointed out that some musicians were attracted to the poem even earlier: Giulio Bonagiunta, 1565; Giovanni Ferretti, 1569; Alessandro Marino, 1571; Tiburtio Massaino, 1571; Gio. Battista Pinelli de Gerardis, 1571; Paolo Fonghetti, 1598; Filippo Nicoletti, 1605, etc.

Perhaps it was this "canzonetta"—in German one would call it a pastoral "*Moritat*," a coarse ballad on a pastoral theme—that suggested the aristocratic madrigalesque narrative to Guarini. But in any case the motif of the concealed observer who witnesses a love scene is found also in Italian tales—for example, in the fifth *Novella* of Pietro Fortini (died 1562)—and in a sonnet set to music by Felice Anerio in his *Secondo libro a cinque* (1585), where it takes on a tragic aspect:

Viddi in mezzo d'un folto et atro bosco
Con un fauno scherzar maligno e fiero
Quella che traviar mi fa dal vero
E mi spira nel sen assentio e tosco.
    Viddi misero ahi viddi e ben conosco
Che fu del respirar chiuso'l sentiero
Ne di gridar mercè diemm'il pensiero
Che perciò venne inebriato e fosco.
    Viddi rapir i bagi e vidd'impresse
Ne bei coralli suoi ferine note
E di spuma letal asperse e tinte.
    Più viddi—e più direi—se mi rendesse
Vita'l pensarvi—ahimè che far non pote
Ch'in me non sien tutti i miei spirti estinti.

Massaino hints at its literary origin when he calls it a *capitolo di quattro parti.* It is in fact a connecting link between the old eclogues from the time of Isabella of Mantua and the new cantata. Similarly, Andrea's music is the connecting link between madrigal and cantata. Andrea stands exactly midway between Alessandro Marino and Massaino, who give the text the form of a madrigal cycle, and Ferretti and the other minor masters who set it partly in the *villanesca* style and partly in the form of duos. Andrea never entirely forsakes the tone of one narrating a sad event, yet he is always ready for tiny bits of tone-painting (*E cader morta*) or equally tiny hints of human sympathy, just as on the technical side he is always ready to change from homophonic, three-voiced recitation to a light motivic texture. No one really knows the art of the sixteenth century until he knows this kind of music. Its relationship to the rich, sumptuous madrigal for many voices is much the same as that of the delightful figurative scenes from Boiardo or Ariosto, attributed to Giorgione, to the great bucolic or mythological paintings of Giorgione or Titian.[5]

It is curious that in 1605 Filippo Nicoletti of Ferrara, choirmaster at S. Lorenzo in Damaso in Rome, set to music almost the same texts that Gabrieli had set, and in the same order, although for two voices—an indication of the far-reaching effect of Andrea's madrigals.

Andrea Gabrieli is also connected with a memorable dramatic and architectonic event of the time, the opening of the Teatro Olimpico built by Palladio at Vicenza. The piece first given was Sophocles' *Oedipus Rex*, as translated by the Venetian patrician Orsatto Giustiniano, and Gabrieli received a commission to compose the choruses: "Chori in Musica composti da M. Andrea Gabrieli, sopra li chori Della Tragedia di Edippo Tiranno. Recitati in Vicenza l'anno M.D. LXXXV. Con solennissimo apparato, Et novamente dati alle Stampe" (printed in 1588, that is, after the composer's death). The assignment was one with which the Venetian musicians were familiar. In an article to which historians of the opera have paid far too little attention ("Le rappresentazioni musicali di Venezia dal 1571 al 1605," *Rivista musicale italiana*, IX [1902], 503ff.), Angelo Solerti has shown that similar performances often took place in the Palazzo Ducale on special occasions—after the elections of the doge, on the occasion of the naval victory at Lepanto, when Henry III of France passed through Venice in 1574 on his way from Poland to Paris, annually after 1578 on St. Stephen's Day (December 26), on St. Mark's Day, and on Ascension Day; of these the music is unfortunately no longer extant, although we have some of the texts. These pieces differ from the later operas only in that they are not yet so called. They anticipate every conceivable type of opera: there are mythological and Christian-mythological scenes (*Trionfo di Christo*, December 26, 1571, by Celio Magno), allegories, pastorals, and burlesques, the last named perhaps related to the madrigal comedy, of which we have still to speak. Solerti has reprinted in full the text of one of these pieces, the *tragedia* by Cornelio Frangipane played before Henry III by the famous Comici Gelosi on July 21, 1574. The composer was Claudio Merulo da Correggio, a pupil of Gioseffo Zarlino. This *tragedia*, so called because it may be said to affect the classical manner, is what the seventeenth and eighteenth century

[5] See Vol. III, No. 64.

would have called a dramatic festival play, a prelude to an opera with mythological figures. If the reader supposes that these pieces were not sung in their entirety he is very much mistaken. "Questa mia Tragedia," the poet explains, "fu recitata con quella maniera, che si ha più ridotto alla forma degli antichi; tutti li recitanti hanno cantato in suavissimi concenti, quando soli, quando accompagnati . . ." — "This tragedy of mine was recited in the manner which most closely approaches the form of the ancients; all performers sang in the sweetest consonance, sometimes alone, sometimes accompanied. . . ." And it is his opinion that Merulo has surpassed the ancients: "Non si è potuto imitare l'antichità nelle compositioni musicali havendole fatte il S. Claudio Merulo, che a tal grado non debbono giamai esser giunti gli antichi come a quello di Monsignor Gioseffo Zarlino, il qual'è stato occupato nelle musiche che hanno incontrato il Re del Buccentoro. . . ." — "In the musical numbers it was not possible to imitate antiquity, for they are the work of Signor Claudio Merulo and the ancients could never have attained his level, any more than they could have attained that of Monsignor Gioseffo Zarlino, who was entrusted with the musical numbers with which the King [Henry III] was received at the Buccentoro." We know what these dramatic and festive choruses were like; as a rule they were madrigals for many voices, designed to be effective in large halls. But what were the solo parts like? The texts of these Venetian festival plays, so far as they have been preserved, and the known settings of ottave rime can give us a clear indication. For with few exceptions the texts of all these solo parts are simply ottave rime, with or without a strict rhyme scheme. The first of the festival plays of 1570 that have come down to us consists simply of stanzas "recitate nel convito fatto dopo la creazione del Serenissimo Luigi Mozanigo," of stanzas by the poet Celio Magno distributed among the mythological *dramatis personae*. Presumably, the singers improvised over a fixed *basso ostinato*, and their improvisations were certainly a step toward the accompanying monody. The composers of these Venetian *rappresentazioni musicali* were the great masters of the city: Zarlino, Merulo, the two Gabrieli, and above all Giovanni Croce da Chioggia, the favorite musician of the powerful and munificent doge Marino Grimani (1595-1605). We should be unfair toward these masters if we were to pass over in silence their part in the creation of the opera. For the opera was by no means a purely Florentine product. The Florentine Camerata was simply more expert in publicity and in draping itself with a "classical" cloak.

Undoubtedly we have one of Andrea's choruses for such a festival play, one on a mythological subject, in a madrigal included in his second book for five voices (1570):

> Non vedi, o sacr'Apollo,
> Com'a gran torto quella benedetta
> Anima langue e'l tuo soccors'aspetta.

Vien, dolcissimo Iddio, ch'a mortal mano
Sanar costei non lice
Ch'è sol da invidia d'altri numi offesa—
La sua rara bellezza è sol radice
Col valor soprumano
Del rio languir—o grat'e bell'impresa
Fia la tua, se diffesa
Havrà da te quest'alma benedetta,
Ch'a torto langue e tuo soccors'aspetta.

The text points to some drama about Psyche or Ino, and Gabrieli has given it a marvelous coloring, setting it for four women's voices and a high tenor; it is a dramatic chorus and evidently accompanied the appearance of the god after his invocation, as a significant pause suggests.

For *Edipo tiranno* Andrea was probably called upon to furnish the choruses. The "solo" in Choro II consists only of a few notes:

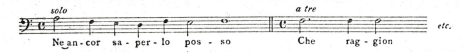

In this respect, then, the work is less important historically than the earlier *Sacrificio* of Agostino Beccari, for which Alfonso della Viola provided music to accompany the scene of the priests (cf. p. 301). None the less, Gabrieli's choruses for Sophocles' tragedy are the high point and masterpiece of the genre. (The print has not come down to us complete; but it is easy to supply the missing voice.) He has aimed at the most extreme simplicity and brevity; the chorus declaims very simply so that every word may tell. Changes in sonority, from two voices to six, and in the distribution of the voices, from high to low, prevent monotony. These choruses do not archaize—they are truly archaic in their grandeur and dignity. Thus Andrea Gabrieli, in other respects the very antithesis of Rore and Lasso, the master of the anacreontic, of the pastoral, of the Venetian festival madrigal, and of the *greghesca* and the *giustiniana*, also made in the choruses for *Oedipus Rex* his contribution to the grandiose and the Michelangelesque.

CONVENTION AND PROGRESS

THE development of the madrigal, like that of every other form of art, is kept in motion by two conflicting forces which by no means cancel one another out: by traditionalism—what we call convention—and by the urge to progress, to shape rather than to be shaped by the demands of the time, to burst the restraining bonds.

The active force is always stronger than the passive; art is not permitted to stand still. But, on the formal side, inertia is still an extraordinarily powerful factor in sixteenth-century Italy, even in the madrigal, which was after all the natural and favorite proving-ground for every innovation. And even where the collapse of the tradition seems most complete, indeed precisely because it is so complete, a reaction is bound to set in. The transition from the song form to the motet form about 1520 had been one of the greatest revolutions in all musical history. The secular counterpart of the motet, the madrigal, had as it were degraded the song forms proper, one after another—the frottola, the *canzon villanesca*, and the canzonetta—to a less aristocratic level, the level of second-rate music. But in being thus crowded into the background—although by no means suppressed—the mysterious resilient force of the song, of the song-like, had actually been doubled. The frottola does not die; it simply becomes submerged, and it transforms itself until at the end of the century it first corrupts the madrigal, then overpowers it, and in the seventeenth century, as the aria, triumphs regally over every other form. Of the motet form, in so far as it gave expression to speech and set the poetic above the musical, nothing is left but the *recitativo accompagnato*, a mere foil for the conquering aria. And yet the madrigal lived on in its original form until well into the time when the cantata was perfected, for it too represents an eternal principle, the principle of part-writing, of polyphony, of counterpoint, even though this principle also underwent a change, the change to the *stile concertante*.

The conflict between old and new, between conservatism and progress, never stops: it is only that it is sometimes more quiet, going on beneath the surface, and that it is at other times noisier and more ostentatious. Benedetto Croce speaks somewhere of the "eternal fact" that is the Renaissance, of the never ending struggle "between worldliness and other-worldliness, between individual strength and a presentiment of a higher power." This formulation will also be true of the music of the sixteenth century if we substitute for Croce's two lofty conceptions the more modest ones of the impulses toward conservatism and innovation. The impulse toward innovation is so strong that at the end of the century it leads to a new musical revolution, to monody, the accompanied solo song, and all their accompanying phenomena. I hesitate to use so strong a word as "revolution" for this change, in view of its academic, philological, literary origin, under the aegis of the Florentine Camerata. But the Camerata's attempt to make the marvelous effects attributed by legend to ancient music available to modern music also was merely the outward sign of a movement which had been long in preparation. At best it may be said to have hastened the advent of monody and of the *stile concertante*.

To begin with, it is essential to understand the character of this revolutionary element in Italian secular music. As in the fine arts, the development leads from rest to motion. I shall not carry the analogy further, for the nature of music is such that one cannot simply transfer to it stylistic concepts borrowed from architecture, painting, and sculpture. He who wishes to call a motet by Josquin or a madrigal by Costanzo Festa "classic" and a motet by Giovanni Gabrieli or a madrigal by Monteverdi "baroque" may do so. Everyone is at liberty to play with words as he likes. But as in the fine arts, there are in music only single Italian masters—above all Rore and Monteverdi—who go beyond the conventional and national, and thus approach the revolutionary. In Italy music becomes national in that it sets limits and respects them. One refines more and more upon what is given, one attaches more and more importance to virtuosity. It is not that as time goes on Italian music and the madrigal gain in truth, in purity, and in depth: in a history of the affective element in music the madrigal would play only a modest part. It is rather that, as the century advances, the affective side of the Italian madrigal becomes increasingly sophisticated but at the same time increasingly shallow and sensual. It is perhaps significant that the century of the madrigal is also the century that called forth the *Exercitia spiritualia* of St. Ignatius and brought them to the highest pitch of effectiveness. For what is the meaning of these "exercises"? To make more vivid the believer's awareness of his every act of faith, to promote "a more lively relation between man and Christ the Lord." The believer engaged in these exercises sees with his own eyes the Stations of the Cross; he hears with his own ears the blasphemies of the damned against the Redeemer and the Communion of Saints—we recall that certain masters of the madrigal set to music the very passage in which Dante (*Divina Commedia*, Inferno III, 22) describes the lamentations of the damned.

Historians have rightly pointed out the connection between the aims of St. Ignatius and the writings of the Catholic mystics of the Quattrocento; they have also stressed their fundamental opposition: the realism, the naturalism, and the conventional clarity of St. Ignatius. Loyola was a Spaniard, a Latin. But the madrigal also stresses Latin conventionality, the tendency to refine upon a form within traditional limits. Wert, Marenzio, and Gesualdo are more "Italian," more national than Monteverdi, who bursts the restraining bonds. This passionateness is not passion. In general, the sixteenth century still rejects raw expression, the barbaric cry, not only in the representative music of the church but also in the madrigal. Otherwise it would not have clung so long to a "neutral" instrument like the polyphonic madrigal for the expression of the most personal feelings. In general it avoids real emotional depth. It does not go beyond the sentimental and the elegiac and prefers to retain the mask of self-representation and self-reflection. The composer writes for the patron or the consumer, and the consumer wishes to see himself in a fashionable, conventional, "ideal" portrait. The formalistic, illusory side of this art is seldom questioned. It is a weakness. But it is also a strength. An innovator like Giaches Wert sets a sequence of stanzas from the *Orlando furioso* in the declamatory style throughout, as *madrigali ariosi* in the spirit of the older music, but for every expressive word he finds at once an equally expressive musical symbol. This was possible only because there was already in existence a supply of ready-made formulas, a sort of musical rhyming dictionary or handbook of musical rhetoric. This very love of formula was—strange paradox— one of the reasons for the overwhelming international success of the Italian madrigal and of the *canzone alla villanesca,* the villanella, and the balletto. Where there are symbols, there is a road from the isolation of nationalism into the universality of the world at large. Marenzio, the personification of stylistic refinement, had a greater international success than Monteverdi, the willful individualist. That we no longer have such symbols today is one of the reasons for the isolation of our art, which is no longer able to find its way beyond the national boundaries and which, even within these boundaries, can no longer address itself to a homogeneous audience.

To give examples for the power of traditionalism, conventionality, and inertia is not necessary: the vast production is in itself a proof. There are "schools" of musicians, of madrigalists, just as there are "schools" of painters: smaller masters group themselves about one of the greater ones and follow his example, though not without developing some degree of individuality. But the interest of history is naturally focused upon the masters, those who provide the impulse, even though it may be an impulse in the wrong direction—in short, upon the masters who write the word "new" on their banners. Giulio Caccini was far from being a great master, but his *Nuove musiche* have made a place for his name in every history of music.

The word "new" has various meanings in the madrigal prints of the sixteenth century. Petrucci was an aristocratic publisher who looked down on advertising, but after Jacopo Junta's *Canzoni novi* or the *Libro Primo della Croce* the phrase *nuovamente stampato* or *nuovamente posto in luce* appears on almost every print of the time. The word concerns us only in so far as it implies a manifesto. Adriano Willaert's *Musica nova* of 1559 heralded the unveiling of a new and lofty art of expression, a music in the service of *poetry*. In exactly the same spirit the Ferrarese musician Giulio Fiesco dedicated his *Musica nova* (1569), a book of five-part madrigals, to Lucrezia and Leonora d'Este, the patronesses of Torquato Tasso. Fiesco's entire works, beginning with his first book of madrigals for four voices (1554), are dedicated to members of the Este family. He is supposed to have been born "about 1519" and to have died "about 1586"; he is also supposed to have been a lutenist. Yet we know only three madrigal prints of his (1554, 1567, and 1569); a fourth, *Madrigali a quattro, cinque et sei, e quattro Dialoghi a sette et due a otto,* is known to us only from the catalogue of the collection of João IV of Portugal. (Eitner invents a second madrigal book of 1554, while other lexicons split the lost print into two distinct editions of 1563 and 1564.)

It is clear that Fiesco was unable to escape the direct influence of Rore, the outstanding musical personality in Ferrara after 1547. His first book of four-voiced madrigals (1554) is already unusually "literary" in Rore's sense. It opens with the dialogue of Montano and Uranio from Sannazaro's *Arcadia*

> Per pianto la mia carne [Fiesco writes *vita*] si distilla.

Beyond this it includes an entire ballata from the fifth *giornata* of the *Decameron* (*Amor la vaga*), Bradamante's lament over Ruggiero (*Orlando furioso*, XXXII, 40), a madrigal and a sonnet from Petrarch, a madrigal by G. B. Strozzi, a stanza by Bernardo Tasso; also a rather "unliterary" compliment, presumably for Alfonso II:

> Se quando per Adone over per Marte
> Arse Venere bella,
> Stato fosti Signor visto da lei,
> Quell'ardente facella
> Sol per te che di lor più degno sei,
> Arsa e accesa l'havrebb'in ogni parte. . . .

Like Rore, Fiesco supplies music for the dramatic performances at the court of the Este family; thus a strambotto, set with great refinement in the style of vocal chamber music, is not a *mascherata* at all, but to be understood only as a motto or introductory chorus for a pastoral play:

> Noi siam Pastori che cantand'insieme
> I nostri amor per queste selve andiamo
> E con pace infinita e gioie estreme
> De soavi desir l'alm'appaghiamo
> Ne invidia ne superbia il cor ci preme
> Chè più lieta fortuna non cerchiamo
> E sol fra noi è quel viver beato
> Ch'altri cercan fra l'or, fra gemm'e stato.

It is also to be attributed to Rore's influence that Fiesco sets an old-fashioned madrigal of Petrarch's and a really modern one, *Bacio soave*, in the chromatic style. The book of five-voiced madrigals of 1567, the texts of which are presumably the work of a single poet unknown to me, is no less "literary." But in 1569, in the *Musica nuova*, there appears for the first time a poet who made history as a purveyor of texts: Battista Guarini, at whose instigation (*ad instanza*) Fiesco has composed his madrigals. In the dedication the composer praises as much the "most prudent judgment" (*prudentissimo giuditio*) of the poet as the understanding and liberality of the two princesses. Guarini, then thirty-one years old, lived and worked as a nobleman in Ferrara, whither he had returned two years before. The book contains only fifteen pieces, fourteen of them bipartite sonnets; the whole is doubtless by Guarini, though only six pieces are surely his in that they occur in his printed editions—for the most part Fiesco has set the earlier text of these poems, not the drastically revised text of the later printed editions. (One of these sonnets, *Lasso, ben può fortuna al viver mio*, is erroneously ascribed by A. Solerti to the young Tasso; it is simply a first version of Guarini's *Più ben empia fortuna al viver mio*.) These poems constitute the "novelty" of Fiesco's madrigals; for in comparison with Cassola's ideal a madrigal like the one which opens the print was indeed "new":

> Avido sonno ingordo,
> Che ne begli occhi di madonna stai,
> Dove ti nutri e pasci,
> E i miei la notte neghittoso e sordo
> A le·lunghe vigilie in preda lasci—
> Fuggi deh fuggi homai,
> Che'l sol già ruota in alto i caldi rai!
> Tu fratel della morte, tu d'errore
> Padre d'ombr'e di fumi
> Che fai dentr'a quei lumi,
> Che son nidi d'amore?

This has elegance, an aristocratic bearing, and a new point, and Fiesco's music is also elegant and pointed, the concluding lines in a homophonic setting. Guarini is even more elegant, fastidious, and "classical" in the following sonnet:

> Fede che nel mio cor t'hai fatto un tempio,
> Qual mai non hebbe il già ben culto Egitto,
> Ch'al gran stuolo d'amor errante afflitto
> S'erge felice e glorioso esempio:—
> Poiche fra le ruine e'l duro scempio
> Che'n lui fa l'amoroso aspro conflitto
> Tanto più saldo ogn'hor sorge e invitto,
> Quanto più fort'è'l mio nemico et empio,
> In lui perche tu Dea l'hagia in governo
> L'altar de la mia fiamma ergo e consacro,
> Che da te sola attende alto soccorso.
> Tu la ristaura sì ch'arda in eterno
> Che qual di Meleagro il tronco sacro
> Questa prescrive a la mia vita il corso.

For us this is extreme Petrarchism, that is, the height of artificiality and mannerism; for Guarini's contemporaries it was the height of virtuosity, if not of wit. All these sonnets cultivate this sort of virtuosity; most of them have a pathetic character; some are outright lyric scenes in fourteen lines; all are stilted and pretentious, even when they strike the motif of amorous confidence or homage. And the character of the poetry has a real influence upon the character of the music. Fiesco permits himself no harmonic innovations and avoids all coarse symbolism. Only when he chances upon the "conflicting emotions" that oppress the heart, does he give way to obvious symbolism:

And yet the fundamental attitude of all these madrigals does lead in the end to harmonic innovations—to cadences on the sixth chord and suspended ninths—and to a livelier rhythm. One of Guarini's sonnets, *S'armi pur d'ira disdegnoso ed empio*—one might call it "The Infuriated Lover"—is already set to music in a *stile concitato*, full of homophony and agitated declamation, with a sweeping, pathetic conclusion that makes full and deliberate use of the power of homophony and of doubly augmented triple-time:

> . . . *E co'l destino il mio voler s'unio* (See example, pp. 557-558.)

This heightening of virtuosity and refinement is one of the components of the progress of the madrigal and hence of its progressive dissolution. Another component is the heightening of expression, passion, and passionateness, of what we call "pathos."

THE RISE OF PATHOS

PETRARCH'S SESTINA

THERE are a few poems that nearly every composer of the sixteenth century attempted to set, just as nearly every painter attempted a Madonna with Child, or every sculptor a Crucifixion or a Pietà. For the madrigal a case in point is Petrarch's Good Friday sonnet:

Padre del ciel, dopo i perduti giorni . . .

in setting which every musician felt obliged to paint the feeling of contrition in the darkest colors at his disposal. But there is perhaps a better example: the second stanza of Petrarch's first sestina (or rather double sestina) on the death of Madonna Laura:

Mia benigna fortuna e'l viver lieto.

It is a better example because it lacks the reference to a holy day of mourning and is thus not held in check by a "spiritual" or even churchly subject, and because the poet has given his sorrow over the death of his beloved the form of an accusation, concentrating it in six terrifying lines:

Crudel, acerba, inesorabil Morte
Cagion mi dai di mai non esser lieto,
Ma di menar tutta mia vita in pianto,
E i giorni oscuri e le dogliose notti.
I miei gravi sospir non vann'in rime
E'l mio duro martir vince ogni stile.

(O cruel, grim, inexorable Death!
How hast thou dried my every source of joy,
And left me to drag on a life of tears,

Through darkling days and melancholy nights,
My heavy sighs no longer meet in rhyme,
And my hard martyrdom exceeds all song!—Tr. Macgregor)

One can scarcely set such a text to music in a purely formal manner and with "neutral" feeling. The musician who chose it, did so because he wished to express the extremity of feeling. The frottola had not yet been capable of this. In Petrucci's ninth book (1508) there is an anonymous setting of the first stanza of our sestina, to which is added the text of several of the following stanzas; only the first is really suited to the music. We have already pointed out (p. 109) that this is by no means a neutral composition. None the less, the expression does not go beyond the general elegiac tone:

There is feeling here, but there is no pathos or even capacity for pathos. Thirty years later another master shows profound understanding for the requirements of the text. In the *Dotte ed eccellente compositioni de i Madrigali a cinque voci* of Verdelot (p. 21) there is a musical setting of the stanza by Arcadelt that belongs to a transitional stage in which a powerful urge toward expression is held in check by the limitations of the medium. Arcadelt, whose four-part writing is clear and transparent, resorts in this piece to a five-part texture that he does not know how to master. And he makes his task more difficult by writing for low voices only: four tenors which are constantly crossing, colliding, and obstructing, and a single bass; he thus obtains a dark tone color:

The beginning is enough to show that Arcadelt either handled the five-part texture very awkwardly or was a bold master who was not afraid to resort to extremes. The collisions in the second and fourth measures are bound to arise if the second and third tenors follow the rules of melody; and that there are no errors here, that everything is deliberately so intended, may be inferred from the literal repetition of these measures at the end of the piece. He who finds these collisions improbable should recall that the madrigal, especially the early madrigal, was in principle melodically conceived, and that the harmony was merely an accidental result of the combining of the parts. (Examples of such collisions from a later period may be found in Ch. Kennedy Scott's sensitive study, *Madrigal Singing* [London, 1931], pp. 9-11.) Every line is worked out with the same "density" and there is no attempt to simplify the task (as might be thought) by making the texture more transparent. If Arcadelt intended all these harsh moments, it would have to be said that, while the brightness and purity of his writing make him a forerunner of Palestrina, his boldness and ruthlessness in voice-leading make him at the same time a forerunner of Rore or of the Marenzio of the *Canzon pietrosa*. But we shall know little of sixteenth century music until we are able to answer such questions with certainty.

We shall not linger over the lesser masters who set this text, among them Joan Bodeo, for four voices (1549) or Jehan Gero, for three voices (prior to 1556, presumably about 1550). But in 1555, in the first book of his five-voiced madrigals, which is filled with enthusiasm for Petrarch, Lasso has set it to a music that shows a real understanding of what it required. The opening itself, with its intentional harmonic instabilities, the harsh "false relation," shows spiritual unrest (see illustration on next page). The rest of the composition shows the same blazing up of feeling, the same dark coloring.

After Lasso comes Rore's setting for four voices (1557), one which we have already attempted to characterize (cf. above, p. 415). This set an example comparable to that set, in the history of German song, by Schubert's *Erlkönig*, which put an

end to the innocuous strophic composition of ballads and which had few competitors.
Rore's setting appears to have fully satisfied the age and to have frightened imitators
away. Not until 1588 does Giaches Wert in Mantua take up the text again, setting
not only the first but also the second stanza of the sestina. He is of course obliged to
outdo Rore, not only in setting the poem for five voices (as against Rore's four),
but also in his expression. The opening with the sixth-chord, the six-four suspensions,
the chromaticism at "... di menar tutta mia vita in pianto," the exploitation of the
lowest registers to express *giorni oscuri*, the breadth of the design—all this stands
already at the dividing line between mastery and virtuosity, between style and
mannerism. A further step seemed impossible.[6] Yet such a further step was taken
by Luca Marenzio, in his last book (1599). We shall return to it later.

One master who goes his own way in the field of pathetic expression is Gioseppe
Caimo of Milan, for whom we shall be obliged to set aside a special place when
we come to our discussion of the new canzonetta. Like a good playwright who
knows how to do justice both to tragedy and comedy, he is a master of both pathos
and humor, and it is surprising that so little attention has been paid to him since

[6] See Vol. III, No. 65.

the outstanding studies of Hol on his mastery of the canzonetta and Kroyer (*Chromatik*, p. 128) on his chromaticism. It is Kroyer's opinion that by 1584 Caimo was already under the influence of the young Marenzio, "whose reputation began to spread abroad with his first madrigal books." But these madrigal books contain nothing that is at once as bold and as regular as Caimo's Good Friday music

È ben ragion se l'eterno motore ...

a piece that arrested Kroyer's attention and was subsequently reprinted by J. Wolf (*Sing- und Spielmusik aus älterer Zeit*, No. 38). No, Caimo himself already stands at the end of a long development and is a pupil—presumably not only a spiritual pupil but also a personal one—of Pietro Taglia (cf. above, p. 425). The stylistic characteristics are the same as in Taglia's madrigals: pure logic, coupled with seeming ruthlessness. Nowhere in his four-voiced madrigals of 1564 does he experiment for experiment's sake. It is as though he wished to protest against Rore when he sets once again the text of Rore's most famous piece, *Ancor che col partire*, and in a much lighter, entirely homophonic style, as if to say: "This epigrammatic, playful text does not deserve more serious treatment."[7]

But he is by no means a superficial composer. His book contains some obviously "scenic" pieces: a prayer to Aphrodite, the *regina di Cipro* (*China le sant'orecchie al canto mio*) and an idyllic classicizing lament of a shepherd, which sounds like the conclusion or climax of an eclogue (a fragment in terze rime):

E se tu riva udisti alcuna volta
Humani affetti, hor prego: O accompagni
La dolente sampogna a pianger volta!
O herbe, o fior ch'un tempo eccelsi e magni
Re fosti al mondo, et hor per aspra sorte
Giacete per li fiumi et per li stagni.

Note how Caimo symbolizes weeping:

[7] See Vol. III, No. 66.

The same piece arrives at the sixth-chord through chromaticism in a wholly novel, though logical, manner:

If we were to "arrange" this composition for soprano and basso continuo, it would be a *lamento* indistinguishable from Monteverdi or Sigismondo d'India.

In content, this work is as varied as one of Taglia's madrigal books: an antiphonal dialogue between donna and signore, a popular ottava (*Li vostr'occhi che sembran due facelle*), complimentary pieces addressed to the sons of the Emperor (cf. below, p. 600) and to a Grazia, a Margherita, an Ippolita, a Chiara, and a Terilla. But it receives its real stamp from the dark and impassioned pieces:

> Piangi colle sacrato opaco e fosco
> E voi cave spelonche e grotte oscure
> Ululando venite a pianger nosco . . .

or the following, in which a whole Inferno is conjured up:

> Andate o miei sospiri ove abelisce
> Con horribil chiome il capo de colubri,
> O l'Hidra, col soffiar incredulisce,
> El faro de Pluton to suoi delubri.
> Aime Caron, già sento che languisce
> D'haverm'in grembo ne stigij lugubri

Ma credo c'haverò tant'acqua a i lumi,
Malgrado d'Atropos che faro i fiumi.

All this is symbolized by the most extreme harmonic means, though not at all in monodic terms: Caimo opens as a rule with an expressive imitation and then continues homophonically and in rapid declamation, as though he had become impatient and was being driven on by his dramatic instinct. A typical piece of this kind is included in our volume of examples.[8]

ARIOSTO AND TASSO

ANOTHER problem in the history of musical pathos is connected with the role of Ariosto and Tasso in sixteenth century music, more exactly, of the *Orlando furioso* and the *Gerusalemme liberata*, a problem on which we have already touched briefly (cf. above p. 209). To deal with it properly, one would have to divide it into two distinct sections, limiting oneself in the first of these to the topic: the epics of Ariosto and Tasso in monody and in improvisation. This first section might begin as early as 1517, with Tromboncino's setting of *Queste non son più lagrime* (p. 206). But here we are dealing only with the madrigal for several voices, always responsive to any external stimulus and particularly so to that of Ariosto's epic. As the century advances, the choice of stanza becomes more and more restricted. Jachet Berchem, one of the first masters to set Ariosto on a large scale, picks out, seemingly at random, ninety-three stanzas of the epic: proverbial wisdom, narrative, lyricism, political matter; yes, even political matter, for example the invective against Spain and against the peoples of Europe who are at one another's throats (XVII, 74 and 75):

Se Cristianissimi esser voi volete,
E voi altri Cattolici nomati,
Perche di Cristo gli uomini uccidete?

In truth, however, Berchem's selection is anything but fortuitous or capricious, although he calls his work a *Capriccio*. In the first of the three books that go to make up this *Capriccio* he considers only the first, eighth, and twenty-third cantos of Ariosto's poem, the only exception being an interpolated stanza from the twenty-eighth (*Che debbo far, che mi consigli, frate*, the turning point in the story of the clever little Fiammetta); in the second book he considers only the twenty-fourth, thirtieth, and thirty-second. Berchem composes *cycles*, choosing the culminating points of the action and concluding with Orlando's recovery of his reason through Astolfo (XXXIV and XXXIX). How carefully he chooses may be seen from the fact that in his *Capriccio* he publishes stanzas 125-126 and 128-133 of the twenty-third canto, but omits stanza 127, which he had already set for five voices in 1546. It is a fair in-

[8] See Vol. III, No. 67.

ference that the music for these ninety-three stanzas, too, had been written long before 1561, an inference confirmed by their style; for Berchem tells his story in the manner of the French anecdotal chanson—rapid, lively, artfully worked out; pathos is still foreign to him. If he is not capricious in his choice of texts, he is very much so in their musical treatment. One needs only to see how he describes Orlando's fit of madness in the second stanza of canto I (as illustrated below).

Berchem also applies this lively, even restless style to pathetic scenes: all in all, he is something of a special case and seems to have believed that an artistically worked-out musical setting was all that Ariosto's poem required. Francesco Corteccia of Florence is already more advanced. In his *Secondo libro a quattro* (1547) he publishes the

first of the stanza sequences, of which Berchem and subsequently (1580) Claudio Merulo set no less than six—the beginning of the *lamento* of the angry Bradamante who waits in vain for the appearance of her Ruggiero (XXXII, 18):

> Dunque fia ver, dicea, che mi convegna
> Cercare un che mi sfugge e mi s'asconde?
> Dunque debbo prezzare un che mi sdegna?
> Debbo pregar chi mai non mi risponde?
> Patirò che chi m'odia, il cor mi tegna?
> Un che sì stima sue virtù profonde,
> Che bisogno sarà che dal ciel scenda
> Immortal Dea che'l cor d'amor gli accenda?

One might suppose that Corteccia would at least assign this stanza to a soprano accompanied by three lower voices. But such is not the case. There are four *voci pari*, that is, three tenors and one bass, and it is not impossible that this choice was partly determined by the word *profondo*, for at this point the bass descends to the low E-flat. Here the pathos takes another form: it may be seen in the dark key which is closely related to G minor, and in the profound emotion and animation of the melody, of which the repetition of the end line will give a good idea:

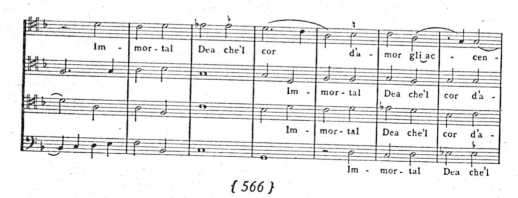

This "neutral" pathos, in which there is already a suggestion of suppressed passion, is completely in keeping with the early period of the madrigal, the period of motet-like conservatism, of artistry, of tender sentimentality.

The setting of stanzas taken from the epics of Ariosto and (later) Tasso now develops in two directions. One stresses narrative: we have already seen the most influential examples in Andrea Gabrieli's three-voiced madrigals (1575, presumably prior to 1575) [cf. above, p. 545]. To be sure, Gabrieli also sets scenes of passion; but he aims only to provide a more artistic dress for the "popular" recitation of such scenes, transplanting and transposing this recitation, at it were, from the canals and the *campieli* of Venice into the *palazzo* and the chamber. It is a combination of the popular and the artistic that we moderns find difficult to imagine. It looks forward to the recitative. The other direction stresses lyricism and looks forward to monody: we already know it from such pieces as the "arias" *Dunque basciar* and *Se tu m'occidi* (*Orlando furioso*, XXXVI, 32-33) in Giaches Wert's four-voiced madrigals of 1561. Although the purely vocal performance of the first of these ottave by four voices is not merely probable but certain, we are reprinting it in the form of an "accompanied monody" in order to show that this style did not need to wait for its "invention" by the Florentine Camerata.[9]

Rore's madrigals for four and five voices "senza battuta" (for example, *Cura che di timor*) have borne early fruit. To be sure, Wert is simpler and more reserved in his harmony than Rore, but the upper voice is already freer, livelier, and more detached from the "accompanying" parts. Above all, the application of this *stile recitativo* to dramatic lyricism is an advance in *aesthetic* insight difficult to overestimate.

This rise in pathos, in the predilection for scenes of agitation, can be followed everywhere in the madrigal prints, and not only in Northern Italy. About 1570 Benedetto Serafico di Nardo, a Neapolitan, sets the outbursts of Olimpia (*Orlando furioso*, x, 24ff.) and Fiordiligi (XLIII, 160f.), designating them expressly as *lamenti*.

[9] See Vol. III, No. 68.

But it was not until they turned from the *Orlando furioso* to the *Gerusalemme liberata* that the musicians of the age—above all, Wert—took the decisive step toward pathos. The change exactly corresponds to the difference in the expression of passion in the two poets and to the decisive change in taste between the first and the second halves of the century. In Ariosto, no phrasemonger, but rather a humane, imaginative, and humorous poet, there is still genuine passion and true feeling. In Tasso, the bigoted, gloomy, humorless pseudo-classic there is *pathos*, that is, exaggeration. For the first half of the century—at least for musical aesthetics as codified by Zarlino in his *Istituzioni* (IV, 32)—Willaert's *Musica nova* embodied the *imitazione delle parole* in an ideal form. For Zarlino, too, music is in the service of *oratione*, of expression; for him, too, the harmony, the rhythm, must follow the *materie*; but as models of the vivid portrayal of emotional unrest he still cites such pieces as Willaert's *I'vidi in terra angelici costumi* ..., *Aspro core e selvaggio* ..., *Ove ch'i posi gli occhi* ..., *Quando fra l'altre donne* ..., *Giunto m'ha Amor* ..., pieces which appear to us as models of classic moderation, at least of emotional restraint. By comparison, Wert seems outspoken to a degree that was bound to seem revolutionary to his contemporaries. He remains faithful to Zarlino's aesthetic code only in so far as he applies extreme, even violent music to the most extreme, the most pathetic, and (for the taste of the time) most beautiful passage in Tasso's epic. It occurs in Canto XII, which culminates in the *Combattimento di Tancredi e Clorinda* and which has supplied music with a variety of examples right down to the nineteenth-century opera. Wert stands at the head of this line of Tasso composers: he set the two stanzas to music and published them (April 10, 1581) even before the appearance of the first authorized edition of the *Gerusalemme liberata* itself (Ferrara, June 1581). Most modern readers will want a summary of the situation. Without recognizing her in her armor, Tancred has killed Clorinda, his beloved, in a duel; before she dies, he has just time to administer the sacrament of baptism. At first disconsolate, he is at length consoled by a vision in which he sees Clorinda blissful in Paradise:

> Consolato ei si desta, e si rimette
> De'medicanti a la discreta aita;
> E in tanto seppellir fa le dilette
> Membra ch'informò già la nobil vita ...

Clorinda's body is buried with solemn and warlike rites, and on the day following:

> ... il cavalier ...
> Di riverenza pieno e di pietate
> Visitò le sepolte ossa onorate.

The two stanzas set to music by Wert and, after him, by twenty others are the following:

Giunto a la tomba, ove al suo spirto vivo . . .
Non di morte sei tu, ma di vivaci . . .

(*Gerusalemme liberata*, XII, 96-97).

How he set them is shown in our volume of examples.[10]

It is the *stile concitato* in all its essentials, long before Monteverdi, now a boy of fourteen, gave it its name. One might call the whole a choral recitative; it is dependent for its effect on its gloomy tone-quality and on its sharp, violent declamation which is ready at any moment for an outburst of pathetic illustration. Everything in these two stanzas is extravagant: the staccato recitation, shot through with rests; the imagery on *sgorgando* and *pianto*; even the harmony with its sixth chords and false relations, although this admittedly avoids extreme tones and modulations. Three years later, in 1584, Luca Marenzio reset these stanzas, adding the two that follow, obviously in rivalry with Wert. But he is merely more the virtuoso—more playful and more sensuous—than Wert, not more grandiose, and certainly less carried away with the inner drama of the scene.

In his eighth madrigal book, published five years later (1586), Wert goes a step further. It contains a few pieces for the "tre gentildonne" of whom we shall have more to say (p. 825), but it is primarily a Tasso work, with half of its contents devoted to the *Gerusalemme liberata*: an epoch-making publication that looks forward to the future and anticipates the vocal concerto and the cantata of the seventeenth century. Though dedicated to Alfonso of Ferrara, it presumably owes its existence to Vincenzo Gonzaga, at that time still the hereditary prince, and not yet the Duke, of Mantua. On November 6, 1584, Vincenzo writes to Wert from Poggio: ". . . Mio carissimo mi farete servitio gratissimo mandandomi quanto prima una copia della musica fatta da voi sopra le stanze del Tasso che cominciano 'Qual musico gentil ch'al canto snodi' et amo qualche altro madrigale novo de vostri se ne havete..." — "My dear fellow, you will do me the greatest service by sending me as soon as possible a copy of the music you have written on Tasso's *stanze*, beginning *Qual musico gentil ch'al canto snodi*, and I should like also to have some other new madrigals of yours, if you have any. . . ." Wert complies with the prince's wish on November 15: "Mando a V.A. le stanze del Tasso con alcune altre composizioni mie." (Cf. A. Solerti, *Vita di Torquato Tasso*, II, 206.)

The eighth book contains this composition (*Gerusalemme liberata*, XVI, 43-47) as one of the chief numbers. Tasso's sixteenth canto is another one of those arsenals from which madrigal, cantata, and opera drew their weapons: Rinaldo's liberation from Armida's snares and the transformation of the fair enchantress into an abandoned fury. Here, too, Wert stands at the beginning of the series that ends with

[10] See Vol. III, No. 69.

Gluck's *Armide,* indeed, with Wagner's *Tannhäuser*. Armida has pursued Rinaldo and his two knightly liberators, Ubaldo and Carlo, to the seashore; now she tries to persuade her beloved to return to her:

> Qual musico gentil, prima che chiara
> Altamente la voce al canto snodi,
> A l'armonia gli animi altrui prepara
> Con dolci ricercate in bassi modi;
> Così costei, che ne la doglia amara
> Già tutte non oblia l'arti e le frodi,
> Fa di sospir breve concento in prima,
> Per dispor l'alma in cui le voci imprima.

There follow three stanzas that begin with injured pride and veiled confession to culminate in mocking challenge:

> . . . Vattene, passa il mar, pugna, travaglia,
> Struggi la fede nostra: anch'io t'affretto.
> Che dico nostra? ah non più mia! fedele
> Sono a te solo, idolo mio crudele.

Wert sets the first stanza quite differently from the following four, as differently as the restricting, neutral medium of the five-voice texture will allow. The first stanza is full of "objective" tone-painting—one might even call it "naïve": *canto* has its long melisma, *ricercate* its positive rhythm, *sospir* its customary quarter rest. But Armida's lines are dependent, not on tone-painting, but on an animated declamation that rises at the end to the point of violence:

After this outburst, this eloquent silence, there follows a broad aria-like setting of the last two lines, with motifs that contrast and intertwine. Wert is already conscious of the opposition of the recitative and aria, but his recitative (the narrating first stanza) is full of tone-painting and his aria full of pathetic declamation. Wert pushes pathos to the limit in setting the stanza (XVI, 40) that describes Armida's outcry as she overtakes the fleeing hero:

> Forsennata gridava: "O tu che porte
> Teco parte di me, parte ne lassi,
> O prendi l'una, o rendi l'altra, o morte
> Dà insieme ad ambe: arresta, arresta i passi,
> Sol che ti sian le voci ultime pôrte;
> Non dico i baci: altra più degna avrassi
> Quelli da te. Che temi, empio, se resti?
> Potrai negar, poi che fuggir potesti."

The opening with the leap of a tenth in all the voices is in itself enough to show how far Wert goes beyond what is usual and appropriate to the style:

Carried away by his subject, Wert sets the entire stanza with the utmost conciseness: if one insists on a literal interpretation of the unusual time-signature, which calls for a rapid tempo, the whole occupies only twenty-three measures. The example is particularly well calculated to show how the concept *musica reservata* is beginning to change. Originally it was broad enough to include without differentiation both genuine expression and mere allegory—"eye-music," intellectual trifling with musical symbols. An exponent of this *imitazione di natura* would have been applauded by contemporary connoisseurs if he had indicated Armida's frenzy by an unusual modulation, a false relation, or some other musical allegory. Wert's music embodies Armida's hysterical outcry directly. The symbol is giving way to naturalism, to genuine passion.

In his ninth book (1588) Wert appears to have returned to a conventional choice of texts: there is a sonnet by Sannazaro (*Ecco ch'un'altra volta*) and several poems from Petrarch (the sonnets *Valle che di lamenti, Vago augellin, Padre del ciel, Quel rossignuol*, and two stanzas of the sestina *Mia benigna fortuna*). But it is only in appearance that he does so, as we were able to show at the beginning of this chapter-division in our discussion of the sestina. The old texts are filled with a new pathos and genuine chromaticism is beginning to creep in (*Ecco ch'un'altra volta*, 2ᵃ parte):

In Petrarch's *Valle che di lamenti* he adheres strictly to the diminished fourth in a "development section" of nineteen measures:

Val - le   che di la - men - ti mieisei pie -   na

In striking contrast to the trend toward exaggerated expression stand the "festive" and "pastoral" trends. For this contrast, too, Wert's eighth and ninth books supply the most instructive examples. The ninth, dedicated to the young Duke of Mantua, Vincenzo, opens with the festive piece Wert wrote for his patron's coronation (1587):

> Hor si rallegri il Cielo e insuperbisca
> Manto . . .

a lively, though wholly neutral, piece of the canzone order. Not to treat his beloved Ferrara in too cavalier a fashion, Wert closes his book with six-voiced settings of Torquato Tasso's madrigals on the pleasure-seat of the Este family:

> Mesola, il Pò da lato . . .

and on Alfonso's third wife, Margherita Gonzaga:

> Ha Ninfe adorne e belle . . .

Again, both pieces are purely decorative. But the two books also contain a number of madrigals that give heightened expression to the opposite of the pathetic—the pastoral. The seventh book had opened with a stanza from the *Orlando furioso* (VI, 21), the beginning of the description of Alcina's garden:

> Vaghi boschetti di soavi allori,
> Di palme e d'amenissime mortelle,
> Cedri ed aranci ch'avean frutti e fiori
> Contesti in varie forme e tutte belle,
> Facean riparo ai fervidi calori
> De'giorni estivi con lor spesse ombrelle:
> E tra quei rami con sicuri voli
> Cantando se ne giano i rosignuoli.

Is it not significant that within a year this one stanza was set to music three times, by Ingegneri, by Pallavicino, and by Wert? Music is seeking new expression for a thrice familiar "category" of feeling—for the idyl and the pastoral. Hence it is that Ariosto, who is thought far too simple, is at once replaced by Tasso, the greater virtuoso (*Gerusalemme liberata*, XVI, 12):

Vezzosi augelli infra le verdi fronde
Tempran a prova lascivette note.
Mormora l'aura, e fa le foglie e l'onde
Garrir, che variamente ella percote.
Quando taccion gli augelli alto risponde;
Quando canton gli augei, più lieve scote;
Sia caso od arte, or accompagna, ed ora
Alterna i versi lor la music'ôra.

Wert at once combines his pastoral mood, his F major, and his three-voiced opening with his contrast of motifs, and before the first line has ended we already hear the beginning of the third:

Not only is this the beginning of the pastoral trend in music; it is also the beginning of musical impressionism. The year before, Marenzio had set the same stanza to music for four voices; his setting, which modern reprints have made widely known, is marked by a sort of childlike merriment and a naïve love of imagery, but it is far less "modern" than Wert's.

In much the same manner we find set to music, in Wert's eighth book, the first stanza of Tasso's Canto XIV, the approach of Night:

Usciva omai dal molle e fresco grembo
De la gran madre sua la notte oscura . . .

and Erminia's lament for her beloved Tancred, in a pastoral setting and a pastoral disguise (*Gerusalemme liberata*, VII, 19-20):

Sovente, allor che sugli estivi ardori
Giacean le pecorelle a l'ombra assise,
Ne la scorza de'faggi e de gli allori
Segnò l'amato nome in mille guise. . . .

Immediately after this, as an extreme contrast, there follows Erminia's lament on finding Tancred wounded and lifeless (*Gerusalemme liberata*, XIX, 106-107):

Misera! non credea ch'agli occhi miei
Potessi in alcun tempo esser noioso. . . .

At the end of the sixteenth century music may be said to have fallen into two categories—the pathetic and the pastoral: one might even say that it took refuge on these safe paths. It was a curse and at the same time a blessing. The pathetic and the pastoral become a convention and remain so for nearly two centuries. If Italian music could no longer give any genuine expression to feeling and simplicity, this convention was to blame; there are a few exceptions, like Monteverdi's *Lamento d'Arianna*, which at once became the starting point for a new convention. For what is the cantata, from the point of view of content, but a combination of the pastoral and the pathetic? And is not Metastasio's opera still a part of this tradition? But only within limits of this kind could form develop. And precisely because there were such limits, Italy continued to retain the leadership in European music in the seventeenth century.

THE STRAGGLERS

IN THE course of the second half of the century the *canzon villanesca alla napoletana* gradually changes its character. It forgets its popular or would-be popular origins. It no longer opposes itself quite so parodistically to the madrigal, and begins itself to approach the madrigal (in so far as its songlike character admits it) by increasing the number of its voices, by motivic animation of its texture, and by "picturesque" details. In all this, the madrigal met it halfway. In the hands of the greatest masters the madrigal always preserved its artistic exclusiveness and its musical freedom. Within the given limits of this art-form and before a sufficiently fastidious and sophisticated audience, one could venture anything at any time. But with Andrea Gabrieli there arises at the side of this exclusive variety, a lighter one: the *madrigale arioso*. The *canzon villanesca* admittedly takes the greater step toward becoming ennobled, for a madrigal is always a madrigal. But when the madrigal begins to repeat not merely its last part but also its first—begins, in other words, to take on the schematic form AA'BCC'—the distinction between the two forms, which had hitherto led an independent and even antagonistic existence, becomes confused and indistinct.

THE THREE-VOICED *CANZON VILLANESCA*

THE three-voiced *canzon villanesca alla napoletana* survived for years, even after the four-part arrangements of Willaert, Perissone, and Nasco; in the middle 'sixties, indeed, it unexpectedly put forth fresh and particularly attractive blossoms and in Marenzio this late flowering reached a new high point, although a purely artistic one. Again, those who resume its cultivation are genuine Neapolitans: Giovanni Leonardo Primavera and Massimo Troiano. Primavera, who was not only something of an author but an unusually prolific madrigalist (his madrigals are often settings of his own poems) was a native of Barletta in Apulia who stood on good terms with Principe Carlo Gesualdo di Venosa, to whom, in 1585, he dedicated his seventh madrigal book. About 1573 he was active as the *maestro di cappella* of the Spanish governor of Lombardy, "dell' Illustriss. et Eccellentiss. S. Commendator maggiore di Castiglia." Schmidl reports that he lived also in Naples and that he founded there a "Camerata di propaganda per l'affinamento del gusto musicale," together with the Principe di Venosa, Luigi Dentice, Rocco Rodio, and other musicians. A more romantic personality is Massimo Troiano, "di Corduba di Napoli." Presumably he received his musical training in Naples, perhaps under Gio. Domenico da Nola; in the 'sixties he is singing alto in the chapel of Johann Jacob Fugger at Augsburg, who apparently allowed him ample leave to see his works through the press: the dedication of his third book of villanelle is signed at Treviso on March 10, 1567, and on November 6, 1568, he is in Venice. Even at this time he was working for Munich as an actor, singer, composer, and "librettist." On the occasion of the sumptuous wedding of Duke William of Bavaria and Renée of Lorraine he furnishes Orlando Lasso with the text of a sort of madrigal comedy, *La cortigiana innamorata*, and describes the festivities in a print which bears in the most interesting way on the history of manners, the *Discorsi de'Trionfi, Giostre, Apparati, e delle cose più notabili fatte nelle sontuose nozze ... nell'anno 1568 il 22 di Febbraro*, and which was reprinted in Venice in the following year, both in Italian and Spanish. In 1568 he becomes a member of the court chapel at Munich. In April 1570, with another singer, Camillo of Parma, as his accomplice, he murders the violinist Battista Romano from motives of revenge, seeks safety in flight, and is pursued by state agents with a warrant. After this we lose all trace of him. But even before this catastrophe he signs his dedications *L'infelice Massimo Troiano*, and I am inclined to suspect that *L'infelice* was his official name as a member of an academy. It now fits him. The ducal warrant briefly and concisely describes his character: "In omnibus verbis et gestibus superbiam et animi fastum ostendit" (cf. *Monatshefte für Musik-Geschichte*, XXIII, 2).

Primavera published four books of *canzoni napoletane* for three voices (1565, 1566, 1570, and 1574) and one book for four voices (1569), in all of which he set aside ample space for his compatriots Troiano and Giovanni Leonardo dell'Arpa, especially the latter. But in these collections the Neapolitan flavor is beginning to disappear. Venice looks on the *napoletana* as a foreign product and modifies it for local consumption:

> Turco Giudeo Moro
> Non ha sì bel tesoro
> Come che *Padoa* bella
> Dove che luce chiara la mia stella....

Giovanni Leonardo dell'Arpa laments the departure of his beloved, though not from Naples but from Venice:

> ... Non sò che pensar de' Venetiani,
> Come t'hanno fatto partir da loro ...
> E vaglion più quest'occhi e questa mano
> Che non Venetia con tutto Morano.

Even the connection with the strambotto is beginning to fade out, though it is still occasionally present, for example in *O Dio se tu conosci quanto t'amo* (II, 3); *Tu m'hai lassat'alla bon'hora sia* (II, 15, by Paolo Gradenico); *Se senza cuore non si può campare* (III, 13, anonymous, a piece noteworthy for the contrapuntal animation of its refrain). To be sure, the canzoni are usually still written in eleven-syllable lines; but the stanzas, even when they are mere couplets with refrain, are no longer connected by rhyme, and tercets and quatrains (a-bb or aa-bb) predominate. A single Neapolitan peculiarity is stressed as never before—the fifths:

Da poi che tu cru-del mi de-sti mor - te Cor - se quest'al-ma per pas-

sar Ca-ron - te Con l'im-ma-gi-ne tua scol - pi-ta al fron - te

> Quando Caronte vide e riguardoe
> L'immagin tua ch'all'alma mia si serra,
> Lasciò la barca e corse verso terra.
>
> E così incominciò a dire forte:
> "Forsi quest'è quell'alma c'ha brusciato
> Tant'alme ch'all'inferno haggio passato?
>
> Torna tu al mondo con questa figura,
> Che s'all'inferno andasse un sì bel viso,
> Diveneria l'inferno un paradiso!"

Besides stanzas that develop a comparison, we sometimes meet with a popular allusion already familiar to us:

Vil - la - nel - la ch'al - l'ac - qua va - i, mo - ro per - te, tu

non lo sa - i; Hai - me ch'io mo - ro pen - san - do a te

At other times the melody is extended by repeating half lines, as for instance in this Venetian genre picture (II, 6):

Na vec - chia - rel - la, Na vec-chia-rel-la al Cam-po di San
Me

Po - lo Ve - den - do che guar - da - vo na ci - tel - la
di - man-da - va se, Me

Me di-man - da-va se, Me di-man-da-va se mi pa-rea bel - la?

Io li risposi se la conosceva
Che a gli occhi mei bella mi parea
Et lei mi disse che non ci vedea.

E poi mi piglia per la cappa e dice
"Se voi che piena te stia la scarsella
Non amar altro che la vecchiarella!"

E poi mi dette in mano un'aneletto
Di rame e d'oro sopra impetenato
Che manco non valea mezo ducato.

Finally, the primitive character of these little pieces is sometimes broken up by a motivic animation, usually in the refrain (III, 17), which goes even further than that in the example just quoted:

Syllabic declamation is the rule in Primavera's little pieces: one will look in vain
for a single melisma. At the end of Primavera's third book Scotto has printed eight
additional numbers, whose simplicity is almost the simplicity of the frottola, so that
they come close to being outright folk-songs, though their texts certainly do not
point to a popular origin (III, 23; as in the frottola, the time-signature is C):

Dammi pur assai dolore
Ch'io giamai non mancarò
D'adorart.'a tutte l'hore
Mentre la mia forza può

Dammi pure dammi guai
Ch'io giamai non cessarò
Di servirte più che mai
Quanto la mia forza può.

Et io sono più che certo
Che la mia sincera fè
Haverà da voi gran merto,
Ch'a chi serve come me,
Non mancò giamai mercè.

Troiano is much more lively and resourceful than Primavera. Presumably he has
written most of his texts himself. This is certainly true of pieces which must be
understood as personal compliments, and in which he speaks of his longing for
Naples (*Primo et secondo libro*, prior to 1568):

Gridando vogli'andar piangendo forte
E in crude rime voltar'il mio stile

Poi che son fuor di Napole gentile.
 Vo star in pianto e in lutto insino a morte,
E per li boschi far stato virile,
  Poi che . . .
 E mai non voglio far felice sorte,
Ma per le selve far mia vita humile,
  Poi che . . .
 Napole bella hoimè, di te son privo,
A voi Prencipe d'Ascol, questo scrivo,
Che senza Napol non voglio esser vivo.

Popular allusion and literary reminiscence are strangely and delightfully interwoven in these little poems, which should assure to Troiano a place in the history of literature at least as honorable as that accorded to many of the frigid sonnet and canzone poets of his time. Irregular, freely invented stanzas alternate with the strambotto; the rhymes are sometimes Sannazaro's *sdruccioli* (III, 29):

 O saporita più che n'è lo Ravano
 E dolce e bianca più che n'è lo Zuccaro
 Tu mi fai gir la notte com'a buccaro. . . .

The *mascherata*, completely absent from Primavera's work, occurs once or twice (*Primo et secondo libro*, No. 4):

 Correti tutt'amanti
 Cha siamo tre mercanti
 Di fuoco fiamma dard' e di saette,
 Che per un gramo vendiam trentasette. . . .

To be sure, this is no longer the genuine scenic *mascherata* but rather a reflection of it in the style of chamber music, as is shown by another example in which there is only one speaker (III, 12):

 Mandato sono per ambasciatore
 Dalle patrone mie Napoletane
 A voi belle signore Venetiane.
  Perche desiamo molto di sapere,
 Se crudeltate o cortesia quì regna,
 E chi mantiene l'amorosa insegna . . .

But a five-voiced piece (III, 33) is again a genuine *mascherata* "alla Turchesca":

 Cinque noi siamo nati a la Turchia . . .

At the end of this third book Troiano achieves a blend of the Neapolitan and the Venetian when he combines a *moresca* in the best style with a *Battaglia della Gatta e la Cornacchia* in the manner of Baldisserra Donato's *Gallina*. The fourth book concludes with a "serious" piece for four voices: Petrarch's madrigal *O passi sparsi* in the Spanish translation of a certain Salamon Usque; only four lines are set to music, as in the older frottola. In general the fourth book tends to take its initial lines from the more serious poets; thus No. 5 draws on a sonnet by Luigi Tansillo: we reproduce it here to show how Troiano gives life to the texture of the *canzon villanesca*.[1] Petrarch is also subjected to this treatment (No. 12, *Vivo sol di speranza*; No. 16, *Chi vuol veder quanta bellezza*); and the humor of these pieces can scarcely be understood without a knowledge of this relationship of theirs to serious literature. The contemporaries were of course aware of it. But this literary allusion to the madrigal is combined with an assimilation of its musical style. The more animated the villanella becomes motivically, the more its fifths disappear and the more it tends to take the form of the canzonetta.

THE TRANSITION TO THE CANZONETTA

It is difficult to do justice to the rich production and to the share of each individual master in the general development. Primavera and Gian Leonardo dell'Arpa seem to have stimulated Giovan Domenico da Nola to fresh productivity for in 1567, after a pause of twenty-five years, he again publishes a *Primo* (sic) *libro delle Villanelle alla Napolitana*, this time for three and four voices, and he includes in it some pieces by dell'Arpa. But these villanelle no longer have the old charm and the old freshness of the Neapolitan coloring. The stanza preferred is generally the new one composed of four tercets, an outgrowth of the strambotto with refrain; it is full of literary reminiscences. Thus No. 15 (*Fuggit'amore o voi che donne amate*) has as its refrain *Che non si vinc'amor se non fuggendo*, a line borrowed from *Alma se stata fossi a pieno accorta*, one of Pietro Bembo's sonnets. One little piece has a certain literary pretension and already shows the empty anacreontic daintiness which dominates the opening of the seventeenth century:

> Signorella, Signorella
> Gioia mia quanto sei bella,
> Tanto dolce saporita
> Che li morti torn'in vita!
>
> Gli occhi tuoi son raggi'ardenti
> Che n'amorano le genti

[1] See Vol. III, No. 70.

E le trezze oro filato
Con che m'hai pres'e ligato . . .
etc.

Another, which has at least the traditional form, recalls the Neapolitan scene and breathes the old aggressiveness (25):

Quando vi veggi'andar donn'in carretta
E con tovaglie vi celat'il viso
Ho gran piacer'e morome di riso.
E sapete ben fare la Civetta
E trasmutate in varie foggie il viso—
Ho gran . . .
Andate in qua e in la come navetta
E vi par sempre stare in paradiso.
Ho gran . . .
Andate per la terra piano piano
S'alcun v'incontra, basciovi la mano
O sia Spagnolo o sia Napolitano.

But Nola has grown old. In general he now leans toward the new, polished, literary trend in the villanella, a trend more in keeping with the last third of the century. With Gio. Leonardo dell'Arpa, Rocco Rodio, and Stefano Lando he is still represented with six pieces (a seventh, attributed to him by Vogel is really by Stefano Lando) in a collection entitled *Corona delle Napolitane a tre e quattro voci* (1570[5]) and brought out by Don Marco Antonio Mazzone di Miglionico, a Neapolitan, who filled it largely (nineteen numbers) with pieces of his own. A last example for four voices will show Nola's new manner; we have chosen it because it still preserves something of his earlier animation and because fourteen years later Claudio Monteverdi will set the same text, again for three voices.[2]

It is a madrigalesque *canzon alla villanella*, far removed from Nola's beginnings. Incidentally, "the unhappy Narcissus" is already made the subject of a comparison as early as 1350, in one of Landino's madrigals (Ellinwood, No. 4):

Non a Narcisso fu più amar lo specchio
Della selvaggia fonte com'è cruda
Questa donna, di me di piatà innuda.
Così sperando per seguirla invechio.
Quella spiatata fugge raguardando
Che io sança merçe mi mor amando. . . .

[2] See Vol. III, No. 71.

The high polish of Nola's piece is common to nearly all of the thirty-eight numbers of Mazzone's influential collection, a regular storehouse from which later musicians often drew their texts. It is not surprising that Mazzone himself should have supplied the final number, a genuine madrigal:

> Se del mio gran tormento. . . .

Nor are we surprised to find the extremes of popular art on the one hand and high artificiality on the other, even in the work of Hubert Waelrant, a Northerner despite his studies with Willaert (*Canzon napolitane a 4 voci*, 1565, not mentioned by Vogel); or to find this distinction broken down in the three books of *canzoni alla napoletana* for three voices published by the printer-composer Girolamo Scotto without date and twice reissued in 1571. The third book concludes with two genuine madrigals by Giovanni Bassano. It is quite in keeping with this change when in the first book of the *Napoletane* of Giovanni Zappasorgo da Treviso (1571) one of Petrarch's sonnets is simply recast as a canzonetta, without any linguistic reminiscence or any intention of parody:

> Vag'augeletto che cantando vai
> Di ram'in ramo così dolcemente—
> Meschino me dolente
> Che giorn' e notte stom' in pen' e in guai.
>   Tu almen la notte sopra un faggio o un pino
> Queto riposi depost'ogni cura
> Et io (ahi sorte dura)
> Lagrim'e piango fin al mattutino.
>   Poi ch'ornata di Rose esce l'Aurora
> Tu cominci'l tuo canto, e le tue note,
> E me sempre percuote
> Duro strale, che m'ange, e che m'accora.
>   O s'io te fossi, e conoscessi lei,
> Che m'arde, e che mi lega, andrei volando
> Subito, e sospirando
> Entro il suo vago seno, e vi morrei.

Another of his texts is simply a variant of a well-known madrigal by Luigi Cassola (I, 3):

> Madonna, io ben vorrei
> Ch'in voi fusse pietà quant'è beltade,
> Ò tanta crudeltade
> Che desse'l fin'a tanti dolor mei. . . .

Zappasorgo's entire print is full of these reminiscences, just as the frottola had been in its day; among all these conventional things one is doubly astounded to come upon an anecdote of the most appalling obscenity (I, 23):

> L'altr'hier vidi una vecchia affaccendata. . . .

Another of his texts (II, 17) can show us how the change from villanella to canzonetta was taking place at this time. In the collection of 1570[5] there is a canzone by an *incerto* (No. 26), whose tone and rhyme scheme clearly reveal its descent from the older strambotto:

> Bon cacciator già mai non perse caccia
> Lo cane che la seguita l'arriva—
> Però voglio seguir per fin che vivo.
>   L'agresta con lo tempo fa guarnaccia
> Pian piano s'ammaturano l'olive
> Però . . .
>   Press'al mal tempo viene la bonaccia
> Da uno sdegno grand'amor derriva
> Però . . .
>   Non vale per combatter una maglia
> E fuggir sempre incontr'a la battaglia
> Ch'al fin la donna vole della quaglia.

Zappasorgo borrows from this only the first tercet and adds to it two wholly neutral stanzas (II, 17):

> . . . Ond'io vo sempre mai seguir la caccia
> E cercar d'accapar la fera mia
> Per poter poi cacciar per fin ch'io viva.
>   O che dolce gioconda, e lieta caccia
> Sarebbe a conseguir la fera mia,
> Che felice sarei più d'huom che viva.

The print concludes with a setting of Tansillo's *A caso un giorno*, proof conclusive that it is now possible to set "popular" ottave rime in two ways: (1) *alla madrigalesca* and (2) *alla villanesca*. With this all distinction between the two classes is at an end.

MARENZIO'S VILLANELLE

IN this crowd of somewhat unpretentious and even unconscious stragglers among the composers of villanelle, one of the greatest masters of the madrigal, Luca Marenzio, comes forward in 1584 with a *Primo libro delle villanelle* and, before 1587, with four further books, making 115 compositions in all. He apparently considered them mere by-products of his workshop and did not even bother to edit them himself. "... È tale l'eccellentia di tutte le compositioni del signor Luca Marentio, che quelle cose ancora che sono tenute in poca stima da lui, meritano esser'haute in pregio da gli altri, come sono le presenti Villanelle composte dall'Auttore quasi per ischerzo, et raccolte da me. ..." — "Such is the excellence of every composition by Messer Luca Marenzio that even the things he holds in little esteem deserve to be prized by others. Such are the present villanelle, composed by their author as a sort of joke and collected by myself. ..." So writes the editor, Ferrante Franchi, in the dedication of the first book. The other four books Marenzio also turned over for publication to friends of his in Rome, Attilio Gualtieri and Christofano Ferrari; he evidently hesitated to make himself publicly responsible for them. None the less, they belong among the more spontaneous products of his genius, and Gualtieri is quite right when in the dedication to the fourth book he praises their *leggiadria* and their *artificio*, their grace and art. It is not easy to place them in a historical context. They are the work of a creative genius who finds recreation in working on a small scale. Marenzio does not write them for "practical purposes"; there is not a single genuine *mascherata* among them. Nor does he cultivate their parodistic relation to the madrigal. Even the fifths have almost completely disappeared and with them the last vestiges of a "popularity" that had long since become fictitious. If Marenzio takes over in his villanella expressive devices characteristic of the madrigal—melismas, chromatic progressions, and rapid, declamatory effects—this is an ironic *jeu d'esprit* that is in keeping with the character of his texts. These must have been written directly for him by his friends. One author was a sceptic, another an anacreontic poet— or were these two authors one person? Unlike Ariosto, he counsels the lover against falling in love with a lady above his station who will grant him a glance "only once or twice a month"; observe how Marenzio reduces his fine-spun chromaticism to a simple formula (1, 2):

Ch'in al-ta don-na hab-bia lo - ca-to il co - re; - re.

don-na hab-bia lo - ca - to il co - re; - re.

Pasce l'alma dolente
Di speme di speranza eternamente,
Ne d'altro sazia le sue voglie accese,
Che d'un sol sguardo, una o due volte il mese.
E s'ella aprendo un riso
Gli volge a sorte, e non ad arte il viso,
Reputa cortesia quel dono che viene
Da puro caso, e se felice tiene.
E poi ch'ha speso il giorno
In girarsi a l'amato albergo intorno,
Passa la notte ragionando in vano
Col ritratto di lei che porta in mano.
Dunque lasciate, amanti,
Questo Amor senza frutto, e da vacanti,
Amate Donna tal, di cui possesso
Prender possiate, e tenir sempre appresso.

Text and music both recall the frottola, the text even in little external traits. Thus Book I, No. 14 (*Fra questi sassi*) is once more an *incatenatura* of the sort familiar to us from the earlier *oda*: the concluding line of each stanza recurs as the opening line of the next. But their resemblance to the frottola is due primarily to inner traits: to their courtly irony, and musically speaking, to their great rhythmic freedom and to their return to the earlier inequality of the voices. The inner voice is more dependent than the outer ones; it is supported by either one of the two, usually by the upper voice, with which it is often paired, as in this case. Genuine, motivic three-part counterpoint is rare. Marenzio does not write genuine trios. The soprano and bass stand at opposite poles. Marenzio's villanelle are all so conceived that they can be sung as monodies to a bass, and in this they became a model for all such products at the end of the century. To be sure, the villanella of those later decades is in another respect as different as possible from the frottola and even from a large proportion of the earlier *canzon alla villanesca*. The refrain begins to disappear, and the villanella becomes a pure strophic song in which the number of lines per stanza may vary from three to six and in which the stanza may be made up entirely of lines of eleven or seven syllables or may mix these two lines together in any conceivable combination. As one result of this, the villanella too begins to describe pastoral scenes:

In un boschetto de bei mirti e allori
All'hor che d'herbe e fior vago è'l terreno
Vidi un pastor a la sua ninfa in seno.
Dicea la ninfa con grate parole:
"Dite, caro mio ben, dolce mio sole,
Dov'è l'anima tua, dov'è'l tuo core?"
Disse all'hor il pastor con un sospiro,
Pien di dolcezza, con affanno mista:
"Tu sei l'anima mia, mio core e vita" (*sic*).
All'hor la vaga ninfa con un riso,
Con vezzose parole, e dolci ciancie
La bocca gli basciò, gli occhi e le guancie.

This does not mean that the villanella altogether abandons the *incatenatura,* which connects the last line of one stanza with the first of the next. Here is the example already mentioned (I, 14):

Fra questi sassi e luoghi aspri e selvaggi
Ove del sol non ponno entrar i raggi
A querci e faggi sfogarò il mio duolo,
Poi ch'io son solo.
Poi che son solo, e tu crudel non senti
Il pianger mesto, e i duri miei lamenti;
Ma questi venti poi per lor mercede
Ne faran fede.
Ne faran fede, e porteranno il pianto . . .

Nor does it mean that the subject-matter of the later villanella is exclusively pastoral. An exuberant operatic Cupid makes his entrance in a trochaic meter and with a new rhyme scheme (II, 2):

Io son A - mo - re Pie - no d'ar - do - re, Con stra - lie l'ar - co Di

Son cieco e gnudo,
Alato e crudo,
Picciol garzone,
Senza ragione,
Che sotto la mia legge
Ciascun si regge
E schiavo stà
In gran calamità.

Mille tormenti
E tradimenti,
Astutie e inganni,
Martir e affanni
A i miseri mortali
Dò con li strali,
Privo di fè
E con poca mercè.

Miseri amanti
Ch'ogn'hora in pianti,
Fiamme e sospiri,
Lacci e martiri
Sete arsi e incatenati
Da me piagati,
Soffrite hor sù,
Ne vi dolete più.

Now he reappears (ii, 10) in another guise, one which would have delighted the Goethe of the *Roman Elegies*:

Io che lo riconobbi al primo incontro,
Per che gran tempo lo portai nel core,
Gli dissi: "ove ne vai, misero Amore?"
    Egli aprendo le labbia in flebil suono,
Disse: "Una donna altiera, e pellegrina
A sì perversa sorte mi destina.
    Ella con gli occhi suoi m'ha tolto il regno,
E però mi convien mendico e tristo
Andar con gli altri poveri a San Sisto."

Though in this respect his touch was of the lightest, Marenzio allowed none of the "picturesque" suggestions of the text to escape him. Such a villanella could be written only by a master of the *madrigal*. Yet it no longer stands in a parodistic relation to the madrigal; it is a little masterpiece of anacreontic music, an original creation whose villanella form seems scarcely aware of its origins. For a striking example of the parodistic relation of the villanella to the madrigal I turn to the number that opens the third book: *Io son ferito e chi mi punse il core*. Every student of Palestrina's music will at once recall, on reading this line, the ottava stanza with the same opening, first published in 1561 in Gardano's *Terzo libro delle muse a 5*; it is one of Palestrina's best known secular compositions, and deservedly so. In it Palestrina re-

nounces all change in expression and seems himself to be using the motifs of a
folk-song, so delicately does he handle (usually in three voices) the beginnings of
the individual lines:

That there is an old ottava tune behind this is confirmed by a setting of the same text
by Jacopo da Nola (1566³), which makes use of the same motifs:

Giovanni Francesco Capuano, of whose life we know virtually nothing, had already
treated the motif in the spirit of the lighter music in 1574 in his *Primo libro delle
Villanelle alla Napolitana a Tre Voci, de diversi Musici di Bari* (p. 36):

In so doing he used the entire text of the ottava, adding a single line to each couplet:
further evidence for the generic connection between the *canzon alla villanella* and
the strambotto. The case is so clear and striking that I must quote Capuano's text in
full; I am printing the lines added to Palestrina's ottava in italics:

Io son ferito hai lasso e chi mi diede
Poi che chieder soccorso non mi giova
Accusar pur vorrei ma non ho prova.

E senza indicio al mal non si da fede
Ne getta sangue la mia piaga nova
Però l'accusa star non pote a prova.

Io pasmo e moro, il colpo non si vede
E benche'l mal ogn'hor più si rinova
La mia nemica armata non si trova.

Che fia tornar a lei crudel partito
E pur d'andarci Amor mi face ardito
Che sol mi pò sanar chi m'ha ferito.

(Anyone wishing to make a study of the melody should look also at the compositions by H. L. Hasler [1590] and O. Vecchi [1597].) In Marenzio's version the villanella becomes a song of praise in honor of a certain Lavinia, a Roman beauty who plays the lute, while the quotation parodies Palestrina.[3] The two villanelle that follow are also dedicated to this Lavinia. In much the same way the first two numbers of the fourth book are written in honor of a certain Laura, while the fifth and last book is evidently a gleaning and no longer quite possesses the qualities of the earlier ones. From first to last, these 115 little pieces are late-comers and have all the iridescent charm and all the tired artificiality peculiar to things born late. Within the narrowest confines are included the most extreme antitheses: short little pieces, syllabically declaimed—longer ones in which single words are over-painted to the point of parodistic exaggeration or in which fragments of the grammatical construction are repeated; pieces that are quite free in their rhythms—little balletti with the swing of the dance; occasional fifths, especially in the last three books—the ultimate refinement in the interweaving of motifs; caricature—the seriously intended pastoral idyl. This same variety of style, in text and music, is found from now on in the work of many of Marenzio's successors and imitators, though they are naturally unable to attain the same virtuosity and epigrammatic grace. It occurs, for example, in Ruggiero Giovanelli's twenty-three *Villanelle et Arie alla Napolitana* of 1588. Here, too, are other familiar traits: the restrained parody of Rore's "romantic" or picturesque madrigal; parodied madrigalesque sentimentality; miniature *battaglie*; the alternation between motivic work for three voices on the one hand and the opposition or *contrapposto* of a supporting bass and two upper voices, animated through imitation or singing in parallels, on the other. Clearly, this sort of music has lost all uniformity. And for Marenzio and his imitators, the choice of the three-voiced texture is already an archaism, a further sign—

[3] See Vol. III, No. 72.

though a purely external one—of the relation of the new villanella to the old *canzon alla villanesca.*

THE NEW CANZONE

GIOVANNI FERRETTI

MEANWHILE the decisive hour for the villanella had long since struck and its *rapprochement* to the madrigal was already an accomplished fact, thanks to the work of a master of international influence, Giovanni Ferretti. His importance for the transformation of the villanella into the canzone stands in inverse ratio to the space usually accorded him in the lexicons. Little is known about his life. Some would have him born in Venice about 1540 (an arbitrary date), while others make him a native of Ancona. We know nothing at all of his musical education. All we know is that in 1567 Giulio Bonagionta, that prolific editor, caused Ferretti's first work to be printed by Scotto and dedicated it to a Paduan nobleman, Benedetto de'Lazzarini. He calls Ferretti an "eccellentissimo musico" without referring to any specific post. Presumably Ferretti was still in Venice at this time as an associate or pupil of Andrea Gabrieli. In 1569, however, he signs a dedication in Ancona, and in 1575 he is the choirmaster at the cathedral of this papal seaport on the Adriatic. From 1580 to 1582 and again from 1596 to 1603 he is supposed to have been the choirmaster at the Santa Casa in Loreto—so Schmidl says, at least, though I do not know on what authority he says so. Actually, from 1569 on, his contacts tend more and more to be with Rome. In that year he dedicates the second book of his five-voiced canzoni to a nobleman in near-by Macerata, Giovanni Ferro by name, and in 1575 he dedicates his second book for six voices to the same Giacomo Boncompagni to whom Palestrina later (1581) dedicated his *Vergini.* In 1586 he makes a contribution in honor of the bride of Giovanni Bardi. Ferretti must still have been alive in 1609, for in that year he set one of the sonnets on the villas of Frascati by the Roman poet Fabio Petrozzi, a collection that appears to contain works by living masters only.

As a choirmaster, Ferretti had no doubt to compose a good deal of church music of all sorts but in secular music he is a specialist. His entire output consists of two books of six-voiced *canzoni alla napoletana* (1573 and 1575) and five similar books for five voices (1567, 1569, 1571, prior to 1573, and 1585). We have only four or five madrigals of his; the madrigal book that haunts all the lexicons (including Riemann) seems to be a "ghost." But of the seven canzoni prints there exist countless editions, and certain pieces from them found their way into reprints issued in Antwerp (from 1583), in London (from 1588), and in Nuremberg (from 1589); these reprints do not cease until 1634. Thus Ferretti's canzoni remained alive beyond the Alps even longer than in Italy itself. They played their part in bringing about the change in the musical practice of Europe; indeed their influence was surpassed only by that of the balletti of Gian Giacomo Gastoldi, in which the canzone turned to a purely instrumental ideal.

To characterize Ferretti's five- and six-voiced *canzon alla napoletana* in a rather general way, we may say that it retains the general form of the villanella (a a b c c), while elaborating the individual lines *alla madrigalesca*. It remains Neapolitan only in name. And this is true also for the texts. There are now very few traces of local dialect or local color; on the purely formal side alone, the "strambotto with refrain" is still frequent (II, 4):

> Non mi date tormento ne più doglia
> Rendetemi il cor mio ch'in voi è posto,
>> Che più non voglio
>> Hor allegro
>> Hor doglioso
>> Nell'amor languire.
> Non tenete ver me si cruda voglia,
> Deh cangiate voler cangiate tosto,
>> Che più . . .
> Se vedete ben mio l'aspra mia doglia,
> Donatemi quel ben ch'in voi è posto,
>> Che più . . .
> Deponete lo sdegno e'l fiero orgoglio,
> Levate la cagion per cui mi doglio.

Most of Ferretti's texts are of this neutral order. An occasional stanza may be livelier in its manner and may seem to be livelier in its content, but the development of the opening motif is always feeble (II, 18):

> Amor sei forse cuoco
> Che butti tanto fuoco
> E non mi vuoi bruciare
> Ma a poc'a poco mi voi consumare.
> Amor non trovo loco
> Ch'in tal martir'un poco
> Non mi fai riposare
>> Ma a poco . . .
>> E son già fatto fioco
> Mentre sovente invoco
> Che pietà vogli usare
>> Ma a poco . . .
>> S'hor per tua festa e gioco
> Ti piace un tanto foco

Almen fammi sperare
Ch'io possa lieto un giorno riposare.

Sometimes Ferretti chances upon a text that strikes a popular note, as in the strambotto *Male per me tanta beltà mirai* (III, 11), published with its music by O. Chilesotti in the *Rivista musicale italiana*, XXII (1905), 115f., after a copy of mine. At other
times his model is the French anecdotal chanson, as in the villanella that opens the
first book of his six-voiced canzoni, *Un pastor chies'ad una ninfa amore*, which is
simply a translation of a chanson set by Thomas Crequillon (Susato, November
1543, *Premier livre des chansons à quatre parties*):

Un gay bergier prioit une bergiere
En luy faisant du ieu d amours resqueste
Allez dict elle tires vous arriere
Vostre parler ie treuve deshonneste
Ne pensez pas que feroie tel default
Par quoy cessez faire telle priere
Car tu n as pas la lance qui me fault . . .

Indeed, I am inclined to believe that Ferretti's canzone derives in part from the
French chanson, with its emphasis on an architectonic form that so frequently
corresponds to that of the *canzon alla villanella*. Elsewhere, however, Ferretti turns
to an actual villanella, such as the anonymous *Hor va, canzone mia, non dubitare*
from the *Quattro libri delle Villotte* (1565) whose melody he uses as the tenor of
his setting of 1568. But the strophic form of these villanelle is in many cases more
apparent than real. Ferretti uses every madrigalesque means of expression and in
so doing thinks obviously of the first stanza only, so that in some cases the adaptation
of the words of the later stanzas leads to absurdities and even impossibilities, for
example (II, 11):

Misero me dolente che lontano
Da voi, dolce mio mal, dolce mio bene

To these lines correspond, in the following stanzas, the words "e sempre in voi pensando," "Senza le belle tue," "Che scolpita nel cor." In many instances Ferretti no longer repeats the music of the concluding line; thus a piece like the one reprinted in our volume of examples (II, 10)[4] is simply a madrigal of the lighter sort. In his six-voiced canzoni Ferretti goes even further in the alternation of divided choirs and in the intertwining of the motifs. J. C. Hol (*Horatio Vecchi's Weltliche Werke*, p. 45) has already pointed out that Ferretti's second and last book for six voices "is distinguished by its greater seriousness and its grandeur and is the one nearest to the madrigal style." In particular, he calls attention to No. 6, which he reprints in his appendix: a dialogue and love scene with a popular text, but with a music that is neither frivolous nor parodistic but treated with passionate seriousness or serious passion— one of those rare compositions in which the century reached out toward grandeur in musical expression. The dividing line between canzone and madrigal is becoming blurred. As though to emphasize it anew, Ferretti includes in the second book of his five-voiced canzoni a quadripartite setting of Tansillo's *A caso un giorno*—in the old *misura di breve*, short, lively, the narrative sections rapidly declaimed and homophonic, though quite madrigalesque.

A genuine madrigal, though at the same time a political one, is the sonnet of the Venetian local poet Zambo del Val Brembana on the naval victory at Lepanto, which Ferretti sets to music at the end of his first book for six voices (1573). It is a scurrilous counterpart to Rore's rhapsodic invocation of the Emperor, *Un'altra volta la Germania strida* (cf. p. 392); the poet makes fun of the defeated sultan Selim, using the coarsest Dalmatian-Venetian mariners' dialect:

> Quae pars est o Selì Salamelèch
> dell'Uniù del hic, et haec, et hoc?
> Sessanta mili de quei to tarloc
> con tresento galer son stag a stech.
>
> E l'anime t'aspetta ilò a Lamech
> d'Alì, Pialì, Caracossa, e Siroc:
> per ghe in Bisanz, nè in Alger, o Maroc
> ti se segur da sti nuof Scanderbech.
>
> Pensavet fors havì a fa co'merlot
> o con zent com t'è ti usag al bif?
> desprezaor del Santo Sabaot.
>
> L'Aquila, col Leò, col bech, e i grif,
> te squarzarà ol cur for del magot
> sta mo a sentì el tof, el taf, el tif.

[4] See Vol. III, No. 73.

(I follow the reprint in Guido Antonio Quarti, *La Battaglia di Lepanto nei canti popolari dell'epoca*, Milano, 1930, p. 189, where the *sesto* of the first part of Ferretti's piece is also reproduced in facsimile, plate 61. Ferretti's text differs in a few details.) Ferretti set the piece in the madrigal style throughout, since its text is not compatible with the form and the style of the canzonetta. Without fear of criticism he could easily have included it in a madrigal collection: it is clear that the distinction has become almost meaningless.

This last observation can also be supported by approaching this matter of the vanishing distinction in the opposite way. An unusually striking piece of evidence is a collection of compositions by musicians of the Bavarian court chapel, edited by Cosimo Bottegari and published by Scotto in 1575 under the title *Il secondo libro de Madrigali a cinque voci*. It contains some highly serious pieces by Lasso, Ivo de Vento (Petrarch), and Gioseffo Guami; but also these verses, set by Antonio Gosswin, which sound like humorously intended personal abuse:

> Non trovo cosa alcuna s'io non pago
> Ne niun mi servirebbe d'un capello
> E tal si mostra mio caro fratello
> Ch'alla botega poi lo trovo un drago.
> S'alcuna volta io compero da lui
> Mi va trovando un parentado antico,
> Dicendo: piglia—io non lo darei altrui.
> Io mi trovo inganato, e poi gliel dico,
> Et lui risponde et domanda: "Con cui
> Vo guadagnar, se non fa col amico?"
> Dicendo ch'il nemico
> Non gli anderebbe mai alla botega,
> Et cosi dolcemente me la frega.

In Giovanni Gabrieli's *Quando io ero giovinetto* Pantalone appears with a burlesque lament, and Antonio Morari sets the following verses to music:

> Sarà pur forz'un giorno ch'io mi sfoghi
> Con queste vecchie brutte malitiose,
> Superbe fastidiose,
> Ribalde dispietate,
> Che poss'in tutte quante esser frustate.
> Sempre m'han posto in qualche strano intrigo
> Con le lor falsitadi et con suoi inganni
> Et già son ben molt'anni

Che per lor pien d'affanni et pianti vivo
D'ogni speranza et di conforto privo.

This abuse of old women is a motif already familiar to us from the *villanella alla napoletana*, where it was a favorite theme of Maio and Nola.

As a last example, how are we to class the following dialogue, set to music by Francesco Mosto? Is it a madrigal or a canzonetta?

"O la, o la, chi mi sa dar novella
D'una crudel e bella,
Che mena seco altiera
Di mortali prigioni una gran schiera?"
"Poch'è signor passò per questa strada
Una che senza spada
E senza arco ne dardo
Dava la mort'a ogn'un con un sol sguardo."

And thus it is only natural that in 1580 an Apulian musician, Cola Nardo di Monte of Bari, should have written four-voiced madrigals on villanelle texts (*con le parole di villanelle*).

GIROLAMO CONVERSI

An attractive successor of Ferretti is Girolamo Conversi, about whose life we know even less than usual. In 1572 he published his first work, a book of five-voiced *canzoni alla napoletana*; by 1589 it had been reprinted seven times in rapid succession; before 1584 there had followed a book of madrigals for six voices. A book of five-voiced madrigals, mentioned by Giunti, has disappeared. And that is all. We know only that he was a native of Correggio and that he dedicated his canzoni to Signor Giuseppe Grassi (the Cat. Bolog., III, 221 says *Corsi*—I can't determine which is correct), saying that most of them are fruits plucked in Grassi's garden in Vigorso(?). In 1584 or earlier Conversi is in the service of Cardinal Granvella, Viceroy of Naples. From then on he disappears from view.

As a composer of madrigals Conversi is highly "literary"—his work is filled with sonnets from Petrarch, Guidiccioni, Castiglione, Bembo, and Luca Contile: living poets do not count for him at all. None the less, he is quite "modern" even in his madrigals, since he tends in them to approach the manner of the canzonetta. In our volume of examples, the reader will find his setting of *Zefiro torna* —among Petrarch's sonnets the one with the sharpest contrast: the octave describes the return of spring, in the sestet the poet himself mourns over his beloved, now lost to him forever. For the first part Conversi uses every device and every rhythm characteristic of the pastoral canzonetta; the second part he at least begins and ends in a broad tempo and in a sonorous G minor that is handled in full awareness of its effect.

In his canzoni—significantly enough, they are no longer called *alla napoletana* after the first edition—Conversi combines a merry "popular" tone with a high order of artistic refinement and shows himself to be quite as aware of the effects of rhythm as of those of harmony. Hol has already drawn attention to the originality of his beginnings and to the striking effect of his contrasts between solo and tutti (*op. cit.*, p. 49):

He has also commented on the aplomb of the homophonic measures and on the thoroughly modern appearance of the thematic work that follows, traits that he justly attributes to the influence of instrumental music. This is a dance song, a recollection of the villotta, for example *Un cavaglier di Spagna*, and a revival in the modern spirit; it also recalls the technique of Maio's and Nola's villanelle for three voices. Hol gives further examples of the rhythmic grace and the harmonic instinct of these canzoni: if Monteverdi was thoroughly familiar with Conversi's madrigal *Zefiro*, then Orazio Vecchi was equally familiar with his canzoni.

GIOSEPPE CAIMO

ANOTHER source of Vecchi's canzone, to which we shall return in another connection, may be recognized in the work of a Milanese master well known to us (all these musicians are North Italians): Gioseppe Caimo *Milanese*, as he styles himself. In 1564, when he published his first book of four-voiced madrigals, he was organist at S. Ambrogio Maggiore; after 1580 he occupied a similar post at the Milanese cathedral. On October 31, 1584, when Pietro Tini published Caimo's second book of *canzonette a quattro*, he referred to him as no longer among the living and as having died a "bitter and unexpected death" ("acerba et impensata morte"). Yet this same Tini is also the publisher of a book of five-voiced madrigals by Gioseppe Caimo, *nobile milanese*, which is provided with a dedication signed by the composer himself on November 20, 1584, three weeks after his supposed death (. . . *ecco vi dedico questo mio Quarto libro di Madrigali* . . .), and until 1588 Muoni continues to list Caimo as cathedral organist in his chronicles. How all these contradictions are to be reconciled, I cannot say. In 1582 an attempt is made to draw him to Munich, but the negotiations come to nothing. He must have been one of the most respected musicians in Milan, for he was entrusted with the composition of the festive music for the reception of the archdukes Rudolf and Ernest, who visited Trent, Mantua (where Ariosto's *Suppositi* with *concerti per intermedii* were performed on December 18), Cremona, Piacenza, and, on January 5, Milan on their way to Spain in 1563 and 1564. This festive music is preserved in the form of a sonnet *Alli figliuoli del Sereniss. Re Massimigliano d'Austria Eccelsa e generosa prole degna* (*Primo libro a 4*, 1564, No. 5)—a fine, sonorous music to be played in the open. The first three books of his madrigals for five voices are lost; his first book of canzonette for three voices (1566) is preserved in one part only—the *canto*, discovered some years ago in Cracow (*Sammelbände der Internationalen Musik-Gesellschaft*, XIII, 384).

Thus Caimo, by a shorter road, made the same transition as Nola: from the three-voiced villanella to the four-voiced canzonetta. This canzonetta is no longer "popular" at all and everything is smoothed out and polished, even in the texts. The abusive treatment of the duenna has disappeared:

> Vorria che si facesse questa legge:
> Che chi geloso fusse della moglia,
> Li fusse tolta con tormento e doglia.
> E poi li fusse posto un capezzone,
> Un freno o morso come si suol fare
> Quando un poledro si piglia a domare.
> E quel che lo domasse fusse Amore,
> Che con gli sproni in vece di saette
> Lo facesse saltar e far corvette.
> E poi che fosse ben e ben domato,
> E tolto il vitio della gelosia
> Se li desse la moglie in cortesia.

If four young men disguise themselves for a carnival celebration, they no longer address the ladies in unambiguously ambiguous language—they pay homage to the chaste Diana:

> Giovani vaghi siam che qui d'intorno
> Sciolti d'ogn'amor vano e notte e giorno
> Cantiam con voce piana
> La figlia di Latona, alma Diana. . . .

Only rarely does Caimo strike a simpler and more cordial note:

> Vengoti a visitar o faccia d'oro
> E portoti sto core per presente:
> Legalo, stringilo, ferilo, struggilo, dagli tormento!
>   Gemme non hò ne arabico odore
> Prendi questo mio core per presente,
> Legalo . . .
>   Ma qual darsi potria maggior tesoro
> Che dar il proprio cor cortesemente,
> Legalo . . .
>   Stendi la bella man per cortesia
> Vieni, lo piglia, o dolce vita mia!
> Legalo . . .

Here the refrain is worked out in the most realistic fashion. The poet has at least provided the musician with "picturesque" materials:

> **Tu *ridi* sempre mai . . .** [also set by Ferretti in 1569]
> Mi vorrei trasformare
> Gri — gri — *gri*llo sol per cantare . . .

When a "picturesque" text is chosen, for example:

> Per solitari boschi,
> Aspri, selvaggi e foschi
> Voglio gir sempre mai
> Per consumarm'ogn'hor in pene e guai . . .

the parodistic intent has virtually disappeared, and the result is a little expressive madrigal in canzonetta form. But Caimo, the musician, is fresher and more naïve than the poets whose texts he uses. His texture is so light and full of grace, so free in the use of unpretentious devices when passing from motivic work to "chordal" declamation, that it is not easy to find comparable examples in the Venetian or Neapolitan music of the time. A delightful example is the first number of Caimo's print, *The Cuckoo*, which we have included in our volume of illustrations.[5]

The little piece is one of the most charming musical products of the pastoral movement—full of natural sounds, sensuality, and archness, and without the artificiality, virtuosity, and pretension only too usual in the pastoral madrigal.

Two pieces in a class by themselves are the last numbers of the print. One of them, the last, is a *mattinata* in which the lover's sentimental farewell is made ridiculous by the coarse refrain ("Coachman, drive on!"):

[5] See Vol. III, No. 74.

Già l'hora è tarda e le minute stelle
Spariscono dal cielo e l'alba appare;
Temp'è da riposare,
Da voi mi part'ò mio bel lum'altiero—
Tocha cochiero! . . .

The other is a charming dialogue between a lover and his sweetheart, a character right out of the *Decameron*; we are including it in our volume of illustrations.[6]

GASTOLDI'S BALLETTO

STILL more influential than Ferretti, Conversi, and Caimo is Giovanni Giacomo Gastoldi da Caravaggio, whose work is at the same time more voluminous and more many-sided than theirs, though he never went beyond the narrow circle of his immediate activity. But he was active at the focal point of an intense musical life, the Mantua of the dukes Guglielmo and Vincenzo Gonzaga. He must have been born about or shortly after 1550 and seems to have come to Mantua early in life. Here he was presumably a pupil of Giaches Wert. For a few years he serves under Guglielmo; toward the end of 1582 he is appointed successor to the invalid Wert as choirmaster at S. Barbara, the family chapel and favorite church of the Gonzaga family, built in 1562. He had taken orders and in 1598 is called *Monsignore*—in a collection of compositions on texts by the pious Angelo Grillo which contains almost nothing but pieces by ecclesiastics. The dedications of his works all attest his unswerving loyalty to the house of Gonzaga. Even in dedicating a book of canzonette to Guidobuono Guidobuoni, the Duke's counselor, he continues to speak of *Serenissimo Signor nostro*. It is said that he continued at S. Barbara until 1609, when Monteverdi was seeking to succeed him, and that he then went on to Milan as choirmaster at the cathedral, but if this were true the Milanese publisher Filippo Lomazzo would scarcely have continued to call him "maestro di capella nella Chiesa Ducale di S. Barbara di Mantova" in reprinting his second book of canzonette in 1615. In 1604, with the eight-voiced *Concenti musicali*, Gastoldi's secular output is at an end and in 1611 he stops writing for the church. As a celebrity he is of course invited to contribute to the most distinguished collections of the time—the *Trionfo di Dori*, for which he writes one of his most successful pieces, *Al mormorar de'liquidi cristalli*, and the *Gloria musicale*, dedicated to Count Mario Bevilacqua, both of 1592. At the court of Mantua, where he is associated with Monteverdi, Pallavicino, Rovigo, Wert, and Striggio, he seems to have gone his own way though he is sometimes obliged to write for the courtly festivities. Literary historians record that in the years 1591 and 1592 a performance of Guarini's *Pastor Fido* was being prepared at the

[6] See Vol. III, No. 75.

court of Mantua and that Giaches de Wert and Francesco Rovigo were entrusted with the composition of the choruses—for as yet there is no question of a genuine opera. One of the singers, Evangelista Campagnolo, was to play the role of Silvio. But the performance did not take place as planned. As a matter of fact, it did not take place until 1598, after the one in Ronciglione (1596) which was presumably the first, for the performances in Ferrara (1584), Turin (1586), and Florence (1588) are not certain. This time Gastoldi seems to have been asked to write the music. At all events, his fourth book of five-voiced madrigals (1602) contains the *Gioco della cieca* and a second chorus from the *Pastor Fido*, beginning *Ciechi mortali*.

Gastoldi published three books of three-voiced canzonette in 1592, 1594, and 1595. These show a certain superficial resemblance to Marenzio's villanelle, works with which they no longer have much in common. In Marenzio's villanelle the ironic musical relation to the madrigal still persisted in a way; they were by-products of the creative activity of a great madrigalist. Gastoldi's canzonette are by-products of his own balletti, and it is no wonder that in the third book of 1594 they begin to be called *Balletti a tre voci*, are provided with a lute tablature, and are expressly designated as suitable for "singing, playing, and dancing"—"per cantare, sonare, et ballare." The texts have become thoroughly conventional, and the connection with the villanella has been completely dissolved. Some of the little pieces still have the form AAbCC, but many are simply AABB. The combination of the parts is the same throughout: two sopranos and a bass, and genuine three-part writing is even rarer than in Marenzio. The upper parts and the bass move on separate planes, producing a new polarity; sometimes (II, 13, *Se ben parto mia vita*) the result is a duet above the bass:

In another case (II, 20, *Vita della mia vita*), a dialogue, the bass immediately assumes the function of a mere supporting voice. But the chief characteristic of these canzonette—and not alone of the balletti—is the heightened vivacity of the rhythm and the clearing up of the harmony. Episodes in triple time are frequent, and up-beats begin to leap about (II, 17):

Once again, as so often in the history of music, a vocal form is determined by instrumental music, by the dance. And for the sixteenth century, with its love of luxury and of rich sonority, Gastoldi's success rests rather on the balletti for five voices than on those for three. It is strange that a priest in Mantua should have created the vocal-instrumental art-form that was acclaimed with enthusiasm in Italy and with even greater enthusiasm abroad, especially in Germany and England. Hans Leo Hasler in Nuremberg and Thomas Morley in London are inconceivable without the priest Gian Giacomo Gastoldi of S. Barbara. The echo of Gastoldi's five-voiced balletti of 1591 even drowns out that of Ferretti's canzoni, and the Venetian reprints are followed by numerous others in Antwerp, Rotterdam, and even in Paris (1614), where the opposition to Italian music was usually strong. That with altered texts two of these balletti were actually adopted by Protestant church music is reported in every lexicon. A third, thanks to Peter Cornelius, who adapted it in masterly fashion to a new and wholly original text, has become one of the most popular pieces of sixteenth-century music: *Armor im Nachen* (beginning "Fahren wir froh im Nachen" and corresponding to Gastoldi's *Amor vittorioso*, beginning "Tutti venite armati"). We can easily understand why Gastoldi's balletti appealed to the Parisians. For, significantly enough, Gastoldi was a native of Lombardy, and the Lombards have always been receptive to the music of their French neighbors. We have already come across a pastoral dance-song among the works of Arcadelt (p. 268); to this I now add a similar piece by Sandrin (Attaingnant, 1548, f. xii) which will perhaps call up an even livelier recollection of the frottola.[7]

One should recall that in the course of the sixteenth century France began to dictate to the world the rules and laws of the dance and that the French dance types by far excelled the Italian in rhythmic definition and individualization. In Gastoldi's five-voiced balletti this influence is unmistakable. They are a triumph of measure, whether of three-four or of four-four, and of a new sort of instrumental

[7] See Vol. III, No. 76.

periodization. The most obvious sign of this instrumentalization is the warbled re-frain *fa la la* which occurs in every piece.

Since Burney, Kiesewetter, Becker, Schneider, and Torchi were satisfied to publish single numbers from Gastoldi's print, it has never been noticed that the collection is an organic whole. It is a forerunner—the most important forerunner—of the *Amphiparnaso* of Orazio Vecchi and the other so-called madrigal comedies by Vecchi and Banchieri, and it might therefore have been as appropriately discussed in another chapter and in another context. (Vecchi's own *Selva*, which appeared four months before Gastoldi's balletti, is, in spite of its opening number, a mere potpourri.) But it is not always possible to separate the lines of development exactly, since toward the end of the century they often cross. To understand Gastoldi's work one must suppose that a merry company has come together to sing, to play, and to dance, and that the revelry has begun to take on the character of a comedy, in that the partici-pants endeavor to represent in imagination every conceivable character. The first number is an *Introduzione di balletti*:

> O compagni, allegrezza, allegrezza,
> Noi siam giunti in Cuccagna
> Ove chi più lavora men guadagna!
> Quest'è quel loco ameno
> Fonte d'ogni piacer, mar d'ogni gioia,
> D'ogni delizia pieno;
> Qui senza alcuna noia,
> Di gelosia, ne di rival sospetto
> Le amate e gli amadori
> Godon de lor amori.
> Hor pront'e lieto ognun di voi si mostri!
> Sù, caccian mano a gli stromenti nostri,
> E per dar lor diletto
> E soniam e cantiam qualche balletto.

And now the various figures make their entrance: L'Innamorato, Il Bell'umore, Il Contento, the Speme amorosa, Lo Schernito, the Gloria d'Amore, Il Piacere, L'Ardito, Amor vittorioso, Il Premiato, La Sirena, La Bellezza, the Caccia d'Amore, Il Martel-lato, and L'Acceso; the finale consists of a tripartite *mascherata* for six voices, a canzone, and a *Concerto di pastori* for eight voices. Even the *mascherata* has become a sort of chamber music—it had long since been replaced by the more sumptuous courtly intermezzo—but it has not given up its textual ambiguities. "Bell'umore" dominates the scene, even when the "Schernito" or the "Martellato" complains of his lot. From time to time Cupid again appears in person as a triumphant victor;

sometimes all join in a hymn in praise of a singing beauty or a pretty Mirtilla. The verse is of no account, but it shows great variety in meter and structure.

The music of these balletti of Gastoldi is still alive today and is perhaps the only music of the sixteenth century that is still familiar to every chorus. It is homophonic; it is also *concertante* in the twofold sense that the compact five-voiced choir is at times split into trios and that the whole is a sort of musical game of ball in which the motifs are tossed from voice to voice. That Gastoldi makes a clear distinction between balletto and canzone is evident from the interpolated six-voiced canzonetta:

> Viva sempre e scolpita
> Vi tengo nel mio cor dolce mia vita.[8]

The characteristics of the balletto, its greater rhythmical definiteness and its instrumental origin, are well illustrated in one of the pieces not heretofore available in a modern edition, the gay "Schernito":

> Se bene vedi, o vita mia.[9]

Writing for five voices was slow to die and still awakens a distant echo in the orchestral dances of Giambattista Lulli.

THE CLEARING-UP OF THE HARMONIC STYLE

THE approaching crystallization of major and minor is so strikingly evident in Gastoldi's balletto that this is perhaps the place to look back upon the road that the harmonic style of the madrigal has traveled in covering the distance from the frottola to the balletto. In a straight line this distance from the earlier light form to the later one is not very great. The frottola had a tendency to use the pure major and minor modes, and if the reader will look into the harmonic situation in such pieces as the anonymous *De nò, de sì, de nò* (Vol. III, No. 4) or Tromboncino's ottava rima *Acqua non è l'humor* (Vol. III, No. 94) he will find that the one is written in a pure C major and the other, as a prototype of the *ciacona*, in a pure D minor that is harmonically no less clear. But aside from this, the frottola may be said to favor a definiteness in cadence even when it does not attain the definiteness in tonality seen in the two passages just cited.

In the madrigal, in the "secular motet," a form on a larger scale than the frottola and, unlike the frottola, not centered in its upper voice but essentially polyphonic, the harmonic situation is no longer so clear and simple. It fluctuates between the "church modes" and modern tonality; as we have already implied in one of our introductory chapters (p. 270), it is at any moment prepared to abandon the highly indefinite tonality that it has announced in order to push forward into unknown

[8] See Vol. III, No. 77. [9] See Vol. III, No. 78.

territory for the sake of individual expression. One would have to examine each individual case to determine whether it represents any real progress on the road toward modern tonality: often the "boldest" chromaticists have the least developed feeling for harmonic logic, and the most intrepid of them all, Carlo Gesualdo, who wrote at a time when this feeling was beginning to clear up, is sometimes more anachronistic than revolutionary. In the course of our investigation, on the other hand, we have been able to follow this process of harmonic clarification step by step in the music of Willaert, Rore, and Andrea Gabrieli. We have seen transpositions of melodic or harmonic "lines"; we have seen wanderings from cadence to cadence that revealed, slowly but surely, a feeling for modulation, and we have seen evidence of this growing feeling even in Willaert and Rore. But the setting in which this harmonic clarification took place was not so much the lofty madrigal, with its passion for tone-painting and for the expression of the single word, but rather the canzonetta, the canzone, the balletto, and that anacreontic, pastoral variety of the madrigal created by Andrea Gabrieli. In particular, the balletto took over from instrumental models its harmonic simplicity and assurance, its well-defined cadences. Gian Giacomo Gastoldi and his German and English imitators, above all Hans Leo Hasler and Thomas Morley, will loom large in every history of harmony.

CHAPTER IX · THE GREAT
VIRTUOSI:MARENZIO, GESUALDO, MONTEVERDI.—
M. DA GAGLIANO

MARENZIO, Gesualdo, Monteverdi: these three names represent the fulfillment and the end of the madrigal. Let no one bridle at our use of the term *virtuosi*. Marenzio, a provincial of humble origin, but an artistocrat in taste; Gesualdo, a Neapolitan *principe* and thus of the highest social rank, but psychopathic; Monteverdi, the son of a humanistically trained and humanistically inclined physician, but a revolutionary: however different in origin and character, these three musicians, as madrigalists, are late-comers who treat a mature form with superior skill, lending it artistic interest only through their personal mastery. This is virtuosity, artistry, and if one may speak of "art for art's sake" anywhere in the history of music it is in connection with the work of these three masters. All three wrote only for connoisseurs—Gesualdo perhaps only for himself. All three, each in his own way, are experimenters. None of them, not even Marenzio with his villanelle or Monteverdi with his *scherzi*, stand in any relation to the open air, to the middle class, not to say to the "folk." All three are closely related, though they come from widely different musical centers: Marenzio became a Roman musician, Gesualdo was a Neapolitan, Monteverdi became a Mantuan. All three look from a distance toward an art center that lies outside their circles of influence—the court of Ferrara. Monteverdi does so least, but only because he was the youngest of the trio and lived for years after the decline of the Ferrarese musical splendor.

Monteverdi's case is in fact a rather special one. He belongs to this triumvirate of virtuosi only during the first half of his career. He is not only one of those late-comers who perfected the madrigal, he is also the man who destroyed it. Thus he must be discussed, not only in this chapter, but also in another one devoted to him alone—not because he survived Marenzio by more than forty years and Gesualdo by nearly thirty, or because he is quite as much a man of the seventeenth century as of the sixteenth, but because his demonic urge carried him far beyond the stylistic limits of sixteenth-century music, just as a similar urge drove Michelangelo Buonarroti beyond the stylistic limits of fifteenth century painting, sculpture, and architecture.

LUCA MARENZIO

THE oldest of the three, whose life still falls entirely within the sixteenth century, is Luca Marenzio of Coccaglio, a miserable little place near Brescia, where (as we now know for certain) he was born in 1553. It has been supposed that he served his apprenticeship in Brescia under Giovanni Contino, the author of several books of church music (all compressed within the years 1560 and 1561) and also of a book of five-voiced madrigals (likewise 1560). (Two books of four-voiced madrigals have been lost, one of them a book listed by Giunti.) Contino is said to have been a singer in the Papal Chapel about 1540; in 1551, however, he is already choirmaster at the cathedral in his native town, a post to which he is reappointed for five years in 1556; in 1561 he goes to Mantua to enter the service of Duke Guglielmo Gonzaga, after which he returns in 1565 to his old post in Brescia once more. On July 30, 1567, he is summarily discharged by the cathedral chapter because of his refusal to give vocal lessons to the clergy "contra conventiones, et spretis multis monitionibus." Thus Marenzio cannot have studied with Contino unless as a boy of twelve to fourteen, and at that age he would scarcely have left school, since he does not come forward with his first work until ten years later. However this may be, as an artist Marenzio has as little to do with Giovanni Contino in Brescia as Richard Wagner with Cantor Weinlig in Dresden, or Brahms with Eduard Marxsen in Hamburg. It is much more probable that he would have gone to Verona, Mantua, or Rome for his further training—as a choir boy or choir singer. Brescia was in those days above all a town for organ music, organ building, and the instrumental canzone; it cannot therefore have held much attraction for a musician so exclusively inclined toward vocal music as Marenzio. A posthumously published youthful work of his, the *Sacrae cantiones* (1616) for five, six, and seven voices, written about 1573 in Coccaglio or Brescia—"in Patria, quo animi gratia per aliquas dies concesserat"— implies an activity or apprenticeship in some place where the situation of church music was far more flourishing than it would have been in Brescia. Two large-scale motets in honor of St. Cecilia (among nine compositions) would seem to point to some place in which this saint was especially venerated. I should conclude that it was Rome, were it not for the fact that the cult of St. Cecilia dates only from 1599, when her corpse was discovered in the catacombs. At all events, the *style* of this youthful motet certainly points to Rome.

As little substantiated as his studies with Contino is Marenzio's appointment as a musician in the service of one of the cardinals Madruzzo—we do not know whether it was the elder, the powerful Christoforo, to whom Rore dedicated a festive motet sometime before 1544, or his nephew Lodovico, to whom Cristoforo turned over the church in Trent in 1567 when he moved to Rome, where he died on July 5, 1578, at the Villa d'Este. But Lodovico also lived in Rome during the 'seventies. That Marenzio's first publication, the madrigal *Donna bella e crudele*, appeared in a Venetian anthology edited by Mosto and Merulo (*Il primo fiore della ghirlanda musicale*, 1577) is at least not incompatible with this supposed appointment, for the collection also contains a piece by another Roman musician—Palestrina. The rest of the contents, however, is largely by Venetians and other composers of Northern Italy.

On August 1, 1579, Marenzio enters the service of Cardinal Luigi d'Este, brother of Duke Alfonso and nephew of the luxury-loving Cardinal Ippolito II, and here he remains until the death of this strange Prince of the Church (December 30, 1586). Luigi's personality is too well known to require any closer examination. He in no way resembled his devout mother, Renée of France, who leaned toward Protestantism. Destined, much against his will, for the church (he was a second son) he fled to Paris where he gave himself up to the wildest dissipations; on being made a cardinal at twenty-three, he proved his aversion for his ecclesiastical dignity by stirring up so much trouble of every sort that he was even threatened with expulsion from the Papal States. When Alfonso d'Este gave up all hope of an heir, Luigi was given an opportunity to put off his priestly robes; but doubtless his own health had by this time suffered to such an extent that there would have been little point in his doing so. He died as a cardinal, leaving enormous debts, although he had had 120,000 scudi to squander annually. No amateur of true art, he was at least an amateur of luxury and pleasure—praiseworthy as the patron of Torquato Tasso, whom he named as one of his *gentiluomini* in 1565; equally praiseworthy as the patron of Marenzio, to whom he paid the miserable salary of five scudi a month, but to whom he evidently granted ample leisure for creative work. In these years the composer Marenzio must be accredited half to Rome and half to Ferrara. We do not know whether, or how often, or for how long he left Rome for Ferrara; what is certain is that, in 1582, he wrote a few things for the three ladies of Ferrara on the Cardinal's order. In the first madrigal book (1580), dedicated to the Cardinal, Marenzio's relation to the two Ferrarese court poets, Torquato Tasso and Guarini, is already established. The second madrigal book (for six voices, 1581) is dedicated to Duke Alfonso, the third (for five voices, 1581) to Lucrezia, the Duchess of Urbino, the vivacious sister of the two princely brothers; Marenzio seems to have seen this second book through the press himself in Venice, for he signed the dedication there in April 1581. Undoubtedly, Marenzio considered himself obliged and attached to the House of Este, and it goes without saying that he was thoroughly familiar with the work of the musicians of Ferrara (and Mantua): Wert, Luzzaschi, and Striggio. His fourth work (*Libro 3 a cinque*, 1582) is dedicated to the members of the Veronese Accademia Filarmonica, which under the patronage of Mario Bevilacqua was then flourishing anew. Other dedications of his point to Paris, to the French Cardinal de Guise, or to the neighborhood of Rome. Another, addressed to Bianca Capello, Grand Duchess of Tuscany, shows that Marenzio smarted under the miserable salary his patron was paying him (*Libro terzo a sei*, 1585); three years later, in 1588, he tired of this and entered the service of the Medici, after efforts, at the Cardinal's death, to obtain a distinguished appointment at S. Barbara in Mantua had come to naught because of a malicious opinion expressed by Palestrina.

But Florence was not the right place for Marenzio: he cannot conceivably have come to terms with the Camerata and with its pedantic and pretentious dilettantism. As Cardinal Medici, the new Grand Duke, Ferdinand, had undoubtedly known Marenzio well in Rome, but seems to have brought him to Florence and to have used him there chiefly for the festivities on the occasion of his marriage to Christina of Lorraine—the famous *Intermedii et Concerti* of May 1589. Toward the end of November 1589, Marenzio was relieved of his duties and returned to Rome. Here he seems to have come under the protection of the cardinals and the great noble families, especially of Virginio Orsini, Duke of Bracciano, and his wife, Flavia Peretti, and to the Duke—a son of the Isabella Medici who was murdered by her husband—he dedicated his *Quinto libro a sei* (1591); an apartment in the Villa Orsini was at his disposal. His earlier patrons must have included Scipione Gonzaga, Tasso's lifelong friend and a cardinal in 1587, to whom he dedicated his four-voiced *Motecta festorum totius anni* in 1585. From 1591 on Marenzio also enjoyed the patronage of Cinzio Aldobrandini, later Cardinal Aldobrandini, one of the two influential nephews of Pope Clement VIII, Tasso's patron and literary heir, who set aside for Marenzio two rooms in the Vatican. There, in September and October 1595, he was for two months the host of the Irish musician John Dowland, then about thirty-two years old, who had come to Rome for the express purpose of studying with him. One would like to know what they learned from one another, this supreme artist among composers of vocal music and this greatest of British song-writers, the real pioneer in establishing a genuine English "monody"—one not contaminated by theoretical speculation. Shortly after Dowland's departure, toward the end of 1595, Marenzio seems to have undertaken a long journey, ill suited to his delicate constitution; it took him to Cracow, where with other Italian musicians he represented the splendor of Italian music at the court of Sigismund III Bathory. We do not know how long he remained in Poland: no trace and no echo of this northern sojourn has survived, and his next work, whose dedication was signed and dated in Venice (October 20, 1598), is dedicated to D. Ferrante Gonzaga and not, as might have been expected, to the Polish king, a music lover and dabbler in alchemy like his colleague, the Emperor Rudolf II. A year later he turned again to Mantua with his last work, dedicated to Duke Vincenzo Gonzaga; three months later, on August 22, 1599, he died "al giardino del Granduca" in the Villa Medici on the Pincio. He lies buried in San Lorenzo at Lucina. That he was at any time an organist or singer in the Papal Chapel is a myth. His whole character and personality have little in common with a church or with the exacting demands of a permanent post. Ap-

pointed with Nanino, Dragoni, and Valesio to the commission charged, after Palestrina's death, with the appraisal of the work done toward the revision of the liturgical chant, Marenzio can scarcely have taken any very active interest in the
proceedings, for he was soon replaced by Giovanni Troiani.

Marenzio is the embodiment of artistry in its purest form; one imagines him, not
at an organ or as directing a choir, but as a dreamer and a sensualist under the
cypresses or beside the rushing fountains of the Villa d'Este at Tivoli; at his desk
before one of the high windows in the Vatican; in the Palazzo Cesarini, filled with
ancient art and the portraits of beautiful Roman women; or among the participants
in the *accademie* in the apartments of Cardinal Cinzio Aldobrandini, together with
the learned Antonio Querengo, Patricio, G. B. Raimondi, Giambattista and Girolamo Vecchietti, Count Serbelloni, D. Mauritio Cataneo, Scipione Pasquali, Simone
Lunadoro, Pier Montorio, and Lodovico de Torres (Solerti, *Tasso*, I, 731). Among
the guests at these *accademie* were the poets Tasso, Guarini, and Guidobaldo Bonarelli. In the dedication of his first book of madrigals for five voices (1593), the
Spaniard Sebastiano Raval conjures up for us a little picture of the society in which
Marenzio moved. Raval had just come from Urbino to Rome; there, in the palace
of Cardinal Montalto, he arranged for the performance of madrigals of his "in the
presence of the one and only Signor Cavaliere del Liuto, of Signor Scipione Dentice,
that rare master on the cembalo, of that divine musician Luca Marenzio, and of my
Signor Stella. . . ." Like his contemporary Torquato Tasso, who died a few years
before he did, near him on the Gianicolo, Marenzio was an artist who could command the patronage of the most wealthy.

His fastidious taste is evident from first to last in his choice of poems; if it is not
his personal taste, it is at least the taste of those for whom he wrote. But we may be
certain that he did not write exclusively to order. He has an innate love of the sensual and of its opposite, the austere; he has an innate feeling for nature, for landscape, for the Roman countryside, a feeling so strong that one might say of certain
madrigals of his that they could only have been written on one of the hills near
Tivoli. No other musician unites such contradictions as he does, no other is so catholic
in his literary taste. Marenzio is indeed far more "literary" than any of his contemporaries in the second half of the century, more so than Lasso and even Palestrina, and he has an even more personal relation to his poets than Wert. He still—
or rather once more—chooses texts from Petrarch, but his choice is not the "classical," balanced choice of Willaert or Lasso or Monte. To be sure, he too set some of
the poems that best reveal the poet's character: the sweet melancholy, the fluctuation
between joy and grief, sensuously supersensual. But what he really seeks in Petrarch
is the pastoral, the playful, the contrast, the pathos, indeed the extreme pathos. In
general, he knows how to reconcile the most violent antitheses: on the one hand he

sets to music the most modern madrigalesque epigrams from Tasso, Guarini, Ongaro, Casone, and Angelo Grillo; on the other, one of Dante's *canzoni pietrose*. His poetic province ranges all the way from 1300 to 1600. In a little provisional study (*Liliencron-Festschrift*, 1910, p. 72f.) I explained some years ago just how Marenzio came to set to music a text by Franco Sacchetti, the caccia *Passando con pensier per un boschetto*, previously (about 1370) set to music for two voices by Nicolò da Perugia: it is included in the poetic anthology edited in 1565 by Dionigi Atanagi, Marenzio's usual vade mecum. His musical activity even reacts upon the poets, especially upon Guarini, Tasso, and Grillo, suggesting to them a new and more outspoken *poesia musicale*. Presumably it was Marenzio's idyl after Sacchetti that prompted Tasso to attempt a new caccia, far inferior to Sacchetti's in point of spontaneity and naïveté:

> Sovra le verdi chiome
> Di questo novo lauro, udite come
> De'canori augelletti
> Altri scherzando van di ramo in ramo,
> Cantando—io t'amo, io t'amo—;
> Ed ei par gli risponda
> Col dolce mormorio
> De la tremante fronda—
> Sì, sì, che v'amo anch'io—;
> Ed altri vezzosetti
> Cantano—quivi quivi—
> Quasi vogliano dire—In questi rivi
> O intorno a queste linfe
> Ti vagheggian le ninfe.

Marenzio is preeminently the musician of the pastoral, of the pastoral in every sense. He revives Jacopo Sannazaro and draws to the full on his *Canzoniere* and his *Arcadia*. It is instructive to compare the relative importance of Sannazaro and Petrarch in the work of Marenzio and of Lasso, to choose a second composer almost at random: for Lasso it is as 1 to 96, for Marenzio it is as 45 to 48. That Sannazaro's *Canzoniere* contains relatively few numbers ought also to be taken into consideration here. It is as yet impossible to say whether Marenzio's interest in Sannazaro is due more to inner inclination or to external circumstances in Rome. But it is surely significant that other Roman musicians are also turning again to Sannazaro, who had of course never been entirely forgotten: Ruggiero Giovanelli, then choirmaster at San Luigi de' Francesi, who published two books of music on the *sdruccioli* of the *Arcadia* in 1585 and 1589, surely one of Marenzio's most successful rivals;

Francesco Soriano, Giovanelli's predecessor at S. Luigi, later choirmaster at Santa Maria Maggiore, who set the *prosa duodecima* (*sic*) from Sannazaro's novel in 1601 —the return of the poet Sincero, who is guided by a nymph to the fountainhead of all rivers and who asks to see not only the great and famous rivers but also the *Picciolo Sebeto* of his native Campania. This preoccupation with Sannazaro is perhaps connected with the relations of the three musicians to Pietro and Cinzio Aldobrandini, the two nephews of Pope Clement VIII; it is perhaps connected also with a peculiarly Roman sympathy for a poem which is actually nothing but a chain of classical reminiscences. Who knows but what this striking revival of the *Arcadia* in the second half of a century that certainly did not suffer for lack of pastoral poetry may not have something to do with Lodovico Domenichi's translation of Polybius (*Polibio historico Greco tradotto . . .*, Venezia, Giolito, 1546)? For it was then that the larger public, and not simply the humanists and scholars, learned what a musical little people the inhabitants of Arcadia had been: ". . . facevano ogni anno i giuochi con canti et con balli al padre Baccho . . . tutta la vita loro si spendeva in queste canzoni, non tanto che si dilettassero d'udire le consonanze, quanto per esercitarsi cantando insieme. Oltra di questo, se vi è alcuno che alcuna cosa non sappia nelle altre arti, non è presso loro di vergogna alcuna. Ma la Musica non è alcuno di loro che non la possa sapere, perchè necessariamente ella s'impara; nè confessare di non saperla, perchè questo appresso di loro è riputato cosa vergognosissima. . . ." (Lib. IV, pp. 181²-182) — ". . . every year they held games with songs and dances in honor of Father Bacchus. . . . Their whole life was passed in such singing, not so much because they delighted in hearing the consonances as to exercise themselves in singing together. Aside from this, if one of them knows nothing in the other arts, it is no disgrace with them; but every one of them knows music, for he is obliged to learn it and may not admit not knowing it, for this they regard as a most disgraceful thing. . . ."

In 1580 Marenzio published his first madrigal book (for five voices) and won with it a tremendous success. Further editions followed in 1582, 1586, 1587, 1588, 1600, and 1602, not to mention the single compositions that found their way into the collections or the later complete editions published in Germany and the Netherlands. The popularity of the first number (*Liquide perle Amor*) is attested as late as 1640 by Pietro della Valle in his *Discorso* on the excellence of modern music (Solerti's reprint in *L'origini del melodramma*, p. 170): "When I was young, Marenzio's madrigals pleased me very much, and because of certain graces that it has, his *Liquide perle*, a piece often sung, pleased me particularly . . ." ("Quando io era giovanetto mi piacevano assai quei del Marenzio, e particolarmente per certe sue grazie quel tanto cantato *Liquide perle* . . ."). J. P. Sweelinck printed an arrangement of this piece at the head of his *Rimes françoises et italiennes* of 1612. Benedetto Pallavicino (*Quinto libro a cinque*, 1593, p. 13) quotes both the text and the music:

> Donne se quel 'ohime' tanto vi piace
> Mentre lieta cantate a tutte l'hore:
> "Liquide perle Amore"
> V'insegnarò cangiate il mio martire
> In un dolce morire
> Che mille volte 'ohime' m'udrete dire.

Another madrigal, *Dolorosi martir*, which became popular in England thanks to Nicholas Yonge's translation (1597), was used by Michael Praetorius as the basis for a six-voiced Magnificat (Winterfeld, *Johannes Gabrieli*, II, 94).

When a work by a new composer enjoys the immediate success of Marenzio's Opus 1, it must necessarily contain something familiar and at the same time something new. The familiar element in this work of Marenzio's is not to be sought in the music of Giovanni Contino, though one of his wedding sonnets (in honor of a certain Fulvia and Nicello) [1566[1]] is not without the charm of colorfulness and a lively rhythm. Quite the contrary, Contino is much too old-fashioned to have had much influence on the young Marenzio. Far more important is the influence of two other masters, one of them rather light, the other rather serious: Andrea Gabrieli of Venice and Marc'Antonio Ingegneri of Cremona. Technically and spiritually, Ingegneri's real pupil was Marenzio, not Monteverdi, who repeatedly acknowledged him as his nominal master. This can be readily demonstrated on the basis of a specific piece, *Dolorosi martir fieri tormenti*, an ottava whose text has been ascribed with some justice to Luigi Tansillo. It is one of the two pieces that are still written in the *misura di breve* in Marenzio's first book. Ingegneri had set it to music and published it half a year before, and his setting was Marenzio's immediate model. A comparison is now easy, for both pieces have been reprinted: Marenzio's in the *Publikationen älterer Musik*, IV, 1 (ed. Einstein), Ingegneri's in the *Istituzioni e monumenti*, VI, 127 (ed. Pannain). The pathos of the ottava drives both musicians to harmonic extremes, to violent expression, but Marenzio goes further than the more conservative Ingegneri; he is more exact, more realistic—one might almost say more naturalistic, more childlike. In the lines

> Ov'io la notte i giorni hore e momenti
> Misero piango . . .

every word is represented *ad oculos*, symbolized through "eye-music," but there is also expressive representation at "Wretch that I am, I am weeping over my lost happiness":

Tansillo's ottava was also set to music by many other musicians. A comparable text is *Quivi sospiri pianti ed alti guai*, a fragment from Dante's *Inferno*, comparable also in that it received musical treatment at the hands of five or six composers who set it to music after 1562: everywhere the same representation of each individual "acoustic image" through daring harmonies, fragmentary declamation, independent voice-leading—one might almost speak of a "dissociation" of the voices. (One of these settings, that by L. Luzzaschi [1576], is reprinted in *The Golden Age of the Madrigal*, No. 7, New York, G. Schirmer, 1942.) Between these two extremes—the crudest sort of "eye-music" and the most refined expression—Marenzio is continually moving back and forth, at least in his earlier work, and his palpable or rather visible picture of night and day is by no means a mere *jeu d'esprit* confined to his lighter pieces, but—as Figura has shown—one that occurs also in his most austere and impassioned music.

The other piece written in the *misura di breve* is a *Rima* by Sannazaro, *Venuta era madonna al mio languire*, an imitation or variant of *I piango ed ella il volto*, the *commiato* of one of Petrarch's canzoni, likewise set to music by Marenzio. He seeks to render the old-fashioned text in an old-fashioned measure. For the rest, however, the piece is as "modern" as possible, rhythmically and melodically: in the barely perceptible distinction between narrative and lyricism (Marenzio seems almost to hover between these two poles) and in the accentuation of feeling in the description of the dream. It is a real *Liebestraum*, as much superior in taste to Liszt's as the sixteenth century is in general to the nineteenth.

Much stronger than the ingredients derived from Ingegneri are those derived from Andrea Gabrieli. Gabrieli gave Marenzio his easy manner, his way of approximating the "scherzando" of the canzonetta—its cheerful, lively play of motifs—without crossing the line dividing the madrigal from its more "plebeian" counterpart. Marenzio's madrigal is always a madrigal, far removed from the architectonic formalism of the canzonetta. At the same time, his sense for architectonics is a little miracle in itself; sometimes he repeats a final line or a concluding couplet, but for the rest he seems to think only of the text and of representing it freely. And yet all his constructions, despite their lightness and transparency, are as solid as a graceful colonnade by Brunnelleschi or a bridge by Ammanati.

A music-historical parallel will perhaps help us to define the nature of the individual, personal element that delighted Marenzio's contemporaries in his first work. It is in some ways comparable to the phenomenon called forth, about 1730, by Pergolesi's music, when the idiom of the opera buffa penetrated the whole melodic style of Italy, even the opera seria, the church music, and the sonata. It was a Neapolitan dialect, but also a personal one—except that Marenzio, over and above the charm of his light and cheerful madrigal, can still write in the older, "serious" style without falling into archaisms, as Pergolesi does when he seeks to make a "learned" impression. And while Pergolesi's buffo style has only one possibility, Marenzio's has a hundred—if one may speak at all of a buffo style in this connection. But what name is one to give a wholly novel, wholly personal charm-style? The famous *Liquide perle* is a sentimental epigram, and Marenzio has given it no deeper content than that of mere civility, of fine chiseling, qualities that reveal themselves particularly in the contest of the two sopranos. In Marenzio's version of Guarini's *Tirsi morir volea* a loving couple speaks, and the repeated use of the two-voiced texture is a symbol that is emphatic in its avoidance of emphasis. The hidden sensuality of the incident is reflected only in a light musical sheen. Our two speakers are not Papageno and Papagena, but they are also not Tamino and Pamina. In *Spuntavan già per far il mondo adorno*, a Mixolydian piece that comes close to being in a pure G major, an unexpected minor six-four chord near the end has the effect of a transparent golden shadow. In *Lasso ch'io ardo* (1, 8), a piece presumably written to order, Marenzio pays his respects to a certain Livia B[ella?]; here the tender passion is of another order than that of the lady herself when, in the guise of a shepherdess, she sends her beloved a wreath:

Questa di verd'herbette
E di novelli fior tessuta hor hora
Vaga e gentil ghirlanda,
Giovin pastor ti manda
L'amata e bella Flora. . . .

She disguises her longing but it is a transparent disguise. The promise ". . . ti vò far felice" is given in a naïve dance-rhythm. Marenzio has a fine feeling for shades of expression. Even when he writes an echo, like the one at the end of this book, for eight voices on a text by Torquato Tasso, he adds grace and wit to his naturalism. Lasso's famous "echo" is by comparison only the joke of a jolly peasant.

Marenzio's first book of six-voiced madrigals, published eight months later, is his book of Roman idyls and elegies. It is nominally dedicated to Duke Alfonso of Ferrara, and it seems likely that the madrigals had been sung in Ferrara before their publication, for in his dedication Marenzio writes: "I should be too bold were I to call unworthy of you a thing already graciously received and approved by your judgment" ("non sarebbe minor temerità di riputare indegna di lei cosa che già sia stata dal suo giuditio benignamente ricevuta e gradita . . ."). But in reality they are secretly dedicated to a Roman beauty, as the first number reveals:

Come inanti dell'alba ruggiadosa
La bella luce sua n'apporta Clori
E de più bei colori
Raccende il ciel con ogni parte ascosa
Indi scoprend'il suo leggiadro viso
Apre quanto di bel ha'l paradiso—
    Così questa di cui canto gli honori
Esce et uscend'il cielo
Scintillar fa de puri almi splendori
A Vener' e a gli amori
Rinforza forza et amoroso zelo
Indi ogni oscuro velo
Ne sgombr'intorn'a l'alma, e al suo apparire
Iacinti gigli e rose fa fiorire.

The initial letters of the poem spell out the name *Cleria Cesarini*—Cleria Farnese Cesarini, the wife of Giuliano Cesarini, a Roman baron who was created Duke of Cività Castellana by Pope Sixtus V in 1585. This is the same Madonna Cleria to whom Pompilio Venturi, a Sienese dilettante, dedicated a book of three-voiced villanelle "fatte in lode di molte Signore, et Gentildonne Romane" in 1571. Venturi sets her above the Colonnas and the Orsinis, even above the Queen of Spain; she must have been known for her special love for music.

"The Book of the Roman Idyls and Elegies"—this means that Marenzio in this second opus of his avoids the region of deeper agitation and passion: his limit is the elegiac sensuality of the ancient world. Thus he sets Petrarch's sonnet *L'aura serena che fra verdi fronde*, a poem seldom chosen, because he has been attracted to it by the thought of describing in music the net in which the poet's heart is caught—the hair of the *Donna amata*:

> . . . le chiome, or avvolte in perle e'n gemme,
> Allora sciolte, e sovra ôr terso bionde . . .

But he brings no depth to the concluding line, with its presentiment of Laura's death—*Che morte sola fia ch' indi lo snodi*. In the few pieces with a more pathetic accent—*O dolorosa sorte!* or the two ottave from an eclogue by Vincenzo Quirini, *Ben mi credetti già esser felice* and *Ahime tal fu d'Amore e l'esc' e l'hamo*—the deeper agitation reveals itself only in the greater harshness of the progressions and in the bolder passing-tones. Marenzio is cautious and determined not to offend his clients and colleagues. Yet he is also bold. How far he is already prepared to go in this direction may be seen in the concluding measures of *Deh rinforzate il vostro largo pianto*, with their incisive passing-tones and sevenths:

One of Quirino's two ottave, *Ben mi credetti già*, has as its last line *Con nove fogge e disusate tempre*; this prompts Marenzio to end his piece at a point on the circle of keys quite different from that at which he had begun. In modern terms, the whole piece is a lapse from D minor to A minor, from a flat key to a key without signature.

Carl von Winterfeld (*Johannes Gabrieli*, II, 92) once drew a striking parallel between Giovanni Gabrieli as a master writing primarily for the church—a somewhat inaccurate characterization—and our Marenzio as a secular master:

"If we compare Marenzio . . . with Gabrieli, we find that what distinguished these two masters . . . was that each had his own field in which he developed his own talent in accordance with the current of his time. Gabrieli's essential being lies in the development of a basic idea, and such a basic idea dominates each of his works, whether it is a mode with all its delicate associations, a rhythmic relationship, or even a single dissonance which, under varying conditions, seems always to underlie the whole. From this center each individual feature takes shape and may even stand out in sharp outlines, though even here its shape is always dependent upon the underlying principle. This is fitting in the domain of the *sacred* art which our master had recognized and chosen as his own, for in this domain everything individual is submerged in the universality of devout exaltation in order that this exaltation may give it new life.

"Things are altogether different with Luca Marenzio. His domain was *secular* music, where the individual takes precedence over the universal; this stands out as sharply as possible in his every creation. Seldom is the mode he chooses grasped in its essential relationships; as a rule, through the correspondence of beginning and end, it serves him only as a general frame for his multifarious, many-colored images, particularly when he openly reveals his desire for the new and unheard of in strange and unusual modulations and in this way endeavors to disclose the sense and spirit of his texts. For the expression of the word in its liveliest, most vivid form is the goal toward which his endeavors are particularly directed."

In our case, it must be admitted, he does not even preserve the correspondence of beginning and end: all formulas and rules are suspended for the sake of a new unity. The whole conception of the madrigal as a polyphonic interpretation, as a musical realization, changes and takes on a new meaning. From Arcadelt, Willaert, and Rore to Lasso, Monte, and Ingegneri every voice in the madrigal has its full share in the whole, its full text, its full right in every musical motif. With Marenzio the individual voices are only parts of a whole; the madrigal becomes more of a symphonic structure in the service of the text; now, as a rule, no one voice has the full text and the full *espressivo* of every motif. And thus the voices begin to combine in two-part motifs or counter-motifs with a view to brevity and striking characterization, for Marenzio is a master of brevity and conciseness. In *Nel più fiorito Aprile* he begins with the four upper voices; the tenor and bass are silent for twelve measures before they are allowed to join the others in a resounding tutti:

It should no longer be necessary to point out to the reader of these pages that Marenzio begins his "narrative" with the motif of the *canzon francese*. But the familiar motif, with its time-honored entrances, has led to something new. The "symphonic," orchestral attitude of the madrigal again stands out with special clearness at the beginning of the last line—*Cantava Clori.*

Extreme naïveté and the most refined taste stand side by side. When Marenzio speaks of the two eyes of the beloved, as often happens, he always "paints" them with two semibreves (◊ ◊); in No. 1 the *oscuro velo* is crudely rendered by black notes, though in No. 2 the *oscure nubi* call forth a fine turn toward A-flat in the low region of the flat keys. Extreme antitheses require extreme expression, thus in No. 3, *Per duo coralli ardenti*, the lines:

> . . . Bramo sentir l'assalto in mezz'al petto,
> Per *morir* e *rinascer* in diletto!

From this it is only a step to the simultaneous elaboration of double motifs, a step
which Marenzio takes in this book in the course of a fine setting of Tasso's *Non è
questa la mano* that is worthy of its text. All the grace, civility, and playfulness of
this madrigal is perfectly reflected in Marenzio's music: as they dance, the poet takes
the hand of his beloved and covers with kisses this source of the rays that have penetrated his heart. In this second work every aspect of virtuosity is intensified, every
sonority refined upon: evidence of this may be seen even in the concluding echo for
ten voices, or rather for two choirs of five voices each.

In Marenzio's third work, the second book of five-voiced madrigals, Tasso is not
represented. Marenzio falls back on older poets: what is more, he also archaizes in
his music. His music on Ariosto's ballata *Amor, io non potrei* and on a text in the
manner of Cassola, *Mi fa lasso languire,* are written in a style—the second piece also
in a variety of measure, the *misura di breve*—that seems like a deliberate return to the
first period of the madrigal: Marenzio was too sensitive a musician not to have
been attracted by the sentimental sensuousness of the madrigals of Arcadelt or the
youthful Palestrina. But Marenzio's "neutral" style is always enlivened by personal
traits. A text in Cassola's manner by his Venetian colleague Girolamo Parabosco—
Amor poi che non vole, a bipartite madrigal with the same concluding line for each

part—is likewise kept within the bounds of this neutrality, but the general style is simpler and more transparent. Three pieces pay homage to Petrarch but these three pieces display a mastery of contrast that can belong only to a late comer standing at the end of an epoch.

Most striking is the setting of the first stanza of Petrarch's "Canzone x in vita di Madonna Laura," *Se'l pensier che mi strugge*, the very stanza that Carpentras and Maio had set to music in 1517 and 1519. "Most striking," we say, because Marenzio has set it for eight voices, in two choirs. To write for a double choir—this is always a temptation to resort to the purely decorative, the superficial, and Marenzio has not resisted it. "If I could find the right words to express my feeling," the poet says, "the ardor that is consuming me would perhaps begin to communicate itself to my beloved." This deeply agitated text demands an agitated musical realization, but Marenzio simply gives it animation, here and there, through the rapid alternation and the give-and-take of the two choirs and emphasizes this or that image—"la dove hor *dorme*," "come un *ghiaccio stassi*"—through the use of the eight-voiced texture and a broad tempo. Was it a patron who persuaded Marenzio to make use of this large body of voices, or was it a desire to compete with another Roman musician— Palestrina? For Palestrina, too, set this stanza to music and published it in 1586 in his second book of four-voiced madrigals. And this is the place to speak again of Palestrina as a madrigalist.

Four-voiced madrigals! For a great master, writing in 1586, this is decidedly an anachronism. But these madrigals of Palestrina are an anachronism from every point of view, a greater anachronism than the first book of 1555, and perhaps the greatest anachronism of all is that they make a uniform impression and do not seem to have been assembled at random from older, scattered pieces. In their expression, too, they are extremely reserved, almost timid. All are in the more modern *misura cromatica*, that is, in four-four time; but this measure is in effect a *misura di breve* reduced by half; the fluctuating rhythm that characterizes the madrigal after Rore is wholly absent. The madrigals are somewhat reactionary and didactic. Many, indeed almost all, are full of charm, grace, and refinement, full of unspeakable beauty in their song-like form; individual pieces are full of art and tender anima-tion. Perhaps the finest piece is *Io ben dovea pensarmi* (No. 8). In a revealing analysis (*Saggio*, II, 72), Padre Martini has called attention to the beauties of one of the others—*Alla riva del Tebro* (No. 15). One of the weakest is our old friend *Se'l pensier che mi strugge*—a formalistic realization of this agitated text. To measure the extent of the change that has taken place, the discrepancy between what has long been superseded and what is most modern, one has only to compare the vir-tuosity of Marenzio's declamation with the almost insensible rigidity of Palestrina's. Nor is this judgment affected by the fact that in one case permitting an immediate comparison Marenzio has adopted an even more archaic manner than Palestrina (see below, p. 659). It would be interesting to know what the Roman musicians thought of these madrigals. No doubt they said what a modern musician might say about a work in the style of Carl Reinecke or Sterndale Bennett: "One can no longer write in this style." The general public took the same view: Palestrina's second madrigal book was never reprinted; Marenzio's second book of five-voiced madrigals went through eight further editions. We can understand why the old master from Palestrina did not precisely regard the young one from Brescia with sympathy.

The second of the Petrarch settings, *O voi che sospirate*, a stanza from the sestina *Mia benigna fortuna*, affords us another parallel. To achieve an extreme expression Palestrina goes as far as the soft suspensions of the seventh and ninth (No. 18):

But Marenzio, mindful of the obligation that Arcadelt, Rore, and Lasso have imposed upon him in their settings of a stanza from this same sestina, actually attains the ultimate extreme. Since its first republication by Carl von Winterfeld more than a hundred years ago (*Johannes Gabrieli*, III, 156, Leipzig, 1834), the piece has become famous, in so far as any madrigal can become famous in the nineteenth and twentieth centuries. It is admittedly extreme, but it is far from being a mere experiment. At the line *Muti una volta quel suo antico stile*, Marenzio risks an enharmonic combination—G-sharp and A-flat, F-sharp and G-flat; it is a passage that shows full comprehension of what we now call equal temperament, a passage that the Principe Gesualdo di Venosa repeatedly imitated, fourteen and more years later, without fully understanding it.

The third Petrarch setting is *I' piango; ed ella il volto*, the *commiato* of "Canzone VI in morte di Madonna Laura" (*Quando il soave mio fido conforto*); it shows Marenzio's personal style in ideal purity. It is one of his shortest madrigals, though not because of the shortness of its text alone. Marenzio is brief because of the wealth of means placed at his disposal by the long history of the madrigal—these include chromaticism and freedom of declamation—and because he is a supreme master in the use of these means for purposes of suggestion. Brevity and resourcefulness are possible only at the end of an epoch. A Schubert song can combine wealth of resource with the utmost brevity. Zelter and Reichardt can also be brief, but their songs are

as simple and poverty-stricken as a frottola. Petrarch's *commiato* was often set to music; I quote the beginnings of several settings by others, Ingegneri, Il Martoretta, and I. Sabino:

Giandomenico Il Martoretta from Calabria, a peculiar man who lived in Venice and by 1554 had made a journey to the Holy Land, is a musician of Arcadelt's circle; he declaims simply and homophonically. Ippolito Sabino of Lanciano (Chieti), a prolific master who is hard to classify, relies on breadth of tone-painting. Closest to Marenzio, and not in time alone, stands Ingegneri of Brescia, with his deeply felt, concise representation of weeping. But Marenzio is not only the most concise and most striking of them all; he is able to re-create the whole situation immediately: the dream, the fine-spun transparent web of illusion that precedes the awakening of the sleeper:

As we have observed before, the name of Sannazaro, the pastoral poet, occurs for the first time in this third work of Marenzio. From his *Arcadia* Marenzio chooses the tercets *Itene all'ombra degli ameni faggi* and sets them to "neutral" music, somewhat formally, like a pastoral manifesto or motto. From this same second eclogue (101-108) he also takes the appeal to Phyllis, *Fillida mia più che i ligustri bianca.* For the rest the book is full of pastoral pieces: there is a stanza from Molza's *Ninfa Tiberina,* another from an eclogue by an unknown poet beginning *O biondo Iddio che con più lungo corso,* a poem printed in an anthology edited by Ercole Bottrigari (1551). Marenzio and A. Gabrieli are the founders of the pastoral style that was to crystallize in the vocal and instrumental music of the 17th century as the *alla Siciliana,* a sort of rocking movement over voices that remain stationary. In Marenzio it is characterized by the lighter rhythm of the canzonetta and especially by the bright, transparent sound of high voices and the high register, and by the vocal *scherzando.* But we already find the bagpipe, as in the trio sonata of Legrenzi or Corelli (Quinto and tenor are silent):

One might say that such a beginning could not have been written in Venice, Florence, Mantua, or Ferrara, but only in Rome, the city of the *pifferari.* The prayer to Helios for a dry and favorable spring (No. 2) points also to Rome:

Perchè di pioggia'l ciel non si distille
E la riva del Tebro tanto inondi . . .

In No. 13 a mention of the Paglia, a tributary of the Tiber, hints at a lady of Aquapendente. No. 7 takes us to Mantua:

Al vago del mio sole
Lucido raggio che'l bel Mincio honora . . .

One might suppose it to be a festive piece written for the reception of the third wife of Alfonso d'Este, Margherita Gonzaga, on her arrival in Ferrara in 1579.

The third book of five-voiced madrigals of 1582 was dedicated by Marenzio in proud yet modest language to the Accademici Filarmonici of Verona; thus he followed in the footsteps of Nasco and Ruffo. He extols the connoisseurship of the members, which had become somewhat "high-brow" since the days of Nasco and Ruffo, and we are thus astonished to find a studious avoidance of "experiment": not one composition even begins to recall the boldness of *O voi che sospirate*. The book shows more virtuosity but it is also shallower than its three predecessors. This is best seen in the one composition on a text from Petrarch, the first sonnet "in morte di Madonna Laura," *Oimè il bel viso*. It paints details instead of recapturing the melancholy or elegiac tone of the poem as a whole, and the master-stroke is of course the tone-painting at *Vento [che] ne portava le parole*. At that, it is still "classic" in comparison with the setting by Monteverdi, thirty years later, in his sixth book of madrigals. Marenzio is more serious and shows more taste in his setting of the madrigal *Caro dolce ben mio*, written in the *misura di breve* which, with him, is always expressive. Here the expression tends rather toward the sharply agitated and the tonality toward B major, although it also touches G minor; for once, the pathos of the close—"Tears that would move rocks to pity"—is genuine, deeply felt and thus fully justified. The other piece in the *misura di breve* is *Se la mia fiamma ardente*, an elegiac epigram. A third piece in the agitated style is a bipartite *lontananza* (No. 6, *Lunge da voi mia vita*), filled with concrete pictures, free in conception, the work of a virtuoso.

For the rest, Marenzio carries his use of expressive devices in the pastoral and the epigram to the point of virtuosity. He pays tribute to Sannazaro's *sdruccioli* in *La pastorella mia spietata e rigida*, a model of lively animation and drastic imagery. Battista Guarini appears twice—*O dolce anima mia* and *Ohime se tanto amate*—and Marenzio understands his epigrammatic side as well as his languor. In the pastoral, canzonetta-like pieces there is added to the *scherzando* rhythm a new element of virtuosity: vocal coloratura used for its own sake, not as tone-painting but as ornament. Perhaps Marenzio's visit to Ferrara may have had something to do with this. All these external and superficial characteristics would tend to give

Marenzio's book at least a lighter specific gravity if it did not contain two pieces that reveal his genius and artistry in all their purity.

One of these is a setting of an ottava from Luigi Alamanni's *Favola di Narciso*:

> Scaldava il sol di mezzo giorno l'arco
> Nel dorso di Leon suo albergo caro,
> Sotto'l boschetto più di frondi carco
> Dormia'l pastor con le sue greggi a paro;
> Giaceva il villanel de l'opra scarco,
> Vie più di posa che di spighe avaro;
> Gl'augei, le fere, ogn'huom s'asconde e tace,
> Sol la cicala non si sente in pace.

It is a picture of the sultry midday heat of the Roman Campagna: Pan is asleep; there is no suggestion of the pastoral, no stage-setting, no pretense—it is a pure idyl. That Marenzio set this text raises him above a hundred of his contemporaries. The same is true of the manner in which he set it. He neglects no detail, but every detail is naïve in the classic manner and never childish; the whole, when properly performed, creates the atmosphere of a vision.

The other is music for Veronica Gambara's madrigal on the eyes of her lover and husband:

> Occhi lucenti e belli,
> Com'esser può ch'in un medesmo istante
> Nascan da voi si nove forme e tante? . . .

Here, as always, Marenzio represents the "eyes" by a pair of semibreves, but this representation has become a spiritual one. The upper voice consists only of semibreves:

The lower parts are the more animated and supply a lively pictorial commentary on the text of the canto. Simultaneous constancy and inconstancy are at once symbolized and made real; the work is a triumph of polyphony, of the madrigal, and of the sensitive artist.

With his next work, the second book of six-voiced madrigals (April 15, 1584), Marenzio returns to the circle of the Este family by dedicating it to the "Cardinal di Guisa." Louis, Cardinal de Guise, was a nephew of Cardinal Luigi d'Este: his mother, Anne, was the elder sister of Luigi and Alfonso and the wife of François de Guise-Lorraine. Four years after receiving this dedication, on Christmas Day in 1588,

the Cardinal was murdered at Blois at the command of his royal master Henri III, the very day after his brother Henri, Duc de Guise, had met the same fate. If Marenzio wrote the dedication in the hope of being called to Paris and had succeeded in realizing this hope, he would not have enjoyed the Cardinal's patronage for long. Nor would the Paris of the St. Bartholomew and of the conflicts of Catholic and Huguenot have been as congenial to him as Rome, though even in the Rome of Sixtus V he might have witnessed any number of bloody executions.

The dedicatory letter contains one striking passage, doubly striking after the frankly hedonistic tone of the preceding book: "So far is it from being the opinion of the learned that the perfect music, as the vulgar suppose, aims solely to delight the senses, that the greatest of the judicious followers of Pythagoras, after holding music up to us as the true means of reducing every essential dissonance of our souls to stable concord, considers it worthy to be called the unique counterpart of temperance" — ". . . tanto è lontano dal parere de savi che la perfetta musica sia, come il volgo s'imagina, indirizzata al solo diletto de sentimenti, che'l maggiore de più giuditiosi seguaci di Pitagora proponendocela per vera strada di ridurre à stabile concordia ogni intrinseca dissonanza de gli animi nostri la riputò degna di esser detta unico parallelo della Temperanza. . . ." Marenzio's soul is divided, torn like Petrarch's between the sensuous and the super-sensuous; accordingly this book is divided between the pastoral and the pathetic. The pastoral is represented by one of Marenzio's loveliest, lightest, most fragrant pieces—*Vaghi e lieti fanciulli*, a birthday greeting for high voices whose bright tone-quality is essential to it. A pastoral farewell (*Filli mia bella a Dio*) whose imaginary scene is laid on the banks of the Arno—probably a piece written to the order of a Florentine patron—is quite playful and cheery: the lovers' pain does not go deep. But even in those pieces that are not pathetic, the canzonetta spirit is negligible. A wedding sonnet, written for a Roman Vittoria (*Cedan l'antiche tue*) fluctuates between small-scale illustration and grandiose conception. Marenzio has attained the ultimate in virtuosity, in the translation of visual impressions into sound. The opening piece of the print sets the prevailing tone. It is an ottava taken from the same anonymous eclogue that we have already mentioned as contained in Bottrigari's anthology of 1551:

> Satiàti Amor ch'a più doglioso amante
> Di me non impiagasti il core ancora;
> Ridi Fortuna che fra tante e tante
> Alme infelici la mia più t'honora;
> Godete Donna sola hoggi fra tante
> Che'l mondo di beltà vanta ed adora,
> Che'n più di mille carte scritto sia
> Vostra durezza con la voglia mia!

No antithesis is sharp enough for Marenzio, and no image or concept seems to him irrelevant:

Marenzio is ingenious, free in his choice of means, in a word, a virtuoso. Nowhere does this stand out more clearly than in the three pieces this book contains on texts by Torquato Tasso, two madrigals and a sonnet. The two madrigals must have been written to order, for they have the same underlying idea: in the old editions *Io vidi già sotto l'ardente sole* is headed "Pallore di madonna desiato," while *Vita de la mia vita* has the heading "Pallore di madonna grato." Marenzio sets them as contrasts, the first in a more playful manner, the second one more serious, but both with the utmost "ingenuity." The sonnet permits a comparison, and thus enables us to see how personal, how brilliant, how overripe Marenzio's style has grown. For two years later Filippo di Monte set the same text to music for five voices in his eleventh madrigal book (1586) which he dedicates to Count Mario Bevilacqua of Verona and in which he has endeavored to write "in the most animated and cheerful style that he could discover" (in quello più vivace et allegro stile, che a me sia stato lecito di poter ritrovare . . .).

Poor Monte! If Marenzio represents the standard of the time, Monte has been left far behind. I must quote the text in full if the connection of the details is to be understood:

> In un bel bosco di leggiadre fronde
> Ch'ombra si fà con le ramose braccia
> Amor che va de l'alme nostr'a caccia
> Tese le reti di due treccie bionde.
>
> Così il mio cor c'havea di due gioconde
> Luci seguita la fallace treccia

Preso restò com'animal s'allaccia
Ne bei legami che ne l'ombr'asconde.
    O dolce laccio, o vaghe reti, o bosco
Vezzoso, o cacciator che mi togliesti
Il core dove l'hai crudele ascosto
    Io pur ritorno spesso a pianger vosco
Et a cercar tra quest'herbette e questi
Vaghi fioretti ov'egli sia nascosto.

Monte's composition requires 108 measures, Marenzio's 152. For both masters the starting point is Venice and the circle of Andrea Gabrieli. Monte does not go far beyond this circle and its style: he is satisfied to give the text a transparent musical dress and to follow up only a few of its pictorial suggestions—the "sweet snare," the *"two* braids," and the zealous "search." For him the madrigal is still a compact whole, and his voices still keep very much together. With Marenzio they have more individual life and a tendency to detach themselves from the ensemble. With Monte the music is subordinate to the poem; with Marenzio the poem is a suggestion for the music and little more. It is almost sufficient to compare the beginnings:

Compared with this, Marenzio's beginning, which is typical for his whole piece, has the air of having been written, not two years earlier, but twenty years later:

Monte tells his story simply, unpretentiously, gaily; Marenzio, although he is as familiar as his listeners with the way in which a canzone is supposed to begin, gives the characteristic rhythm to the upper voice alone and writes below it a pseudo-canonic duet. Every concept is illustrated; the ensemble is so free and easy that it is in danger of crossing the boundaries of the *stile concertante*. If straightforwardness and simplicity are the characteristics of the purer, nobler work of art, Monte's piece is to be preferred to Marenzio's by far. Marenzio is a late-comer, a virtuoso.

The book strikes a more serious note in certain pieces that are not only written but also conceived in the older measure, the *misura di breve*. One madrigal is worked out on a grand scale and in a grandiose manner:

> Tutte sue squadre di miserie e stenti
> Ben mi cred'io c'hor seco
> Giù dal più basso addolorato speco
> Il duol condurre a mio gran danno tenti . . .

It is of course for low voices, though without illustration. *Nessun visse giammai più di me lieto*, another stanza from Petrarch's sestina *Mia benigna fortuna*, also set to music by Palestrina, Lasso, Monte, and others, fluctuates between mere symbolism —there is also an example of pure "eye-music"—and genuine grandeur of expression. *Del cibo onde 'l Signor mio sempre abbonda*, a sonnet from Petrarch in which the dead Laura appears to the poet in a dream, dries his tears, and consoles him, becomes a *madrigale spirituale*: Marenzio substitutes Mary for Laura. In all these pieces Marenzio seems anxious to prove that he is also perfectly able to write in the old, almost impersonal style.

As though to quiet every dissenting voice, Marenzio concludes this book with an exceptional piece: a setting of Franco Sacchetti's caccia *Passando con pensier per un boschetto* in three sections. He had found it in the second book of the poetic anthology brought out by Dionigi Atanagi, and as we have already explained, this anthology must have served Marenzio as a sort of vade mecum, for it is also the source of many of his other texts. But Marenzio's setting has nothing to do with the Old Florentine caccia on the same text by Nicolò da Perugia, preserved in the famous Squarcialupi Codex (f.35), reprinted by Johannes Wolf in his *Sing- und Spielmusik* (No. 7), and by W. Th. Marrocco, *Fourteenth-century Italian Cacce* (Cambridge, 1942, The Medieval Ac. of America, No. 14), and one would be on the wrong track if one were to try to use this piece as a link between the Trecento and the Cinquecento. Marenzio again stands out from among the hundreds of madrigalists in that he was the first and only Italian to whom the idea of setting this text occurred. Not until 1598 did his example bear fruit in the eight-voiced setting of the English Peter Phillips. The poem takes us back to a purer and more youthful period in Italian poetry:

> Passando con pensier per un boschetto,
> Donne per quello givan fior cogliendo,
> To quel, to quel, dicendo,
> Eccolo, eccolo,
> Che è? che è?
> È fior di liso.
> Va là per le viole,
> O me che'l prun mi punge.
> Quell'altra me v'aggiunge,
> U vò, che è quel che salta?
> È un grillo.
> Venite qua, correte,
> Raponzoli cogliete.
> E non sono essi.
> Si sono.
> Colei, o colei
> Vien qua, vien qua per funghi;
> Costà costà pel sermollino.
>
> Noi starem troppo, che'l tempo si turba,
> Ecco balena, & tuona:
> Et vespero già suona:
> Non è egli ancor nona:
> Odi odi

Il lusignuol, che canta,
Piu bel ve, piu bel ve;
Lo sento, & non so che,
O dove è, o dove è?
In quel cespuglio:
Tocca, picchia, ritocca:
Mentre che'l busso cresce,
Et una serpe n'esce,
O me trista, o me lassa.

Fuggendo tutte di paura piene
Una gran piovia viene
Qual sdrucciola, qual cade,
Qual si punge lo piede:
A terra van ghirlande:
Tal, ciò c'ha tolto, lascia, & tal percote:
Tiensi beata chi più correr pote.

Si fiso stetti il dì, ch'io lor mirai,
Ch'io non m'avvidi, & tutto mi bagnai.

(I follow the reading of Atanagi's anthology. The poem has been translated into English by D. G. Rossetti, *The Early Italian Poets*, London, 1861, p. 179)

As I walk'd thinking through a little grove,
Some girls that gather'd flowers kept passing me,
Saying, "Look here! look there!" delightedly.
"Oh here it is!" "What's that?" "A lily, love."
"And there are violets!"
"Farther for roses! Oh the lovely pets—
The darling beauties! Oh the nasty thorn!
Look here, my hand's all torn!"
"What's that that jumps?" "Oh don't! it's a grasshopper!"
"Come run, come run,
Here's bluebells!" "Oh what fun!"
"Not that way! Stop her!"
"Yes, this way!" "Pluck them, then!"
"Oh, I've found mushrooms! Oh look here!" "Oh, I'm
Quite sure that farther on we'll get wild thyme."

"Oh we shall stay too long, it's going to rain!
There's lightning, oh there's thunder!"
"Oh shan't we hear the vesper bell, I wonder?"
"Why, it's not nones, you silly little thing;
And don't you hear the nightingales that sing
Fly away O die away?"
"I feel so funny! Hush!"
"Why, where? what is it then?" "Ah! in that bush!"
So every girl here knocks it, shakes and shocks it,
Till with the stir they make
Out scurries a great snake.
"O Lord! O me! Alack! Ah me! alack!"

They scream, and then all run and scream again,
And then in heavy drops down comes the rain.
Each running at the other in a fright,
Each trying to get before the other, and crying
And flying, stumbling, tumbling, wrong or right;
One sets her knee
There where her foot should be;
One has her hands and dress
All smother'd up with mud in a fine mess;
And one gets trampled on by two or three.
What's gather'd is let fall
About the wood and not pick'd up at all.
The wreaths of flowers are scatter'd on the ground;
And still as screaming, hustling without rest
They run this way and that and round and round,
She thinks herself in luck who runs the best.

I stood quite still to have a perfect view
And never noticed till I got wet through.

All the naïve description, all the realism that Marenzio can command are in their right place here; everything is full of musical life and musical refinement. I forego citing specific details, since it would be necessary to reproduce the entire piece and since a complete edition of our composer is bound to appear some time. Uncritically considered, the piece might also be assigned to another context, namely to convivial music, somewhere between Striggio's *Cicalamento* and *Gioco di primiera* and Vecchi's *Convito musicale* (cf. p. 766f.). But its level is much higher. It lacks

the elements of self-parody, "entertainment," and fun. It is rather a work of the purest and noblest grace and of the purest and noblest poetry.

The *madrigale spirituale* after Petrarch in this *Secondo libro a sei* prefigures another of Marenzio's works, the *madrigali spirituali a cinque* which he dedicated, only nine days later (Rome, April 29, 1584), to Lodovico Bianchetti, Chamberlain to Pope Gregory XIII and brother of Cardinal Lorenzo Bianchetti, auditor of the Rota under Sixtus V. Marenzio had no difficulty in finding texts for this book of devotions. He drew chiefly on Sannazaro, whose sestina *Non fu mai cervo sì veloce al corso* concludes the print impressively, and from whom the Good Friday sonnets *Le dubbie speme* and *È questo il legno* are also taken. The book begins with a sestina stanza, *Grazie renda al Signor*, by Benedetto Guidi; Torquato Tasso, too, is represented by a penitential sonnet, *Padre del cielo, hor ch'atra nube il calle*. We shall not go into the "spiritual" side of the book as fully as it deserves. For the present we shall say only that Marenzio usually set the sonnets in the *misura di breve*, and that the sonnets are always at least reserved, sustained, and somewhat archaic. The texts in madrigal form, on the other hand, are set in four-four time and with as much animation and insistence as his secular works. There is, for example, a madrigal on the Annunciation ("sopra la Sacratissima Annunciata") by the Roman author Aurelio Orsi:

> Quasi vermiglia rosa,
> Humile e in se nascosa
> Sedea la bella donna in atti schivi
> E in pensier casti e divi,
> Quand'il ciel rise, e fu mirabil cosa:
> Ch'io vidi nel bel seno
> Lampeggiar un sereno,
> Che Dio direste in esso, e ben fu Dio,
> Che scendendo nel grembo a lei s'unio.

Marenzio received this text directly from the poet, for it was not printed until a year later in Cesare Caporali's *Le piacevoli rime*, Milano, 1585, where it is found on p. 206. The musical setting is thoroughly in keeping with the poem and is as worldly, as realistic—one might even say, as insistent—as possible. It already shows the same lack of reverence for the Divine Mystery that the seventeenth century was later to carry to intolerable extremes. Also for the Annunciation, and belonging to the same class and probably to the same poet, is the madrigal *Qual mormorio soave*; Good Friday claims the madrigal *Il dì che di pallor la faccia tinse* and an ottava painting all the phenomena attendant upon Christ's Passion, *Sento squarciar del vecchio tempio il velo*; the madrigal *Vergine gloriosa e lieta, oh quanto* is for Easter Sunday. Between the two styles, the sustained and the animated, stands Sannazaro's sestina in seven sections, evidently written for five singers who were masters of rapid declamation and elegant ornamentation.

The fourth book of five-voiced madrigals, dedicated on May 5, 1584, to a Signor Girolamo Ruis, otherwise unknown to me, is one of the four publications by Marenzio whose dedications are signed in Venice. To judge from this dedication, Marenzio must have traveled from Rome to Venice in less than ten days, by no means an impossibility at that time, but it is also conceivable that the reference to the place of dedication is fictitious, as is so frequently the case. However this may be, within twenty days Marenzio has published three separate works: he is now riding the crest of the wave, confident of success.

On the whole, the book has no uniform tendency and consists largely of occasional pieces. But one tendentious piece stands at the head—the sequence of four stanzas from Torquato Tasso's *Gerusalemme liberata* (XII, 96-99), of which we have already spoken in another connection (cf. above, p. 568f.). Three years earlier, two of these stanzas had been set to music by Giaches Wert, with whom Marenzio was probably now competing, perhaps at the request of Duke Guglielmo of Mantua or of his own patron, Cardinal d'Este. As previously pointed out, Marenzio outbids Wert but does not outdo him. He is no dramatist; what matters to him as a virtuoso is picturesque description, and this interests him far more than the lament of the unfortunate Tancred, which he treats somewhat homophonically. He is less concerned with emotion than with artifice—one might almost say, with mere dexterity.

But Marenzio is alone among his fellows in setting to music an extremely personal, artificial madrigal of Tasso's, *Disdegno e gelosia*, in which the poet speaks of himself as having become the prey of the hunter and the target of the archer. Marenzio's music mirrors this artificiality, this outward animation, this personal style, without even attempting to portray the inner drama. Marenzio has reached a limit—the limit of his own style. One calls this mannerism, and he has indeed become a mannerist. This is only too evident in another piece from this book, the madrigal *Vaghi augelletti che per valli e monti*, previously set to music by Andrea Gabrieli, likewise for five voices (*Secondo libro*, 1570). Gabrieli chooses the *misura di breve*, for he is anxious to avoid any suggestion of the canzonetta; he is far more "archaic" than Marenzio, but there is in his work a trace of humor and amiability that Marenzio lacks. His vocal writing, too, is more refined and more genuine. Marenzio is much more the deliberate virtuoso, but already he is also somewhat cold and mechanical—somewhat mannered. For purposes of comparison I have included Gabrieli's composition in the volume of illustrations.[1]

Another opportunity for comparison is presented by the sonnet *Real natura, angelico intelletto*, by G. B. Zuccarini, a miserable writer of occasional poems; Marenzio

[1] See Vol. III, No. 79.

set it to music on the occasion of the wedding of Bianca Capello. Two years later Zuccarini himself published Marenzio's piece again (Vogel, 1586⁴) under the title *Corona di dodici sonetti*, together with settings of other poems of his by Palestrina, Monte, Andrea and Giovanni Gabrieli, Claudio Merulo, Orazio Vecchi, and five other lesser masters. Those of two Venetian musicians, Giovanni Gabrieli and Vincenzo Bell'Haver, have been reprinted by Torchi (*Arte musicale in Italia*, II, 149 and I, 405): they are simply decorative and thus in keeping with the occasion. (Incidentally, the twelve compositions were not composed *for* the wedding, which had taken place in 1579, but in *honor* of it.) But Marenzio's piece, for high voices, is more than decorative; it has virtuosity, which is lacking in the work of the two Venetians. Palestrina's contribution has almost no bearing on the comparison. Baini departs from his usual adulation to pronounce a harsh judgment on it that it by no means deserves. But it is written in the "timid" style of the second madrigal book and the timorous coloratura and the triple time at the beginning of the second part are at best attempts at festivity, not festivity itself. Palestrina has ceased to understand the times—even to understand the world.

It is a part of the manneristic side of Marenzio's writing that he is still (or perhaps already) using certain stereotyped formulas for particular images. Two madrigals, *Scendi dal paradiso* and *Corran di puro latte*, the one written for a wedding in Rome, the other for one in Ferrara, contain almost identical turns of phrase:

> . . . l'anime belle
> D'Amarill'e di Tirsi son'unite
> *Al nodo sacro e santo* . . .

and

> . . . le lor alme e i cuori
> Leghi Imeneo *con casti nodi e santi* . . .

These are set to almost identical music:

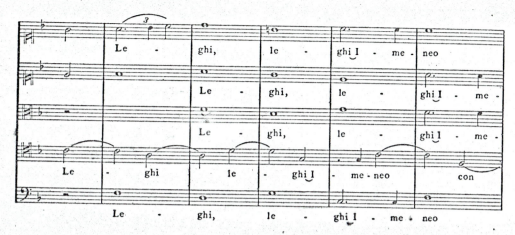

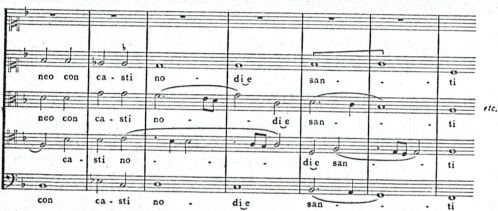

Is this a matter for blame? One might say equally well that where the circumstances are the same, Marenzio's imagination reacts in precisely the same way; even J. S. Bach, in his cantatas, operates with such formulas—for example, with the stereotyped musical treatment of the verb "to bind."

What is noteworthy is that Marenzio in this book never goes beyond the conventional in harmony. Even the threnody on a young woman who has met a violent death—*Filli, l'acerbo caso*—avoids extremes (although the *crudel ferro*, the "cruel steel," was no idle threat to the aristocratic ladies of those days) and remains a virtuoso-piece of chamber music with a conclusion that dies away in a *pianissimo*. Its counterpart is the madrigal *Cadde già di Tarquinio al cieco errore*, written in praise of a certain Tarquinia (there is a Tarquinia del Cavalliero among the Roman ladies in Stefano Venturi), a piece in solemn alla breve, but quite free and likewise in the chamber-music style. More in the spirit of "open-air" music is the madrigal *Spirto a cui giova gli anni a buona fine*, which celebrates the distinguished intellectual attainments of someone who is not named—the text hints that it is a mem-

ber of the Polo family; here Marenzio literally repeats the music of the last couplet. *Ecco l'aurora con l'aurate fronte*, an ottava from a pastoral eclogue by Vincenzo Quirino, is unique in form in that Marenzio uses exactly the same music for the last four lines as for the first four. It is a genuine *canzon francese*, conceived in a wholly instrumental style; Marenzio has given it the form of a canzone because of its narrative content, beginning and ending it with the typical tone-repetitions:

Without its text, the piece might have found a place in the *Canzoni francesi* of Florenzio Maschera, first published in Brescia this same year (1584). Even Ariosto's *Quando vostra beltà, vostro valore* is shot through with instrumental characteristics; its most striking detail is reserved for the end, where the path that is "too steep and too long" for Hope to climb is represented by a repeated descending scale in an interlocking arrangement for two voices while the three remaining voices provide a contrapuntal accompaniment. As though in compensation for this, other numbers of the book are the more effectively written for voices, now hastening, now delaying, filled with poetic applications of motifs and countermotifs, for example the moving, sentimental *Senza cor, senza luce* or *Sapete amanti perche ignudo sia*, a madrigal by Valerio Marcellini drawn from Atanagi's anthology (I, 191) in which Marenzio has substituted "la mia bella donna" for "Virginia," the name of the lady addressed.

Not more than six months intervened between the publication of the fourth book of five-voiced madrigals and that of the fifth, dedicated by Marenzio on December 15 to Nicolo Pallavicino, a Genoese nobleman to whom Antonio Dueto, a canon of the cathedral in Genoa, also dedicated a book of madrigals in 1584. Marenzio's dedication thus seems to point to a connection with Genoa regarding which we lack further details. But a long time—nearly ten years—will elapse before Marenzio's next book of five-voiced madrigals, and this striking circumstance requires an explanation.

External reasons will not account for it. It is as though Marenzio had realized that he had reached a limit: in the variety of its contents and style the book testifies to one of those crises that were as common in the music of the older masters as they are among the moderns and ultra-moderns. The familiar contrast of time-signatures is still present: for Marenzio the *misura di breve* (¢) is still the pathetic measure and he prescribes it for two sonnets by Giovanni della Casa, *Quella che lieta del mortal mio duolo* and *S'io vissi cieco et grave fall' indegno*, one of them solemn and amorous, the other almost spiritual. In the second of these, the effect of the sustained tempo is intensified by the transposition to a darker tonal region with a two-flat signature (its first occurrence in Marenzio), but although there is graphic illustration (*lungo calle*) and harmonic expression (*piangone tristo*) in both sonnets, the expression has become more moderate and the luxuriance of the naïve description has been checked. Evidently there has been criticism of Marenzio that has made him stop to reflect. He is still crude in his use of "eye-music," for example at "Di *color* persi, variati e gialli" in his setting of *Liete, verdi, fiorite et fresche valli,* a sonnet by Sannazaro, or—to take a more serious case—at "Ratto, com' *imbrunir* veggio la sera" in Petrarch's *Consumando mi vò di piagg' in piaggia,* a sestina stanza which in general prompts him also to pure, descriptive virtuosity. But in both instances he avoids the extreme. The same is true of Sannazaro's sonnet *L'alto e nobil pensier che sì sovente,* of which he sets only the octave: admittedly, the poet's rapture is reflected in the music by the considerable instability of the tempo and by a certain restlessness that swings back and forth between homophony and motivic development, but when the poet feels his blood run cold the climax is only a B major chord:

Sola angioletta starsi in treccia a l'ombra, the sestina by Sannazaro that opens the book, is almost neutral in its expression, striking only in its use of the high register and its fondness for equally neutral ornament; it was perhaps written to order for the patron to whom the book is dedicated. *Il suo vago gioioso e lieto manto,* a sestina stanza that one might entitle "Springtime in Tuscany," shows us the Marenzio we know, as does Guarini's madrigal *Oimè l'antica fiamma,* the one a pastoral idyl distinguished by the most delicate sort of description, the other witty and epigrammatic, a musical justification of the poem. But epigram becomes virtuosity in the setting of *Chi vuol veder Amore,* a completely worthless text; here Marenzio seems to make a principle of working with paired voices, for the full five-voiced sonority comes always as a surprise. Such indeed is his general principle; he aims to create a light, transparent sonority and his technique turns on an interplay of motifs that is by no means to be understood as an anticipation of the *stile concertante.* All this is well illustrated in his setting of the madrigal *Dolor tant' è la gioia che mi dai,*

a poem that might almost have been written by Cassola and that might thus have already been set to music by Arcadelt or Verdelot. But what would have been the amazement of these two masters, could they have foreseen the effortless mastery of means to which their beginnings would lead in less than fifty years!

This fifth book of five-voiced madrigals reveals a number of strange connections with three older masters: Palestrina, Andrea Gabrieli, and Giaches Wert. That with Palestrina is wholly external. Marenzio sets Ariosto's sonnet *La rete fu di queste fila d'oro*, in the most graceful style, with delicate imagery and sentimentality. But when he comes to the passage beginning "*Io son ferito*, io son prigion per loro" he makes a bow to his distinguished colleague:

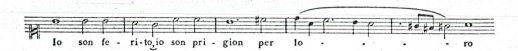

As we know, this compliment failed to win Marenzio Palestrina's favor.

The second connection goes deeper. Marenzio set Petrarch's sonnet *Due rose fresche e colte in paradiso*, one often used for weddings and presumably so intended in this case. He might have followed twenty models, but he pays tribute to Gabrieli, who had set the sonnet to music in 1572 (*Primo libro a cinque*):

Marenzio uses Gabrieli's opening as a sort of motto, and the motivic relationships are easy to follow from here on; one has the impression that Marenzio aims to prove that the sonnet can be reduced in music to a shorter and more concise formula than Andrea's. At the same time the connection does not bespeak rivalry but rather esteem for the older master who has shown him the way.

The connection with Wert stands out particularly clearly in *Occhi miei che miraste sì bel sole*, a threnody in the form of a sonnet on a departed loved one. Its basis is Wert's rapid and homophonic manner of reciting, and only where an image urgently requires it does this declamation broaden out into "picturesque" imitation.

The second half of the print is largely written in this style. *Basciami mille volte*, in keeping with its text, retains the homophonic, anacreontic manner throughout; in *Se voi sete cor mio* the first soprano frequently stands out in contrast to the more compact leading of the lower voices while the second soprano either competes with it or follows a parallel path. But the clearest illustration for this new experimental style is Cesare Pavesi's *Filli tu sei più bella*, a text for which Marenzio has turned again to Atanagi's anthology (II, 168, where the first line reads "Cinthia tu sei più bella"). Marenzio's choice of this text, like his choice of Sacchetti's caccia is a fresh proof that he relied on Atanagi to supply him with new verse forms. For what is the form of this poem? Not a canzonetta, surely, for four stanzas of similar structure (a a′ b B′ c C′) are followed by a four-line *commiato*. It is a canzone in miniature, an anacreontic canzone.

Marenzio is aware of its novelty and gives it the heading "Aria." And he makes of it a sort of hybrid between madrigal and canzonetta by giving the same music to stanzas 1 and 2 and again to 3 and 4—a completely homophonic *four*-voiced music; only at the accents does five-part writing come into play. The time-signature (¢) comes as something of a surprise, but it has a new meaning here: it is to guarantee the freedom of homophonic declamation. Strictly speaking, it is wholly superfluous—just as superfluous as it was in Rore's recitative-like madrigals for four and five voices (cf. above, p. 420), or in the analogous experiments in scansion attempted by the French musicians who followed Ronsard and the Pléiade. These "anacreontic" pieces of Marenzio's call to mind a whole series of ancestors, beginning with the French chanson and leading to Domenico Ferabosco and beyond. We have already quoted (p. 311) Ferabosco's piece (1554: *De diversi autori il quarto libro de madrigali a 4 voci a note bianche . . .*) and it is most unlikely that Marenzio did not know it:

Ba-cia-mi,   ba-cia-mi   mil-le, mil-le vol - te;   Ba-cia-mi,   ba-cia-mi   *etc.*

Naturally, Marenzio uses five voices and more artifice than the older master does.

With his "Aria" Marenzio has predecessors also. In 1555 the Roman singer and publisher, Antonio Barre, brought out a collection of four-voiced madrigals under the title *Primo libro delle Muse*; the book was repeatedly reprinted, its contents repeatedly altered. This has the subtitle "madrigali *ariosi* di Antonio Barre et altri." It is no mere trade-name. If we look closely, we shall find that Barre has included in the print the "aria" of Bradamante from the *Orlando furioso* (XXII, 18-21), set to music by himself, and the heroine's oath of fidelity (XLIV, 61-62), set to music by Ghiselino Danckerts. Both works make use of the "aria" melodies to which the folk sang Ariosto's verse; this stands out particularly clearly in Danckerts' music. But to the use of these melodies Barre has added the principle of rapid homophonic declamation that the impassioned scene requires. Without being aware of the peculiar character of this music, Peter Wagner has fortunately reprinted all four stanzas of Barre's sequence (*Vierteljahrsschrift für Musikwissenschaft,* VIII, 468-475); thus the reader can easily satisfy himself that the pieces belong to pre-monodic monody, that they are madrigals which in spite of occasional imitative and illustrative episodes concentrate their expression in the declamation of the upper voice. Thus the concept of the *madrigale arioso*, the madrigal on a folk-song, is combined with the concept of the *madrigale cantabile*. Stefano Rossetti of Nice, a strange personality and a prolific madrigalist who wrote in Florence for Isabella de' Medici, wife of the Roman Duke Orsini, and for the house of Savoy, includes a number of pieces specifically labeled *madrigali ariosi* in his first book of four-voiced madrigals (1560), written at Schio in the Veneto. Among them are two sonnets and Petrarch's *Con lei foss' io*, a sestina stanza often set to music. They are free declamation in the same sense as the Ariosto scenes of Barre and Danckerts. Thus it is not surprising that Rossetto should end his career with a madrigal book entitled *Il lamento di Olimpia* (1567) in which the first stanza of canto X from the *Orlando furioso* is followed by the great scene of the abandoned Olimpia (X, 19-34) —an Arianna scene long before Monteverdi's. It is a great madrigal cantata, a passionate narrative interspersed with passionate arias in the form of the ottava. Marenzio adopts this style for his "aria" but makes it pastoral or anacreontic rather than pathetic. In so doing he becomes in turn a model for other masters, for example Giovampier Manenti of Bologna, a musician in the service of the Grand Duke Francesco, who publishes a book of *Madrigali ariosi* in 1586. This centers around Sannazaro with his *Per pianto la mia carne si distilla*, the shepherd's lament from the *Arcadia* (Ecloga II), although it concludes with *capricci* "sopra i cinque tempi della Gagliarda," lively little pieces of considerable charm which go to show that the influence of instrumental music upon the madrigal begins well before Gastoldi.

The connection with the court of the Medici which Marenzio had begun with his

wedding madrigal for Bianca Capello on a sonnet by Zuccarini is strengthened by
the dedication of the third book of six-voiced madrigals to the Grand Duchess on
February 12, 1585. (Three days earlier Marenzio had dedicated his book of motets
to Scipione Gonzaga, the friend and patron of Torquato Tasso, then not yet cardinal
but simply Patriarch of Jerusalem.) In his dedication he emphasizes on the one hand
the many reasons that make him desire the favor and protection of Bianca Capello
("quanti . . . cagioni ho io di bramar la grazia, e protezione, e favor suo"); on the
other hand he also emphasizes that he is doing well in the service of his Cardinal,
who affords him ample leisure for his creative work ("potrò con l'ocio tranquillo
concessomi dalla benignità dell'Illustrissimo e Reverendissimo Cardinale d'Este
mio Signore applicare l'animo ad opre più degne e capace del favor suo . . ."). This
was only prudent, for in view of the none too friendly relations between the Este
and the Medici it would have been unwise to dedicate a work to the one without
making a bow to the other. No work of Marenzio's has greater uniformity than this
third book of six-voiced madrigals. This is already apparent in an external characteristic that is less external than it seems: it contains only compositions in the
misura cromatica, in four-four time, and thus, logically enough, no pathetic pieces
and no harmonic audacities. Its tone is wholly sensuous and hedonistic. But within
these limits there is room for variation—the basic color is susceptible to shading. One
madrigal represents an extreme beyond which even Marini did not venture:

> Stringeami Galatea
> Fra le sue nude braccia
> Com'hedra suol che'l caro tronco allaccia,
> E co'l nettar de baci
> E rapidi e tenaci
> Tal gioia mi porgea
> Ch'ebro da la dolcezza
> Hebb'in quel punto di morir vaghezza.
>   Ella che se n'accorse, i dolci rai
> Chiuse pietosa in languidetti giri;
> Poi disse a me: "Cor mio, lascia c'homai
> L'anima tua nella mia bocca spiri."

The seed of Guarini's *Tirsi morir volea* has borne fruit, and Marenzio has certainly
done nothing to discourage its growth. Tone-painting and symbolism stand side by
side: the treatment of *stringeami* would deserve a place of honor in a history of
obscenity in music, along with the last measures of Mozart's "catalogue" aria, while
the word *ebbro* is symbolized by two voices several octaves apart; just as the
drunkard no longer knows what he is doing, so the music seems to have lost control

of itself. On the harmonic side, however, Marenzio does not go beyond the B major chord (*baci!*). An equally sensuous text is a madrigal by Girolamo Casone, which in 1590 was also set to music by Monteverdi:

> Quell'ombra esser vorrei
> Che'l dì vi segue, leggiadretta e bella
> Che s'hor son servo, i sarei vostr'ancella:
> E quando parte il sole,
> M'asconderei sotto que'bianchi panni.
> Lasso! ben ne gli affanni
> Ombr'ignuda d'huom viv'Amor mi fai,
> Ma non mi giungi a la mia Donna mai.

One regrets that in the next to the last line the "naked shadow" to which Cupid reduces the lover calls forth a crude example of "eye-music" which, by introducing a dance rhythm in triple time, openly contradicts the meaning of the words. But the symbolism of the opening is delightful:

Only the three upper voices have the essential first line; the bass takes no part at all in the first third of the piece, that is, in the first seventeen measures of the fifty-three. Nor is this the only piece that seems to look furtively toward the three ladies of Ferrara despite its dedication to the Grand Duchess. Another, more striking example is the one madrigal on a text by Torquato Tasso that the book contains, a sonnet presumably addressed to one of the members of the trio:

> Su l'ampia fronte il cresp'oro lucente
> Spars'ondeggiava . . .
> Che mi fu per l'orecchio il cor ferito,
> Ei detti andaro, ove non giunse il volto.

This is a piece in which tone-painting and "eye-music" (*Rinchiusi i lumi . . .*) are carried to extremes, for example in the representation of the waving golden curl. Noteworthy also is the way in which the two highest voices alone are involved in the "expression" of the following line:

But this madrigal is the one example that carries the painting of details to such a length. Generally speaking, it shows an extraordinary concern for architectonics, a new sense for form. Marenzio chooses texts in which the first and last lines or couplets are identical, and as a matter of course he gives them the same music:

> Io morirò d'amore
> S'al mio scampo non vien sdegno e furore,
> Poi che Madonna alla mia vera fede
> Solo di finto amor vuol dar mercede;
> E perche del mio foco
> Prende solazzo e gioco,
> Se qualche gel non tempra tant'ardore
> Io morirò d'amore.

Or, to quote another example:

> Posso, cor mio, partire
> Senza farvi morire.
> Ch'Amor, giusto signore,
> Vuol, che se meco porto il vostro core,
> Con voi ne rest'il mio,
> Onde non morirem ne voi ned'io.
> Posso dunque partire
> Senza farvi morire.

One might say that for the sake of these "architectonic" texts Marenzio even sacrifices his refined literary taste. But the tendency toward a new solidity of form goes even further. From an anthology edited by Lodovico Domenichi (*Rime diverse di molti autori*) and reprinted in Venice in 1546, Marenzio chooses (I, 253) a sonnet by Bartolomeo Gottifredi to which one might give the sentimental title "Wish in Springtime." Marenzio gives the two quatrains exactly the same music, adding a little coda the second time. Is this a return to Verdelot? By no means; it is a new sense of form, a renunciation of detailed tone-painting, a recognition of a new and more temperate ideal if not a rejection of the old luxurious one. It is in keeping with this that in his narrative madrigals, in his pre-monodic cantatas, Marenzio now begins to make a much sharper distinction between the descriptive sections and the lyric. He uses his six voices to produce the most refined and most varied divisions into half-choirs of three, four, and five voices; the madrigal, we repeat, is no longer a union of equally privileged voices, each of which has the complete text, but a choral symphony to which each voice makes its particular contribution without having any claim to a particular share. Narrative and description are blended in the music of the following ottave, which doubtless owe their existence to a specific order and to a special situation:

> Danzava con maniere sopr'umane
> D'amorose donzelle allegro coro,
> E si stavano l'aure immote e piane,
> Intente forse al bel grato lavoro;
> Ed ascondea nell'alt'onde oceane
> Il gran celest'Auriga i bei crin d'oro,
> Quando di sdegno e di pietad'accesa
> Ver me l'alma mia Dea disse: "Son presa."
>
> "Son presa," disse, e a me rivolse in giro
> Vergognosetta le ridenti stelle,
> Da quai per quanto d'ogn'intorno miro
> Non veggio le più honeste e le più belle.
> L'alma mia all'hor accolta in un sospiro,
> Sentendo raddioppiar strali e facelle:
> "S'io son," mi disse, "in simil laccio involta,
> Tu ne sospirarai più d'una volta."

For the whole first half of the second ottava four voices suffice; thus the "tutti" produces a fresh effect. A similar treatment is given to two ottave from Molza's *Ninfa Tiberina*, beginning *Con dolce sguardo alquant'acerb'in vista*. Recitative and aria are sharply distinguished in the following *madrigaletto*:

> **In un lucido rio**
> Mirando il suo bel viso

Così doleasi un pastor d'Amore:
"Misero perche anch'io,
Quasi un nuovo Narciso
Non mi converto lagrimand'in fiore?
Ch'in quella form'almeno
Mi raccorrebbe la mia Donna in seno."

The recitative is for three voices only, though not without some picturesque details; we are still a little distance from the bald narrative tone of the cantata. Yet we no longer have far to go, as will be evident from the following little "cantata," whose text we print by way of introduction:

Piangea Filli, e rivolte ambe le luci
Al ciel ch'anch'ei piangea—
"O Tirsi, o Tirsi," pur mesta dicea,
"O Tirsi, o Tirsi," mormoravan l'onde,
"O Tirsi, o Tirsi," i venti,
"O Tirsi, o Tirsi," i fior l'herb'e le fronde.
Ei sol que' duri accenti
Ei sol non udia lasso,
E pur sen giva e pur doppiava il passo.

It is a *lettera amorosa* from a lady to her cavalier:

The lament of the shepherdess, literally repeated again and again, is not unworthy of being considered a forerunner of Monteverdi's *Lasciatemi morire* in its combination of naturalism with beauty of sound. (Incidentally, the descending whole tone step in the bass as the foundation for a succession of two major triads is typical of Marenzio.) A similar little masterpiece, playful and artistic, is the setting of *Donò Licori a Batto*, a pastoral scene from Guarini in which Marenzio has changed the pastoral names to Cynthia and Damon.

Exactly six months after the appearance of the third book of six-voiced madrigals Marenzio published his only book of madrigals for four voices; the dedication.

dated July 15, 1585, is addressed to his patron at the papal court, Monsignore Marc'Antonio Serlupi. It was printed in Rome by Alessandro Gardano. Two years later, Ricciardo Amadino and Giacomo Vincenti issued a pirated edition in Venice, and Vincenti provided his print with a new dedication to Michele Booth, evidently an Englishman then residing in Venice. It is a sure sign that Marenzio was already in demand in Venice—within five years of his first appearance. In the sixteenth century fame was established more quickly and more securely than it is in the twentieth, supposedly the century of all-powerful publicity.

This book of four-voiced madrigals contributed more than any other to the revival of interest in Marenzio and his work at the end of the eighteenth century and at the beginning of the nineteenth, at a time when the four-part texture was considered the norm. Hawkins (III, 198ff.) reprinted one madrigal from it (*Dissi a l'amata*), Padre Martini (*Saggio*) a whole series; they were followed by Kiesewetter (*Schicksale und Beschaffenheit*) and others, while Winterfeld (*Johannes Gabrieli*, II, 93) singled out one number for severe criticism. For Marenzio, five-voiced writing was the norm, four-part writing the exception. Accordingly, this work has a special character, both in its choice of texts and in its musical workmanship. The preferred poets are Sannazaro and Petrarch; also represented are Giovanni della Casa with a sonnet, Torquato Tasso with the famous stanza describing the spell of Armida's gardens (*Gerusalemme liberata*, XVI, 2), and Marenzio's Roman colleague, Giovanni Battista Moscaglia. In this same year (1585), Moscaglia also published a book of madrigals; the texts were entirely his own, but since his "multifarious duties" did not permit him to set them all himself, he turned some of them over to other Roman musicians. Thus his print contains works by Macque, Nanino, Giovanelli, Stabile, and others, among them Marenzio with his *Dissi a l'amata mia*.

Moscaglia dates his dedication 1582, but even without this indication we should suspect that the composition of these twenty-one four-voiced madrigals by Marenzio spreads over a considerable period. They are unequal in style and merit. But in certain respects they are all alike: Marenzio avoids all harmonic extremes and experiments, and it is obvious that he is searching for a special type of pastoral expression suited to the four-voiced texture. Of the four "madrigals" contained in Petrarch's *Canzoniere* he sets no less than three to music, evidently because of their pastoral atmosphere, and he exhausts the possibilities of Sannazaro's *Arcadia* in his hunt for pastoral and idyllic themes. He finds the sought-for pastoral note in rhythm and in the musical reproduction of the *sdruccioli*. Philological considerations must also have played a part in this attempt to recapture the antique spirit. Interest in antiquity was by no means confined to the Florentine Camerata. A skipping rhythm is maintained from beginning to end in the setting of the eighth eclogue of the *Arcadia* (vv. 142-147), verses that proudly proclaim their descent from Horace:

Here one has at one time every characteristic of the pastoral style: the high register, the leading of the voices in pairs, the transparent texture, the skipping rhythm, the discreet tone-painting. The book is full of such pieces from the *Arcadia*: *Madonna, sua mercè* (Ecloga VII, stanza 5), a companion piece to Petrarch's *I' piango* and Marenzio's own five-voiced setting of the poet's vision of Laura—although the dream is wholly ignored in this playful, superficial piece; then *I lieti amanti* (Ecloga VI), with outright triple time for the *sdruccioli*; and *Menando un giorno* (Ecloga I), Ergasto's complaint in a thin setting that relies in principle on the two-voiced texture and in tone maintains a studied naïveté. The tendentious character of this style is particularly evident in *Vienne Montan, mentre le nostre tormora*, a tripartite piece from the ninth eclogue (IX, 37-75). Let us try to determine what is at stake. Sannazaro's eclogue in terze rime is an imitation of those ancient eclogues whose archetype may be recognized in the *Comatas and Lacon* of Theocritus: two simple shepherds are contending for a prize to be given to the best singer, while a third, an old man called Morson in Theocritus, acts as judge. In Sannazaro the shepherds are Ofelia and Elenco, the judge is Montano. Marenzio sets the high point of the competition, distinguishing the several roles in the third section of the piece and even causing lines to overlap that in Sannazaro simply follow one another. One might say that the madrigal has become a duet. But it is only an "ideal" duet, for Marenzio feels at liberty to introduce picturesque and naturalistic details at any time and to return whenever he pleases to his usual madrigalesque style. When he comes to a sestina stanza in Sannazaro's sentimental style, as for example *Chi vuol udir i mei sospir in rime* from the fourth eclogue of the *Arcadia*, he sets it in his sustained manner, in the *misura di breve*, with passing dissonances and livelier episodes.

To Petrarch, Marenzio turns not only for "madrigals," but also for other poems which he sets in the same "pastoral" style, for example the sonnet *O bella man, che mi distringi 'l core*, a trifling piece but also a lyric one. And besides this style the

four-voiced madrigal also uses the style of motivic contrast, which presupposes a sharper chiseling of the motifs. An example will clarify the procedure. Marenzio sets Petrarch's third "madrigal" to music:

Nova Angeletta, sopra l'ale accorta,
Scese dal cielo in su la fresca riva
Là'nd'io passava sol per mio destino.
Poichè senza compagna e senza scorta
Mi vide, un laccio che di seta ordiva,
Tese fra l'erba, ond 'è verde 'l cammino.
Allor fui preso, e non mi spiacque poi;
Sì dolce lume uscìa degli occhi suoi.

The poem had been set to music dozens of times since the beginning of the century, and perhaps even earlier. Musicians were no doubt most attracted by the fifth and sixth lines, in which the poet describes the silken snare that his beloved has spread on the grass. When he sets this for four voices (1562), Filippo di Monte is already modern in that the correspondence of lines 4-6 with 1-3 no longer exists for him; the music is concerned not with form but with content. But he still respects the poet's division into lines:

The snare of love is just barely indicated by the imitation and coloratura, and no violence is done to the text. Twenty-three years later—one might almost say, at the same time, for Monte's first book of four-voiced madrigals was reprinted in 1586— Marenzio is more "old-fashioned" than Monte in so far as he prescribes the *misura di breve*, which in the present case can only indicate a lively tempo. But he draws the first word of the fifth line forward and interweaves the motifs:

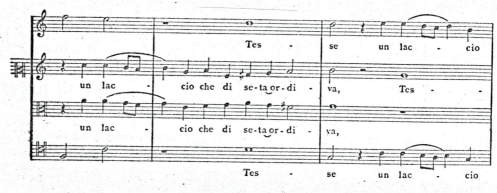

Marenzio's "visual" inclination leads him to represent both the "snare" and its "weave," and the visualization of the "weave" is already a sort of higher musical symbolism. Thus it is strange that he disregards the "descent from heaven" which Monte has discreetly illustrated.

As though it were a manifesto announcing a new program, Marenzio chooses the working-out of a double motif of this sort for the first number of his book: it is a fragmentary setting of the opening lines of a stanza from Petrarch's canzone *In quella parte dov'Amor mi sprona:*

The ending is even more instructive: here Marenzio first presents the "theme" by itself, in a homophonic version for four voices, and then combines it with the concluding line as in a double fugue:

A structural intention, or at least an instrumental one, is evident in this "working-out," which is surely not based upon "tone-painting" or "poetizing." Thus if this four-voiced madrigal book contains pieces of naïve description, it also contains sentimental pieces in which there is no trifling. Sharply contrasted are the consecutive settings of two sonnets from Petrarch, *Tutto'l dì piango e poi la notte quando* and *Zefiro torna e'l bel tempo rimena*. We have already mentioned Winterfeld's criticism of the second of these for its extravagant and distracting painting of details. But the first sonnet renounces tone-painting; it is lugubrious, iridescent in its harmonies, and archaistic. The same may be said of *Ahi dispietata morte*, a fragment from Petrarch's canzone stanza *Amor quando fioria*. Here an unexpected opportunity for comparison presents itself, since this canzone stanza was set to music in its entirety by Palestrina, likewise for four voices, and published in 1586,

only one year after Marenzio's setting. Marenzio's music can be consulted in Padre Martini's *Saggio* (II, 78), Palestrina's in Haberl's complete edition (XXVIII, 107). In this instance Palestrina is more "modern" than Marenzio. A brief quotation will suffice to prove this; we give it on two staves, since both scores are of easy access:

Marenzio uses the older sort of measure here, as he generally does in setting an impassioned text; Palestrina uses the "modern" measure and is also bolder in his harmonies than Marenzio if the accidentals I have supplied are valid—they probably are, for the singers of the 'eighties were not much troubled by our concern for the "purity of the Palestrina style."

We have already said that throughout his career Marenzio's choice of texts bespeaks a fastidious taste. For the fourth book of his six-voiced madrigals this statement requires some restriction: the volume contains a number of pieces on texts so trite and commonplace that they fall distinctly below Marenzio's usual level:

> La dipartita è amara . . .
> Vattene, anima mia . . .
> Crudel perchè mi fuggi. . . .

Can this have anything to do with its dedication to the Marquis of Pisani, "Cavaliere degli Ordini del Re Christianissimo, Consegliero de Stati, et Ambasciatore di Sua Maestà"? In the dedicatory letter, dated December 10, 1586, there is a reference to the ambassador's return to Rome; thus the Marquis is probably identical with the Jean de Vivonne to whom all this applies. He would accordingly have been a foreigner. Marenzio foresaw the death of his patron—Cardinal Luigi d'Este died within twenty days after the date of this dedication—and seems to have gathered together a number of miscellaneous pieces with a view to securing another patron. It is also possible that the dedication is dated in advance, for the print did not actually appear until 1587. Incidentally, Vogel's duplicate edition with the Amadino-Vincenti imprint is nonexistent. Under No. 11, Vogel has listed (I, 394) five pieces for six voices and one for eight, beginning with *Deh se 'l fetor* and ending with *S'il dolor*. These pieces are not by Marenzio at all, but belong to D. Francesco Farina's first book of madrigals for six voices, a book otherwise lost. As Dr. Egon Wellesz has kindly verified, pages 15 to 20 are missing in the Oxford copy of the canto of Marenzio's madrigals, and the English binder has erroneously put pages 15 to 20 of Farina's madrigals in their place.

No doubt the dedication to the Marquis also explains the inclusion of two occasional pieces: *Trà l'herbe à piè d'un mirto che copriva*, a wedding sonnet whose text Marenzio may have found in Domenichi's anthology (I, 248) and in which the bridal couple are compared to Venus and Adonis; and *Donne il celeste lume*, a *mascherata* for nine voices in the form of a madrigal, likewise a wedding piece. The first is very rich and written with great virtuosity in the chamber-music style; the second is quite in the Venetian style, though somewhat less decorative and more lively in its expression.

Likewise Venetian and in Gabrieli's manner is one of the most delicate numbers in the book, Guarini's *Dice la mia bellissima Licori*, wholly in Andrea's anacreontic style, though even lighter and livelier and more inclined toward virtuosity. Indeed the whole print is anacreontic; it avoids every harmonic innovation and aims at brevity. And to attain this brevity Marenzio relies to a large extent upon homophonic choral declamation, upon the give-and-take of choral masses as a principle, though not as a rigid principle to be blindly followed. For the expression of heightened feeling Marenzio can always fall back on imitation. The two procedures are freely combined in *Crudel, perchè mi fuggi*, for expressive reasons the one piece in the entire book that is written in alla breve. The choral writing is enlivened and as it were disguised by little liberties of voice-leading in Guarini's *O che soave e non inteso bacio*. In the paired madrigals then so much in vogue and consisting as a rule of the question and answer of shepherd and shepherdess, of *proposta* and *risposta*, the sought-for brevity brings with it a fresh inclination toward dramatic lyricism, though

this of course remains within the limits of the madrigalesque and of Marenzio's own style; an example is the *partenza*:

> Caro Aminta, pur vuoi . . .
> Non può, Filli, più il core . . .

Other pieces carry on the development of the "visual," picturesque, personal side of Marenzio's art and bring it to the threshold of the baroque; the classic examples are Torquato Tasso's two sonnets *Arsi gran tempo, e del mio foco indegno* and *Di Nettare amoroso ebbro la mente*. The first is a lover's denunciation, a denunciation so sweeping that it is almost pathological; Marenzio is able only to parody it by translating its grandeur into baroque terms. Nowhere does the whole artificiality— the superficial, conventional character—of the madrigal's symbolism reveal itself more clearly than in such pieces: no wonder that after 1600 all these symbols became unintelligible. When Tasso speaks of oblivion "in the bottomless pit" (*ne' più profondi abissi*), Marenzio as a matter of course descends to the low D, a tone above the lowest string of the violoncello—a German bass would say "a third below Sarastro's lowest 'Doch.'" Even more artificial is its companion piece, a sonnet that "tells how the poet saw two ladies whom he loved kiss one another" (*descrive l'atto nel quale vidde baciarsi due donne amate da lui*). Four voices carry the actual narrative; for the rest, two-part writing predominates for symbolic reasons, though at "ò fra le due fa terzo" a third voice is added as a matter of course. Each single detail of the happening is illustrated, and while the symbolism of the piece is obscene, the music is not. Five years later, Monte also set this favorite text to music for six voices, but unfortunately we are unable to determine how he succeeded with it, for only half the part-books have been preserved. A third sonnet, *Ne fero sdegno mai, Donna, mi mosse*, is an avowal of fidelity in the style of Ariosto's *Ruggiero* or that other ottava by Bernardo Tasso, often set to music; in this case "symbolism" and "expression" are in perfect harmony:

The book also makes extensive use of the double motif. The single voice comes to mean less and less, the ensemble more and more; sometimes one voice is strikingly overemphasized, almost independent, while others have only fragments of the text and of the thematic material. This last holds true particularly for the bass, whose entrance invariably has a secondary coloristic effect. A piece distinguished by great virtuosity, but also by great harmonic interest, is the setting of *Questo ordìo 'l laccio*, a delightful text by the Florentine poet Giovan Battista Strozzi (1504-1571), who occupies a relatively honorable place in the otherwise depressing literary history of the madrigal; it is perhaps the ideal representative of this central lull in Marenzio's productivity.

Exactly a year after the dedication of this fourth book for six voices, Marenzio signs the dedication of a new madrigal book, his *Madrigali a quattro, cinque, et sei voci libro primo*; it is dated "Venice, December 10, 1587," and addressed to Count Mario Bevilacqua in Verona. The book is the fruit of a sojourn of his in the city of the Accademia Filarmonica and of a journey to Northern Italy, doubtless undertaken primarily with a view to sounding out the situation in Mantua, for Duke Guglielmo had died on August 14, and his successor Vincenzo was reputed to be even more sumptuous and liberal than his father. It occupies a special place in Marenzio's work, not only because it is the only one that was never reprinted—which means that it was unsuccessful—but also because its contents are arranged not according to the number of voices but according to style. As the dedication explains, Marenzio has thus far been unable to repay Bevilacqua for his kindnesses unless by his sincere and grateful affection; now, on the occasion of his journey through Verona, he deems it proper to offer to the Count certain madrigals recently "composed in a manner very different from my former one in that through the imitation of the words and the propriety of the style I have sought a sort of melancholy dignity that will perhaps be prized the more highly by connoisseurs like yourself and the members of your

distinguished assembly" — "composti con maniera assai differente dalla passata, havendo, et per l'imitatione delle parole et per la proprietà dello stile atteso ad una (dirò così) mesta gravità, che dagl'intendenti pari suoi, et dal virtuosissimo suo ridutto sarà forse via più gradita." What has happened? Has Marenzio realized the "sensuality" of his most recent production? Or is the book the result of conversations with Torquato Tasso? About 1584 Tasso had written his dialogue *La Cavaletta*; he published it two years later (cf. Solerti, I, 396). In this dialogue he speaks in a derogatory way of the degeneracy of modern music, which has in his opinion become soft and effeminate and which ought therefore to be brought back to its ancient dignity (*gravità*) by such serious musicians as Striggio, Wert, Luzzasco, "e alcun altro eccellente maestro di musica eccellente" (cf. above, p. 219f.). It is not improbable that Tasso's unnamed "maestro" was none other than Marenzio, and that he refrained from naming him only in order not to arouse the jealousy of his three friends, the "Ferrarese" musicians. Marenzio's "mesta gravità" and Tasso's "gravità" are so similar that there must be a connection of some sort between them.

However this may be, this book of madrigals is a work with a program—esoteric, designed for connoisseurs, not addressed to a larger public. There are fifteen pieces in twenty sections. For once, Vogel's table of contents is unreliable (I, 398); it follows the Bologna catalogue blindly (III, 100), fails to indicate the "seconde parti," and altogether omits the "prima parte" of Sannazaro's sonnet *Fiere silvestre* (seconda parte: *Ecco ch'un'altra volta*). The only poets represented are Sannazaro, Petrarch, Della Casa, and Girolamo Troiano (a sonnet, again taken from Atanagi's anthology); the ottava *Piango; che Amor con disusato oltraggio* seems to have been taken from an eclogue and the source of the one madrigal in the entire collection is also unknown to me:

> Come ogni rio che d'acque dolci e chiare
> Porge tributo al mare,
> Giunto in quelle voragini profonde,
> In amare si cangia e torbid'onde:
> Così ogni ben ch'è buono per natura,
> Giunto nel mar de la mia pena cura,
> Si cangia in male amaro, e divien tale
> Per l'amaro infinito del mio male.

A text as dark and austere as this is out of the ordinary. Yet it is in keeping with the rest, for Marenzio has searched through his favorite classics, Sannazaro and Petrarch, for expressions of hopelessness and pessimistic melancholy, moods that he could not have found in such purity and concentration in the modern poets Tasso and Guarini.

The deliberate, one-sided, tendentious character of this exceptional work could scarcely have been carried further. It is at once archaic and modern. Its archaic qualities are superficially revealed in the exclusive use of the *misura di breve* (¢), which with him is always a sign of agitation, of pathos, of violence. But in this case it is also a sign of a uniform tempo. In the fourteen or fifteen pieces Marenzio does not allow himself a single acceleration or fluctuation of the tempo, even for one measure; the expression lies almost exclusively on the harmonic side. It is an opus that is half constructive, half expressive. Marenzio naturally finds it impossible to renounce tone-painting altogether: when the word *ghirlanda* occurs, the voices adopt ornamental figures, though without any change in the tempo, and in Sanna-zaro's sonnet *Ecco ch'un'altra volta*, at the line "the fishes will hearken to my lament" ("I pesci al mio languir staranno intenti"), the four lower voices begin to weave about below the smooth surface of the soprano. In one instance, Sannazaro's *Senza il mio sole*, there is even a crude example of "eye-music," called forth by the tempt-ing image *Chiuse le luci.* But these are exceptions. The musical expression of the "mesta gravità" lies in the stately, deliberate, uniform course of the declamation, which in taking on these qualities yields no part of its refinement and flexibility, and in the free and daring treatment of the tonality and the suspension and of every sort of dissonance, particularly the passing dissonance. It is the fulfillment of every-thing that Rore had begun. Marenzio is no longer an experimenter; he is never bold for the sake of being bold. The conclusion of the stanza *Fuggito è'l sonno* (from Petrarch's sestina *Mia benigna fortuna*) is typical of the whole:

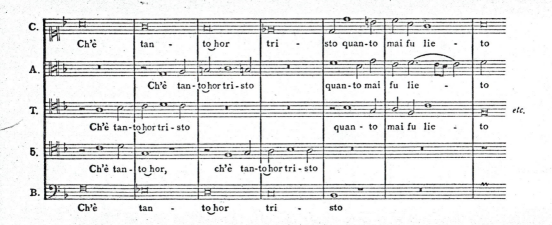

Or, as an example of Marenzio's more temperate and regular "chromaticism," I add the conclusion of the octave from Petrarch's sonnet *Se la mia vita da l'aspro tormento*:

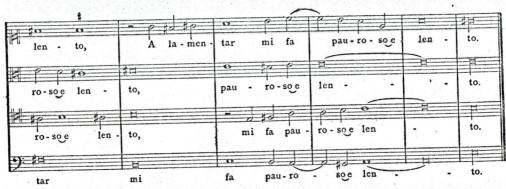

Almost every text in the book plays in some way on the change in Marenzio's style: thus the first of the five-voiced madrigals includes the line "Fuggito ... è 'l suon usato alle mie roche rime," while at the head of the whole collection stands this question, likewise from Petrarch's sestina of mourning, *Mia benigna fortuna*:

> Ov'è condotto *il mio amoroso stile* ...
> Hor non parlo ne penso altro che pianto!

This text was also set to music for four voices by Lasso (1562); superficially considered, this setting is more "modern" than Marenzio's, for it uses the *misura cromatica*, but in comparison with the work of the later master it seems flat and lacking in insight. There are in these madrigals passages of the utmost grandeur, for example this passage in *Senza'l mio sol*, the sonnet by Sannazaro already mentioned:

> ... in solitario orrore
> Trapasso i giorni et i momenti e l'ore.

Here the quinto (or second tenor) descends step by step to the ninth below while the other voices declaim in counterpoint against it: it is the path into the unknown, into the night. All six voices travel together on this path at "Valli *riposte* e sole," the opening line of a canzone by Sannazaro that in 1510 had been set to music by a certain Franciscus F. in the usual manner of the frottolists. And at the end of this piece, at the line "Ma quì si stia sepolta ogni mia doglia," Marenzio finds an expressive symbol for the eternal night of the grave—an organ point sustained for ten long measures. He sets only the first quatrain of Sannazaro's sonnet *Interdette speranze e van desio*, but gives it such majestic breadth that to go on to the end would have exceeded all reasonable proportions and limits. He reaches the limit of the style in his setting of *O fere stelle omai datemi pace*, the third stanza from Sannazaro's *Spent'eran nel mio cor l'antiche fiamme*. At the invocation "E tu, fortuna, *muta il crudo stile*" he finds his way into the gloomy region of B-flat minor and D-flat major; the allusion to Cupid's ruthless onslaught carries him as far as the dazzling brightness of E major. The piece represents the extreme development of Marenzio's new style, and for this reason we have included it in our collection of illustrations.[2] But here Marenzio parts company with this style. The last number of the book, for ten voices, or rather for two choirs of five voices each, brings a return to a familiar idiom:

> Basti fin quì le pene, e i duri affanni
> In tante carte, e le mie gravi some
> Haver mostrate, e come
> Amor i suoi seguaci al fin governa:
> Hor mi vorrei levar con altri vanni
> Per potermi di Lauro ornar le chiome:
> E con più saldo nome
> Lassar di me qua giù memoria eterna.

In this fragment from the third stanza of Sannazaro's canzone *Sperai gran tempo, e le mie Dive il sanno*, each single word is given a biographical or stylistic application, half grandiose, half humorous. For Marenzio begins majestically in the *misura di breve* only to return in the fourth line to his canzonetta-like pastoral style. In this the piece recalls Schubert's *An die Leyer* (after Anacreon):

> Ich will von Atreus Söhnen,
> Von Kadmus will ich singen!
> Doch meine Saiten tönen
> Nur Liebe im Erklingen.

Marenzio's prophecy proved right in the end: his immortality rests, not on this work, but on his "flight on other wings."

Marenzio must have been bitterly disappointed by the failure of this exceptional book. To this period belongs his stay in Florence, but after the festivities connected with the wedding of the new Grand Duke in 1589 his duties there cannot have

[2] See Vol. III, No. 80.

made any unusual demand upon his time. Nor do we know of any other external circumstance that would explain why he remained silent for three full years, until the beginning of 1591, when he again published a new work, the fifth book of six-voiced madrigals, dedicated to Virginio Orsini, the Duke of Bracciano. In the dedication he calls the Duke's protection a friendly refuge in adversity (*in ogni mio accidente*), doubtless a reference to his recent experiences in Florence. With a single exception, the book contains no direct reference to Florence, and during the remainder of his life Marenzio dedicated no further work to the Medici, though there were further dedications to the Estes and to the Gonzagas.

The book is thoroughly Roman in character; thus it opens with a bipartite madrigal in honor of Virginio Orsini and Flavia Peretti, in whose palace it had been written (. . . *queste mie timide muse, . . . nate, et nudrite in casa sua . . .*):

> Leggiadrissima eterna primavera
> Vive scherzando a questi colli intorno . . .
> Fiammeggia il ciel di più pregiati odori
> Che'l tutt'adorna, il tutt'informa e accende
> L'honor ch'in Flavia e ch'in Virginio splende!

If this is a wedding madrigal it must have been written in Florence, in the spring of 1589, for in that year Flavia Peretti, one of the grandnieces of the powerful Pope Sixtus V, was married by proxy at the beginning of February to the Duke, who made his entry into Rome on April 8 (cf. Pastor, *History of the Popes*, Engl. ed., xxi, 70; here we also learn the address of the palace where Marenzio lived with the young couple—8 Via Parione). The second number, *Leggiadre ninfe e pastorelli amanti*, is also a wedding piece, one written by Marenzio at the request of the Venetian patrician Leonardo Sanudo. A year later it was reprinted in the *Trionfi di Dori*, and from a remark of the printer's in his dedication to Sanudo, it is clear that Sanudo had been displeased by Marenzio's premature publication of the piece. In this collection all twenty-nine madrigals, by twenty-nine different poets and twenty-nine different musicians, conclude with the same refrain—*Viva la bella Dori!*—a salute to the bride. And if the rhythm of this refrain has somehow imposed itself upon each of the contributing musicians, Marenzio has managed to give his version of it a pastoral touch and a refinement that approaches that of chamber music. (The contributions of Striggio, Gastoldi, Asola, and Vecchi are reprinted by Torchi in his first and second volumes, Gastoldi's also by Barclay Squire.) A third piece of the same sort is *Spiri dolce Favonio Arabi odori*, a sonnet written by Girolamo Troiano for the wedding of a certain Annibale Gattola to a Lucrezia. Marenzio has changed the names to Thyrsis and Amaryllis to make the piece suitable for any wedding.

The entire book has a pastoral, hedonistic stamp. There is no experiment, no duality of measure, no pathos, but in compensation there is a heightened sensuousness of sound that manifests itself in a refined technique of choral division. A good example is No. 10, a lascivious madrigal by a poet unknown to me:

> Con la sua man la mia
> Madonna un dì m'avinse,
> E così dolce strinse
> Che mi sentia—dal gran piacer morire.
> Ella che se n'accorse,
> Tosto la sua sù la mia bocca porse
> E suggendo involò li spirti miei,
> Ond'in me morto hora mi vivo in lei.

The first six lines maintain a rapid homophonic declamation and are divided among contrasting half-choirs of four voices each; only at *e suggendo* do all six voices enter with imitations, and the effect has a sensuous charm of which the first and second generation of madrigalists would not have dared to dream. Here we are not surprised to find Marenzio choosing two texts by Torquato Tasso, whose headings speak for themselves: "Amoroso godimento" and "Desiderio d'amor reciproco," the first a frank imitation of Guarini's *Tirsi morir volea* in the form of a sonnet—homophonic, naturalistic, sometimes quite in the manner of the canzonetta. Marenzio reaches the high point of this style in a five-voiced setting of Guarini's "Canzon de'baci" (*Baci soavi e cari*). Guarini did not see fit to include this canzone in his collected poems, presumably because he anticipated trouble with the censors, but it is found repeatedly in manuscript copies, for example with some variants in Codex 1171 of the Biblioteca Universitaria in Bologna (reprinted by L. Frati in his *Rime inedite del cinquecento*, Bologna, 1918, p. 142). But of the sixteenth-century madrigal one may say, as of the nineteenth-century opera, that what may not be spoken becomes innocuous when it is sung. Did Marenzio's music really make Guarini's poem innocuous? I am not sure. Even if we concede that the unambiguous use of two voices alone at certain points is as usual a mere symbol and that Marenzio's art has ennobled many of Guarini's expressions, for example his ever-changing apostrophe *Baci soavi e cari, Baci amorosi e belli, Baci affannati e ingordi, Baci cortesi e grati*, many another expression has been raised to the level of drama and can never fail to make a dramatic effect provided the performers have the virtuosity that this piece of highest virtuosity demands. Other high points of a less dubious order are Girolamo Troiano's sonnet *Ecco che'l ciel a noi chiaro e sereno* ("Per la primavera"), della Casa's canzone stanza *Come fuggir per selv' ombrosa e folta*, and finally the

ottava *Giunto a un bel fonte il trasmutato in fiore* ("Favola di Narcisso"), a grandiose piece of imagery.

The third number of the book is a madrigal by a certain Antonio Bicci, *Candide perle e voi labbra ridenti,* and in his later books Marenzio included other madrigals by this composer. Bicci—the name is Florentine—must have become acquainted with Marenzio during his stay in Florence, and it is in keeping with this that other madrigals by Bicci are found scattered among the works of various Florentine musicians—Luca Bati (1594), Santi Orlandi (1602), and Stefano Venturi (1596 and 1598). He seems to have been an aristocratic dilettante, and his pleasant, though shallow and musically uninteresting composition shows where the imitation of Marenzio could lead, indeed was bound to lead.

Three years later—after a long silence that is not easily explained—Marenzio returns to five-voiced writing: his sixth book *a cinque* is dedicated to his new patron, the great Cinzio Aldobrandini, who had meanwhile become Cardinal of San Giorgio. The collection seems to contain no personal reference to his patron: the last number, *Cantiam la bella Clori,* a fairly conventional wedding piece for eight voices in two choirs, seems even to be still an echo of the wedding of the "fair Dori" of the Sanudo family—this time the refrain is *Viva la bella Clori.* Another piece points unmistakably to Ferrara; it is a setting of *Hor chi Clori beata,* a dialogue by G. B. Strozzi which we may already refer to as a "madrigale concertato." *Mentre qual viva pietra,* No. 13, is perhaps the only "Roman" piece and the strangest and most personal one in the entire book; it begins like a *canzon francese* and includes sections that are structural in function—the scale at the end, which descends in the soprano with deliberate steps—but it seems intentionally to avoid reconciling its contradictions. And at the end of a curve that began with Rore stands the setting of Annibale Caro's sonnet *Ben ho del caro oggetto i sensi privi,* a lovely *lontananza* whose somewhat old-fashioned style was perhaps suggested by the patron who ordered it. An equally harmonious adjustment of rest and motion characterizes two other madrigals—*Amor se giusto sei* and *Voi bramate ch'io moia.* In contrast to the last book of six-voiced madrigals, Marenzio again alternates between C and ₵, deliberately and with consummate art.

The novel side of the work has to do with Battista Guarini and his *Pastor fido.* Marenzio discovers the pastoral *tragi-commedia* and comes to terms with it. Guarini shows him the pastoral in a new light. It is no longer a game that finds its elements of expression in the canzonetta; it is a new lyricism. Marenzio no longer pays any substantial tribute to the canzonetta, not even in G. B. Strozzi's *Ecco maggio seren,* a genuine Florentine *maggiolata* which swings back and forth in a sort of stylistic middle ground between dance-song and madrigal.

Literary historians tell us that the *Pastor fido* was first performed at Crema as late as 1596, though it was begun about 1569, had been virtually completed by 1583, and had come in fragments to the attention of musicians before it appeared in print at the end of 1589. It supplied Marenzio with Dorinda's lament *Anima cruda si* (IV, 9), Mirtillo's *Udite lagrimosi* (III, 6) and *Ah dolente partita* (III, 3), and the *Deh Tirsi anima mia* (III, 4) of Amaryllis. But the four pieces are by no means uniform in style. Some of them—and other similar pieces, such as the rhymeless *Donna dell'alma mia*, surely an excerpt from some pastoral comedy, G. B. Strozzi's *Clori mia*, Livio Celiano's farewell-scene, *Rimanti in pace*, Antonio Ongaro's *Stillò l'anima*, or another farewell, *Clori nel mio partire*—are actual scenes in which distinct preference is shown the upper voice, even though they are far from being monodies in disguise. They are sentimental, lyric, and they completely renounce all the detailed tone-painting and drastic symbolism upon which the younger Marenzio was so dependent. But other pieces—and precisely the most pathetic ones, such as Mirtillo's invocation of the Underworld—are madrigals, not scenes, and the text gives rise to all sorts of harmonic audacities and exaggerations, even to exaggerations in the literal sense of the word. There is a new and closer relationship to the text, a new rhetoric. (Since the entire book has been reprinted in the *Publikationen älterer Musik* [III, 2; ed. Einstein], quotations will be unnecessary.) He who studies these pieces attentively will discover that the years from 1591 to 1594 were decisive for Marenzio. In this book he becomes one of Monteverdi's immediate forerunners. Had he had the good fortune to survive the end of the century by a decade, history would perhaps need to consider him, with Monteverdi, as a composer of opera.

With his sixth book of madrigals *a sei* Marenzio returns to Ferrara. He dedicates it on March 30, 1595, to Margherita Gonzaga and speaks in the dedication of his "antica divotione, et servitù verso la Serenissima Casa" of the Gonzagas and the Estes. And he opens it with a bipartite festive piece, taken from an eclogue that Guarini had written in 1579 for the wedding of Margherita and Duke Alfonso:

> Lucida perla a cui fù conca il cielo
> E tu di lui tesoro
> Tu pria con luminoso alto decoro
> D'Iddio fregiasti la coron'e'l regno
> Poi sul Mincio prendesti humano velo.
> Hora il più ricco pegno
> Del Rè dei fiumi, e nostra gloria sei
> E sarai madre ancor di semidei.
> Oda'l Ciel questi voti,
> E tu, nel canto di tua gloria indegno

Gradisci i cor devoti
Che son nel ver troppo sublimi some
L'erger al Ciel di Margherita il nome.

It would be a mistake to suppose this piece to have been written for the wedding itself, that is, as early as 1579: it is pure chamber music, in a mature and luxuriant style, with ample coloratura for the three ladies and their companions, worked out at great length and with great brilliance.

This opening number stands in the sharpest possible contrast to the two pieces that follow: a complete setting in seven sections of Petrarch's second sestina "in vita di Madonna Laura," *Giovine donna sott' un verde lauro*, and Luigi Tansillo's gloomy *partenza* in terze rime, *Se quel dolor che va innanzi al morire*, a capitolo already set to music in 1577 by Wert. It is the first time that Marenzio has worked with the cyclic forms on so grand a scale: it is as though he had hesitated to do so until after the death of Lasso and Palestrina. These are not "Ferrarese" works, or if they are it is only in the sense that they are barely possible for amateurs and require sure-footed, experienced, professional singers, such as could then be found only in Ferrara and Mantua, Rome and Venice. Marenzio no longer aims to be "popular," and with these madrigal cycles he no longer influences the public at large, the amateurs; he influences only a few of his fellow artists—Monteverdi, Schütz, Gagliano, and one or two monodists. It is most significant that, unlike the Marenzio of the 'eighties, this new Marenzio no longer makes any impression upon the Elizabethan madrigalists. As long as Marenzio remains a miniaturist, they follow him; they translate his pastoral idiom and his virtuosity into the language of English society. But Marenzio does not limit himself to miniatures. In these highly personal works, written in complete isolation, he permits himself the utmost liberty in applying all the means at his disposal: the technique of the divided choir, of the double motif, of the fluctuating tempo. The fusion of the *misura di breve* and the *misura cromatica* is now complete. The time-signature invariably indicates the *misura cromatica*, but the basic tempo is a Largo—a mean tempo from which the road is open in either direction. In a similar way, the basic or mean principle of the texture is an interweaving of the voices and not homophony; in Tansillo's capitolo it is a use of dissonance and not the static consonant chord. It is really amazing that Artusi and his fellow critics should not have made Marenzio as well as Monteverdi the butt of their indignation, for Marenzio is quite as bold as Monteverdi and it was Marenzio who gave Monteverdi the courage for his final audacities.

Marenzio's harmonic boldness is of course noticeable in the sestina. What induced Marenzio to add another setting to those of Andrea Gabrieli (printed in 1589 but composed before 1555), Vinci (1583), and many others, can only be guessed: it was presumably not so much the poet's promise to be faithful "until the last day shall

close these eyes" ("fin che l'ultimo dì chiuda quest' occhi"), as it was his confidence
in his immortal fame:

> Di tal che nascerà dopo mill'anni,
> **Se** tanto viver può ben culto lauro. . . .

This is the passage that Marenzio particularly emphasizes: the sustaining, "eternal"
voice is first the soprano, then the tenor:

Contrasts of tempo—of breadth and rapidity, and of simultaneous rapidity and
breadth—constitute the essence of the music of this sestina; only once, when the poet
contrasts the dark hair of youth with the white hair of old age, does Marenzio fall

back on "eye-music." Within the given range of the basic tempo, the third stanza, *Ma perche vola il tempo, e fuggon gli anni*, can only be characterized as "hurried."

Still more personal is the music for Tansillo's *partenza*. This is no longer a game, no longer *imitazione della natura*; it is *expressione* from beginning to end. In his own day, Baldisserra Donato had set this first pair of tercets to music:

His setting is beautiful, dignified, and genuinely felt, with the open fifths at the beginning, the sixth-chord in the third measure, the conflict of G-sharp with C and the false relation in the fourth. But compared with Marenzio's music, it is primitive:

Needless to say, this no longer bears the slightest resemblance to the style of the "pathos" book of 1588. New is the extreme plasticity of tempo, new is the extreme freedom in the use of all the usual devices of the madrigal and of all the special devices that Marenzio has developed; everything "pastoral" or canzonetta-like has been discarded. And it is not simply that these devices are used indiscriminately one after another—though we shall see later on that this is true of the dilettante Gesualdo, whose genius is rooted in his pathological personality; if Marenzio's style is subjective, it is also organic. It must be admitted, however, that this style can be understood only by those who have followed the whole artificial evolution of the madrigal, an evolution that seems almost to be a result of inbreeding. It is a style that carries expression to its utmost limit and that stops at nothing, not even at the illogical—for example, Marenzio does not hesitate to make the voices completely incommensurable. The ending of Tansillo's *Ottava parte* reads as follows:

... Ma'l bel guardo divin per cui m'alzai
Fin sopr'il ciel è quel che più m'atterra,
Mirando de bei lumi i dolci rai,
Voce par ch'oda *ch'ivi dentro gridi*:
"Questi son gl'occhi ove tu lunge andrai" ...

The poet's inner cry is for Marenzio a state of insanity in which no voice has further relation to any other:

When a genius is great enough, such things are possible, even in the harmonious, southern, "geometrical" art of Italy.

As though to conclude the book on a harmonious, Italian, "Ferrarese" note, Marenzio ends with two madrigals by Torquato Tasso, *La dove sono i pargoletti Amori*, a hunting scene for amoretti in the style of one of Albani's paintings, and the "echo" *O verdi selve, o dolci fonti, o rivi*—both in a bright high register, both filled with luxuriant coloratura, both pieces of the most refined virtuosity, the jubilant "echo" once again a piece especially designed for the Duke of Ferrara's bird-like singers.

This sixth book concludes Marenzio's production in the field of the six-voiced madrigal. From here on, up to the time of his premature death, there follow three books of five-voiced madrigals, of 1595, 1598, and 1599. The first of these (Book VII) was dedicated, shortly before Marenzio's departure for Cracow, to the major-domo of the Pope ("intimo Cameriere participante, et assistente di N. Sig."), Diego de Campo, evidently a Spaniard.

In content it is essentially a continuation of the sixth book: the chief poet is Guarini with his *Pastor fido*, who has completely crowded out Sannazaro and his *Arcadia*. The very first piece is a half "pseudo-monodic," half madrigalesque setting of Mirtillo's confession of despair (1, 2):

> Deh [Guarini has *Ma*] poi ch'era ne fati ch'io dovessi
> Amar la morte e non la vita mia . . .

Indeed the entire book is devoted to the pastoral *tragi-commedia*, and its final number is a tendentious piece designed to reestablish the emotional equilibrium of the listener or singer after the impassioned and idyllic scenes that have gone before:

> Ombrose e care selve,
> Se sospirando in flebili sussurri
> Al nostro lamentar vi lamentaste,
> Gioite anco al gioire, e tante lingue
> Sciogliete, quanti frondi
> Scherzan al suon di queste
> Piene del gioir nostro aure ridenti.
> Cantate le venture e le dolcezze
> D'Amarilli e di Tirsi
> Avventurosi amanti.

This is a wedding madrigal, and it may be that the whole book is a description in pastoral terms of the vicissitudes of a love affair. For the *Pastor fido* has certainly not been chosen out of respect alone. Marenzio has not hesitated to alter the text of Guarini's *tragi-commedia*, and drawing also on another pastoral poem which I have been unable to identify, he takes what he pleases and uses it to express feelings that are quite personal and sometimes extremely intense. This expression leads him to set the most extreme antitheses side by side, to permit himself the utmost liberty in the use of harmonic devices, to animate his way of speaking, to dissolve his form— in short, to what one might call a sort of madrigalesque *pointillage*. The predilection for combining double motifs, indeed everything "constructive," every "instrumental" trait, has disappeared; what is left is pure expressionism. Consider, for example, the beginning of the "conversion to love" from the first scene (1, 1) of the *Pastor fido* (Marenzio has changed the name "Silvio" to the more neutral "Thyrsis"):

This is a refinement, a personal mode of expression unsurpassed in its lack of concern, yet at the same time a thoroughly Italian mode of expression; one will not find it imitated by anyone, even by the boldest of the Elizabethan madrigalists. Six years before the *Nuove musiche* this mode of expression already has the characteristic combination of exclamation, declamation, and coloratura for the cadence, except that the coloratura (No. 6) still retains its expressive value:

But the most striking characteristic for the modern listener is the harmonic intensity of these madrigals. With the utmost ease Marenzio begins and ends a madrigal (*O disaventurosa, acerba sorte*) with the B major triad, symptomatic of this animated *stile concitato*. There are progressions and suspensions of the most unusual sort, yet they are logical; they are not hatched out on one of those "chromatic" or "enharmonic" keyed instruments that had existed since Vicentino and Zarlino, but conceived in a pure and completely vocal idiom. I need only quote the conclusion of Mirtillo's monologue (*Pastor fido*, 1, 2) *Cruda Amarilli, che col nome ancora* (see illustration just below).

Ten years later (1605), when Monteverdi opened his fifth madrigal book with a setting of this same monologue, he took care not to set the second part to music, for it

would have been difficult to surpass Marenzio in this. In the first part, however, he openly paid tribute to Marenzio, thus acknowledging him as his predecessor in the *seconda prattica*. In the examples that follow I do not think it is necessary to include the text:

Cruda Amarilli

The similarities are as characteristic as the differences, and it is most characteristic that while Monteverdi rests his a cappella composition on a bass which will soon become a basso continuo, Marenzio remains within the stylistic limits of his more refined and nobler century, a century of vocality.

In the pastoral anecdotes that the book contains, for example in Ergasto's narrative *O fido, o caro* [Guarini has *forte*] *Aminta* (*Pastor fido*, I, 2), Marenzio is again a child of his century in that he distinguishes sharply between recitative and aria, between antiphonal declamation and full lyric expansion, without ever venturing beyond the limits of the madrigalesque style. *Al lume delle Stelle*, a little pre-monodic "cantata" of Tasso's, shows the same distinction though it has more of the canzonetta spirit. The whole book is full of hidden drama, but the presentation of the actual scene or monologue is always madrigalesque, even where there is a real temptation to dramatize, as in *Care mie selve addio*, the farewell lament of Amaryllis (*Pastor fido*, IV, 5), where the text has again been slightly altered to give it a more general application. Every madrigalesque device is used with the utmost freedom. Restlessness and contrast are so intensified as to bring Marenzio dangerously close to the stylistic border-line. But he does not cross it.

The eighth madrigal book, published in 1598 and dedicated to Ferrante Gonzaga of Guastalla, the grandson of the Ferrante Gonzaga who was the first patron of the young Orlando di Lasso, seems actually to cross the line. In only two of the seventeen pieces in the book is it still possible to recognize the Marenzio of Book VII, the Marenzio whose style includes the most extreme antitheses. He is most readily recognizable in the last number, *Laura, se pur sei l'aura*, a piece worked out at con-

siderable length, less readily in the delicate polyphonic animation of *Care lagrime mie,* a poem often set to music. Both texts are from the pen of Livio Celiano, with whose poetry Marenzio must have become quite familiar between 1595 and 1598, for the eighth book includes several other pieces of his:

> Provate la mia fiamma ...
> Ahi chi t'insidia al boscareccio nido ... (a sonnet)
> Questi leggiadri odorosetti fiori ...
> La mia Clori è brunetta. ...

In Comin Ventura's *Rime di diversi celebri poeti dell'età nostra* (Bergamo, 1587), Celiano appears in the company of a number of poets who play a role in Marenzio's work—Guarini, Torquato Tasso, Giuliano Goselini, and Angelo Grillo, one of whose rare non-devotional poems Marenzio now sets to music:

> Quand'io miro le rose,
> Ch'in voi natura pose,
> E quella che v'ha l'arte
> Nel vago seno sparte,
> Non sò conoscer poi,
> S'ò voi le rose ò sian le rose voi.

The remaining texts of this book include monologues, narratives, passionate outbursts from a pastoral *tragi-commedia*—an imitation of the *Pastor fido* that I have been unable to identify—and a scene (IV, 9) from the *Pastor fido* itself. And for once it really is a scene, a part of the dialogue between the wounded Dorinda and her cruel Silvio, in the course of which Silvio repents and is accepted by Dorinda as her lover. In choosing such a scene Marenzio becomes a successor of P. Simone Balsamino, the Venetian choirmaster who published in 1594 a setting of a scene and an entire dialogue from Tasso's *Aminta*, written some years earlier for an *accademia* in Urbino, his native town. (Cf. A. Einstein, "Ein Madrigal-Dialog von 1594," *Zeitschrift der Internationalen Musik-Gesellschaft,* xv, 8.) In general Balsamino divides his six-voiced chorus into two half-choirs of three voices each which carry out a sort of dialogue; relying largely on homophony, he succeeds in giving the long scene a relatively rapid tempo. But Marenzio is much more radical, for Balsamino is sometimes unable to resist treating a given passage in a madrigalesque fashion, making it picturesque, symbolic, or half contrapuntal.

Of the seventeen pieces in the book, fifteen represent a new departure, and in these Marenzio relies throughout on homophony, on the free declamation of the upper voice in which the expression is concentrated, and on the colorful harmonization provided by the various choirs formed by the accompanying lower voices. There is no longer any contrasting of means, any "painting," any symbolism. The one exception is Celiano's *La mia Clori è brunetta*; as already mentioned (cf. p. 242 above), this is written throughout in black notes, a final humorous tribute to "eye-music." The bar-line becomes superfluous; the antithesis of C and ₵ has been annulled. It is significant, and perhaps an indication that Marenzio has taken his cue from Balsamino, that in one of his two scenes from the *Aminta*, Satiro's monologue, Balsamino has likewise used the direction "Music to be sung without measure or rests" ("Canto da cantarsi senza battuta e pause"); instead of rests, the part-books have cues.

Like Balsamino, Marenzio makes the dialogue of Dorinda and Silvio a great madrigalesque scene, omitting the conclusion of Dorinda's first lament which he had already set to music in 1594. But at this point the parallel ends. For Marenzio is a far greater master of declamation and his "harmonization" is far more sensitive. I shall quote only one passage, reproducing it at once in the form of an "accompanied monody" without indicating the voice-leading and the rests, not in the mistaken belief that it is no longer a genuine madrigal, but simply to show how small a step still remained to be taken by the Florentine Camerata:

This declamatory style is a blend of the very old and the very new: on the one hand it recalls the frottola and the formulas of Tromboncino and Cara *per sonar strambotti, sonetti, terze rime*; on the other it recalls Rore's choral recitatives for four and five voices and looks forward to the *stile nuovo* of the Florentines. For our example forecasts a monodic madrigal of the seventeenth century. And wherever a rhythmically regular text calls forth a rhythmically regular and dance-like music, as in Grillo's *Quando miro le rose* or Celiano's *La mia Clori*, the aria-canzonetta—the primitive aria—arises of itself. Marenzio may have taken Grillo's text from the first book of five-voiced madrigals by Serafino Cantone (1591, not listed by Vogel), but what a difference there is between his music and the setting by the worthy organist of Milan's San Simpliciano! Where Marenzio takes only twenty-one measures, Cantone takes eighty, meanwhile destroying the poem's epigrammatic spirit with his three- and four-fold text repetitions and weighting his airy nothings with lead. All these madrigals of Marenzio are short: in the scenes he quickly disposes of an enormous number of lines; fragments of the text are never repeated, and there is no emphatic use of polyphony. Where quasi-polyphonic episodes occur, they seem intended merely to remind us that this is still choral music and not yet genuine monody. But it is "ideal" monody: we stand on the threshold. I need only quote the text of the third number to show that the cantata, with its differentiation between recitative and aria, is knocking at the door:

> Filli, volgendo i lumi al vago Aminta,
>   Dal profondo del cor trasse un sospiro
> E disse: "Aminta, io t'amo e questa mano
>   Sia pegno del mio amor, della mia fede,
>   Con ch'ora a te mi lego e per lei giuro
>   Che d'altri non sarò, se tua non sono!"
> Tacque, e i begli occhi gravidi di perle,
>   Di purpureo color fur tinti intorno,
>   E'l fortunato Aminta a lei sol rese
>   Per parole sospir, per gratie pianto.

On May 10, 1599, just three months before his death, Marenzio dedicates his last madrigal book, the ninth, to Duke Vincenzo Gonzaga, who had asked him to send on some of his music a few months before. Thus Marenzio returns to Mantua, the city in which he had begun his career as a madrigalist, and to Giaches Wert. One looks in vain in this book for a direct connection with the most extravagant prince in Italy, whose erotic prowess filled the *chronique scandaleuse* of all Europe. For the book is a return to the highest artistic ideals and to the highest seriousness. Certain pieces from it determined Marenzio's musical portrait as it was known to the eighteenth and nineteenth centuries: Padre Martini, Burney, and Torchi offered a choice of pieces that was to be reprinted and admired over and over again.

If the eighth book was devoted to homophony, hedonism, and the pastoral, the ninth aspires to the highest possible specific gravity, both in its choice of texts and in its musical treatment of them. This is sufficiently clear from the opening and closing numbers alone. The book begins with a setting of the first stanza from Dante's "canzon pietrosa," *Così nel mio parlar voglio esser aspro,* a text that no musician had thought of for eighty years. (Cf. A. Einstein, "Dante im Madrigal," *Archiv für Musikwissenschaft,* III, 405, and "Dante on the Way to the Madrigal," *Musical Quarterly,* xxv, 142.) If in his day the composer of the old canzone of 1520—Bernardo Pisano or whoever it may have been—set this stanza in the neutral motet style, Marenzio takes the poet's *durezza,* his austerity, in dead earnest; the audacity of his harmony and voice-leading is not to be surpassed. A false relation, an unusual suspension, a strange series of harmonies—one shock follows another. It is both expression and *imitazione della natura,* both personal expression and affectation, it brings an artificial style to the sharpest possible focus. The concluding piece is a setting of Guarini's madrigal *La bella man vi stringo* (Torchi, *L'arte musicale in Italia,* II, 224f.). Here again Marenzio goes back to the beginning—to Arcadelt, Corteccia, and Rore—in that he leads the soprano and alto in canon at the lower fourth at the interval of a semibreve and works out the three lower parts thematically. It is as though he were saying: I am a master; I can do everything you others can and more; therefore I can allow myself the utmost liberty and option and the most personal style.

And in this swan-song he allows himself everything. In one number he returns to the Bevilacqua madrigals of 1588, the stepchild of his success, by setting to music a further stanza from Petrarch's sestina *Mia benigna fortuna;* as before, he writes in the *misura di breve,* maintains a broad tempo that becomes more animated only towards the end, and permits himself the most incisive and relentless chromaticism. Thus his *Crudel acerba inesorabil morte* represents the final stage and highest point in the history of pathos that we have already carried up to Wert (cf. p. 561 above); at this point a reaction was bound to set in. Marenzio writes in another and more personal style in setting three further stanzas from the same sestina:

> Se sì alto pon gir . . .
> Amor i'hò molt'e molt'anni pianto . . .
> Chiaro segno Amor pose alle mie rime . . .

How personal it is may perhaps be shown by comparing the first of the three with the setting of the same stanza written by Lasso in 1563 (*Works,* IV, 59). Lasso in his day is himself quite "modern" and colorful in his harmony: Petrarch's *mutato stile* takes him to B major; he is already sufficiently free and characteristic. And

yet his music is primitive and "compact" when compared with the sensibility and the dissolution or disintegration of every means in Marenzio's. There is an analogous difference between Marenzio's second stanza and the setting by Monte of 1562. For all his lively "expression," the old master, who was still living in 1599, remains a "constructor" beside Marenzio, who goes straight from exclamations of extraordinary vehemence to simple recitative:

The third stanza, finally, has a most intricate texture, doubtless suggested by the word *penosa*. But it is no longer dominated by any external tone-painting, as in the earlier Marenzio, but by an extraordinary psychological penetration.

Tradition has it that Marenzio fell in love with a young lady of the Aldobrandini family and that he lost the favor of the Pope "for overmuch familiarity" with her. Such, at least, is the report of Henry Peacham in his *Compleat Gentleman* of 1622. (Cf. Grove, III, 322, under *Marenzio*.) Marenzio's choice of a fragment from Petrarch's *Trionfo d'Amore* (III, 148f.) in his ninth book seems at first glance to bear this out:

> Dura legge d'Amor! ma, benchè obliqua,
> Servar conviensi; perocch'ella aggiunge
> Di Cielo in terra, universale, antiqua.
>
> Or so come da sè il cor si disgiunge;
> E come sa far pace, guerra e tregua;
> E coprir suo dolor quand'altri'l punge:
>
> E so come in un punto si dilegua,
> E poi si sparge per le guance il sangue,

> Se paura e vergogna avvien che'l segua.
> So come sta fra'fiori ascoso l'angue;
> **Come** sempre fra due si vegghia e dorme;
> **Come** senza languir si more e langue.

But more probably this piece is itself responsible for the tradition and owes its existence to the example of Wert, who had set the same text to music as early as 1561, likewise for five voices. Yet not until 1599 could it be set with the necessary subjectivity, a subjectivity able to paint in bold strokes the state of being in love and the pallor and blushes of those thus affected (see example below).

The three other madrigals of the ninth book that were published by Torchi in the second volume of his *Arte musicale in Italia* are certainly calculated to support the legend of Marenzio's hopeless love and to present him as a harmonic innovator. The last of these is a setting of a sonnet by Petrarch, *L'aura che'l verde lauro e*

l'aureo crine, a text so seldom chosen—from the time just before Marenzio we have only the settings of Ippolito Sabino and Pietro Vinci—that one might even suppose Marenzio to have shared the poet's wish to die before his beloved. It is worked out on a grand scale, using the technique of the double motif, and is filled with striking contrasts of tempo, with baroque coloratura, and with unusual harmonies, for example at the word *pellegrine*, where two seventh chords occur in succession. But even so there is more art than expression. The same is true of the setting of another sonnet of Petrarch's, *Solo e pensoso i più deserti campi*, whose beginning, with the soprano's chromatic scale in even semibreves, rising to the ninth and then falling back to the fifth against the commentary of the four lower voices, has been a constant source of amazement and admiration. And rightly so: perhaps without even intending it, Marenzio here succeeds in depicting both the subjective mood and the landscape—the lonely wanderer in the deserted fields. The technique is familiar to us from Marenzio's setting of the madrigal by Veronica Gambara (cf. p. 628 above); here, however, everything is even more individual, including the intensified coloratura. Also familiar is the technique used in the first of the three pieces, *Il vago e bell' Armillo*. It is another of Livio Celiano's pre-monodic cantatas, this time with a maritime scene: Marenzio assigns the narrative to divided choirs or gives it an informal motivic treatment and holds the full choir in reserve for the outburst of the *pastore-marinaro*. It is an aria in madrigalesque disguise.

Having already devoted so much space—perhaps altogether too much space—to one man, we can afford to pass quickly over the remaining pieces of this book: *Vivo in guerra mendico e son dolente*, a sonnet by Antonio Ongaro, who has given it the title "Idolatrice d'amore"—all nature comes to life at the thought of the beloved; *Fiume ch' a l'onde tue Ninfe e Pastori*, a second sonnet by the same poet; and two further madrigals by Guarini, *Parto ò non parto* and *Credete voi ch' io vivo*. The last opens ostentatiously like a *canzon francese*, but soon takes on a freer and more subjective character rich in contrasts. Throughout this book one has the impression that it is a last work, the climax and more than climax of a wholly personal style, just as one has this impression of Wagner's *Parsifal*, which could likewise have been followed only by repetitions. Marenzio himself was not of this opinion: in his dedication to Vincenzo Gonzaga, he expresses the hope that his feeble intellect, stimulated by the favor of his patron, may in future produce something more worthy ("il debole intelletto mio fomentato dalla gratia Sua, produchi per l'avvenire parti più degni dell'A.S. . . .") From the letters of Angelo Grillo, we know that after the publication of this ninth book Marenzio wrote several further madrigals, most of them to poems by Grillo himself. (Cf. A. Einstein, *Kirchenmusikalisches Jahrbuch*, XXIV, 152.) They seem to be lost and Marenzio did not live to dedicate them to the Duke. But it sometimes happens that Fate knows best when to close the circle.

CARLO GESUALDO DA VENOSA

MARENZIO, "il più dolce cigno d'Italia," has come down in legend as a somewhat romantic figure in an unhappy love-affair which probably has little basis in fact. Carlo Gesualdo, Prince of Venosa, was in his day a figure in the *chronique scandaleuse* of Naples, of Italy, in fact of all Europe, and in his case, unfortunately, the basis is real enough. His extravagant music has shed light upon his personality; while his extravagant deed—the murder of his wife and her lover—has drawn attention to his music. Cecil Gray and Philip Heseltine (*Carlo Gesualdo, Prince of Venosa, Musician and Murderer*, London, 1926) have tried to characterize the man and the musician. His deed is the subject of a masterly little story in the *Puits de Saint Claire* by Anatole France, where it is treated in the manner of Stendhal, that is, without any pretense of historical accuracy.

Born about 1560 as the second son of Fabrizio Gesualdo—a member of one of the

oldest families in the kingdom of Naples, who had himself maintained a musical *accademia* at his house—Carlo Gesualdo seems to have been able to devote himself to his love or passion for music from childhood on, both as lute virtuoso and singer to lute accompaniment, and as composer. Naples was in these days full of musicians to guide him and to serve him as colleagues. In all probability, his actual teacher was Pomponio Nenna, "cavalier di Cesare," a native of Bari, who dedicated his first madrigal book (1582) to Fabrizio Carafa, Duke of Andria, who was later to be the Prince's victim. That Nenna and Gesualdo were intimately associated as artists is more than suggested by their choice of texts: by my count, they have no less than nine in common. For the rest, the famous old Domenico da Nola was still living in Gesualdo's youth as choirmaster at the Annunziata, though he was now feeble and delicate and as a musician a figure of the past. A new star was also rising on the Neapolitan horizon—Giovanni Macque of Valenciennes, whom Gesualdo must have known. Gesualdo's own circle, his *accademia*, included such names as Giovanni Leonardo Primavera, Muzio Effrem, Rocco Rodio, Scipione Dentice, Stefano Felis, and above all Scipione Stella, who constitutes the link with Roman music—we have already met him in association with Marenzio.

But this life for art alone is soon at an end. In 1585 his elder brother Luigi dies, and Gesualdo, to his misfortune, now becomes head of the family and is obliged to marry. In 1586 he chooses as his bride, Donna Maria d'Avalos, like himself a member of an old Spanish-Neapolitan family, a beauty of irresistible attraction to men. Despite her youth, she had already buried one husband—contemporary gossip makes him a victim of her insatiable sexual appetite; a second husband had managed to save himself from a similar fate by a timely divorce. Gesualdo was soon presented with an heir, but by the time his second child, a daughter, was born, he was no longer sure whose child it was. For in the meantime Donna Maria had secretly entered into an intimate and ardent relationship with Don Fabrizio and had ended by acknowledging it so openly that Gesualdo had no alternative but to avenge his honor in the manner prescribed by his time. On October 26, 1590, came the catastrophe. The pair were caught in the very act. The adulterer was shot; the adulteress had her throat cut as she lay in bed; the two bodies were cruelly mutilated. After the deed, Carlo took refuge in his castle at Gesualdo, where he awaited the possible consequences. Contemporary sympathy lay entirely on the side of the murdered couple, but perhaps only because the murderer was a pathological weakling and an unchivalrous avenger of his honor. As Brantôme tells us, the chief complaint against Gesualdo was that he had caused his wife and her lover to be put to death by his servants instead of attending to the matter himself.

Apart from this objection, the affair was quite in order. Gesualdo had nothing to fear from the authority of the State. When there seemed no longer to be any likelihood of a private revenge on the part of the Carafa and Avalos families, he went on to Ferrara, where early in 1594 he married Eleonora d'Este, a sister of Cesare d'Este, heir presumptive to the throne of Ferrara and later Duke of Modena. He left Ferrara at the end of 1596—shortly before that city's musical splendor came to an end. He then returned to Naples, honored as one of the greatest nobles in the kingdom, hated by his own household, a miserable invalid who for reasons of health submitted himself to daily flagellation; a medical writing of the time reports (Gray-Heseltine, p. 51): "Princeps Venusiae musica clarissimus nostro tempore cacare non poterat, nisi verberatus a servo ad id adscito." He died in 1613, though it was said that this was not without the help of his distinguished consort, who survived him for many years and to whom Muzio Effrem dedicated a posthumous madrigal book of her husband's in 1621. Paolo Quagliati, a Roman musician of high rank, celebrated another event in the Gesualdo household: the wedding of Isabella, the elder daughter of Carlo and Eleonora, to Nicolo Ludovisi, a nephew of Pope Gregory XV (Alessandro Ludovisi, 1621-1623). In Quagliati's *La sfera armoniosa* of 1623 there are no less than five compositions written in honor of this festivity: at the beginning two large cantatas, a ballet (*Ballo delle Stelle*) and a sort of festival play (*La Nave felice*), and at the end a chamber duet, all of this in the most modern style. This effectively does away with the fable of the Neapolitan chronicler Don Ferrante della Marra, who says that the marriage took place against Gesualdo's will (Gray-Heseltine, pp. 49ff.). For by this time Gesualdo had been dead for years.

Gesualdo was on intimate terms with another pathological artist of the time, Torquato Tasso, at least in so far as this was possible in view of the difference in rank between a prince and a simple nobleman. Tasso had come to Naples early in 1588 and on this occasion had made the Prince's acquaintance. They came to know one another better in February and April 1592, when the poet visited Naples a second time, and when late in 1593 or early in 1594 Gesualdo left for Ferrara and his second wedding, Tasso wished to accompany him. From here on his verses record every event in the Prince's private and public life: not only does he celebrate the Prince himself in the two sonnets *Alta prole di regi eletta in terra* and *Carlo, il vostro Leon c'ha nero il velo* and in the canzone *Musa, tu che dal cielo il nome prendi,* he also immortalizes Maria Avalos and her unhappy end; he writes a group of ottave "nelle nozze di D. Carlo Gesualdo . . . e di Donna Leonora d'Este" (*Lascia, o figlia d'Urania, il bel Parnaso*); he supplies the composer Gesualdo with about three dozen texts of which eleven have been preserved with music (the list given by Gray-Heseltine, p. 10, is not complete); finally, he writes letters to the Prince (cf. *Lettere,* ed. Solerti, v, 1423, 1424, 1427 and 1428) which tell us something about his views on *poesia musicale.* Of special interest is the self-criticism in his observation that some of his texts contain too much hidden erudition. For the rest, the

composer Gesualdo pays little attention to the literary quality of his texts. Sometimes he also favors Tasso's rival, Guarini, but he shows little respect for Guarini's poetry. Thus he sets Guarini's *Tirsi morir volea* in a mutilated form, omitting the end entirely. The remaining texts he set to music are for the most part worthless doggerel, evidently obtained from complaisant rhymesters. He sets no sonnets of Petrarch, no stanzas of Ariosto and, strangely enough, nothing from Tasso's *Gerusalemme liberata*. To him the text is merely the occasion, the necessary and indispensable raw material of his aristocratic music. His relation to his poets is thus the direct opposite of the relation of the minstrel to the troubadour: this time it is the musician who rides the high horse while the poet holds his stirrup. Gesualdo's texts had first and above all to be short: they had to give him the opportunity to shape his music as he pleased by repeating parts of the text, and a longer poem would have made this impossible. Gesualdo rarely set a sonnet and never a canzone, a sestina, or any other cycle; he is an egotistical musician who thinks only of himself and never of his poet.

To a certain extent, Gesualdo's work has been made available in reprints by Keiner, Gray-Heseltine, Kiesewetter, Ambros, Torchi, Pizzetti, and Weismann. The richest of these, that by Pizzetti, has unfortunately lost some of its value through its unnecessary reduction of the note values. A list is given by Gray-Heseltine, pp. 135ff.; it needs only to be supplemented by the eight (or rather six) pieces subsequently published by W. Weismann (Peters Edition, No. 10879). What sort of musician was Gesualdo and what was his place as an individual musician and as a link in the chain of musical development? His contemporaries thought him a great man, but their judgment is visibly influenced by his princely rank; indeed it would have been dangerous to criticize Gesualdo as Muzio Effrem criticized Marco da Gagliano, and as Giovanni Maria Artusi criticized Claudio Monteverdi. The opinion of posterity is divided. For Burney, Ambros, and Eitner, Gesualdo is a dilettantish experimenter; for Leichtentritt, Keiner, and Heseltine he is unquestionably a genius. Ambros, to be sure, was too artistic and independent a critic to misjudge Gesualdo altogether and would never have subscribed to the stupidities of Eitner, whose offhand dismissal of Gesualdo reads as follows: "With a perseverance that is positively plebeian, the Prince turned out innumerable madrigals whose harmonic idiom made them real monstrosities for their time. Closer examination perhaps reveals a predilection for Cipriano Rore, a harmonist of genius, but His Highness did not have talent enough to imitate Rore with success." Innumerable madrigals? There are only seven books, the last of which was published posthumously (1594, 1594, 1595, 1596, 1611, 1611, and 1626), with about 150 pieces if we count as separate numbers the subdivisions of those madrigals that have more than one section. This is a relatively modest number. A harmonic idiom that made them real monstrosities for their time? We shall come back to this charge later. But did he write only madrigals? This is not true, at least not in the literal sense: Pomponio Nenna, in the eighth book of his madrigals (1618), prints two of Gesualdo's five-voiced canzonette —two completely "normal" yet highly personal little pieces, similar in form to those of Ferretti and Vecchi, but more delicate than the average. Admittedly they are casual products. But beyond these we now know three books of church music by Gesualdo: motets *a cinque* (*Sacrae cantiones*) from 1603; motets *a sei* (including one *a sette*) from the same year; and responds *a sei* from 1611. From the first of these, Guido Pannain has reprinted fourteen out of nineteen numbers in the *Istituzioni e Monumenti dell'arte musicale italiana*, v (1934), invaluable material for the objective appraisal of this much debated musician. Evidently he was no one-sided madrigalist but a man of some versatility. And apart from this, has anyone ever criticized Chopin for not having written a symphony or a string quartet? What is more, Gesualdo distinguished carefully between the secular and sacred styles. This is evident even in externals, for without exception his madrigals have the time-signature C and thus stand in four-four time, while the recently reprinted motets are all in the *misura di breve*. In addition to this, the freedom or fluctuation of the tempo in his madrigals is carried to an extreme, just as it is in Marenzio, though Gesualdo's unit is even smaller than Marenzio's—where Marenzio uses the half-note, Gesualdo uses the quarter. Yet in the motets the uniformity of the tempo is hardly ever disturbed. At the same time, anyone determined to connect the music of Gesualdo's motets with his life would find them richly rewarding. They consist of nothing but cries of anguish, self-accusation, and repentance—settings of such fragments from the Psalter and the Song of Songs as *Peccantem me quotidie; Laboravi in gemitu meo; Heu mihi, Domine, quia peccavi nimis in vita mea; . . . miserere mei, Domine; O vos omnes qui transitis; Exaudi Deus deprecationem meam;* together with ecstatic invocations of Our Lady. The whole is, as it were, a musical reflection of the famous altar-painting in the Capuchin monastery at Gesualdo (reproduced in Gray-Heseltine, plate IV), which shows us the composer, under the patronage of his uncle, Carlo Borromeo, being commended by the Saints and by Our Lady to the mercy of the Saviour. This is a painting with a secret personal content, and the same holds true for these motets; it is as though personal suffering and personal anguish sought purification, relief, and "objective" expression. This characteristic attitude stands out when we compare Gesualdo's motets with those of his Neapolitan contemporaries, for example those published by Giovanni Maria Trabaci in 1602, a number of which have been reprinted with Gesualdo's in the *Istituzioni e Monumenti*. This Neapolitan school of Macque, Nenna, and Montella stands somewhat closer to Venice than to Rome: its writing is rich in harmonic clashes resulting from suspensions and in colorful high lights, but it avoids all ex-

aggerated subjective expression. In a word, it is church music. But Gesualdo's motets
are church music and something else besides; they are more than church music and
at the same time less. They are more, if we allow the musician writing for the church
to use a personal idiom; they are less if we hold that this departure from "objectivity" is already the first step toward the irreverence of seventeenth-century church
music in the presence of the divine and unapproachable. In illustration I quote from
Pannain's reprint one of the invocations of Our Lady. The motet is in two sections,
a first section with considerable contrapuntal animation:

> Ave dulcissima Maria,
> vera spes et vita,
> dulce refrigerium!

and a second, more "homophonic" section, which is repeated:

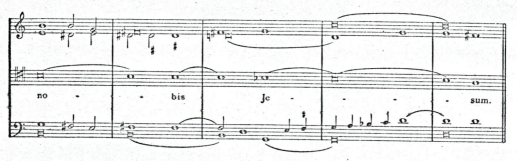

This is a passage full of truth, depth, and reverence, full of harmonic assurance and beauty, full of awareness of the expressive value of chords, both on the brilliant side and on the somber—for it embodies a decrescendo to pianissimo that is realized with the help of chords and not through dynamics alone—and he who wrote it was no "knight errant staggering about in a harmonic wilderness," but a real musician. In a similar way, Gesualdo's contemporary El Greco was a real painter and a great one, although—or rather because—his religious ardor did not express itself within the confines of the canonical sacred art of Raphael and Guido Reni. There are also distortions and examples of "want of style" in Gesualdo's motets, for example in the first number (*Ave regina coelorum*), which begins imitatively in the Mixolydian mode and in Palestrina's classic manner, when the *Ave* and the *Ora pro nobis* take on a warmer expression and begin to become iridescent, chromatically and harmonically; or in the *O vos omnes*, at "videte si est dolor *sicut dolor meus*," when the harmony becomes almost a gesture in its chromaticism and its clashes. But this is genuine exuberance, and the musical devices used are not determined by the indifference of a dilettante who feels free to indulge his every whim. Gesualdo's independence is also visible in his church music. If Pomponio Nenna was really his teacher, Gesualdo shares his colorful harmonic style—I need only refer the reader to the selections Pannain has reprinted from Nenna's responds of 1607, especially to Christ's words on the Mount of Olives, *Tristis est anima mea*—but this is simply the general chromatic mannerism of a school, for Gesualdo is more impassioned, more moved, more a part of his music. This is evident above all in his renunciation of all external, visual appeals to the imagination, of all that his time considered "picturesque," a trait in which he differs from Nenna who, to retain the same example, naturally sets the word *fuga* as a "fuga" in the reproach of Jesus, at *Vos fugam capietis*. Gesualdo was unquestionably influenced by Marenzio, whose book of *mesta gravità* had been available since 1588, not to mention other pieces of the highest pathos. But what he had heard in them was simply the emotional vibration communicated through the use of novel harmonic devices, for he failed to experience —or else ignored—the graphic or visual components. With all his taste, Marenzio was a practical musician, not a humanist. Gesualdo, on the other hand, as a member

of the high nobility had received the education of his class and had undoubtedly read and understood Vincenzo Galilei's mocking diatribes against "eye-music" and other forms of symbolism. In all his work there is hardly a single example of this sort. When in his *Languisco e moro* (III, 3, 1595) all voices but one are silent at the word *solo*, it is no play of words, but a reflection of genuine feeling. He is a pure expressionist.

And an expressionist he remains from first to last. He underwent a "development" in so far as his "wedding trip" to Ferrara and his stay in that city make a division in his creative life at the year 1594. His first two madrigal books, edited for and dedicated to him by Scipione Stella, his house musician, stand somewhat apart from the rest of his work; of the two books, the *Secondo libro* is properly the first and was so numbered in the famous edition in score prepared in 1613 by the Genoese choirmaster Simone Molinaro. In this book Gesualdo is still fairly reserved, in terms of his own later style or of the style implicit in certain extreme audacities of Marenzio and other forerunners and contemporaries. But even here he takes things more seriously than others: his mind is gloomier and his means of expression show more virtuosity. Yet this is not apparent in his setting of the mutilated *Tirsi morir volea* (Pizzetti, pp. 18-30). If anywhere, it is here that we see the high-born dilettante whom no one dared to criticize. In this piece Gesualdo admittedly cultivates the contrast of written-out chordal *ritenutos* and the polyphonic elaboration of rapidly declaimed motifs, but these motifs are dry and prosaic, and there is no feeling for the pastoral sensuality of the scene, a sensuality which is its life and justification. Gesualdo is not the man for the pastoral or for a mere game. A good example of his manner is the setting (II, 4) of Torquato Tasso's *Gelo hà Madonna il seno, e fiamma il volto*, one of the pieces not written to a text intended expressly for him, since it had repeatedly been set to music before (Bellasio, 1578, Merulo, 1579, Caimo, Cavalieri, 1585, Macque, 1587, and Monte, 1590). Monte, who provides the most suitable material for comparison in his fourteenth book, takes the text for what it is— an epigrammatic compliment—and gives it a short, light setting, half canzonetta-like, in the Venetian style. Gesualdo gives it a more complex, more refined treatment (see illustration on p. 696).

Here in a nutshell is the early, pre-1594 Gesualdo. He certainly does not make matters easy for himself and from the very outset avoids all obvious use of homophony, without giving up any of the refinements of declamation or of the carefully treated spoken accent. The light text is labored and weighed down with feeling. Gesualdo is aware of this and compensates for it on the architectonic side through repetition; thus he begins the first line in the region of G minor and B-flat major, repeating it in a somewhat varied and richer form in the region of D minor and F major. With sovereign indifference he starts from the sixth chord on G;

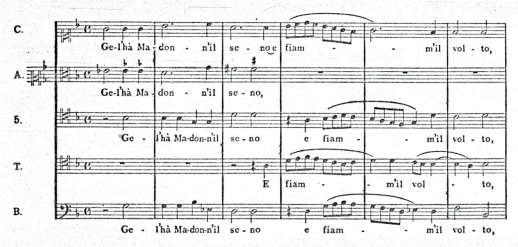

indifference is indeed the chief characteristic of these first two books—not audacity or extreme expression, as might be supposed. Where the *nobile dilettante* betrays himself is in certain awkward and clumsy details—the overcrowded voice-leading, the clashing of the voices, which betrays a strangely defective ear, the insensibility toward false relations, an insensibility characteristic of the whole century, though especially of the time before 1560. In his own time Gesualdo is not surpassed in this by any of his colleagues. "Picturesque" traits such as the coloratura at the word *fiammeggiar* fall more and more into the background as his work progresses, while such symbolisms as the use of two voices at *fra due mi tieni* (in II, 3: *Com'esser può ch'io viva*) eventually disappear almost entirely. But in contrast and in the fluctuation of the tempo Gesualdo hardly goes beyond Marenzio, yet even here one has already the impression of a more pronounced dissociation between the motivically animated sections and those which for expressive reasons are restrained or over-

laden with harmonic allurements. Sometimes his dependence upon Marenzio is thoroughly obvious, for example at the end of the second section of *Baci soavi e cari—Cibi della mia vita*, the first number of the *Secondo libro* (in Pizzetti's reprint), where one voice leads and a pair of voices follow. But despite Marenzio, Gesualdo's own personality already stands out very prominently in these first two books, and it would perhaps be idle to look for further models, just as it is idle to look beyond Tintoretto for El Greco's models.

None the less, the attempt to find such models must be made. They are not to be discovered in Naples. I cannot believe that Giovanni Macque made much impression, even though he worked close at hand, but I cannot be quite certain, since I unfortunately neglected to provide myself with a sufficient number of scores from Macque's madrigal books (the first dated 1576, the last 1613). Maldeghem's reprints of three pieces (VIII, 15-17), one of which does not even have its original text, are utterly useless. Thanks to U. Prota-Giurleo's "Notizie sul musicista belga Jean Macque," a paper printed in the Report of the First Congress of the International Society for Musical Research (Liége, 1930, pp. 191-197), we are now quite well informed about Macque's life. He was born at Valenciennes about 1552 and came to Italy early in life, probably as early as 1566; there he became a pupil of Filippo di Monte—presumably in Rome. At all events, it is in Rome that he signs the dedications of three early madrigal books in 1576, 1579, and 1582, the second one addressed to Scipione Gonzaga, one of Marenzio's patrons. He must at that time have been a member of Marenzio's inner circle for he collaborated with Marenzio, G. N. Nanino, Moscaglia, Soriano, and Zoilo, Roman colleagues of his, in setting Horace's dialogue *Donec gratus eram tibi*: his contribution was the music for the fourth stanza of the Italian translation by Luigi Alamanni, *Hor' un laccio, un'ardore*, written in a refined, easy style—freer than his teacher Monte and more reserved than his rival Marenzio. In 1586 he comes to Naples and enters the service of Fabrizio Gesualdo, the father of our Carlo, who must by this time have been an accomplished musician. In May 1590 he is second organist at the Annunziata, where his associates are Scipione Stella, the first organist, and old Nola, the choirmaster. In 1592 he marries Isabella Tonto, a Neapolitan, and in so doing assumes the obligation never to leave Naples, an obligation that cannot have been much of a burden to him. For in September 1594, on the recommendation of Bartolomeo Roy, he is appointed successor to the Spanish organist of the Royal Chapel, Cristóbal Obregón, and in 1599 he becomes its choirmaster. He died in September 1614. Macque is the last of the Italianized Netherlanders and the teacher of an entire generation of Neapolitan musicians: Trabaci, Francesco Lambardi, Maione, Montella, Spano, Falconieri, and Luigi Rossi. Through Rossi he also becomes one of the ancestors of the "Roman School," which besides Rossi includes Giacomo Carissimi, Tenaglia,

Manelli, and Savioni. But he can scarcely have been Gesualdo's teacher, either directly or indirectly. From the incipits of the motets of 1596 that Pannain has given (*loc. cit.*, pp. xxxiiiff.), it is clear that he was a master with "colorful" tendencies, but at the same time a distinctly temperate individual; the instrumental canzoni that have been preserved (cf. *Monumenta musicae belgicae*, IV, 1938, ed. J. Watelet) reveal a musician of considerable naïveté, gaiety, and folk-like simplicity who is in many respects the direct opposite of Gesualdo. The following madrigal books have been preserved: two books for six voices of 1576 and 1589, the second of which is dedicated to Gesualdo's father, one book for four voices, of 1579, four out of six books for five voices of 1587, 1597, 1599, and 1613 (the first and fifth are lost), two out of three books for four voices of 1586 and 1610 (the second is lost), and two books of six-voiced *madrigaletti e napolitane* of 1581 and 1582. From these it appears that Macque is rather a pupil and successor of Monte than a forerunner of Gesualdo and rather a contemporary of Ingegneri and Wert than a contemporary of Marenzio. His favorite poets are still Sannazaro, Petrarch, and Bernardo Tasso; even from Torquato Tasso he selects remarkably little. Late in life Macque does seem to have come closer to Gesualdo's style. In Bernardo Bolognini's first book of madrigals for five voices (1604, not listed by Vogel) is included his *Chi vuol veder un Sole*, which clearly resembles Gesualdo in its alterations of rapid contrapuntal weaving and harmonically emphasized *ritenutos*, in its combination of rhythmic and harmonic freedom. But Macque is more moderate, more harmonic, and more "normal." This is necessarily a general appraisal, but one which more detailed investigation should confirm.

However this may be, the true Gesualdo, the Gesualdo who made the impression upon the following generation and upon posterity in general, does not appear until after 1594. It is a piece from his sixth book of which Pietro della Valle writes in his famous letter to Lelio Guidiccioni: "For its pitying and compassionate expression I particularly liked the Prince of Venosa's *Resta di darmi noia*, a famous piece" (". . . per affetto pietoso e compassionevole [mi piaceva] *Resta di darmi noia* del Principe di Venosa, famoso madrigale..."). And significantly enough it is a piece that is most extreme in its attitude. What caused this radical change in Gesualdo? Or ought we rather to ask what caused this development of the eccentric side of his nature? Was it his acquaintance with the music and musicians of Ferrara? Luzzasco Luzzaschi, who stood at the head of the Este court music, dedicated his fourth book of madrigals to Gesualdo on September 10, 1594, less than a year after Gesualdo's arrival in Ferrara. This is striking, and it is still more striking that until now no one has ever looked into this book in connection with Gesualdo. For in the dedication Luzzaschi expressly says: "Inasmuch as Your Excellency has in various ways made known to the world, both far and near, that you esteem my compo-

sitions, feeble though they be, I have resolved to dedicate to Your Excellency the first appearance of these madrigals, which now leave my hands" — "Havendo Vostra Eccellenza con diverse maniere, mostrato al Mondo di stimare, et lontano, et vicino, le mie, ancorche deboli compositioni: . . . ho resoluto di consacrarle il parto di questi Madrigali, che hora escono dalle mie mani. . . ." Thus the Prince must already have known Luzzaschi's madrigals in Naples. In his second book of 1576 (the first seems not to have been preserved), Luzzasco was already giving free rein to his tendency toward extreme expression in his setting of Dante's terze rime (*Quivi sospiri*). The third book, too, contains such somber pieces as the sonnet *Quest'è, fortuna ria, quella ferita*, with an epitaph in "black" notes at the end, but it also contains one of Petrarch's most attractive sonnets (*Per far una leggiadra sua vendetta*) and a number of playful, pastoral pieces that are almost cantatas:

> "Fuggiti dal mio raggio,
> Pastor gentil e saggio;
> Fuggiti da quest'onda,
> Che l'un'abbruccia troppo e l'altro innonda,
> E vattene all'armento,
> Se non vuoi quì restar di vita spento!"
> Così dicea Licori,
> Cogliend'erbette e fiori.

Like Marenzio, Luzzasco often descends to "eye-music."

None of this looks very much like anticipation of Gesualdo, and the book of 1594 with its dedication to Gesualdo also falls short of our expectations on this point. (Incidentally, it contains one palpably older piece, *Tu ribello d'Amor*, which had already appeared four years earlier [1590[5]] in a Venetian collection.) In this book Luzzasco appears partly as a follower of Giaches Wert and Ingegneri, particularly in the pieces written in the *misura comune*, in the ₵ measure, which he regards as the most suitable for pathetic texts, as do Wert and Marenzio. His setting of *Dolorosi martir, fieri tormenti* (No. 14), a stanza by Tansillo, looks as though he had intended to outdo Ingegneri and Marenzio (cf. p. 615 above), and if this was his intention, he has certainly succeeded.[3]

But this fails again to make him an example or model for Gesualdo, either in its melody or in its chromaticism, for the Prince is working in a totally different direction. Yet in another respect he is most decidedly a model, namely in his tendency to repeat certain sections of the text in elaborated form. Our example (No. 3) points in its opening measures to the "three ladies":

[3] See Vol. III, No. 81.

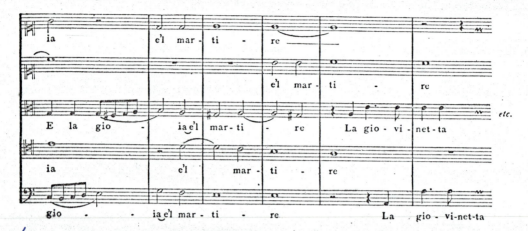

Things of this sort made an impression on Gesualdo, though he prefers to transpose the repetition at once and though he cultivates a closer and more compact texture: with him everything is from the first more energetic, restless, and impassioned than it is with Luzzasco, who tends to be more quiet and harmonious. Yet this connection between Luzzasco and Gesualdo is no idle construction of ours. It rests above all on Luzzaschi's one extant posthumous work, the *Seconda scelta delli madrigali* of 1613, published in Naples by Giovanni Giacomo Carlino six years after the composer's death. Significantly enough, Carlino was Gesualdo's publisher, and it is not improbable that Gesualdo paid for the printing of Luzzasco's book. It is evidently a selection from pieces written at different times, and it is at least possible that some of these may belong before 1594, just as it is also possible that Luzzasco himself may have learned something from Gesualdo. At all events, the close relationship between the two masters is only too evident in the following example of "elaborated repetition" (No. 11):

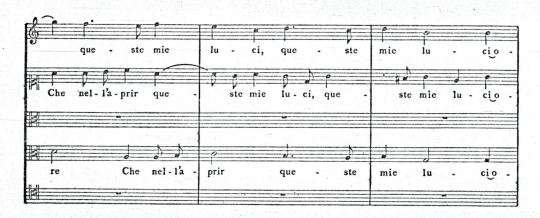

The resemblances and differences are obvious enough: Gesualdo is to Luzzasco about what Tintoretto is to Titian or El Greco to Tintoretto: from the outset he goes further harmonically, his motifs are less simple and "diatonic," he avoids pairing his voices. But fundamentally the two styles are the same. In both there is the same breaking-up of the piece by rests in all the voices, both have the same motet-like expositions in close imitation and the same epigrammatic brevity. And that there are no written-out repetitions of endings in this posthumous book of Luzzasco's makes it seem even more epigrammatic. Perhaps this was due to economic considerations; if Luzzasco had been able to publish the book himself, he would no doubt have expanded the single pieces by repeating the music for the last couplets in a more or less elaborated form, as is Gesualdo's almost invariable practice.

How closely Gesualdo approaches the Ferrarese madrigal style can be seen in the work of a musician who represents this style in its purest form. This is Count Alfonso Fontanelli, who cannot very well have studied with anyone but Luzzasco.

A Ferrarese nobleman, Fontanelli was a dilettante like Striggio, Gesualdo, Del Turco, and Guglielmo Gonzaga, but he was perhaps more gifted than any of these —one might call him Gesualdo's harmonious and well-balanced counterpart. In 1595 he published his first madrigal book at Ferrara—anonymously, though the signatures on the gatherings reveal his name. A second edition appeared in 1603, edited by no less a person than Orazio Vecchi, who calls it "full of novelty, dignity, grace, and temperament" ("piena di novità, di dignità, di diletto, e d'affetto"). A second book of 1604 went through three editions. As the printer explains, Fontanelli has in this book deliberately avoided uniformity in style and has even lowered the general level with a view to pleasing various tastes ("l'autore schivando a studio l'egualità dello stile, anzi alcune volte artificiosamente abbassandolo, [per] dar sodisfatione a tutti, secondo la diversità de gusti loro . . ."). Fontanelli was admired not only by Vecchi but also by Peri and Monteverdi, and this is easy to understand. The verb *abbassare* by no means implies the adoption of a popular style; Fontanelli uses it only for gay pieces and handles it with extraordinary ease, grace, and fluency.

In Luzzasco one can also find parallels for Gesualdo's experiments in harmony. But in this respect he is less one-sided than the Prince, and it must be admitted that he is also less insistent. A piece like *Gioite voi col canto* (No. 13) is shot through with "linear" chromaticism of the sort that Gesualdo seldom uses (see example below). But *Itene mie querele* (No. 17), a piece reprinted in our volume of illustrations,[4] could almost be by Gesualdo himself, despite the notation in the *misura comune*, if Luzzaschi had only made more frequent use of the alternation of agitated, extravagantly harmonized choral declamation with imitative expositions. Incidentally, the use of this written-out *ritenuto* in connection with harmonic audacities is not only characteristic of Gesualdo and his circle, it is also characteristic of the later madri-

[4] See Vol. III, No. 82.

gal in general. A striking illustration occurs among the four-voiced madrigals of Antonio Buonavita (1587) in *Tu che fai ghiaccio il foco,* at "Alla mia cruda pena al mio dolore." Buonavita was a nobleman of Pisa, a Knight of St. Stephen ("nobile pisano, cavaliere [di Santo Stefano]"), and a cathedral organist; he cannot have been influenced by Gesualdo and can scarcely have influenced Gesualdo himself.

On the whole, however, it seems to me that the most likely explanation for the change in Gesualdo's style is that he discovered Nicolo Vicentino's "archicembalo" in the famous instrument collection of the Dukes of Ferrara and that he made himself familiar with it. Ercole Bottrigari gives an account of this instrument in his *Desiderio* (reprinted in the *Veröffentlichungen der Musik-Bibliothek Paul Hirsch,* No. 5, 1924, ed. Kathi Meyer, pp. 40f.) and classes it among the instruments "not used," since it was rarely played because of the difficulty of mastering it, tuning it, and keeping it in tune. But a few pages later on he tells us that Luzzaschi played it perfectly and that he composed special pieces for it (". . . il Luzzasco Organista principale di sua Altezza, lo maneggia molto delicatamente, con alcune compositioni di Musica fatte da lui a questo proposito solo . . ."). Vicentino's instrument was not unique. From the Opus IV of Martino Pesenti, the lovable blind composer and clavier master of Venice in the first half of the seventeenth century, we learn of a similar *clavicembalo,* built by Vido Trasentino in 1601; we know also of Zarlino's chromatic and enharmonic clavier, which Pesenti characteristically preferred to Vido's (cf. Cat. Bologna, IV, 136/137). Burney saw it in Florence in 1770 (*Present State . . . ,* p. 253). In Pesenti's "enharmonic" music there is of course no question of a full understanding of equal temperament and the possibilities of modulation seventy-five years before the time of Bach, but it shows some understanding of transposition, for example when a Corrente is printed first in D minor and immediately afterwards in A-sharp minor.

It would perhaps be too much to expect the same understanding from Gesualdo in 1594. Yet many passages seem to show it, and traces of an acquaintance with some chromatic-enharmonic instrument are found in his later work on every hand. Did it lose by this? Did it gain by this? I am inclined to think that it did both and to consider this the solution of the "Gesualdo controversy." He is an insufferable mannerist when, with his predilection for the extreme, he uses his extreme style for the sake of the style alone; he is a genuine artist when he finds ways of using it with feeling, with significance, and with force. Posterity's attitude toward him will continue to change and will depend always upon the extent to which his expression is held to be truthful and sincere; it is not surprising that he should have fared worse in the time of John Christian Bach, in Burney's *History of Music*, than he fares today in the time of Stravinsky and Schönberg. Perhaps the pendulum will swing to the other side again before long.

The third and fourth books of 1595 and 1596 were still published in Ferrara and as usual are dedicated to the composer himself, this time by one Ettore Gesualdo, perhaps a relative or a member of his household; they contain a number of older pieces that the Prince has carelessly left lying about ("lasciati andare per le tavole trascurati"), as we learn from the dedication to Book IV. To this category belongs the bipartite madrigal (III, 10) *Meraviglia d'amore* (Pizzetti), a piece marked by certain archaistic traits, for example the B-flat triad on *dolce*, the angularity of the declamation, which moves by fits and starts, and the strange harmonies, perhaps unintended, as at *ma spiri l'aura*. It is a compliment to a lady—a Laura—and contains no reference to death or dying, something most unusual with Gesualdo. Only at these associations does his imagination take fire, as for example in (III, 3) *Languisco e moro! Ahi cruda* (Pizzetti); here the vocal line becomes marvelously free, the harmonic conflict at *dolorosa morte* is genuinely felt, and through choral responses the whole takes on a certain "static" or architectonic quality. It has a hidden affinity to monody, though Gesualdo has nothing to do with monody and monodists: he requires richer means of expression. He clings to the madrigal, and this, too, is significant for his ambiguous historical position: on the one side, that of harmony, he is extraordinarily modern—on the other side he is already out-of-date. And unlike Monteverdi, Gagliano, and their fellow innovators, he has no operatic safety-valve.

A companion piece to *Languisco e moro* is (III, 9) *Non t'amo ò voce ingrata* (Torchi, V, 1; also Pizzetti). The text is an epigrammatic trifle:

> "Non t'amo," ò voce ingrata!
> La mia Donna mi disse,
> E con pungente strale
> Di duol e di martir l'alma trafisse.

Lasso, ben fu la piaga aspra e mortale;
Pur vissi e vivo; ahi non si può morire
Di duol e di martire!

But for Gesualdo "death" and "pain" always have their full literal meaning; the words themselves are enough to stimulate him. In this case he distinctly overdoes the chromaticisms, the unprepared six-four chords, and the passing dissonances, but despite the ninth-leap in the bass, the ending is restrained and conciliating, in Marenzio's style. It is a forced antithesis. In compensation, Gesualdo shows real understanding for the madrigal style in the last number of the book (Torchi, v, 7), a piece for six voices:

Donna, se m'ancidete,
La mia vita sarete ...

The recurrence of this opening couplet at the end of the piece, with the lines in inverse order, rounds out the form of the whole. It is as though Gesualdo had arranged a monody for six voices, just as Monteverdi later arranged his *Lamento d'Arianna* as a five-voiced madrigal. The first soprano by itself would make an expressive monody:

Don - na,   se m'an - ci - de - te,   La mia vi - ta sa - re - te...

But it is no more expressive than the other voices or than the whole, the ensemble, which contains no special audacity unless the suspended sevenths are to be so considered. From this piece we may perhaps form an idea of what Gesualdo's lost book of six-voiced madrigals must have been like; of the book itself, posthumously published in 1626 by the reactionary Muzio Effrem, we have only the Quinto.

The fourth book has as its first number another formal masterpiece, *Luci serene e chiare* (Weismann 1). It has a canzonetta text—a further indication of how "unliterary" and violent the musician Gesualdo is: three stanzas of three lines each in the form a a B! Poetically, the second stanza is a mere variant of the first, and Gesualdo accordingly makes its musical setting a variant, a modified second *Stollen*, in order to reserve the full force of the expression for the *Abgesang*; this is likewise repeated in the form of a heightened variant. Although each word receives its emotional accent, the whole does not suffer as it so often does with Marenzio. This applies also to the bipartite madrigal *Io tacerò, ma nel silentio mio* (Weismann IV/V and Pizzetti; the first section also reprinted by Andrea della Corte in his *Scelta di musiche*, 1928, No. 45, with a horrible misprint on page 77 in measure 5). It is significant that Gesualdo resorts to the naturalistic rest at the word *sospiri*, though only once and in the soprano: he is not above using any device that is expressive or expressionistic. Everything in this piece is expressive, almost exhibitionistic; it is as though some indiscreet, shameless, uncompromising person were making a painful, public confession. It ends with a tortured false relation. There follows a vision in the manner of El Greco, a spiritual madrigal (IV, 8; Pizzetti):

> Sparge la Morte al mio Signor nel viso
> Tra squallidi pallori
> Pietosissimi orrori.
> Poi lo rimira e ne divien pietosa:
> Geme e sospira, e più ferir non osa.
> Ei, che temer la mira,
> Inchina il capo, asconde il viso, e spira.

As Gesualdo's counterpart in the field of the fine arts, El Greco is perhaps too classic a master for a piece like this and one ought rather to think of Bernini: Grim Death beholds the Saviour on the Cross and dares not strike again, but moans and sighs. The text is not from Angelo Grillo's *Essequie di Giesù Cristo*, as one might suppose; Tasso's friend was a man of taste. Gesualdo was not; he spares us nothing, not even the most violent expression. Such is the music with which Good Friday was celebrated in Gesualdo's chapel. In comparison with this, our next number (IV, 13; Pizzetti) is a mere game in which the use of the word *morte* is purely literary:

> Arde il mio cor, ed è sì dolce il foco,
> Che vive nell'ardore,
> Onde lieto si more.
> O mia felice sorte,
> O dolce, o strana morte!

Its effect is heightened by an elaborated repetition of the three lines at the beginning (in so far as one can speak in this connection of beginning and end) and by an emphatic repetition of the last couplet; the tonality is retained throughout. To deal with the word *strano* Gesualdo has of course the ideal equipment. After this, it is not easy to understand why Gesualdo should be in dead earnest when he comes to this wholly similar text (IV, 12; Weismann, No. 2):

> Ecco morirò dunque
> Ne fia che pur rimire
> Tu, ch'ancidi mirand'il mio morire.
> Ahi, già mi discoloro, ohimè, vien meno
> La luce a gli occhi miei, la voce al seno.
> O che morte gradita,
> S'almen potessi dir: "moro, mia vita!"

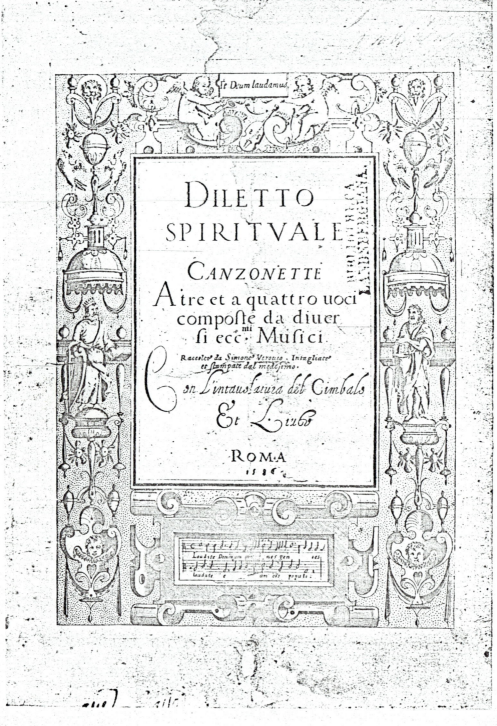

Title Page of "Diletto spirituale." Rome 1586. Simone Verovio. One of the
first specimens of engraved music

A tre soprani

Terzetto for Three Sopranos with Accompaniment of the Harpsichord,
by Luzzasco Luzzaschi. Rome 1601. Verovio.

This combines—or rather, fails to combine—extreme antitheses of tempo and harmony: this last heightening of the *espressivo* brings about the complete disintegration of a style that had once been style. An intermediate stage in this process of disintegration may be seen in what is perhaps Gesualdo's most familiar madrigal (IV, 9), *Moro, e mentre sospiro* (Martini, *Saggio*, II, 198, and Kiesewetter, *Schicksale*, No. 35; cf. also Winterfeld, *Johannes Gabrieli*, III, 118); here the contrast between the weighty harmonies of the Largo and the imitative Vivace is defined with all possible sharpness.

There is an interval of fifteen years between the appearance of Gesualdo's fourth madrigal book and that of his fifth and sixth (1611), both of which were edited by a certain Don Giovanni Pietro Cappuccio, who dedicated them to their composer. But his style no longer changes in any essential respect. Neither one contains a single bipartite piece; his texts become shorter and shorter and more and more epigrammatic; they are now mere excuses for the music with which he provides them. The fifth book contains a single text by Guarini (*T'amo mia vita*, the final number), while the sixth book does not contain one literary name worth mentioning. The poet has merely to supply the oxymora—the stark contrasts of images, feelings, and ideas. And to call Gesualdo "the musician of the oxymoron" would be to give him the most concise characterization possible. Thus a text that is barely more than the empty shell of something that may once have been a thought or a poem can call forth the most animated and uncompromising sort of music (v, 5; Pizzetti):

> O dolorosa gioia,
> O soave dolore,
> Per cui quest'alma è mesta e lieta more!
> O miei cari sospiri,
> Miei graditi martiri,
> Del vostro duol non mi lasciate privo,
> Poi che sì dolce mi fa morto, e vivo!

Another example for the growing antagonism between harmonic audacity and the linear, for Gesualdo's stylistic dualism, and for the irreconcilable contrast is (v, 15) *Tu m'uccidi, o crudele* (Pizzetti): still another is the following (v, 11; Keiner and Pizzetti):

> Mercè grido piangendo,
> Ma chi m'ascolta, ahi lasso—io vengo meno!
> Morrò dunque tacendo!
> Deh, per pietade almeno,
> Dolce del cor tesoro,
> Potessi dirti pria ch'io mora: "io moro."

The "expression" in this sort of piece is astonishing, but it would be difficult to determine exactly where sincerity of feeling ends and mannerism begins. Another number is distinguished by sheer virtuosity (v, 3; Torchi, and Weismann, No. 7):

> Itene, o miei sospiri
> Precipitate il volo
> A lei . . .

In this Gesualdo has in his own way unquestionably surpassed Marenzio by over-doing the contrasts and by exaggerated and exceptional treatments of such words as *sospiri, volo, bella, cangerò* (a change to triple time, following a model by Luz-zasco), and *canto*. It has a sort of parallel in (v, 4) *Dolcissima mia vita, a che tardate,* a piece now available in three modern reprints (Torchi; Schering, *Geschichte der Musik in Beispielen*, No. 167; Weismann vi). This, too, is still in Marenzio's style, but still more in Gesualdo's own: to Marenzio belong the runs in sixteenths on *ardo, fuoco, bramare,* and *desire,* to Gesualdo the violent chromaticism. In the interests of a quite personal—one might almost say "egotistical"—style, all the hard-won means of expression that had been developed in the course of a century are here exploited to the limit; applied to a text that cannot tolerate such excessive treatment, the style becomes absurd.

In the sixth book *Itene, o miei sospiri* has another parallel in *Già piansi nel dolore* (Torchi, iv, 13); and this perhaps explains why the piece was omitted in the second, Venetian edition of the book, along with *Quando ridente e bella*. In this farewell book, the dualism that runs through Gesualdo's entire work repeats itself on a grand scale. One has the impression that the unknown poet (for the whole seems to be the work of one and the same person) was asked to supply only two kinds of verse and to supply these in equal proportion—that half the pieces were to contain the word *morte* or *morire*, that the other half was to consist of lively pastoral pieces, and that the whole was to be as epigrammatic and as full of oxymora as possible. But Gesualdo is now less than ever the man for pure joy, for the idyl, for innocence. Pizzetti has reprinted one of these pieces, *Volan quasi farfalle*—this time without reducing the note values—and one can see from this example that Gesualdo succeeds only in being restless and capriciously nervous. Other pieces of this sort are *Al mio gioir il ciel si fa sereno, Alme d'amor rubelle,* and *Candido e verde fiore.* In every one Gesualdo is hemmed in by his own manner. He is happier—and we are happier with him—only when his text meets him halfway with something piquant, as in the madrigal on the gnat, the pseudo-Vergilian *culex,* a tiny creature who plays a great role in Italian poetry:

Ardita zanzaretta
  Morde colei che il mio cor strugge e tiene
  In così crude pene.
Fugge poi e rivola
  In quel bel seno che'l mio cor invola.
  Indi la prende e stringe e le da morte
  Per sua felice sorte.
Ti morderò ancor io,
  Dolce amato ben mio,
  E se mi prendi e stringi, ahi verrò meno,
  Provand'in quel bel sen dolce veneno.

The opening could not possibly be more lifelike:

The suspended ninth in the soprano against the bass entrance is just as permissible from the point of view of vivid tone-painting as the stubborn declamation of the tenor in the fourth measure. Equally vivid and naturalistic, almost pathological, is the conclusion:

As expression this is inimitable, even today. But in other instances the same sort of thing leads merely to a baroque exaggeration that is outright mannerism, for example in the very next madrigal:

> Ardo per te, mio bene, ma l'ardore
> Spira dolc'aura al core;
> Moro per te, mia vita, ma'l morire
> Gioia divien, dolcissimo il languire.
> Felice stella, ancor ch'io ard'e moia,
> L'ardor divien dolc'aura, e'l morir gioia.

This stanza, or one very much like it, might even have been set to music by Arcadelt, who would have represented "joy" by a gentle melisma and "sweetness" by an inclination toward the E-flat major triad. Here is what Gesualdo does with it:

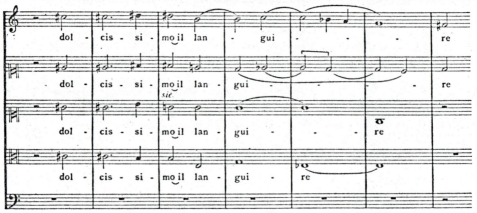

A popular Petrarchism—"sweet bitterness" or "bitter sweetness"—has finally found its full musical expression. Where this kind of contradiction is involved, there is no rule that Gesualdo does not violate. In the style of the time, one poem develops this pretty theme—a lover's kisses stifle his beloved's "no":

> Quel nò crudel, che la mia speme uccise
> Ecco che pur trafitto
> Da mille baci di mia bocca ultrice
> Qual fiera serpe in mezz'a i fiori essangue
> Tra quelle belle labbra a morte langue.
> O vittoria felice!
> In quel vago rossor gli amanti scritto
> Leggan di quel bel volto: hà vinto Amore!
> Amor vinc'ogni core.

The beginning says a great deal in a few notes, resembling in this the beginning of the *Tristan* prelude:

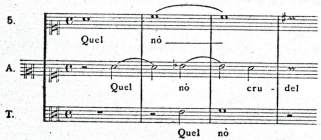

The whole book is full of these harmonic refinements and extravagances. There is scarcely any possibility that Gesualdo did not use at one time or another. In this book his special predilection is a change of harmonic function in the bass or in some other stationary part. *Deh come in van sospiro* contains a short example of this:

There is a longer one in *O dolce mio tesoro*:

It is impossible to sing three such pieces one after the other without being seized by a sort of nausea or musical sea-sickness, for the dose is too strong and the unsteadiness too prolonged. They are effective only when considered one at a time and as a final consequence of a one-sided development, as a special case. But they have an overwhelming effect when the text is one that has moved Gesualdo deeply and when all frivolity is put aside. This is the case with the madrigal *Resta di darmi noia*, which Leichtentritt (Ambros, IV, 211) and Pizzetti have done well to reprint:

> Cease now, no longer plague me,
> Deceitful thought and cruel,
> For I can never be what you desire.
> Dead is for me all joy;
> And never may I hope
> To know what gladness is.

Tortured harmony and restless declamation have been transformed from mannerism into full-blown expression, and this expression is the more affecting if one considers the piece as an autobiographical confession. And why should one not allow music, in Gesualdo, what one has so often allowed the fine arts and poetry, in Michelangelo and Rembrandt and in Goethe and Shelley? Autobiographical confession is unquestionably present in No. 10:

> Io pur respiro in così gran dolore—
> E tu pur vivi o dispietato core?
> Ahi che non vi è pur spene
> Di riveder il nostro amato bene!
> Deh morte danne aita,
> Uccidi questa vita,
> Pietosa ne ferisci, e un colpo solo
> A la vita dia fin ed al gran duolo.

Where are we to draw the line in this between stark naturalism and highest expression, between symbolism and self-confession? The laborious "breathing," the "pain," the agitated invocation of Death—everything is depicted, and the concealing of "un colpo *solo*" in a single voice can only have been symbolically intended. But it has also an uncanny effect when it is declaimed by a murderer who is haunted by the memory of his victim's wounds (see example on pp. 716-717).

Here one has the expressionist Gesualdo, Prince of Venosa, in a nutshell. He stands at the end and at the peak of a long development, which began with Willaert and Rore and in which every madrigalist has played his part, great or small. The development ends in a blind alley: beyond the peak yawns the abyss. And as their escape is cut off, the desperate ones hemmed in lose themselves in lofty aspirations.

Every chord is tested, every transposition permitted. But the little modulations from C major to G, such as occur in the canzonette of Ferretti or Orazio Vecchi, point the way to freedom and the future, and are worth more historically than all Gesualdo's audacity. It is not correct to say that Gesualdo had neither imitators nor successors: he certainly had both, at least among the composers of accompanied monody, and it is highly significant that the most outspoken and unmistakable of them all, Sigismondo d'India, was likewise a South Italian, a Sicilian. In Naples and Palermo the most extravagant baroque flourishes in church and palace and in music. But in the history of the madrigal Gesualdo is really an end.

CLAUDIO MONTEVERDI

IT has already been explained (p. 608) that the present chapter can cover only a part of Monteverdi's contribution to the literature of the madrigal—that part in which the composer still keeps within the traditional limits of the style and in which he may still be considered the contemporary of those other great virtuosi, Marenzio and Gesualdo. This is possible only in his first four madrigal books, of 1587, 1590, 1592, and 1603. For with the fifth he takes the first step towards a break with the past which is and remains a break, no matter how carefully it has been prepared by his own efforts and those of a number of his contemporaries.

What are Monteverdi's origins? He was born in 1567 in Cremona, where he was a pupil of Marc'Antonio Ingegneri of Verona, a man of great character and personal charm who had settled permanently at Cremona about the time of his great pupil's birth. Monteverdi, a child prodigy, published his first work at the age of fifteen (*Cantiunculae sacrae*, for three voices, 1582), and for years to come, indeed until 1590, he continued to acknowledge his indebtedness to Ingegneri. This should suffice for the present. Ingegneri himself had been a pupil of our old friend Vincenzo Ruffo during the decade when Ruffo was the choirmaster at the cathedral in Ingegneri's native Verona (to 1563); in the years that followed he had been privileged to be the intimate friend and personal pupil of Cipriano Rore in Parma, as he proudly and reverently acknowledges.

But Monteverdi has little more in common with Ingegneri than Philipp Emanuel with Johann Sebastian Bach or Hector Berlioz with Lesueur and Reicha. The two generations to which they belong are too different, and the possibilities of musical development were now too varied and too extensive to permit the character of the younger musician to be exclusively determined by his teacher. Monteverdi does not even follow his master in external things. Ingegneri never stooped to write villanelle or canzonette, but Monteverdi's first secular publication (1584) is a collection of twenty-one canzonette for three voices, sparkling with life, witty, informal in their technique, modeled in a general way on Primavera and dell'Arpa. Ingegneri publishes a book of madrigals for four voices in 1578 (his first work, actually written about 1565) and another in 1579, a book of madrigals for six voices (1586), and five books of madrigals for five voices (from about 1569 to 1587). Monteverdi publishes a book of madrigals for five voices in 1587 and adheres to this standard combination of voices for the remainder of his life. (The complete works of Monteverdi have been available since 1926 in an edition by G. Francesco Malipiero: *Tutte le opere di C. M. . . . Nuovamente date in luce.*)

Above all, however, the inner natures of master and pupil are diametrically opposed. This can no longer be questioned since the publication of a considerable—though by no means sufficiently comprehensive—selection from Ingegneri's four- and five-voiced madrigals in the Italian "Denkmäler" (*Istituzioni e monumenti dell'arte musicale italiana*, vi, ed. Cesari and Pannain), to which may be added Ellinor Dohrn's *Marc'Antonio Ingegneri als Madrigal-Componist* (Hanover, 1930). Even more than Lasso or Monte, Ingegneri belongs among the immediate followers of Cipriano Rore, to whom he stands in about the same relation as Fra Giovanni Angelo da Montorsoli, with his statues of SS. Cosmas and Damian, to Michelangelo, with his representations of Night and Morning in the Sagrestia Nuova in Florence. In either case there is an undeniable relation of pupil to master and an undeniable similarity in style; in either case the work of the younger man reveals a certain smoothness and elegance when it is compared with the rough-hewn grandeur of the work of the older man. Ingegneri divides his music into pieces in the *misura comune* and pieces in the *misura cromatica* just as Rore does, and like Rore he tends to use the one measure for the pathetic and expressive pieces, the other for the less grave ones. Ingegneri shares Rore's predilection for daring, extreme harmonies, but he is smoother, more harmonious, less experimental than his uncompromising master.

Ingegneri shares Rore's seriousness in the choice of texts and, like Rore, turns very rarely to Petrarch, all the oftener to Bembo, and draws frequently on Ariosto, but also on Vittoria Colonna and Parabosco and on Guarini and Torquato Tasso among the living. Spiritual madrigals are characteristically frequent and Ingegneri betrays his North Italian origin by his liking for the *canzon francese*, which he uses as a setting for narrative ottave; there are even two genuine chansons in his third book of five-voiced madrigals, and the first book of his madrigals for four voices contains two "arie di canzon francese" which are not so much instrumental music as they are schemes to be adapted to texts in a specific form—that of the ottava rima. Ingegneri is one of the most skillful of those who brought the madrigal to perfection: for all his gentle agitation he is always self-possessed; for all his high seriousness he is always judicious and tasteful; he is a pure classicist, a master of form.

Of Monteverdi, on the other hand, we may say that from first to last he was the very opposite of a classicist. Thus in his first madrigal book he is already as unlike his teacher as possible. This is even evident in an external trait that is in reality not external at all—he no longer uses the *misura comune* and knows only four-four time. On opening his book, one has the impression that it is a collection of canzonette. The very first number, *Ch'ami la vita mia nel tuo bel nome*, is a musical dedication whose text plays on the name "Verità"; it begins in the spirited, buoyant manner of a villanella for three voices, but the significant thing is the way in which he underscores "the afflicted heart"—the phrase is stated twice, in a slow tempo that stands out from the context and with incisive harmonies:

One need pay no attention to the thinly disguised fifths in the first measure; in general, Monteverdi's part-writing is not free from slips, especially outright octaves.

Generally speaking, the basic attitude of this madrigal book is anacreontic, though there are frequent overtones of passion and tension. A piece like No. 12, *Uscian ninfe omai*, maintains the light pastoral style throughout, but its loving elaboration of occasional details prevents its becoming a mere canzonetta. Another piece (No. 8) is a "parody":

> **Poi che del mio dolore**
> **Tanto ti nutri, amore,**
> **Libera mai quest'alma non vedrai,**

Fin che per gl'occhi fuore,
Lasso, non venga il core!

The "original" of this stanza was often set to music:

Poi che'l mio largo pianto,
Amor, ti piace tanto,
Asciutti mai quest'occhi non vedrai,
Fin che non mandi fuore,
Ohimè, per gli occhi il cuore!

Monteverdi begins rather seriously in a sustained style but is unable to resist the temptation to introduce certain lively canzonetta-like details. Ingegneri seldom if ever does so. In his choice of texts, Monteverdi is surprisingly independent, unconventional, and modern. Ingegneri is still quite as literary as Rore: he clings to the ottava and the sonnet, even to the sestina. But Monteverdi has whole-heartedly adopted the epigrammatically pointed madrigal of Guarini and Tasso and their imitators, and it is a rare and exceptional thing for him to set a sonnet or an ottava. Not until the end of his career does he take up the sonnet and sestina again—we shall see why. It is characteristic that one of his texts is already a little cantata, though it was first published in 1565 in Atanagi's *Rime* (1, 15ª), two years before he was born:

Fumia la pastorella
Tessendo ghirlandetta
Sen gìa cantando in un prato di fiori;
. . . .
Ella rivolta al Sole
Dicea queste parole:
"Almo, divino raggio
. . . .
Deh quel, che sì ci annoia,
Cangia in letitia, e'n gioia."
Allhora i pastor tutti
Del Tebro, et Ninfe a schiera
Corsero a l'harmonia lieti, e veloci. . . .

This tripartite text, the work of Antonio Allegretti, had been set to music as early as 1582 by Pietro Bianco (*Primo libro a 4*) as a canzone for a wedding celebration; his second stanza is for three voices only, and the whole is madrigalesque and somewhat neutral. With Monteverdi the piece becomes a pastoral idyl that has the swing of a canzonetta. This first book of Monteverdi's is entirely free from literary pre-

tension, and it seems almost an accident that it should contain settings of G. B. Strozzi's *Questa ordì 'l laccio* or of Guarini's *Baci soavi e cari*, a text that he could have found in Girolamo Belli's madrigals of 1582—almost an accident that it should conclude with Guarini's *Ardo sì, ma non t'amo*, a text set over and over again; to this Monteverdi adds Tasso's "risposta" and "contrarisposta," making a little cycle of the whole that is already in a sort of *stile concitato*, agitated and epigrammatic— already a cycle of little character pieces. Monteverdi dedicates this first work of his to Count Marco Verità, who figures as a poet in Carlo Fiamma's great collection of madrigal texts (1610-1611), but he seems never to have set to music a single line by this patron. In a word, the break with the past is already an accomplished fact in these first madrigals, written in the composer's twentieth year: like Gesualdo, but *before* Gesualdo, Monteverdi has no respect for literary quality as such—to him a text is simply a text, and not a poem. He chooses them for their anacreontic content and for the possibilities they afford him to indulge his predilection for dissonant tensions and clashes, for from the first he has a liking for motivic combination and harmonic coloring. He is Ingegneri's pupil only on the title page. And he is a second-generation pupil of Rore's only in so far as he acknowledges no tradition and stands out as a distinct personality in his first madrigal book. For Rore knows neither the pastoral nor the anacreontic madrigal. It is a strange crossing of relationships: Ingegneri's real pupil is Marenzio, with his fine sense for literary values, a man who is still loyal to Petrarch and Sannazaro; Monteverdi, on the other hand, seems more dependent on Andrea Gabrieli and his fellow Venetians, at least in so far as they cultivate the pastoral and enliven their madrigals with style-elements borrowed from the canzonetta.

Monteverdi's second madrigal book was published in 1590 with a dedication dated January 1, that is to say after an interval of three years, a considerable period in view of his rapid development. He seems suddenly to have become "literary," though not at all in the sense that he turns back to the "classical" period of Italian poetry— with one strange exception. He has discovered Torquato Tasso. No less than eleven texts, out of a total of twenty-one, are the work of Tasso, among them the opening sonnet, and at least five of these had never been set to music before. The change doubtless has something to do with Tasso's renewed relations with Guglielmo Gonzaga and with his son Vincenzo, who succeeded him in the early autumn of 1587. Tasso, released from his prison in Ferrara, had come to Mantua in July 1586, and he remained on friendly terms with Vincenzo even though he did not stay in Mantua for long. Thus it seems likely that Monteverdi was commissioned to set some of these poems as soon as they were received. Other poems in the book are by Girolamo Casone (*Bevea Fillide mia, Non giacinti ò narcisi,* and *Quell'ombra esser vorrei,* a text set to music by Marenzio as early as 1585), Filippo Alberti (*Tutte le bocche belle* and *Ti spontò l'ali amor*), and Ercole Bentivoglio (*La bocca onde l'asprissime parole*); the last text in the book is by Pietro Bembo (*Cantai un tempo*), so that there remain only three anonymous pieces.

Critics have wondered why Monteverdi set this last piece of Bembo's in a style quite different from all the rest; it is an archaistic motet-like style with luxuriant melismas and an uninterrupted flow of the five voices, somewhat in the style of the Rore of 1542 or 1544 or of Willaert's *Musica nova*. He did so simply because the sonnet was an "old" one, written nearly a hundred years earlier than his music. Monteverdi set only the quatrains to music. How differently he proceeds when he turns to a sonnet by a contemporary, for example the opening number, Tasso's *Non si levava ancor l'alba novella*! This is a show piece, half in the style of the *canzon francese*, half freely madrigalesque, and quite like Marenzio in its broad treatment of the situation and character of the two lovers who figure in this *partenza*; it is one of the few examples in Monteverdi to show him under the influence of Marenzio. The opening with its double motif is quite characteristic:

Non si le - va-va an - cor l'al - ba no - vel - - - la   etc.

Monteverdi is obliged to paint the rising dawn in accordance with the conventions of the madrigal, but he adds a descending motif in order to give the necessary negation: "*Not yet* has risen the new dawn." Marenzio's influence is also to be observed elsewhere in this restless and heterogeneous book, for example in *Mentre io mirava fiso*, another of its outstanding pieces, a humorous affair in which the bass and soprano have descending scales in half notes (*Facendo mille scherzi e mille giri*) while the inner voices frolic about in the intervening tonal space. In this book, written at twenty-three, one can already observe that the madrigal is approaching its final disintegration, even apart from the archaistic setting of Bembo's poem. For where there is archaism, there is also stylistic dualism—one looks back after attaining a new height. Certain numbers still hesitate in their tone between the canzonetta and the madrigal, for example *Non giacinti o narcisi*, *Dolcissimi legami*, and *Tutte le bocche belle*. There are still pieces like *S'andasse amor a caccia*, so light and accentuated in its rhythms that it must have been inspired by the French chanson; there are still pieces like *Donna nel mio ritorno*, with a veritable orgy at the cadence; there is even an elegy, *Se tu mi lasci*, a strictly madrigalesque affair that relies entirely on the alternation of half-choirs of two, three, and four voices with the five-voiced tutti—it is all sound and color, as are so many madrigals in the Venetian style. At the same time, two characteristics betray the growing disintegration of the style, and it is precisely in the most important pieces that they are most evident. The one

characteristic is the "monodic" invention of the motifs, particularly of the "narrating" motifs, which are constantly being recombined in the interests of broad description, as in *Ecco mormorar l'onde*; this characteristic also reveals itself in the free use of abrupt changes of expression and of means: coloristic treatment of the lower voices, coloratura, "scherzando" effects with little motifs, harmonic colorings, contrapuntal interweavings, and finally all those dynamic contrasts that the old editions leave to the discretion of the performers. If we put all these things together, we have a piece like *Dolcemente dormiva la mia Clori*. The other characteristic is Monteverdi's impatience: he is becoming increasingly fond of beginning a madrigal with a *contrapposto* of different parts of the text, a procedure almost identical with that polytexture which was later so strongly condemned in the Gloria and the Credo of the mass. Only in the continuation does he begin to elaborate the individual motifs. This "impatience" is of course a reflection of the poetic oxymora, but at the same time it introduces into the madrigal a combinative, instrumental element that is not in harmony with the classical ideal. Monteverdi is not yet actually seeking out extravagant harmonies as direct bearers of the expression, but he is already using austere passing dissonances in Marenzio's manner.

Monteverdi's third madrigal book, which appeared two years later (1592), is a duplicate of the second in so far as it has the same transitional character and shows the same inner conflict. To be sure, it contains no such contrast as that in the second book between the archaistic setting of Bembo's quatrains and the rest of the contents. Although Monteverdi again includes a poem of Bembo's, *O rossignuol che 'n queste verdi fronde*, the first stanza of a canzone, he sets it in a personal, if somewhat neutral style. The opening number, which has the character of a dedication, is in much the same vein:

> La giovinetta pianta
> Si fa più bell'al sole
> Quando men arder suole . . .

For in the actual dedication to his patron, Duke Vincenzo Gonzaga, Monteverdi also speaks of the "pianta che non sia sterile, come dopo i fiori produce i frutti," and goes on to compare his new madrigals to fruits. But despite the dedication to the Duke, this book seems to me to stand in much the same relation to Ferrara as Giaches Wert's eighth madrigal book of 1586: it is filled with the presence of the *tre dame*, the three singing birds at Alfonso's court. No student of these madrigals can have failed to have been struck by the prominent position they give to the soprano trio; that the already-mentioned stanza from Bembo begins with a trio of this sort, twenty-two measures long, is altogether typical. But in these pieces Monteverdi differs decidedly from Luzzaschi and even from Wert. There are few concessions to the ladies' fondness for coloratura; the one exception is No. 14, *Lumi, miei cari lumi,* which is as it were shot through with coloratura and saturated with it. On the contrary, his motifs come more and more to take on the character of impassioned, concentrated declamation, as may be seen from an opening to be quoted later on (p. 734), or from the following:

Or to take another example, consider this motif from No. 13, *Vivrò fra i miei tormenti e le mie cure*:

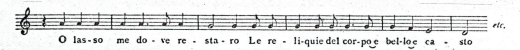

Is this still the thematic or motivic material of the madrigal? To be sure, Monteverdi weaves such a motif into a polyphonic texture, but the effect of the whole is that of frustrated monody. For monody, still the prisoner of the traditional polyphonic way of working, is beating against the bars of its cage, and its melodic idiom is already that of recitative and exclamation. Apart from this, Monteverdi is still using the choral recitative, and in so doing he betrays his dependence on Giaches Wert, a dependence that characterizes this book as a whole. For another thing that connects this third book of madrigals with Ferrara is that Monteverdi as it were discovers in it the two poets who served the house of Este—Guarini and the Tasso of the *Gerusalemme liberata.* From Guarini he takes the following texts:

> O come è gran martire . . .
> O dolc'anima mia . . .
> Stracciami pur il core . . .
> O primavera gioventù dell'anno . . .
> Perfidissimo volto . . .
> Ch'io non t'ami . . .
> Occhi un tempo mia vita . . .
> Lumi miei, cari lumi. . . .

The fourth of these is the first setting of Mirtillo's lyric monologue from the *Pastor fido* (III, 1), a text that will be set to music dozens and dozens of times in every conceivable form, up to and including the setting by Paolo Quagliati in 1623. Yet there

Portrait of an Unknown Italian Composer. *Unknown Master*
Paris, Private Collection

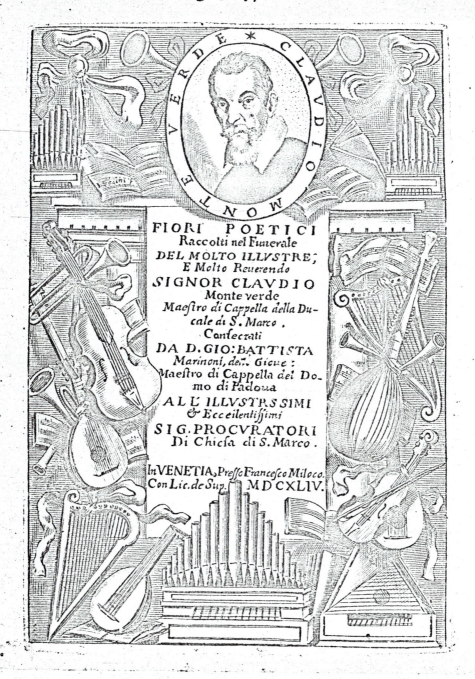

Title Page of the "Fiori poetici" (Venice 1644) on Claudio Monteverdi's
Death, with His Portrait

is not the slightest difference between Monteverdi's treatment of the text of this monologue and his treatment of the following madrigal (*Perfidissimo volto*), to choose a second example at random. Both texts provide opportunities for combining the motifs of successive lines; in either case the opening combination is developed for twenty-eight measures. But with Tasso the situation is a little different. There are two tripartite cycles: (1) Armida's curse upon the faithless Rinaldo (*Gerusalemme liberata*, XVI, 59, 60, and 63); (2) Tancred's lament over the slain Clorinda (*ibid.*, XII, 77-79). Monteverdi was thus already occupied with the lines that were to inspire him thirty-two years later to write his *Combattimento*. From Stanza 78 of this lament we have already quoted one motif in illustration of Monteverdi's polyphonically conditioned monody. This stands in the same relation to genuine monody as Monteverdi's own five-voiced arrangement of the *Lamento d'Arianna* to the original, and this arrangement proves that Monteverdi by no means considered his polyphonic works to have been "dated" or superseded by the rise of the monodic style. Monteverdi's age was not yet an age of naturalism, and it did not object to the presentation of Armida's passionate curse by a five-voiced choir that included two men. It was used to such things. As early as 1575 Andrea Gabrieli had created this "pre-monodic secular oratorio" with his music for Ariosto's *Orlando*; Wert had followed him in 1581 and 1586 with music for Tasso's *Gerusalemme*. And in his *Armida abbandonata*, in the half chromatically animated, half chorally homophonic narrative of the third stanza, Monteverdi again reveals his affinity to Giaches Wert.

A brief consideration of Monteverdi's *Rimanti in pace* will reveal similarities and differences between his work and that of another master—Marenzio. This sonnet by Livio Celiano, a *partenza* in the form of a dialogue, is one of the many imitations of Guarini's *Tirsi morir volea*. Marenzio set this text to music somewhat later (*Sesto libro a cinque*, 1594)—evidently without knowing Monteverdi's piece, for minor variants show that he used another source. The differences are much more striking than the resemblances. We tend to associate the two musicians, for their dates and places of birth lie close together. Yet their styles lie far apart, at least in this instance. Marenzio deliberately looks back and summarizes; this is already evident in his choice of the archaistic time-signature. His piece is a high point in lyric vocality, a picture in bright iridescent colors, an example of vocal impressionism. Monteverdi's piece is conditioned by his interest in the viola and his instrumental upbringing. He blends Marenzio's manner with the spirit of the canzonetta, his contrasts of tempo are sharper, and he has already given up that unity of vocal style which Marenzio is still intent on preserving. Even in this book Monteverdi still shows an aptitude for fluent vocality, as in No. 11 (*Ch'io non t'ami*) and No. 12 (*Occhi un tempo mia vita*), and in this he resembles Marenzio. But Marenzio is never as broad as Monteverdi, who with all his "impatience" needs time for his technique of combination and for the exposition, expansion, and recapitulation of his motifs no matter whether his purpose is descriptive painting or whether it is purely musical. An instructive example is No. 5, *Stracciami pur il core*, in which the rising and falling scale-motif plays almost an abstract role.

An interval of eleven or twelve years lies between the appearances of the third and fourth books of madrigals, an interval marked by the deaths of Palestrina and Lasso, of Wert and Marenzio, and properly regarded as a turning-point in the history of music. This time Monteverdi addresses himself directly to Ferrara in his dedication: Being no longer able, he says, to dedicate his work to Duke Alfonso in person "per la sopravegnente sua morte," he wishes at least to dedicate it to the Accademici Intrepidi of Ferrara, who have placed him so much in their debt and who are residents of a city towards which he is most inclined and which he has no wish to leave ("Ho stimato convenirmisi il non dipartirmi dalla . . . Città, alla quale sono molto inclinato"). No doubt this inclination had increased in 1596, when Wert died and Monteverdi was obliged to give way to Pallavicino and to see him appointed choirmaster in Mantua; this must have been a deep disappointment to him, and it is not surprising that he should have transferred his allegiance to Ferrara and Duke Alfonso. We do not know that Monteverdi was a member of the Accademia degli Intrepidi and the information we have about the founder and foundation-date of this musical society is full of contradictions. The *Enciclopedia italiana* names as its founder the famous architect G. B. Aleotti detto d'Argenta and gives the date of its foundation sometimes as 1597, sometimes as 1600. Vogel (*Vierteljahrsschrift für Musikwissenschaft*, III, 339) names as the founder Francesco Saraceni and as the orator who pronounced the inaugural address (on August 26, 1601) Count Guidobaldo Bonarelli, the author of the pastoral comedy *Filli di Sciro*. This sounds much more probable, and it may be presumed that some of the texts of this fourth book are his work.

But most of the others are again Guarini's, and this time not one but three numbers are from the *Pastor fido*, among them the very first piece:

> Ah dolente partita!
> Ah fin della mia vita!

These are Mirtillo's last words after being dismissed by Amaryllis. Monteverdi was not the first to choose this text: Marenzio had already set it in 1594 (*Libro sesto a cinque*), and Monte set it for seven voices in 1600. And Monteverdi knew Marenzio's piece: his rhythmic treatment of the words *E sento nel partire* is almost identical with Marenzio's, and the irregularly resolved leading-tone (H. F. Redlich's *abspringender Leit-Ton*) is likewise a feature of Marenzio's style (see page 727). But apart from this, what a difference there is between Marenzio's simple, sweet

lyric flower and Monteverdi's violent outburst! (We shall not deal with the elaborate, half-ornamental version by the elderly Monte.) Monteverdi again uses the first four lines of the text for a long development on interwoven motifs extending over fifty-six measures, basically sentimental in coloring; there follows a short middle-part that has the character of a canzonetta; at the end, *vivace morire* and *morir immortalmente* are treated as counterpoints to one another, as a sort of *contrapposto*, the one rhythmically animated, the other a sustained motif built around the interval of the diminished fourth. Monteverdi has absorbed something of Gesualdo's restlessness, though it must be admitted that Monteverdi is never as radical as Gesualdo in splitting the tempo into two contrasted types of movement, a lively allegro and a harmonically pungent largo.

Monteverdi offers us another opportunity for comparison in No. 16, *Anima dolorosa*, a love lament of a shepherdess, also set to music as early as 1586 by Filippo Monte in his eleventh book for five voices. With Monte it is still a madrigal with a free flow, and though each detail is delicately expressed, it is a polyphonic whole. With Monteverdi it becomes an actual scene in which choral recitation and pseudo-polyphonic episodes are sharply contrasted; the five voices are in reality only one, for the four lower voices are almost completely subordinated to the soprano; the piece is the apotheosis of the rhetorical question. Every element of the madrigal has become involved in the process of disintegration. In No. 4, Rinuccini's *Sfogava con le stelle*, Monteverdi resorts to choral psalmody for the narrative sections and in so doing approximates the style of the Improperia; it is as though he no longer thought it worth while to give such words a madrigalesque elaboration. But in the ottava *Piagne e sospira*, a text not found in Ariosto or Tasso, he goes to the opposite extreme and carries the chromatic realization of the opening line to enormous lengths; the chromatically rising fourth-note motif with the "sigh" that succeeds it is combined with the motifs of the following lines right down to the concluding couplet without the slightest regard for the proportions of the whole. The *contrapposto*, the contrasting of one voice with a group of voices, is very old—as old as the madrigal itself —but never before has it been carried as far as it is in No. 3, *Cor mio non mori*, in which the possibility of a return to the madrigalesque, to the equally privileged status of all the voices, is practically ruled out. Polyphony becomes a matter of combining and interweaving; imitation becomes a game with sequential chains of parlando motifs, as in No. 5, *Volgea l'anima mia*. The epigram becomes more than epigram in No. 11, Guarini's *Ohimè, se tanto amate*, a text often set to music; here the free dissonant entrances of the exclamation, repeated over and over again, lead to exaggeration and turn the piece into a *scherzando*. Sweetness, too, becomes the very opposite of sweetness; how remote from the early madrigalists, with their innocent flatted harmonies on *dolce*, is Monteverdi's *dolcezza* in No. 15, *Sì ch' io vorrei morire*:

Harmonic tension is often carried to extremes, for example in No. 9, Guarini's *Voi pur da me partite*. And one can understand why guardians of tradition like the worthy Artusi were incensed at such unheard-of innovations. The motif of straightforward recitation and the exclamatory melos stand side by side, as in genuine monody. One piece may turn on the combining of motifs and must accordingly be worked out at length; the next may be a concise little piece like No. 8, *La piaga ch'ho nel core*. The five-voiced texture is now invariably informal, and invariably some one voice—least often the bass—now takes over the role of *primus inter pares* or, as *primus*, ruthlessly proclaims its uncontested supremacy. Yet in No. 13, *Quell'augellin che canta*, a text from the *Pastor fido* that has obviously been set to music with a view to its performance by the three ladies of Ferrara, the bass takes no part in the coloratura and the tenor does so only once, almost as though inadvertently.

It is a dissociation of the parts of the whole, a disintegration that was bound to bring about a transformation of the classical madrigal and to lead to the *madrigale concertato*. In the fifth book of his madrigals Monteverdi himself will take the decisive step.

ALTHOUGH Marco da Gagliano is one of the most famous names in musical history, no musical lexicon or history has anything—sensible or foolish—to say about him as a madrigalist. Torchi alone has reprinted two pieces from his sixth madrigal book (*Arte musicale in Italia*, IV, 23 and 27), but unfortunately they are not madrigals at all. In this respect his fate has been not unlike that of J. S. Bach, for the first choral work of Bach's to be published after his death was a mass for double chorus that is certainly not by him. Indeed one may say that Marco's reputation stands in inverse proportion to the knowledge posterity has of his works.

The story of his life has often been retold since the publication of Emil Vogel's essay (*Vierteljahrsschrift für Musikwissenschaft*, V, 396f.), which straightened out all the early mistakes. He was born about 1575 as the son of a certain Zanobi whose family name we do not know, and as a native of Gagliano, a few Italian miles north of Florence, he was entitled to call himself a Florentine. His teacher was Luca Bati (died 1608), choirmaster at San Lorenzo, the household church and sepulcher of the Medici, and also at their court chapel; Marco succeeded him in 1611, and in so doing joined that procession of Florentine masters which, in more than a century, included only these five: Corteccia, Malvezzi, Bati, Gagliano, and Filippo Vitali. Marco now becomes a priest, and later he is appointed a canon at San Lorenzo; in 1614—like Agostino Steffani—he is even raised to the rank of Apostolic Prothonotary. He is thus one of the few musicians to succeed in combining artistic and clerical distinction. Surrounded by the members of the Camerata—Caccini, Peri (with whom he is joined by ties of reciprocal friendship and admiration), Rinuccini, Alessandro Striggio the Younger, Giovanni del Turco, and the rest—he cannot avoid being something of an aesthete, and after the death of Jacopo Corsi, presumably in 1604, he founds an academy of his own, the Accademia degl' Elevati, and assumes the academic name of "L'Affannato"—"The Distressed One." Until his death in 1642 he is the official court composer of the Medici, and it becomes his duty to provide the music for every state occasion, whether joyful or solemn: thus he writes operas, oratorios, tournaments, ballets, intermezzi, and solemn funeral pieces. But his reputation rests chiefly on an opera written for the Gonzagas, his *Dafne*, performed at Mantua in 1607 and published in 1608. The libretto was a slightly altered version of the libretto by Rinuccini that had been previously set to music by Peri.

Much of Marco's work has been lost, though what is left is still a good deal—apart from church music, there is even a book of vocal chamber music in the monodic style. He began his career with a book of madrigals for five voices in 1602, and this was followed by five further books in 1604, 1605, 1606, 1608, and 1617. The first is dedicated to Rudolf of Anhalt, a German prince, and the fourth to Don

Ferdinando Gonzaga, a great patron of Marco's and himself a composing dilettante —he is the composer, not only of certain arias in Marco's *Dafne*, but also, as Vogel has shown with a good deal of probability, of the tripartite setting of one of Petrarch's sonnets in Marco's sixth book. But one cannot call Marco a successful madrigalist: when he began, the madrigal already belonged to the past. Only two of his books, the first and last, went through a second edition, and one or two are preserved only in a single copy.

With Marco da Gagliano Florence has a master madrigalist again, after having been relatively inactive since the time of Corteccia, when it had surrendered the initiative to other cities—Mantua, Ferrara, Venice, Rome, and Naples. It is significant that until the 'eighties—before Cristofano and Giorgio Marescotti—Florence was without a music-printer, and that even later, during the monodic period, this trade failed to prosper. Corteccia's works, though they are certainly very Florentine in spirit, were all printed in Venice, and we could say the same of Striggio's works if we were willing to consider him a Florentine. Stefano Rossetto of Nice, who is definitely a member of the Florentine circle, has his works printed in Venice and Rome. His *Lamento di Olimpia*, a piece we have already mentioned above (p. 545), exemplifies a peculiarity of the Florentine madrigal that goes back to Corteccia's time. It is somewhat "cloistered," it tends to be rather emotional, and it entertains decided literary pretensions. This is also true of the madrigals of Giovanni Piero Manenti of Bologna, a musician in the service of the Grand Duke: he not only writes *madrigali ariosi* (see above, p. 645), he also sets Sannazaro's Arcadian lament *Per pianto la mia carne si distilla* and a stanza from Tancred's lament for Clorinda (*Gerusalemme liberata*, XII, 97); his music is somewhat in Wert's style, colorful though reserved, one might almost say "aesthetic." And it is true of Cristofano Malvezzi of Lucca, the choirmaster to the grand-ducal court and the chief author of the famous *Intermedii e concerti* written on the occasion of the wedding of Ferdinando de' Medici and Cristina of Lorraine and performed three times in 1589—on May 2 in connection with Girolamo Bargagli's *La Pellegrina*, on May 6 in connection with the *Zingara* played by the Comici Gelosi, and on May 13 in connection with Isabella Andreini's *La Pazzia*; it was printed in 1591. He is the composer of a book of madrigals for six voices (1584) and two books (1583 and 1590) of madrigals for five voices, of which the last is dedicated to Emilio de' Cavalieri. It contains pieces of great charm, notable for their blending of the recitative-like and the pathetic, for example a setting of Guarini's *Tirsi morir volea*, and there are others that have a certain freshness, like *La pastorella mia spietata e frigida*, on Sannazaro's *sdruccioli*, but the whole lacks independence and strikes no really personal note. The Reverendo Padre Mattia Mauro, a friar of the cloister de' Servi in Florence, can scarcely have been an exception to the general rule. He is the composer of two books of four- and

five-voiced madrigals (1571), of which the second is dedicated to Pandolfo Bardi de' Conti di Vernio; the first book is still filled with settings of Petrarch, like a madrigal book of the 'fifties.

Surely the most striking figure among all these musicians is Vincenzo Galilei, the father of the great Galileo, the composer of the first works in *stile rappresentativo*; as a member of the Florentine Camerata, he has been dealt with appropriately in the *Istituzioni e monumenti dell'arte musicale italiana* (vol. IV, ed. G. Fano). In 1930 the Florentine section of the Associazione dei Musicologi italiani even published four of his madrigals in a more or less questionable reprint. We know only two madrigal books by Galilei, one of pieces for from three to five voices, of 1574, the other of pieces for four and five voices, of 1587, published four years before his death. Of the first we have only one part-book but one number (for three voices) has been preserved complete, thanks to Galilei's having included it in his *Fronimo*; this is *Qual miracolo Amore* (reprinted by O. Chilesotti in his *Saggio sulla melodia popolare del cinquecento*, p. 31). The loss is greater from the biographical or historical point of view than from the musical, for the essential part of the contents (two numbers are exceptional) consists of four multipartite canzoni in honor of Bianca Capello, to whom the book is dedicated. The dedication is unusually concise: "Alla clarissima signora Bianca Capelli gentildonna venetiana essempio rarissimo d'ogni regia virtù. Vincentio Galilei divotissimo suo servitore, questo primo libro di suoi madrigali a quatro, et cinque voci gli da, dona, et dedica." As though in compensation, the contents of the second book show considerable variety. It is dedicated to the "bellissima, et virtuosissima Madonna Ippolita Zeferini" on the occasion of her taking the veil (*elezione*) and contains two Latin pieces, one on the Immaculate Conception of the Blessed Virgin and one (for eight voices) on St. Andrew, which were presumably performed on that solemn occasion. Galilei tells us that the madrigals of this book were often sung in Siena during the summer of 1586 in the garden of Ippolita and her father, Pietro Lazzaro Zeferini, and certain complimentary pieces that the book contains enable us to name some of the other ladies, friends of Ippolita's, who must have been present: there is a Malaspina (*Nel bel giardin*, written in the manner of a *canzon francese*); there is an "amorosetta e candida Viola" (*Voi caduchi ligustri*); there is a "dura Pietra," while among the gentlemen, besides the older Zeferini (*Spirto sovran*), there is also the madrigalist Pietro Vinci of Nicosia in Sicily, then choirmaster in Bergamo (*Vinci te stesso*), for there can scarcely be any other reason for his inclusion. Another occasional piece is *Dolcissimo riposo*, a setting of one of the several poems that Giovanni Battista Strozzi had had written on a Florentine garden. Musically the most impressive piece in the book is a half worldly, half spiritual sestina in seven sections. And as a Florentine, Galilei too is "cloistered": although he has learned genuine chromaticism and the use of color from the Venetians—supposedly from Zarlino—he is stricter and more austere than many of this school, among them Andrea Gabrieli. He seems to have been a little ashamed of his dilettantism and anxious to free himself from this reproach, for he begins his book with a strict five-voiced canon as a sort of musical dedication:

Ippolita gentil, saggia e pudica,
Di verità, di fede, e d'amor tempio!

The tripartite *Poca fiammella accesa*, likewise written for some special occasion unknown to me, is unusually animated motivically. But the really "Florentine" pieces are those that show a more homophonic tendency. Galilei promises Ippolita that he will soon bring out his *intavolatura di liuto*, and one has the impression that a number of these madrigals were actually written as vocal models to be arranged later for accompanied solo voice. They are *madrigali ariosi* quite like those of Manenti and his fellows (cf. above, p. 645). In this style he sets not only Strozzi's madrigal, but also two stanzas from the *Orlando furioso* (*Cantan fra i rami*, XXXIV, 50, and *Alcun non può saper*, XIX, 1), the second in the form a a b, and one from Bernardo Tasso's *Amadigi* (*La pastorella con la verga in mano*, LVII, 1). Several pieces are quite short and we have included one of them in our volume of illustrations.[5]

The piece is extremely simple and for its late date, deliberately so, but it is characteristic with its mixture of old-fashioned false relations on the one hand and "modern" sixth chords on the other, with its awkward *unisono* between measures 5 and 6 on the one hand and its unerring sense for the form of the madrigalesque epigram or epigrammatic madrigal on the other. We stand mid-way between Arcadelt and monody, and it is this aspect of Florentine music that we have called "cloistered," for such pieces can scarcely be found elsewhere. They conform exactly to the theoretical requirement formulated by Galilei in his *Dialogo della musica antica e moderna* that all music should have a dramatic character, even the madrigal.

If Vincenzo Galilei is a gifted dilettante, Luca Bati, Gagliano's teacher and predecessor, is again a master. All the lexicons repeat the same biographical data, based on an article in the *Gazzetta musicale di Milano* (VI, 22) and on Emil Vogel's paper on Gagliano. He is accordingly said to be the composer of the music for *Le Fiamme d'Amore*, a *mascherata* by Gino Ginori (de gli Accecati)—this was a float or *carro* drawn through the streets of Florence on February 26, 1595; the intermezzi for *L'esaltazione della croce* (1589), a sacred representation; finally, in collaboration with Stefano Venturi del Nibbio and Pietro Strozzi, the choruses for Caccini's *Il Rapimento di Cefalo* (1600). Vogel was the first to draw attention to his two madrigal books of 1594 and 1598, of which the first is dedicated to Jacopo Corsi,

[5] See Vol. III, No. 83.

and he expresses the opinion that Bati "belonged to the strict contrapuntal school."

"The strict contrapuntal school?" Bati wrote no monodies that we know of—I do not think that Vogel intended to say more than this. A number of his polyphonic pieces were included by Gagliano in his madrigal books. But Bati is no more "strictly contrapuntal" than Striggio and Marenzio. In 1589 Marenzio had been active in Florence and it is impossible that he should not have exercised his personal and musical influence upon his Florentine colleagues. We have evidence of this in the person of Antonio Bicci, whose madrigals Marenzio, Bati, and Venturi use in their own collections. But Bicci was an imitator of Marenzio, the "pastoral" Marenzio, the Marenzio of hedonism and sensuality. And so is Bati in his madrigal book of 1594, which is unfortunately the only one preserved in a complete copy. As with Marenzio, we are on the road to the *musiche nuove* in so far as polyphonic pieces can be "new music"; otherwise this generic term must be restricted to monody. Bati's madrigals are either definitely pastoral or definitely expressive. The very first number, the sonnet *Questo fonte gentil non versa stilla*, is a pastoral idyl in the form of a narrative, with the typical paired sopranos and a concerto-like conclusion that suggests the canzonetta. An excellent example of the other extreme is the beginning of No. 5:

Caccini, Peri, and Gagliano take over these expressive formulas and restate them monodically without adding to them. Each voice in our example is already actively expressive, already *rappresentativo* before the *stile rappresentativo*. Bati is both pastoral and expressive in No. 7, *Filli, deh non fuggir*, a sonnet by Benedetto Varchi that was often set to music, likewise in No. 8, *Il più bel pastorell' e 'l più gentile*, and in No. 15, *Ben sei Tirinto*, with its concluding, cantata-like tercets:

Così piangendo e signozzand'in guisa
Ch'avrebbe rotto di pietà gli scogli,
Dicea vicin'al *Ren* la vaga Nisa.

The last line suggests that this is a piece written to order for a patron from Bologna.

Marco da Gagliano is a faithful pupil, more gifted than his master. In his first book of 1602 he includes a piece by Bati which is hardly distinguishable from his own work, unless in its lack of melodic and harmonic freedom. It would be a mistake to suppose that, as a monodist, Gagliano followed Galilei's example and began by cultivating the homophonic style in his madrigals, allowing the melody to lead and taking the accompaniment for granted. Like Bati, he is fond of interweaving the voices, but he is more delicate, more precise, more animated, and freer in his declamation. These madrigals have the effect of polyphonic, imitative arrangements of monodies: a beginning such as the following would also be perfectly adequate as monody:

Scher-za Ma-don - na e di - ce, Hor l'un in me gi-ran - d'hor
l'al - tra stel - la: "Mi - ra, co-m'io son bel - la!" *etc.*

But he works it out as an anacreontic madrigal with an animated texture. The print is opened and closed by two of Dorinda's outbursts from the *Pastor fido* (II, 2) —one might call them monodies in madrigalesque transposition. Motifs of pure declamation and of pure expression are interwoven; there is not a single cheap or transparent effect. Marco's pathetic style reaches a high point in the second number, a setting of della Casa's *O sonno, o della placida*, the last a cappella composition on this text, first set by Rore. It is in two sections, and we have included them both in our volume of illustrations.[6]

It is a musical manifesto, uncompromising in its expression, and an indication that Marco is already acquainted with Monteverdi, though he prefers more compact, more concentrated, writing.

But, as was the case with Bati, the expressive, emotional pieces in this first work represent only one side of its character. The other side is epigrammatic and anacreontic; natural declamation, light parlando, free little melismas, and unaffected chromaticism are woven together to form a fluctuating, specifically vocal style that is sometimes restless—quite unlike Marenzio's style, which with all its vocality is

[6] See Vol. III, Nos. 84 and 85.

sometimes moved by impulses that are instrumental in origin. The chief characteristic of these madrigals is not tone-painting, though this is not avoided, or anything "constructive," such as the double motif or the *contrapposto* of the voices, but lively and essentially expressive declamation.

I am unfortunately unable to give detailed accounts of Marco's second and third books of 1604 and 1605, for I failed to score these from the copies at the Liceo Musicale in Bologna, the only ones extant. The second book, dedicated to Marco's pupil Giovanni del Turco, contains several pieces on the death of Jacopo Corsi, the patron of the Camerata; some of these are by Marco himself, others are by Pietro Strozzi and Giovanni del Turco. Turco reprinted his own contribution in his second madrigal book; it is a short though not unworthy composition written as it were in a simplified form of his teacher's style. The text reads as follows:

> CORSO hai di questa vita
> I primi arringhi e colto i primi pregi;
> E per la tua partita
> Non hà più Flora onde s'adorni e fregi,
> E le Muse e le Gratie insieme accolte
> Son con teco sepolte.

But despite these threnodies, despite a tripartite setting of a sonnet by Petrarch (*In qual parte del ciel*), this second book seems to strike a lighter note, and the third book is still lighter: among other things the second book also contains an excerpt from Sannazaro's *Arcadia* and the triumphant song of Corisca, the *intrigante* in the *Pastor fido* (IV, 4):

> Cingetemi d'intorno,
> O trionfanti allori,
> Le vincitrici e gloriose chiome . . .

Besides two madrigals from Torquato Tasso and one from Livio Celiano, the third book contains a canzonetta by Chiabrera, *Vaga su spina ascosa*, set to music as a bipartite madrigal, while another text is a pure canzonetta:

> Vaghi rai, mercede, aita
> Giù nel sen; mirate il core
> Tutto fiamma e tutto ardore!
> Foco, e fiamma è la mia vita,
> Tutte piaghe o'l cor nel seno,
> Ma d'un guardo almo e sereno
> Si consola ogni ferita.

Vaghi rai, mercede, aita
Giù nel sen; mirate il core
Tutto fiamma e tutto ardore!

One will note that the form and spirit of the Metastasio aria existed long before his time.

Marco's fourth book (1606) is basically epigrammatic and in the lighter style. The single exception is the last number, a setting of Petrarch's Good Friday sonnet *I vo piangendo*, which has a long and venerable line of musical ancestors. It is for six voices and evidently intended for an important and more or less public occasion, perhaps to be performed in the Sagrestia vecchia of San Lorenzo or in one of the apartments of the Palazzo Pitti. It is at once very sustained and quite personal, at once motet-like and madrigalesque, with a more agitated ending, almost in a pure D minor. Two pieces that belong together but do not quite fit within the general framework are (1) a ten-voiced choral dialogue and (2) *Quel vivo sole ardente*, a six-voiced tribute to the ladies. The dialogue begins as follows:

Ove si lieti, o bel drappel d'Amanti,
Hor che la notte asconde
Col maggior lume i rai del vostro Sole? . . .

Both are *mascherate* in the cultivated, courtly style appropriate to the Florence of the princely Medici; musically, too, they show more refinement and are more elaborate than similar pieces from Venice. But the remaining eleven numbers are mere epigrams, their motifs mere declamation. Their parlando style permits the graceful interweaving—or better, the motivic animation—of the voices, but it also restricts the use of ornamental melismas and rules out all tone-painting whatsoever. The authors of the texts are Guarini, Marino, and Chiabrera, the two last mentioned being personally connected with the Medici and with Florence. But Guarini, despite his witty conceits, is already too involved and too long-winded for this generation. Marco sets one of Guarini's best known madrigals in the following abbreviated form:

Perfidissimo volto,
Ben l'usata bellezza in te si vede,
Che mi consuma il core,
Ma non l'usata fede.
Ah, se tu perdi Amore,
Perche seco non perdi ancor vaghezza,
O non hai pari alla beltà fermezza?

As set to music by Filippo di Monte (eleventh book, 1586) and many others, Guarini's original text reads as follows:

Perfidissimo volto,
Ben l'usata bellezza in te si vede,
Ma non l'usata fede.
Già mi parevi dir: Quest'amorose
Luci che dolcemente
Rivolgo a te sì belle e sì pietose
Prima vedrai tu spente,
Che sia spento il desio ch'a te le gira.
Ahi che spent' è'l desio,
Ma non è spento quel per cui sospira
L'abbandonato core.
O volto troppo vago e troppo rio,
Perche, se perdi amore,
Non perdi ancor vaghezza
O non hai pari a la beltà fermezza?

To compare Marco's opening with Monte's is to recognize the progress that has been made towards harmonic freedom; Marco's declamation is the more pointed and rigid of the two (see example at the bottom of this page and also at the top of page 738).

With Monte the madrigal still retains its indefinable unity and fullness; with Gagliano everything has become epigrammatic and dialectic, witness the many cadences followed by rests in all the voices and requiring a fresh start. Marco's No. 9 is a

setting of the first of the three stanzas of a real canzonetta by Gabriello Chiabrera:

> Hor che lunge da voi
> Movo bei lumi, ove hà riposto Amore,
> Il più caro, e'l più bel de'lumi suoi
> Chi da conforto al core?

He continues with one of the specific idioms of impassioned monody:

All this is sometimes highly concentrated and not merely brief; sometimes it is highly modern, as in the first piece (*seconda parte*), at the reference to the *palidette viole*, the pallid viols, where there is an inflection towards the A-flat region. But such things are infrequent: Marco was thoroughly familiar with certain pieces by Venosa—this may be seen most readily in their common tendency to repeat settings of entire lines in transposition—but as a Florentine, he is restrained and well behaved. The same may be said of the other three musicians whose art stands close to his and whose music the book includes: Giovanni and Lorenzo del Turco and Luca Bati: around 1600, one may also speak of a Florentine school in connection with the madri-

gal. The boldest of the three is Giovanni, with his little chromatic audacities. Bati, the eldest, is broader and less epigrammatic and favors a more song-like melody.

Marco's fifth book (1608) no longer contains anything like his earlier setting of a Petrarch sonnet. To be sure, there is still a sonnet, *Seccasi giunta a sera in un momento*, but like *Vattene o felice alma*, the bipartite madrigal that precedes it, a threnody "in morte del Conte Camillo della Gherardesca," it is surely intended for performance as chamber music in Marco's *accademia*. Marino is represented by two poems: *Quì rise, o Tirsi*, a pastoral madrigal, and the rather too epigrammatic *Mori mi dice*. Marco's brevity—one might almost call it haste—in setting these texts and others like them is scarcely to be surpassed; it sometimes happens that two voices begin the first line and are immediately interrupted by the other three voices with the second. One of the prettiest texts requires only twenty-five measures:

> Fuss'io pur degno, Amore,
> D'esser com'altri già cangiato in fiore—
> In fior fuss'io rivolto
> Da te, da Filli mia gradito e colto.
> Oh che lieto fioretto,
> S'io fussi a Filli in sen racchiuso e stretto!

Yet the last two lines, first presented by three and four voices, are repeated by five; for the first three and a quarter lines three voices suffice, as in a *canzon villanesca*, and the bass is kept busy for just ten measures. The madrigal has become a musical epigram and is being treated with more or less indifference. Marco's voice-leading is often thoroughly disagreeable, and his lack of sensitivity towards false relations is very striking in this late period, when the basso continuo is beginning to clarify the harmonic logic. At the same time the influence of the basso continuo is already making itself felt. Marenzio could never have written a passage like the following, from *Quì rise, o Tirsi*, in which the bass is a mere prop and remains rooted to the spot:

Marco seldom employs unusual melodic intervals as he does in Marino's second madrigal:

"Mori," mi dici, e mentre
Con quel guardo crudel morir mi fai,
Con quel dolce parlar vita mi dai—

The only typical things in his setting of this text are the concise parlando, sometimes homophonic, sometimes imitative, the false relation, and the varied repetition in the manner of Luzzaschi or Gesualdo (see example, this page, and top of p. 741). Even in his moments of pathos Marco remains within bounds, unlike Gesualdo, who even injects pathos into the pastoral.

Two pieces are written for particularly festive occasions—the tripartite *Su la sponda del Tebro* (No. 12) and the seven-voiced *Altri di beltà vaga* (No. 15). The first is obviously written for singers like Francesca and Giulio Caccini, Vittoria Archilei, and Francesco Rasi: it is filled with virtuoso parlandos and virtuoso coloratura—a festive, baroque piece. And in the second we find at last the direction that is as it were the madrigal's epitaph—"per cantare et sonare." It has a basso continuo

and is written in the *stile concertato*, with a tutti and a three-voiced virtuoso episode. It is a courtly procession, intended for one of the many grand-ducal festivities in the Palazzo Pitti or at the Poggio Imperiale.

Between Marco's fifth madrigal book and his sixth and last published in 1617 lies an interval of nearly ten years. As the composer says in his dedication to Cosimo del Sera, it had been written the year before (*l'anno passato*) for del Sera's *camerata*. It is a late-comer in every sense. For between the fifth book and the sixth lies not only Marco's great operatic success in Mantua, the *Dafne* of 1607, but also his *Missae, et Sacrarum Cantionum 6 vocum* of 1614, and his *Musiche a una, due et tre voci* of 1615. The mass and the motets of 1614, which rank among his most comprehensive and important works, are written in the *stile concertato* throughout: they give us a picture of the novel and festive manner in which the church year was then being celebrated at San Lorenzo. And the *Musiche* teach us how serious Marco's interest in monody was and how much the general interest had shifted from the madrigal to the *nuove musiche*. The choice of texts is in itself significant: Marco begins with a duet on Bembo's sonnet *Cantai un tempo e se fu dolce il canto*, continues with canzonette by Rinuccini and Chiabrera, sets to music a sonnet by Petrarch and two stanzas from Petrarch's canzone on the Blessed Virgin, and writes a monody on Luigi Tansillo's picturesque sonnet *Valli profonde al sol nemiche*. Even the festival play by Alessandro Ginori which Marco reprints, the *Ballo di donne turche* from the carnival of 1614, is a piece of an altogether different musical caliber than the similar pieces in the madrigal books.

The sixth madrigal book contains only two "literary" pieces. One is Petrarch's *Io vidi in terra angelici costumi*, but as Vogel has convincingly demonstrated, this is almost certainly not by Marco but by Cardinal Ferdinando Gonzaga, the Prior of Barletta, Marco's music-loving and musical patron, who was then given free rein to his aesthetic inclinations at the Florentine court. In 1615 Marco had published the same sonnet as a monody. The other "literary" piece is the opening number, Torquato Tasso's *La bella pargoletta*. It was this book that provoked Muzio Effrem to publish his violent attack in 1623, an attack in which he reproaches Marco with his failure to preserve the modes, his faulty voice leading, his defective cadences, and his tendency to confuse the madrigal with the canzonetta. All this is perfectly true from the point of view of a reactionary and might even have been said of some of Marco's earlier madrigals, and it is of little importance that Effrem was not the man best qualified to make these criticisms of Marco and of Marco alone. Marco's reply was weak, perhaps because he did not himself attach much value to the defense of works in an outmoded form.

We have already mentioned Torchi's publication of two numbers from this book. In the first of these, *Evoè Padre Lieo*, Marco invades Orazio Vecchi's province; it is a *musica da concertarsi co'l bicchiere*—a tutti in the modern yet not-so-modern triple time of the frottolists and monodists begins the piece and returns after each of three duo episodes. The Hellenistic text is in itself enough to show that the piece was intended, not for Vecchi's gay company, but for the banquets of some Florentine *camerata*. The music, too, especially the duos, is somewhat forced and stiff. The second piece, *Su l'affricane arene*, belongs to the history of opera: it is the final chorus of an intermezzo for Rinuccini's *Mascherata di Ninfe di Senna* of 1611, to which Peri also contributed some music. (Cf. Solerti, *Albori*, II, 277 and 291; also his *Musica, ballo e drammatica*, p. 74.)

CHAPTER X
MUSIC IN COMPANY: STRIGGIO, VECCHI,
AND BANCHIERI

IN THE sixteenth century the several forms of secular music—the madrigal and the various classes related to it—are neither private nor public, but occupy an anomalous position halfway between the two. Solitary and completely intimate art, such as that of the Preludes and Fugues of the "Well-Tempered Clavichord" or certain sonatas of Mozart, Haydn, and Beethoven, is unthinkable. It would stand in complete contradiction to the function of sixteenth-century music, whose aim is not emotion, not edification, uplift, or self-improvement, but to serve as entertainment at best, and often enough as a prelude to Venus, an accompaniment to eating and drinking, or a mere pastime. What public music the age brings forth in the way of festival motets and festival madrigals is strictly segregated in its style and attitude from the great mass of the production—the chamber madrigal. But the chamber madrigal requires no audience. The four, five, or six singers are as self-sufficient as two chess-players or a group at a card-table, where "kibitzers," although they may stand by, are uninvited and a general nuisance. For the madrigal this character of companionable entertainment is essential. Only after the foundation of the *accademie* do we begin to meet with "art for art's sake" and with the Horatian hatred of the *profanum vulgus*.

But it is precisely these same *accademie* that create and cultivate the madrigal as a social game. Within the great general category of the "madrigal as entertainment" a whole series of works embodies in the most striking manner the joys of singing and playing in company. These works have their roots in the arrangements of folk-songs from the turn of the century, in the quodlibet, in the dance song, and in the musical parody. They are a residue and at the same time a continuation of everything that the sentimental madrigal of 1535 excluded.

MUSIC AS ENTERTAINMENT AND THE QUODLIBET

WE have an early indication of the connection between music as entertainment and the quodlibet in a collection of villotte by M. Mathias Fiamengo, choirmaster at the cathedral in Milan, which was published by the Venetian printer Antonio Gardano (1549) under the title *La bataglia taliana*. As Miss Cecie Stainer has shown in her excellent article for *Grove's Dictionary*, this M. Mathias of Flanders is Master Mathias Werrecore, who was appointed to his post in Milan at the beginning of 1523 and who was an eye-witness and perhaps a participant in the battle of Pavia two years later. He reorganized the chapel in 1534 and seems to have died shortly before

1558. He was above all a composer of church music: in 1555 the brothers Fr. and Simone Moscheni published a splendid edition of his first book of motets for five voices. But a few madrigals by a "Mathias" are printed in the madrigal books of Maistre Ihan (1541) and Arcadelt (*Primo libro*, ed. of 1559) and cannot very well be by anyone else. He is the one master in the first half of the century, before Pietro Taglia, who keeps alive the musical glory of the unhappy city of Milan, the unfortunate victim of the struggle between France and the Pope, between Francis I and Charles V.

For its time, Gardano's print of 1549 was almost an "unearthing of old music." For the most famous piece which it contains, the "Italian Battle," which Gardano had heard sung at the house of Messer Alessandro Giamberti in Venice by "M. pre Sebastiano" and three companions, celebrates a victory of Duke Francesco Sforza over the French, probably the victory at Bicocca (1522) rather than that at Pavia. Not only does the victory at Pavia (1525) properly belong to the Emperor's Spanish general, but from this time until his death in 1535 Francesco was no longer anyone in whose honor it was wise to be singing songs; thus the year 1525 would seem to be the latest possible date for this musical battle-piece. It was first printed as early as 1544 in a Nuremberg collection by Petreius; cf. Vogel, II, 387. Its composition has a political background. It goes without saying that Mathias' *Battaglia* is a companion-piece to Janequin's *Bataille* on the victory of Francis I over the Swiss mercenaries at Marignano (1515), a piece that became so extraordinarily famous and familiar, even in Italy, that the Italians determined to beat the hated French at their own game. Mathias' battle-piece is in three sections, and one need only glance at Kade's reprint of the first section (*Mattheus le Maistre*, Mainz, 1862, Musik-Beilage No. 1) to see that Janequin has decidedly the better of it. In both cases there is the same liveliness and the same complication in the rhythm. This complication rests on the simplest harmonic basis. The real effect of this primitive program music depends not only on the striking and naturalistic rhythm, but also on the onomatopoetic plasticity of the text. To these factors Mathias adds the tumult of the calls and cries and scraps of songs of the various nationalities—Italian, French, Provençaux, and Swiss and German mercenaries, all singing at once. Thus his piece reveals a relation to the quodlibet that is barely evident in Janequin's.

Long before 1550, in the 'twenties and 'thirties, Mathias also wrote the three villotte that Gardano prints with the *Battaglia*. These aim to make fun of the folk-song and to use it for obscene allusions, and they are obviously connected with the satiric frottola that ends with a street song. Four boisterous companions (they are men, in spite of the high clef combination in two out of the three pieces) sit down together and amuse themselves with well-known melodies and texts. The humor

lies in the way the quotations turn up unexpectedly and in the secondary meanings and ambiguities:

> Horsu horsu compagni stat'attenti
> Ad ascoltare li canti nostri varii
> Che vi faran legrare tutti quanti
> Dico se gian boccal haret'alzato
> Che senza lui non si puo ben cantar
> E da noi scaccia molte fantasie
> Si che da lui s' ha buona compagnia
> Cancaro li venga a chi sta' n fantasia
> E se noi vogliam stare tutti contenti
> Cantarem mattin'et sera allegramente
> Et per dar fin'a questo nostro sgallezzar
> conciatevi in quattro
> Che queste nostre canzonette alla villanescha
> vogliam cantar:
>
> > Mi levava l'altra mattina
> > piu per tempo che non soleva
> > E la vecchia mi diceva
> > che la putta non voleva
> > star salda alla passion
> > Fa ri ra ri ra ri ron
> > canta su bel compagnon
> > Tandare col boccalon
> > Deh dormenton
> > che dormi sotto la scala
> > fa li la li lon
> > harestu mai sentu la mattinada.

(2nd part)

> Cantar vogli'una canzon—
> "Cantane una cantane due
> cantane pur quante tu vuoi"
> > O donne belle guardeve la pelle
> > per il prete del canton
> > c' ha larghe le cost'e grass' i rognon
> > "va su villan va su poltron
> > el canta sempr' una canzon"
> > Io adoro la monicella

et di santo Costantin
L'altra notte da mattutin
el mio amor senti cantare:
Vrai dio d'amor chi mi confortera
che'l mi' amor si m' ha lassa
O fa ri ra ri ron
ch'io son fora di pregion
o fa ri ra ri ron
voglio cantar ser'et matina
E la bella Franceschina
che la piang'e la sospira
che la vorre mari.

(3ʳᵈ part)   Hoime de cha vo mori
se non ho quel che vorref
se l savesa ve l diref
a vorref a so ben mi
Bertolina Bertolina
tu mi schizzi trop i bis
stu me prometi la matina
Et la sera tu desdis
el me par a me devis
sel saves che lef canta:

       El marchese di saluzzo
       da mattina che'l se ne va
       el marchese di saluzzo
       cazza pur la pur la
       Et da mattina che'l se ne va

se non dormi donn'ascolta
la passion che mi tormenta
Hora mai saria ben tempo
da far quel che si fa nel fin d' amor
Donn' hormai fa mi contento
questo mond'e pien di vento
el cervel mi frulla sempre
ogn'un dice ch'io ho bon tempo
forsi che si forsi che no
Al dispetto d'un bechazzo
cha gl' ha strazza' l mostazzo

o che gran poltronazzo
o che visazzo
E voio cantar ogn' hora
Quando sara ch'io mor' amore
su la panz' a la mia signora
al hora diro sempre Viva viva'l mio amore.

It would be a mistake to regard this villotta as a quodlibet in the musical sense. The quodlibet is a polyphonic variety; essential to it is the humorous confusion that arises from the simultaneous singing of different texts and the combining of familiar melodies; its performance requires expert singers. But this villotta is intended for dilettanti; it is essentially homophonic; all the voices sing the same text, and imitation in two or three voices occurs infrequently, usually at the beginning of a section. In compensation, the villotta is intensely alive in its rhythms and its tempo: duple and triple time are constantly alternating, and the tempo is sometimes pushed to such a point that it becomes a mad helter-skelter. It is a nonsense that makes sense, a lark that has meaning, the end of a merry drinking-bout, the Italian counterpart to the caterwauling of Sir Toby Belch and his companions. And it would take some time to identify all the allusions in such a piece and to point out all its shifts and changes in attitude. It begins with mutual exhortation, a sham question, and a jubilant assent in which all concur.

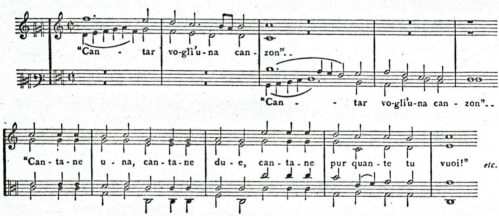

Then follows the warning against the village priest—surely a folk-song. The villotte are as interesting for their folklore as for their music, and they have preserved for us a wealth of material bearing on the history of the Italian folk-song in the fourteenth and fifteenth centuries, a history that has yet to be written. They are wholly formless and "unliterary," as in the introductory exhortation in our example, which is almost pure prose, but for this very reason they are an unexplored source for the history of literature.

Of the same sort, though perhaps still more promiscuous in their choice of ingredients, are the other two villotte by Master Mathias that Gardano prints, a long
one in four sections and a shorter one in a single movement. The one in four
sections tends to use rhymed seven-syllable couplets for the connecting story:

> Una leggiadr'e bella
> E vaga pastorella
> Accorta villanella
> Piu ch'altra di pavana
> A pie d'una fontana
> Con l'altr' in un ristretta
> Tutta vergognosetta
> Cantava in sua favella:
>> "La via della fiumana voglio fare
>> Per l' herba fresca fa dolce dormire"—
> Et cosi nel finire
> La dolce canzonetta
> Distesa su l'herbetta
> Si mess'a riposare;
> Et io nel trapassare
> Vedendola distesa
> Quasi dal sonno presa
> Da l'amoroso foco
> Fatto sicur'un poco
> A dirgl'incominciai:
>> "O villanella quand'a l'acqua vai
>> Dimmi se fresca torni come vai? . . ."

La via della fiumana and *O villanella* are two of the most popular street-songs of the
Quattrocento, and our villotta goes on to quote a whole string of them—the melody
of *De voltate in qua, e do bella Rosina* to the words *Et infra—infra l'Aprile e'l
Maggio*; the dance-song *Donne venite al ballo*, preserved in several manuscripts and
even in print (1531[1]); the frottola-refrain *La non vuol esser più mia*; and many
others. We have not hesitated to quote the opening lines of this bucolic anecdote,
which follows the pattern of the French chanson and develops coarser and coarser
situations as its plot unfolds; at length the idyl is disturbed and interrupted by the
appearance of a hunting-party, with the sounding of horns, the barking of dogs,
and the cries of the hunters, a scene that naturally calls for increased contrapuntal
animation—it is a resurrection of the old caccia in a new form.

It is impossible not to think of the satiric frottola in this connection; in this particular case there is an obvious relation to a piece by Nicolo Pifaro (VIII, 23):

South where all foolishness of this sort was usually put in the form of the *moresca*. "No authors are named," says Vogel but, so far as any conclusion can be drawn from the two (of four) part-books that have been preserved, it is not a miscellany but a collection of pieces by one man, and an able and accomplished one at that. Who was he? And why did he (or Gardano) conceal his name? He must have been from Mantua. It can scarcely have been Duke Guglielmo himself, although he arranged to have his own five-voiced madrigals printed without his name in this same year by this same printer, but it may perhaps have been Alessandro Striggio or Giaches Wert, great masters of serious music who would not have cared to acknowledge a publication of this sort.

Whoever wrote them, these eight pieces—most of them in several sections, the last a six-voiced dialogue—have considerable historic and folkloristic importance. One or two of them still preserve all the old vulgarity and parodistic banter, thus No. 3:

> Io mi levai una bella mattina
> Sol per andar a lo bello giardin
> E m'incontrai una bella fantina
> E li bacciai il suo dolce bocchin
> E lei mi pres'a dir—Amor mio caro amor mio fin
> Quando ritornarastu a me?
> Io li risposi: doman da matin.
>> E mentre in tal dolcezza
> Gioendo stava pieno di vaghezza,
> Venne da un'altro lato un giovinetto
> Ch'interroppe mia gioia con diletto
> Il qual poi che vicino
> Mi si fece, Ripresi il mio camino
> Ella rivolta al ciel sereno e chiaro
> Dicea con stil amaro:
>>> Tu ti parti cor mio caro
>>> Et mi lasci in piant' amaro
> E senza alcun riparo
>>> Deh non ti partir da me
>>> Caro cor per la tua fe
> Ma fu interrotta
> Da un gargion ch'in fretta
> Passò cantando questa canzonetta:
>>> Bianca Lucia fatte alla fenestra
>>> Con le tue mani scarga la balestra

E qui staremo un gran pezzo a cianciare
Quattr'o sei volte amor ti vo baciare.

(2nd part)　　　Io mi fermai un poco, e mentre stava

Intento a udir cio che'l gargion cantava
Ei si rivolse et presso l'acqua assiso
Vidde una pastorella
Tutta leggiadr'e bella
A cui disse con grat'e dolce risa:
Mi lavaresti un po la mia camisa
o lavandera
Si che la lavaro stu mi contenti
corin mio bel o viva l'amor
Ella di rossor tinta e di vergogna
Alzando il viso grato
Con un ton disusato
Rispose col cantar questa canzon:
Tu starai su la tua porta
E mi staro—ne—no sul mio canton
E per farm'ogn' hor piu accorta
Ti trattaro—ne—no da Babion
Ma poi fermossi e con disdegno et ira
Volgendo gli occhi alquanto
Udi da un'altro canto
Cantar un Pastorel con dolce lira
lira lira lira
Nuova canzon d'amor e nuovi versi
A cui vicine fersi
Molte Ninfe leggiadre
Che con due vaghe squadre
D'amanti rissonar faceano il cielo
Cantando pieni d'amoroso zelo:
Fami la Pidra Antonia
Falala lalala la.

This gay nonsense, reminiscent of nursery rhymes and improvised doggerel, is
naturally meaningless without the music, without the quotations of familiar
melodies, without the alternation of half-madrigalesque narrative and half-popular
coarseness. But that things of this sort were actually written in the second half of
the century is evident from another group of pieces in which the connecting narrative has a pastoral character. The very first number is one of these:

Damon Pastor gentil con la sua Clori
Stav'apoggiato a un'Elce antiqua e ombrosa
E di face amorosa
Ardendo ivi fra verd' herbett'e fiori
La cara amata Nimpha riguardava,
Che dolcemente una canzon cantava
In voce pur'e schietta:
  Io mi son giovinetta e volentieri
  M'allegro e canto in la stagion novella
  Merce d'Amor e de dolci pensieri.
Tacque la Nimpha bella e con vezzoso
Parlar al suo Pastor dolce ridendo
Disse: Caro Damon, dì ancor tu quella
Che nel ritorno tuo cantasti al' hora
Tutto gioendo da pensier geloso
Sciolto vivendo fuor di gelosia:
  Cara la vita mia egli è pur vero
  Ch'altra fiamma d'amor non v'arse' l petto
  In tanto tempo si turbato e fiero.
Così dicea'l pastor ma fu interrotto
Da un grosso stuol di Nimph'alm'e leggiadre
Che con pastori in dolce unite squadre
Passando risonar faceano intorno
Il ciel e l'aria con cantar adorno,
Spargendo voci in queste parti e'n quelle;
Quando le vaghe stelle
Nel bel sereno cielo
Con la ruggiata e' l gielo
Cadon'insieme alhora
Che spunta fuor l'aurora.

It is the same thing on a higher level. To the more elegant pastoral setting correspond the more elegant quotations: these are no longer folk-songs and street-songs but famous madrigals, known to everyone—Domenico Ferabosco's madrigal on Boccaccio and Giaches Wert's *Cara la vita mia*, from his first madrigal book for five voices (1558), a piece frequently used for *missae parodiae*, together with other madrigals by Filippo di Monte and Claudio Merulo. (I shall not venture to decide the question whether the quotation from *Cara la vita mia* favors or contradicts the thesis that Wert is the author of these villotte; a self-quotation is quite as likely as an *omaggio* to a musical acquaintance. But the presence of such a quotation in the very first number of the book might well be a concealed reference to its author.) Here again, as in the canzonetta, there is a mixture of styles: the villotta takes on a madrigalesque appearance, begins to resemble the pastoral dialogue, and looks forward to the cantata. If we substitute the "aria" for the quotation, we have the cantata of the seventeenth century in all its essential features.

Yet it is precisely in this play of allusions that the wit of music-making in company consists, and the sixteenth century carried its enthusiasm for quotation-making to an extent that is difficult for us to understand today, deprived as we are of a common popular heritage. The sixteenth century considered it perfectly legitimate for Fra Lodovico Balbi, choirmaster at the Santo in Padua and earlier a singer at San Marco and choirmaster at the Cà Grande in Venice, to take over the upper voices of twenty-seven famous madrigals for four voices and to make them into five-voiced madrigals by adding four lower voices of his own. And it was legitimate, for his time attached far less importance to what we call *invention* than we do. At the very least these pieces presuppose a certain connoisseurship on the part of the listener—a knowledge of the literature and the capacity to appreciate the new setting and its new inflections. For us today, the interest of Balbi's work lies in its choice of composers and pieces: besides Arcadelt's *Il bianco e dolce cigno*, Rore's *Ancor che col partire*, and Verdelot's *Quanto sia liet'il giorno*, we are surprised to find names and compositions unfamiliar to us but evidently more than familiar in their day. In general a knowledge of certain famous pieces is taken for granted. Seriously intended quotations occur even in Marenzio, and it is astonishing to find this master of sophistication associating himself with the austere Cipriano by introducing a literal quotation from one of Cipriano's posthumous madrigals for four voices (1565) in the seventh number of his *Primo libro a sei* (1581):

> Al suon de le dolcissime parole
> Et agli ultimi accenti
> Ster queti et fermi i venti,
> E più chiaro e più bel si fece il sole,
> Ond'ella come suole
> Tornò a ridir: "Non mi tolga il ben mio
> Chi non arde d'amor come faccio io."

And what is one to say of the *Furti* of Girolamo Belli d'Argenta, which textually and musically are wholly made up of nothing but "stolen goods"? They are the musical counterparts of the literary *centoni* of the time, poems consisting wholly of quotations, like beggars' coats patched together from stolen scraps. Girolamo Belli was born a subject of Duke Alfonso of Ferrara, to whom he dedicated his first work

in 1583, a book of six-voiced madrigals whose chief and central number is a setting of Guarini's *canzone dei baci* and which also contains a text from Tasso. But he spends part of his time in Mantua, where he is said to have been a singer, and in 1584 he dedicates his second madrigal book for six voices—the *Furti* already mentioned—to Duke Guglielmo; three years later he republished it in a new edition with nine new numbers and a new dedication. And it is surely no exaggeration when he says in this second dedication that his madrigals have already overrun all Italy ("i miei madrigali che per l'adietro per esser solo dedicati a V.A. hanno così felicemente scorta tutta la Italia"). Later on he seems to have returned to Ferrara: as though in anticipation of coming events he prudently dedicates his third madrigal book for six voices to Cardinal Pietro Aldobrandini, nephew of Pope Clement VIII, the future vicar general and grave-digger of the duchy of the Este, to whom Luzzaschi, who is supposed to have been Belli's teacher, also dedicated his *madrigali concertati* (cf. below p. 834). Belli's activity as a madrigalist extends well into the seventeenth century: as late as 1617 a ninth book of five-voiced madrigals, some of them already in the *stile concertato*, appeared as Opus XXII. On the title-page Belli styles himself "L'Elevato" as a member of the Accademia degli Armonici in Cesena.

Belli was a serious musician and a prolific writer of church music, and his *Furti* were seriously intended and seriously received. Unquestionably they were considered quite clever, although—or rather because—they consisted wholly of allusions. A text like the following, which we repeat, is patched together from Petrarch, Bembo, and Boccaccio:

> Questa crudele e dura—
> Tu'l scerni Amore (Ahi misero mio stato)—
> Tuo regno sprezza e del mio mal non cura!
> Che giova posseder cittadi e regni
> E mille haver vittorie e fregi degni
> Se Donna sol Qual bella pargoletta
> Ch'ancor non sente Amore
> Schernisce il tuo valore
> Tratta contro quest'empia per tu'honore
> L'arco tuo saldo e qualch'una saetta.

But Belli's "thefts" extend also to the music, and as we have already pointed out (p. 212 above), his *Flora di vaghi fiori il crine adorno* combines quotations from the two most celebrated madrigals of Palestrina. The element of parody is not altogether lacking. Thus the following piece begins with the *capoverso* of one of Petrarch's most serious canzoni and ends by singing the praises of a local beauty:

> Standomi un giorno solo alla finestra
> Dal Po con degn'honori,

Verso la sponda destra
Vidi una bella Ninfa sorger fuori.
Sorgean seco scherzando
Mille amori, e cantando
Pareano dir ver me: quest'è il tesoro
Ch'all'alma mia darà dolce ristoro!

The reader may determine for himself to what extent Belli has utilized the most grandiose of Lasso's madrigals (*Works*, II, 89), from the second book for five voices of 1559:

At the second line and the beginning of the "pastoral" atmosphere, Belli changes, without any indication, from ₵ to C, and the tempo changes from sustained to lively, from Largo to Vivace—a procedure familiar to us from the villanella. The metrical situation is just the opposite of that in the *Meistersinger* Vorspiel, where at measure 27 Wagner changes, likewise without any indication, from an alla breve to a genuine four-four. I call it the opposite situation in that with Wagner there is an involuntary slowing-up of the tempo at the shift to four-four time.

How completely alien and unintelligible to us today is a work of art that presupposes an exact knowledge of another work and that does not lose in value as a result of this knowledge! Of course, a quotation is at the same time a tribute. Thus, in the dedication of his second edition, Belli admits that he has taken special pains to "steal" from the madrigals of Duke Guglielmo.

We turn now to another form of music in company, a form related to that prac-

ticed in all but the most "high-brow" of the academies—to the music of the university students in Padua, Bologna, and Siena, particularly of the students in Padua, who seem to have been the ones most given to musical merry-making. In this field Francesco Portinaro of Italy (cf. p. 471 above) finds a rival in Filippo Duc of Flanders. We know next to nothing about his life: we do not even know what town he came from, when he arrived in Italy, or who his teacher was, although it was probably a Venetian. The first work of his that we know, a book of four-voiced madrigals "con una serenata et un dialogo a otto nel fine" (1570) is dedicated in a cordial and touching letter (Bologna catalogue, III, 66) to his compatriots, the Flemish students in Padua; a book of spiritual madrigals (*Le vergini*, though not Petrarch's) of 1574 is dedicated to two counts Montfort of Vorarlberg who must have been students in Padua at the time; his last publication, finally, is dedicated in 1586 to Johann Jacob and Karl Kisl, sons of the treasurer to Archduke Carl of Graz. His work is a cross section of what the young noblemen sang during their student years in Padua.

There is no lack of edifying pieces and invocations of the Muses, or of settings of texts by Petrarch (*Deh hor foss' io*) and Torquato Tasso (*Non è questa la mano*), but the real emphasis is on gaiety and on the vocal *collegium musicum*. The five- and six-voiced pieces in the collection of 1586 are all of them written to order—serenades, a gallant comparison of a Paduan beauty to the rising sun with Apollo withdrawing in shame behind a cloud (*Luce de gli occhi*), a farewell, always a favorite theme with students, and so forth. A tripartite piece (*Non ha potuto in cotanti anni*) is dedicated to a student, Leonardo Mercherich (Leonhard Merkerich), to judge from his name a native of the Lower Rhineland: one of Cupid's victims begs him to aim also at his beloved. Everything is concise, colorful, and plastic, though by no means artless. And that the work is intended for young noblemen, who are not fond of difficulties, is reflected in the notation, which meticulously indicates every accidental, even the "self-evident" ones. The last two numbers take us to the heart of student life. One of them is a hymn to Bacchus, half Latin, half German:

> Sequamini, o socii
> Zu einem guten vullen wein
> Laetamini vos ebrii
> Und lasst uns frisch und frelich sein . . .

The other is a canzonetta "alla napolitana" whose "Neapolitan" characteristics are neither formal nor linguistic and must therefore lie in the rapid declamation and in the quasi-dramatic, dialogue-like alternation of the divided choirs with the tutti.

Sapete voi qual sia
Donna la pena mia?
Ben so che lo sapete
Ma voi non lo credete—
Onde di novo ve lo torn' a dire:
Voi mi fate morire.

Among Duc's earlier madrigals for four voices the most remarkable piece is the serenata especially mentioned in the title. The text reads as follows:

L'aria s'oscura e di minute stelle
Già si dipinge il ciel & in ciascuna
Parte i bei raggi suoi scopre la luna;
Ogni fiera selvaggi'il sonn'affrena—
Sol'io piangendo e sospirando dico:
 Chi passa per questa strada e non sospira beato se—
Ma tu crudel nemica di pietade,
Più sord' assai ch'un aspe od ors'alpestra,
Di me ti ridi e stand'alla finestra
Mi chiami e poi t'ascondi,
Ond' io piangendo humilmente dico:
  O sorte o Dio
  Dite che v' ho fatt'io
  Che si contraria sete al voler mio?

(2nd part) Ma tu per dar al cor magior tormento,
Mi dici in voci colme di lamento:
  Dhe non t'affliger tanto vita mia—
  Non sai tu ben ch'io son la Margherita
  Che chi mi don'il cor gli do la vita
   Meschin' oime
Et poi dall'altra parte,
Usand'ingann' et arte,
Chiamar ti fai da certa vecchiarella
Ch'in freta dice: O Polissena bella,
Tua madre ti dimanda
E'n modo tal col far da me partita
  Di fuor mi lasci a lamentarmi forte
  Di te d'amor e di mia acerba sorte.

{ 758 }

(3rd part)   Apri homai l'uscio o mia gentil signora,

Ne in stato tal non mi lasciar perire,

Mentre poi dar soccorso al mio languire,

Et s' hora che son tre giorni

Ch'io mi partei di Franza

Cara speranza

Solo per tuo amore

Non mi lasciar piu in doglia qui di fuora,

E se la voglia tua pur si compiace,

Che cosi pera senz' haver mai pace,

Non consentir almeno

Che quella tua vecchiazza dispettosa

Con voce rantacosa

Mi dica col fuggirsi dal balcon

O che naso o che nason!

Ma riprendend'il suo malvaggi'ardire,

Mostr'a ciascun ch'alberg'in questa via

Ch'io sia'l tuo amante & tu la donna mia.

(4th part)   Oimè ch'io spasmo—apri la port' omai,

Dolce mia pastorella,

E mentre sei de piu verd' anni tuoi

In la stagion novella,

Dona omai pac'all'affannato cuore

Ne por l'affett'a questi spensierati

Che van di nott'armati—canticchiando:

Chi zapparà la melica

un bel bas' havrà da me,

Rispose messer lo zanni,

la zapparò ben mi messer lo zanni,

Zappe la melica mariola

da un bas'a me

a me si

Sangue de mi

mai non ti vidi

Manc'un baso ti promisi no.

No no no no de mariola

No che non volendo compiacerl'ogn' hora

Se n'andran sempr'in tuo disnor gridando:
   Che t' haggio fatto o ladra traditora.
Però gentil signora
Apri la port'omai
E mentre poi scorgend'il mio dolore
Don'omai pac'all'affannato cuore.

Wherein lie the meaning and humor of a piece like this? In the constant alternation between the sanctimoniously sentimental narrative—or rather the lament of the languishing lover beneath the window of his lady, who is not exactly a lady—and the coarse street-song, the vulgar allusion. It is a new testimony to the love of parody characteristic of the time—its lack of seriousness, its skepticism, and its indecision. With Duc, even the sentimental framework is parodistic: it abounds in exaggerated little phrases, pathetic cross-relations, ritardandi and accelerandi, in short in "madrigalisms," in so far as the rapid tempo admits of such. The most violent contrasts clash with one another in the last section, where the sentimental conclusion follows immediately after the absurd episode of Zanni and Mariola, one of those dialogues or *mariazi* that were especially popular in Padua, where the folk-singers acted and sang them in a most dramatic fashion in the public squares (cf. V. Rossi, *Storia della letteratura italiana*, II, 2). In this piece Duc has preserved for us just such a scene.

The words of this serenata were set to music often—for example, as No. 7 (a bipartite setting) of the *Villotte mantovane* of 1583, a collection already mentioned. And from this second setting we learn something curious: the sentimental framework is the same, but the quotations, the street-songs, have changed. Instead of *Chi passa per questa strada* the sentimental tone continues; the end of the third section is completely different and introduces the folk-song about "La Girometta"; the spirit of the whole is more uniformly *alla villanesca*, and at several points the new version resorts to the comic stuttering of the *giustiniana*. In this respect, the piece is related to the *commedia dell' arte*, for there too the situations are always the same, while the *lazzi*, the jokes, are subject to constant change at the whim of the improvisers.

We have anticipated a little in order to be able to deal in a connected fashion with the work of Alessandro Striggio, the strange musician who made the most numerous and most important contributions to music as entertainment of anyone before Orazio Vecchi. In his first madrigal book for six voices of 1560 our serenata is the concluding number, more or less exactly in the textual version of Filippo Duc, who must certainly have known Striggio's setting. But Striggio's distribution of the emphasis is different from Filippo Duc's and even more varied than that of the Anonymous of the *Villote mantovane*. Striggio sets the first two sections for five voices, the last two for six, and thus makes use of the more complex and most

complex apparatus of the madrigal; in his setting the emphasis falls accordingly on the pseudo-sentimental sections. (J. C. Hol has reproduced the folk-tunes of Striggio's serenata in the appendix to his monograph on Vecchi, pp. 2ff.) Thus the contrast between these sections and the homophony of the street-songs stands out more sharply than ever, especially since Striggio tends to accentuate his homophony by giving it the added impact of triple time. Later on Striggio made a specialty of writing music for entertainment in company, among other things, and if we were asked why he did so, we should answer that it was because he was a courtier and not a professional musician.

ALESSANDRO STRIGGIO

ALESSANDRO STRIGGIO occupies a special place among the musicians of the sixteenth century, one only comparable—and even then not wholly comparable—to that of the Principe Gesualdo da Venosa. No dilettante, he was an excellent musician; at the same time he was a Mantuan nobleman—he is said to have been born at Mantua about 1535—and for this reason he never accepted a professional post. Not one of his works is provided with a letter of dedication. We do not know who his teacher was; perhaps it was Rore, though more probably Wert. I should be inclined to identify him with the "Sandrino" who is represented by a single madrigal in Rore's fourth book (in the editions of 1557 and 1563), and to regard this madrigal as Striggio's earliest work, one that would coincide in time with the conjectural publication date of his first madrigal book, if the publication of the work of a nobleman under a nickname were not on the whole improbable, and if it were not for the existence of a more likely candidate, a certain Alexandrino Venitiano, presumably a resident of Rome. But however this may be, Striggio published his first book of five-voiced madrigals about 1557 or 1558 (only the reprint of 1560 has been preserved), and this was followed by several further reprints and four additional books. In 1560 and 1571 he published two books of six-voiced pieces; he is also represented in the anthologies of the time by a whole series of isolated numbers. He wrote almost no church music; the few masses and motets listed by the bibliographers seem in part to be *contrafacta*—madrigals to which a Latin text has been adapted.

On the title pages of his madrigal books Striggio regularly styles himself "gentil'huomo mantovano" and "servitore dell'Illustrissimo et Eccellentiss. Cosmo de Medici Duca di Firenze e di Siena." This was a post of composer to the family and court that did not prevent his undertaking long journeys. Between May and August 1567 he was in England, and it is tempting to imagine for oneself what his political and musical experiences may have been during these months. After a journey through Flanders and France he arrived in Milan again about the middle of August, and on August 20 promised the Duke to return to Florence by way of Mantua (cf. *Rivista musicale italiana*, xx, 527ff.). He always remained a loyal servant of the Medici, though he never broke off his relations with his native city and with the Gonzaga family, and though he seems also to have been employed at one time by Duke Guglielmo. Later on we shall learn (p. 846) that in the summer of 1584 he spied upon the singing of the *tre dame* at the "enemy" court of the Este in Ferrara and then attempted to exploit his discoveries in compositions of his own. He seems to have been an accomplished player on the lute and "viola," and to the nobleman and virtuoso all doors stood open.

Striggio began his career as a "viola" virtuoso; as early as 1567 Cosimo Bartoli praises him as such in his *Ragionamenti*: "Io havevo in vero sentito molto lodare uno Alessandro Strigia da Mantova, non solo eccellente, ma eccellentissimo nel sonar la viola: et far sentir in essa quatro parti a un tratto con tanta leggiadria et con tanta musica, che fa stupire gli ascoltanti, et oltre a questo le sue composizioni son tenute cosi musicali et buone, come altre che in questi tempi si sentino. . . ." — "In truth, I have heard high praise of a certain Alessandro Striggio of Mantua who is not merely excellent but even more than excellent in playing the 'viola,' and he plays on it in four voices at one time with such elegance and fullness of tone that he amazes the listeners; his compositions are considered as musical and as good as the others that one hears these days. . . ." Striggio's instrument is described in some detail in a letter written by Duke William V of Bavaria to his father Albert V on August 3, 1574 (Munich, Geheimes Hausarchiv, Akt 597, vi): it was a large lira da gamba with a considerable number of strings. Striggio must accordingly have been well known at the Bavarian court. First a player on the "viola," later a composer, Striggio opened up a path that Monteverdi followed after him; the transition was not altogether unusual, as we learn from Giovanni Rovetta in the strange preface to his *Salmi concertati* of 1626 in which he defends his transition from instrumentalist to composer by saying that before him Giovanni Priuli, Giovanni Valentini, and Signor Striggio had done likewise. On September 22, 1587, Striggio is said to have died in Mantua. But it is just possible that this is an error: on the one hand, he is represented as late as 1592 by a contribution to the *Trionfo di Dori*, a collection of pieces written to the order of Leonardo Sanudo; on the other hand, these pieces were written some time (*di qualch' anno*) before their publication, as the dedication explains. His last three madrigal books were published in 1596 and 1597— strangely late—by his son Alessandro Striggio the Younger, a librettist and producer of operas whose name will be forever associated with the immortal Claudio Monteverdi and his *Orfeo*.

Alessandro Striggio the Younger ("Sandrino") was a librettist by inheritance. For in the service of the Medici his father had made a specialty of the composition

of music for dramatic intermezzi, an aspect of his work that belongs in its entirety to the preliminary history of opera. The series begins with the intermezzo *Psiche ed Amore*, written in 1565 in collaboration with Corteccia for the *Cofanaria* of Francesco d'Ambra and performed on December 25 in the Sala vecchia. It continues with the intermezzi for the *Fabii* of Lotto di Mazza, written in 1567 on the occasion of the christening of Leonora Medici; for the *Vedova* of Giovambattista Cini, performed on May 1, 1569, in the great hall of the Palazzo vecchio in honor of an illustrious guest, Archduke Charles of Graz—perhaps the most interesting of these is the *Transformation of the Peasants into Frogs*, after Ovid, which can hardly have failed to include a monodic *preghiera di Latona*. The series ends with Striggio's contribution to the wedding music for the marriage of Francesco Medici and Bianca Capello, the "daughter of the Republic" of Venice, in 1579, and the first, second, and fifth intermezzi for the *Amico fido* of Count Giovanni de'Bardi, the patron of the Florentine Camerata, on the occasion of the wedding of Don Cesare d'Este and Virginia de' Medici in 1586.

With all of these essays, Striggio was surely one of those who helped to bring monody into being, and had he lived longer, his name would perhaps be coupled with Giulio Caccini's and even with Claudio Monteverdi's. In his own period, from 1560 to 1590, he stands as a madrigalist between Rore and Monteverdi, and not (as might be thought) between Gabrieli and Marenzio. He is anything but a pastoral madrigalist. He remains quite serious and is reserved in his animation, even when he writes a wedding piece in the form of an anacreontic scene, as he does in his earliest work (before 1560):

> Mentre la donna anzi la vita mia,
> Misti a le rose i gigli va tessendo,
> Vide fra l'herb'e i fior ch'Amor dormia,
> Et lui lieta legò dolce ridendo.
> Sciolgersi di tal nodo Amor volia
> Ma chi l'havea legato poi vedendo:
> "Va," diss', "o madre, cerc'un nov'Amore,
> Perch'il mio regno quì sarà maggiore!"

Likewise thoroughly un-Venetian and as delicately wrought as chamber music are the two festival pieces of 1571 and 1586 that Torchi has reprinted (*Arte musicale in Italia*, I, 333f.) among other things of his—*Di questa bionda e vaga* and *Ninfe leggiadr' e belle*. For an exemplary piece of his one should turn to the six-voiced madrigal *Nasce la pena mia*, a piece used by Filippo di Monte as the basis of a celebrated mass, likewise for six voices (*Works*, ed. Van den Borren and Nuffel, No. 16): it is an elegiac piece with a quiet movement, characterized also by its rich sonority and its delicate, rarefied harmony, and by the repetition of the concluding lines which is also typical of Monte. He is severe in his choice of texts: some are from Petrarch, others from Ariosto and the stanzas of Bernardo Tasso, but there is nothing from Guarini or Torquato Tasso, though he must have known both of them intimately. Yet it may be that this reserve on the part of a servant of the Medici may also have had a political basis. He chooses no authors later than Guidiccioni and Tansillo, whose sonnet *Amor m'impenna l'ale* inspired him to an especially grandiose composition. In a similar way, he does not go beyond Rore on the rhythmic side, and on the harmonic side Rore leaves him far behind. There is nothing "experimental" about his work, but an indefinite hesitation or hovering between the two varieties of measure is characteristic of him. An amateur, he is fond of contrapuntal weaving, even entangling; he is almost a mannerist in stretto. Despite the occasional use of divided choirs and paired voices, his voice-leading is basically homophonic in its motivation in five Petrarch settings of his first book for six voices:

> I dolci colli ...
> Lasciat' hai morte ...
> Là ver l'aurora ...
> Che fai che pensi ...
> Amor io fallo. ...

As a half-spiritual madrigal, *Lasciat'hai morte* moves quite uniformly in the alla breve measure. One is almost astonished to find the crudest sort of "eye-music" in his setting of a text that seems like a remote anticipation of the "day and night" dialogue in Wagner's *Tristan* (*Primo libro a cinque*, before 1560):

> *Notte* felice aventuros'e bella,
> Che dopo tante pene e dolor tanti,
> Dopo singolti e pianti
> Pur mi guidasti in bracci'alla mia stella,
> Ove donasti alla virtù smarrita
> Sì dolce e cara vita!—
> Ma'l sol poi troppo caminando forte
> Tosto conduss'il giorno ond'io hebbi morte.

To be sure, the "eye-music" is offset by the pronounced dramatic movement of this strange piece. In violent contrast to the writing of the Striggio who is a disciple of the austere Rore, stand such completely baroque details as the naturalistic sighs and the portrayal of Cupid fanning the flame of love with his wings in the six-voiced setting of Ariosto's *Questi ch' inditio fan del mio tormento*, a stanza from the *Orlando furioso* (xxiii, 127), or the beginning of Ariosto's stanza *Non rumor di tamburi*, a passage already discussed (cf. p. 232 above). Apart from the aesthetic

observation that the madrigal is inclined to represent a negative by an exaggerated positive, one might make the biographical one that Striggio was probably a pupil and surely an imitator of Giaches Wert, and the historical one that the piece in question is to some extent a recollection of Janequin's *Bataille* and in this sense a connecting link with Striggio's naturalistic works. This same book of 1571 (*Secondo libro a sei*) contains another contrapuntal *tour de force* of Striggio's, a setting of a stanza from Bernardo Tasso:

> Ahi dispietato Amor, come consenti
> Ch'io meni vita sì *penosa* e ria. . . .

To a five-voiced piece, complete in itself, Striggio has added a *sesta parte si placet* which, in keeping with the meaning of the text, winds its way laboriously and painstakingly through the other voices, in constantly changing rhythmical variants of the ascending and descending hexachord:

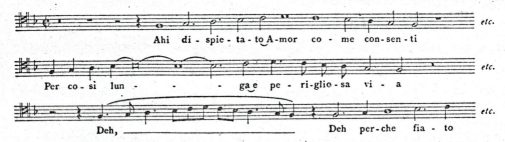

Here the medieval or constructive point of view comes into direct contact with the modern or expressive one.

Striggio achieves a perfect balance by concluding this book with a setting of the two first stanzas from Canto XLVI of the *Orlando furioso*:

> Hor se mi mostra la mia carta il vero
> Non è lontan a discoprirsi il porto . . .

In effect, he says: "I approach the end of my labors." How personal this is, and how much one would distort it by detaching it from its context and publishing it as a separate piece without any explanation! Surely this is proof conclusive that not every book of madrigals is a haphazard assortment of unrelated pieces. By way of contrast, Striggio's *Secondo libro a cinque* (1570) really is a haphazard assortment of unrelated pieces—pastorals, festive madrigals, and so forth, and it is significant that only one of these pieces has a "literary" text, *La pastorella con la verga in mano*, a stanza from Bernardo Tasso's *Amadigi* (LVII, 1). In setting the two stanzas from the *Orlando furioso*, Striggio gives his music a firm rhythmic pace and strikes a note of confidence and victory; at *Odo di squille, odo di trombe il suono* the sound of the trumpet is represented as a matter of course.

These realistic features in Striggio's "serious" production do not wholly explain how and why he became the master of the naturalistic scene. That from the very first he entertained a fondness for the bizarre and a tendency to question the concept of sentimentality in the madrigal, is evident from his serenata of 1560, and his French journey of 1567 may perhaps have intensified his love of the *battaglia*, the *caccia*, and similar descriptive fancies. But his most famous work, the "Chatter of Women at Their Washing" is not (as might be thought) a result of his visit to France, for on September 12, 1567, its publisher Giulio Bonagionta had already signed the dedication of the first edition—*Il cicalamento delle donne al bucato et la caccia di Alessandro Striggio, con un lamento di Didone ad Enea, per la sua partenza, di Cipriano Rore. . . .* Two further editions, without Rore's piece, but augmented by Striggio's *Game of Cards*, appeared in 1569 and 1584.

The *Cicalamento delle donne* has been reprinted by Domenico Alaleona and Angelo Solerti (*Rivista musicale italiana*, XII and XIII), but this is a documentary reprint and not a musical one, and it is offered in a misleading way as a document bearing on the preliminary history of the opera. Nothing could be more erroneous, and it is unfortunate that in the early 1900's no piece of music that had the slightest scenic or dramatic character could be studied from any point of view but that of operatic history. The *Cicalamento* is a madrigalesque entertainment and not a "forerunner" of musical drama. From the historical point of view, it is a descendant of the caccia of the Trecento and an ancestor of certain humorous pieces of the seventeenth and eighteenth centuries, such as Carlo Grossi's festive gathering of the Jews (1681) or the vocal and instrumental peasant pieces by Valentin Rathgeber and Leopold Mozart.

This much is true: in Striggio's serenata the setting was still a narrative; in the *Cicalamento* it has become a scene—once more a scene, as it had been with Janequin, who seems in his hunts, his battles, his bird-songs, his street-cries, his *Caquet des femmes* (Striggio's immediate model) to make us eye-witnesses of actual happenings. But what was new and artistically stimulating for the end of the sixteenth century was not the scene, but the narrative or framework; not the aria, but the recitative. To regard the first operas as musical drama is to impose on these early beginnings the operatic concepts of the eighteenth and nineteenth centuries; like classical tragedies, the operas of Caccini, Peri, Gagliano, and the early Monteverdi culminate in the narrative—the recitative—and not in the powerful dramatic scene.

It would be useless to search for Striggio's text in any of the literary sources of the time. It is *poesia per musica*, and its models are to be found only in other music books. Thus one of the most charming poems of the supposedly so "classical" six-

teenth century remains anonymous. It begins, as do Nasco's and Ruffo's "cantata" texts, with pure narrative:

> Nella vaga stagion`....`
> Mi trovai presso a un chiaro e vivo fonte. . . .

And now follow the four sections of the naturalistic scene: While industriously splashing away at their work, the women chatter, laugh over village scandal, and scream at the appearance of a bird of prey; the scene culminates in quarreling, abuse, and reconciliation; it ends with farewells and an agreement to meet again the next morning at the village bakery.

It is easier to describe this piece than to understand it historically. It comes from a variety of sources. One of these is, of course, the canzone of Nasco and Ruffo, with its division into several sections, the single sections characterized by changes in the number of voices. The *introduzione*, the narrative that introduces the scene, is for four voices, simple but not homophonic: Striggio narrates somewhat circumstantially, and with many text repetitions, features pointing clearly to an origin in the canzone and in the *canzone alla villanesca*. The intention is not entirely naturalistic. But sometimes it is so and in Janequin's style, for example in the working-out of the scene with the bird of prey or at the climax of the quarrel, when the women come to blows. But in general it is partly realistic and partly in fun: the fashionable company that sings this work is amusing itself at the expense of the lower class. And in the second and final sections, two quotations affirm the connection with Striggio's serenata and its predecessors: a few of the buxom dames suddenly fall to singing folk-songs which stand out by reason of their triple time from the conversation in duple time that runs on against them. These folk-songs are Tuscan *rispetti* or Roman airs: the second is simply the well-known *romanesca*:

There is little tone-painting, but not even Striggio can resist "laughter," and the suspect indisposition of one of the women tempts him to modulate toward the gloomier side of the mode. Elsewhere the prevailing characteristics are a recitative-like melody and the simplest possible tonal relationships, as in Janequin. But there is no textual onomatopoeia and no realism or humor as such. It is not easy to bring the *Cicalamento* to life as humor—not to say comic opera: we shall have to wait until Orazio Vecchi for the introduction of this ingredient.

Striggio takes us into a different social sphere, though one seen no less naturalistically than the last, in his "Card-Game" or *Gioco di primiera*, the forerunner of such modern scenes as the game of skat in the *Intermezzo* of Richard Strauss or Igor Stravinsky's *Jeu des cartes*. In the sixteenth century *primiera* was the card-game of the upper classes: we have commentaries on it in the *Capitolo del gioco della primiera col comento di messer Pietropaulo da San Chirico* (Venice, 1534) and the popular *Gioco di Primiera con una nova gionta composta per Benedetto Clario Cieco Venetiano* (Bologna, 1550), and everyone who has studied the diaries describing the life at the courts of Ferrara, Mantua, Florence, and papal Rome knows that almost all evening entertainments, including musical ones, ended at the card table with *primiera*. Nor was the motif of card-playing altogether new to music: in Petrucci's sixth book of frottole (No. 32) it is already treated by Francesco Veneto (Francesco d'Ana):

> Se le carte me son contra
> Gia non voglio disperarme
> Ma per meglio governarmi
> Che poi pegio non me incontra. . . .

Ideally, the rules of the game require eight players. Striggio is satisfied with five in either section of the scene, although in his *Cicalamento* and *Caccia* he had gone as far as seven. Since we have reprinted the piece in our volume of illustrations[1] no detailed discussion will be necessary. There are two parts. First comes a short introduction; then the "clean" deck is brought in and shuffled and the players are warned to be "good" losers, even if there should be laughter at their expense. Then follows the game itself with all its dramatic details; one has the illusion that each of the five players is an individual. The scene is unsurpassed in liveliness and naturalism. If we may be permitted to draw a parallel between the tempi of music and painting, we shall say that this is one case in which music leads the way. Michelangelo Merisi, surnamed Caravaggio, the first painter of naturalistic scenes of card-playing and other games, was not born until the year in which Striggio's "Card-Game" was printed—1569. But he comes from the same region as Striggio and the naturalistic, anti-pastoral scene in music—Lombardy, Mantua, Bergamo, and above all Modena. More than a hundred years later another North Italian musician, Carlo Grossi, wrote and published a second *Gioco di primiera*, in his *Divertimento di Tavola, All'uso delle Reggie Corti*, Op. ix (1681), a work that combines naturalism with moralizing arias. Grossi's piece was presumably known to Antonio Caldara when he wrote his cantata *Il giuoco del quadriglio* for the Archduchess Maria Theresia and her sister Maria Anna, another work that describes and depicts a game of cards (MS 17646 of the Vienna National Library). Grossi attains the height of naturalism in a similar

---

[1] See Vol. III, No. 86.

piece, the *Gioco della Morra*, a game still played today just as it was played in 1681 and presumably just as it was already being played in Imperial Rome.

One of the musicians who stands between Striggio and Vecchi in point of time is that strange figure, the Reverendo Monsignore Lodovico Agostini of Ferrara, Apostolic Prothonotary, and a chaplain and musician in the service of Duke Alfonso II. I hesitate to say that he exercised much influence on Vecchi but he was surely an admirer and imitator of Striggio, whose *Nasce la pena mia* he parodies in a canzone of his own (1581) and whose style he also takes as a model in other madrigals (*Dolce Lucrezia*, 1583—"Ad imitazione del S. Al. Striggio"). He belongs to the circle of Luzzaschi and Wert and to the brilliant musical life of Ferrara and Mantua. He dedicates a madrigal to the singer Laura Peperara (*De l'odorate spoglie*, 1583); but even so he is a somewhat isolated figure in Ferrara as elsewhere, his works have no far-reaching success, and the anthologies also ignore him almost altogether. In spite of his high ecclesiastical dignity, Agostini did not leave a single piece of church music, and to atone for a disturbingly exuberant early work he wrote only a book of spiritual madrigals, the *Lagrime del Peccatore* after Tansillo, his last work. (He died on September 20, 1590, at the age of fifty-six and lies buried in the Santo Spirito in Ferrara.) The exuberant early work in question is a *Musica . . . sopra le rime bizzarre di M. Andrea Calmo, et altri Autori* of 1567, dedicated to the poet himself four years before his death and printed and dated in Milan, strangely enough, and not in Venice. For these jokes in dialect, travesties of Petrarch (*Paxe non trovo*, cf. V. Rossi's *Calmo*, p. xcii), mascherate (*Quanti sono saltatori*, cf. F. Ghisi, *loc. cit.*, p. 150), and serenades belong to the sphere of the Venetian villotta and Castellino's Ferrarese imitation of it; like Castellino's pieces, they do not go beyond simple homophony, though they contain many "chromatic" jokes (cf. Hol, *loc. cit.*, pp. 59ff.). These crudities were later (1583) offset by more pretentious "chromatic" pieces and works for double chorus "in which the natural replies that an echo will make to anyone's voice are artificially imitated" ("ne'quali sono artificiosamente imitate le risposte, ch'Echo suol fare naturalmente alla voce altrui"). Agostini remains wholly preoccupied with the bizarre, and it is significant for the taste of the time that he has so little success. In his "Musical Riddles" of 1571 there occur the following texts:

Madonna un mio pensiero
Scoprir vorrei; Ma poi non v'adirate,
Se con voi dico il vero!
Dico ch'io penso et voi non vi pensate
Ch'iscusar non potrete il vostro errore,
Se a un simulato Amore

Voi crederete hor quest'è il pensier mio—
Intendami chi può che m'intend'io.

    Un mal è che mi rende afflitto, e mesto;
Un remedio può sol farmi contento
Un Rè mi tien oppresso, et m'è molesto,
Un Rè mi fà gir fuori di tormento;
Un Rè mi fà sol lieto à tutte l'hore;
Un Rè mi fà sol lasso, e quest'è Amore.

The first is a parody of a sentimental madrigal; the second, filled with puns on the solmization syllables, is like a parody of the madrigal contrived as a mere *jeu d'esprit*. Works of this sort are more noteworthy as a part of social history than as music. In *Le notti piacevoli*, the collected *novelle* of Straparola, each *giornata* concludes with an ambiguous and suggestive riddle—the intentions of Monsignore Agostini are not very different. This is music as entertainment, as a game to be played in company. And if Agostini was one of Vecchi's actual models—and this needs further investigation, as does the whole personality of this outsider from Ferrara— it will have been only in the extremely superficial sense that he prompted and encouraged one of the many sides of the many-sided master whose work reflects and sums up the whole development of the madrigal and its related forms and brings it to a brilliant and jovial conclusion—Orazio Vecchi.

But before we turn to Orazio Vecchi we must mention one more piece which definitely belongs to the sphere of social merry-making—*A Segnor Hermano io digo*, a dialogue for ten voices by Michele Varotto, church choirmaster in Novara. Varotto is primarily a composer of impressive church-music—six-voiced masses (1563), five- to ten-voiced Magnificats (1580), five-voiced hymns (1590), and so forth—and apart from this dialogue, published in the anthology 1586[5], his only secular works are a setting of Tasso's *Ardo sì ma non t'amo* and a canzone in many sections. He can scarcely be identical with the Michele Novarese mentioned in Antonfrancesco Doni's *Dialogo* of 1544, although Vito Fedeli has so assumed (*Le cappelle musicali di Novara*, in *Istituzioni e monumenti*, III, p. 57): "Michele Novarese . . . . non può essere altri che il Varotti." What interests us in the piece is its birthplace: Novara, situated between Milan and Turin in Lombardy on the plain to the south of the Alps, the region in which this sort of music was particularly at home. It is a scene with figures from the *commedia dell'arte*, a chance meeting of strollers and pairs of strollers, presumably on the Piazza di San Marco. A visitor from Genoa asks a Sicilian for information about a certain Franceschedda; a Spaniard obtains similar information about a certain Isabella from an extremely obliging Neapolitan;

the "Magnifico" (Pantalone) confides in Zani about his short-comings as a lover; Doctor Gratiano from Bologna questions a visitor from Milan about a certain Catarina; and against the background of this verbal skirmishing of the lower voices a gypsy and a Frenchman sing their songs without concern for those around them. The whole is a loosely constructed scene—salutations, introductions, a tutti, a return to "il nostro proposito," farewells and another tutti, textually and musically rather pointless and without any real comic impact. By far the most delightful detail is the gypsy's lullaby:

> Cingarin del babo,
> Cingarin della mama,
> Cingarin galante,
> Cingarin polito . . .
> Quando meteva man al pistolese
> Tutte Bologna facea tremare—
> Se tu roberai tu sara impicato,
> Cingarin del babo,
> Cingarin della mama . . .

Also attractive is the chanson of the Frenchman with its pretty tune:

Varotto borrowed this text—and perhaps this melody, though of this I cannot be certain—from Andrea Antico's *Canzoni francesi* of 1535. He has an imitator in Johann Eccard, who includes a *Zanni e Magnifico*, a dialogue for five voices involving a similarly diversified company in his *Newe Lieder* of 1589 (cf. Eitner's series of publications, xxi [1897], 95f., also J. C. Hol in *Rivista musicale italiana*, xliii, 21). In Eccard's bipartite composition the two highest voices represent Zanni (*O messir, o patru, o non pos plu cantar*), the tenor is the abusive Magnifico (*Che distu, che fastu*), while the bass is the *Tedesco*, drunk as usual (*Mi star bon compagnon*); against this background the quinto keeps repeating a folk-song, now at one level, now at another:

> E la bella Franceschina—
> Ninina—bufina—
> La filibustachina. . . .

Obviously, this is a quodlibet rather than a dramatic dialogue, a musical joke rather than a dramatic or naturalistic scene. And Eccard is far more musical than his model from Novara. Where his text came from we do not know—whether he obtained it from his teacher Lasso (if Lasso really was his teacher), or from Teodoro Riccio, whose successor he became, or during his years of service with the Fuggers in Augsburg, a city dominated by Italian influences.

Teodoro Riccio of Brescia, later choirmaster to the Duke of Prussia, is himself the composer of a piece belonging to this group; it stands at the end of his *Primo libro delle canzone alla napolitana* of 1577. He calls it a "Ballata," presumably because it has the form of a folk-tale, for this tripartite piece for six voices has nothing whatever to do with dancing:

> D'una bella mattina mi levai,
> E dove l'amor mio si m'aspettava,
> Allegro me n'andava
> E dir incominciai:
> Deh non mi dar più guai,
> Contentami cor mio ch'homai
> Il temp'è ch'io goda
> dolce mercè del mio servire.
> Ella non vols'udire i prieghi miei
> Al fin cortesemente
> Volendosi partire
> Un bascio mi donò sì soavemente,
> Che l'alma per partir fu immantinente.

The musical treatment is quite unpretentious, half antiphonal, half madrigalesque, half popular, half serious. There seem to be no quotations, and there is only the barest trace of any intention to find amusement at the expense of the "folk."

ORAZIO VECCHI

STRIGGIO was a serious master. He did not write a single villanella or canzonetta, and in discussing his work under the head of "music as entertainment" we have done him something of an injustice: his naturalistic scenes constitute only a fraction of his output, an appendix to his contribution to the festive and sentimental madrigal. This cannot be said of the master whose work constitutes not only the high-point of this chapter but also an end-point of the madrigal's entire history: Orazio Vecchi of Modena. With Vecchi the center of gravity is "music as entertainment," however great and serious a master he may have been otherwise. His so-called "madrigal comedies," which are anything but comedies and which have no more to do with the theater, the stage, or the birth of the opera than Striggio's *Cicalamento*, follow

after a long and fruitful preoccupation with the canzonetta. Striggio is altogether devoid of humor—another point in which he resembles the painter Caravaggio: he is interested only in the fidelity, the naturalism, and the vividness of the scene. But everything of this sort that Vecchi writes is not only wonderfully observed but also gilded over with the magic of laughter and even of genuine humor.

Modena, then a part of the Este domain, a modest provincial town of second-rate importance as long as Ferrara was shining in the glory reflected by the court of the ruling house, produced in Orazio Vecchi her first great musician. (In the seventeenth century, as a princely residence, Modena became a new musical center, especially for instrumental music, and despite the dangerous proximity of Bologna it exchanged roles with Ferrara, a sad and deserted place.) Here Vecchi was christened on December 6, 1550—the baptismal certificate was found as recently as 1928 by Monsignore Evaristo Pancaldi, the choirmaster at the cathedral of Modena. His teacher was Salvatore Essenga, a Servite monk, the author of two books of madrigals for five voices (the first is lost, the second was published in 1561), and one of madrigals for four voices (1566): essentially, these are collections of multipartite canzoni and not of single pieces. In his book for four voices Essenga already includes a madrigal by his pupil, then a boy of sixteen: this is *Volgi cor lasso*, and unfortunately it has not been preserved complete. Considerable time passes before Vecchi comes forward with a work of his own, for it is not until 1578 or 1579 (the first edition is lost) that his first book of canzonette appears. To the intervening years belong two sonnets in the *Quinto libro delle muse* (1575), one of them on a text by Francesco Coppetta. But even at this early date, works of his must have been spread all over Italy in manuscript, and at the same time he was acquiring a wide reputation as a desirable companion, a poet-musician, a singer, a ball-player, and a conversationalist—all this despite his having taken holy orders. In 1577 he travels into the northern parts of Lombardy in the company of Count Baldassarre Rangoni, a member of one of the most illustrious noble families of Modena. They go first to Brescia; from Brescia they turn westward to Bergamo, where Pietro Vinci was then officiating as choirmaster; and from Bergamo they presumably went on to Venice; on the way there, Vecchi visited Verona, where he was the guest of the Count Mario Bevilacqua to whom he dedicated his Opus I. In 1579 he collaborates with Andrea Gabrieli, Vincenzo Bel'haver, Claudio Merulo, Baldisserra Donato, and Tiburtio Massaino in the composition of a sestina in honor of the wedding of Bianca Capello and the Grand Duke Francesco (with the key-words *alba, oro, rosa, Arno, giorno, cielo*) which was printed by Scotto with other festive pieces under the title *Trionfo di musica* and dedicated to the "vera et particulare figliuola" of the Venetian republic. This indicates that Vecchi's reputation was well-established and well-developed and that he had already been accepted as a member of the Venetian circle. J. C. Hol, the author of the excellent biography of Vecchi, does well to emphasize that as a musician Vecchi is no mere provincial talent from Modena, Reggio, or Bologna, but one of the great "Venetians." If Striggio is Rore's spiritual pupil, Vecchi is Andrea Gabrieli's—and perhaps his personal pupil as well.

On February 16, 1583, Vecchi is appointed choirmaster at the cathedral in his native town, but he is so poorly paid that the very next year he is obliged to appeal to the charity of his local admirers in order to assist his impoverished, ailing father, and on January 1, 1586, he resigns his post to become choirmaster at the cathedral in Reggio. Here too he remains only a few months, for here too the pay is insufficient, while the social life of the little town, the seat of a bishop, is even less stimulating than that of Modena. Therefore he accepts an appointment as canon at the collegiate church in Correggio, and in so doing he leaves the Este domain for the first time, for Correggio as a fief was dependent upon the House of Habsburg. The death of his father prompted Vecchi to write and publish his first sacred work, a setting of the Lamentations of Jeremiah dedicated to Sisto Visdomini, Bishop of Modena. In 1589 he begins his association with Mantua by dedicating a book of five-voiced madrigals to Duke Vincenzo Gonzaga, who had just visited Correggio where he had heard certain works of Vecchi's without meeting their composer. But in time he also tires of the tranquillity of Correggio. In 1590 he dedicates his first book of motets to Duke Wilhelm V of Bavaria and in his letter of dedication intimates very plainly that he would be pleased to enter the Duke's service—evidently reports of Lasso's imminent physical and mental collapse must already have reached Italy. He expresses a similar wish in dedicating his *Selva di varia ricreatione* in the same year to the brothers Jacob and Johann Fugger in Augsburg, men of considerable influence at the court of Munich. But Vecchi's appeals fall on deaf ears. Although he was now (1591) an archdeacon in Correggio, and although his circumstances there were now quite comfortable—he lived in a house of his own—Vecchi returned to Modena in 1593.

Thus Vecchi is once more a resident of his native town during the last twelve years of his life. These years are embittered by secret and open enemies: we know that on February 5, 1594 "a hore 22" he was attacked by an unknown assassin—fortunately he escaped unharmed. Among his open enemies was Fabio Ricchetti, the organist of St. Agostino, a pupil of Luzzaschi in Ferrara, who quarreled with him over questions of competence and liturgical usage. Vecchi must also have been deeply grieved by the ingratitude of his pupil Geminiano Capilupi, who was indebted to him for his introduction into the musical world and who thanked him by laying a trap for him in order to succeed him as choirmaster at the cathedral. In this he was only too successful: disregarding an express prohibition by his bishop (no longer the benevolent Visdomini), Vecchi had been imprudent enough to conduct

the music in a nunnery and was accordingly removed from his post on October 7, 1604. By this time he was a sick man, and it must have been a bitter disappointment to him that he was no longer able to accept an appointment as successor to Filippo di Monte at the Imperial court when it was offered to him in May 1604. Vecchi died on February 19 or 20, 1605. Among the sorrows of his last years, about which the faithful chronicle of his compatriot Gio. Batt. Spaccini (1588-1636) informs us in detail, must be counted the adultery of the wife of Vecchi's brother Girolamo, an affair which led to a bloody domestic scandal (June 18, 1595). Yet these last years in Modena were not wholly lacking in compensations. He finds some diversion in visiting Venice to oversee the printing of his works; on February 26, 1597, he returns from such a trip in the company of Count Alvise Montecucoli. In 1598 Cesare d'Este, the new Duke, appoints him choirmaster and music teacher to his children "con provigione di scuti 80 l'anno," and he thus becomes associated with the beginning of a new flowering of music at the court of Modena, the heir, as it were, of the musical splendors of Ferrara. Throughout his life he stood on the friendliest of terms with the Benedictines of San Pietro, and the tranquillity of his existence in Modena was interrupted only by journeys. Thus in May 1595, at the head of the Compagnia di San Gimigniano, he made the pilgrimage to Loreto that he later described in his *Breve compendio del pellegrinaccio di Loreto*; in 1599 he traveled to Rome in the company of the newly hatched Cardinal Alessandro d'Este, who sends his half-brother Cesare his warmest thanks for this well-bred, ingenious, and versatile companion in a letter dated May 22, 1600. (Cf. J. C. Hol in *Rivista musicale italiana*, XXXVII, 4; also Scheurleer *Gedenkboek*, 1925.) Vecchi's superior qualities must have been at once fascinating and provoking to his contemporaries: he was a merry and a pious priest, not a misanthrope of the Counter Reformation like the elderly Lasso or a hypocrite like Palestrina; a man of broad culture, but not a pedant or a "humanist"; an artist who had reflected on the laws of his art in a thoroughly independent spirit, uninfluenced by the authority of the ancients and in this wholly unlike the members of the Florentine Camerata; an altogether original figure, but not a revolutionary.

What makes Vecchi independent and sets him apart from the group of the three "great virtuosi" is his status as poet-musician. He is wholly independent of literary fashions and reputations, which he surveys from a distance, from an objective point of view. He is the author of his own texts. I do not mean to say that he can do entirely without Petrarch, Torquato Tasso, and Guarini, or to deny that he too suffered for a time from the fashionable pastoral disease. His *Convito musicale* includes a setting of Petrarch's sestina *Chi è fermato*, and in other pieces too he chances, as it were, upon texts by Guidiccioni and Tasso; at other times he sets texts out of politeness, for example the sonnet written for him by his friend Giovanni

Battista Zuccarini of Feltre (*Corona di dodici Sonetti*, 1586) as a fresh tribute to Bianca Capello. In the foreword to his *Veglie di Siena*, he even quotes one of Marini's comparisons—the spheres are God's strings and the heavens are His lyre—thus proving his familiarity with the work of the author of the *Adone*. But he set only one text by Marini—*Di marmo sete voi*. Vecchi was highly cultivated, well read in the works of ancient and modern authors, but he remained unaffected by fashion and pedantry. Near the end of the foreword to his *Veglie di Siena*, he gives us himself a useful hint about his reading. This is a quotation from the *Hospitale de' pazzi incurabili* by Tommaso Garzoni (1549-1589), and it suggests that he may also have known some of the other writings by this bizarre author.

His creative work centers in the four larger compositions in which he mingles the gay (*piacevole*) with the grave (*grave*), following an aesthetic principle of his own: the *Selva di varia ricreatione* (1590), the *Amphiparnaso* (1594, printed in 1597), the *Convito musicale* (1597), and the *Veglie di Siena* (1604). He was well prepared for either extreme: for the gay by his six books of canzonette, four for four voices, one for six, and one for three; for the grave by two books of madrigals, one for six voices (1583) and one for five (1589), in addition to which a large number of scattered pieces are found in the anthologies of the time.

He began before 1580 with the publication of a book of canzonette, although as he explains in his dedication to Count Bevilacqua, most of these pieces were already scattered throughout Italy in manuscript and under the names of other writers— "essendo sparso per molti luochi d'Italia la maggior parte delle presenti mie Canzonette, sotto nome di diversi autori; mi è paruto à proposito, di far sapere al mondo, co'l mezo della stampa ch'elle sono le mie, come in effetto sono . . ." In these canzonette he intentionally avoids the five-voiced texture that had been sanctioned for this sort of music by Ferretti, Regnart, and others, and returns to composition for four voices, as more popular and less madrigalesque—less suited for performance before an elegant company. His immediate model is Gioseppe Caimo. But if Caimo is already vivid, Vecchi is still more successful in "imitating things to the life" (*di meglio imitar le cose al vivo*):

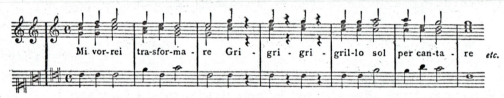

Caimo is somewhat richer, somewhat more "artistic"—in so far as it is possible to speak of "art" in this connection—he leans a little toward the madrigal with his naturalistic tone-painting. Vecchi, as it were, frees the canzonetta from any madrigalesque admixture; he is simpler, more straightforward, more popular, though he sacrifices no part of his uncompromising realism. This, in a general way, is his formula: to be as simple, straightforward, and striking as possible. I do not mean to say that his canzonette are all alike; on the contrary, they sum up the whole development—the canzonetta has become a play on itself, has made itself its subject. Madrigalesque traits are not altogether absent (*O tu che vai per via*, I, 18). He amuses himself with the *sdruccioli* of Sannazaro's *Arcadia* (II, 2):

> Hor s'io son gionto quivi
> Fra questi boschi e rivi
> E quest'herbette tenere
> Io vo cantar del fier fanciul di Venere. . . .

He imitates Guarini's *Tirsi morir volea* and in so doing falls into dialogue and parody (III, 13):

> Con voce dai sospiri interrotta
> Dicea un pastor dolente:
> "L'alma vicin'a mort'homai si sente!"
> Disse la Ninf'al'hor con gran desio:
> "Non posso più tardar: i'moro anch'io!"

There is no denying the parodistic intention, the exaggeration, the roguish mockery of Petrarch and Della Casa in the following (II, 6):

O donna ch'a mio danno i ciel ti denno
Le belle treccie d'oro e'l petto d'ira,
D'amor amar'ohime ch'io moro, mira!
    Et se m'ha svelto il sonno, et svolto il senno,
Tua gratia, ch'in te spera, spara, e spira
        D'amor . . .
    Lo spirto esperto è sparto, e a ogni tuo cenno
Vola veloce ove tua voglia il tira
        D'amor . . .
    Se'l tuo decoro ho caro, et cura il core
N'ha perche ardire hor dir non deve ardore
Mira ch'io moro ohime d'amaro amore!

Here is a further illustration (II, 20):

Opache selve et cavernose grotte
Albergo di serpenti et crude fiere
Deh ribombate alle mie stride altere. . . .

Whether such verses are by Vecchi himself is an open question, although he speaks in the dedication of his *Libro terzo* of presenting and consecrating both his rhymes and his songs—"le dono dunque e le consacro queste mie rime, e questo canto." But precisely this book is full of borrowings from the canzonette of Caimo and others. Yet only a musician could have written the text and music of the canzonetta that follows:

Fammi una canzonetta capricciosa,
Che nullo o pochi la sappian cantare,
E al tuon di quella si possi ballare.
    Non ti curar di tuono ò d'osservata,
Che questo è meglio che tu possi fare
        E al tuon . . .
Falla come ti dà la fantasia
E affretta il corso col bel solfeggiare,
        E al tuon. . . .

It goes without saying that Vecchi depicts the word "capricious" by a cross-grained polyrhythm, with a complex intertwining of the voices in the second line, and the refrain by a gay dance-rhythm. A second example is reprinted in our volume of illustrations. We can understand the exuberance and the quiet mockery of this

little piece,[2] which must be seen in the original notation and not merely heard, and whose note values cannot be altered "for practical performance" without destroying its meaning. It is half trifling, half amusement at the expense of the old sentimental, sleepy madrigal of Arcadelt's time that Vecchi criticized, half in homage and half in rivalry, in his recomposition of the *Bianco e dolce cigno* of D'Avalos-Arcadelt. He strikes much the same note in another piece (*Canzonette a tre*, Nö. 33) when he advises a beauty not to hold out too long:

> Udite, udite, amanti,
> L'amor di donna è qual musica nova,
> Ch'ogni cantor di gran piacer vi trova.
> Ma quel che dianci egli cantò con gioia,
> Dipoi gli vien per la vecchiezza a noia. . . .

The variety of the text is equaled by the variety of the music. The whole is a little rhythmic feast, a feast of lively simplicity, with unexpected little pranks, parodistic features, allusions, and impertinences on every hand. I shall give no further examples, since a number of these canzonette have been reprinted (Torchi, II, 253f., has two for four voices and one for six voices; cf. also Hol, Velten, Schwartz, and others) and since Italian scholars are about to stop concentrating their whole attention on the *Amphiparnaso* and are now planning an edition of Vecchi's complete works.

In his canzonette for six voices (1587) Vecchi outdoes his model Ferretti in his sense for sonority, animated dialogue, and delicate workmanship. In those for three voices (1597), in which he includes a number of pieces by his pupil Capilupi, he makes the transition from Marenzio's villanelle to monody. This book has a lute accompaniment, and the lute is essential:

> Deh cant'Aminta un'aria alla Romana!
> "Io son contento
> Ch'io ne ho ben cento:
> Ma pria m'ascolti, e tien l'orecchie intente
> A queste uscite in luce novamente!"
> Ecco ch'assiso ascolterò il tuo canto,
> A punto L'AURA
> Dolce ristaura,
> Cosi CORTESE e leggiermente spira,
> E veggio a tuo favor ch'Apol t'inspira.
> Ma se desij di contentarmi a pieno
> *Prendi il Liuto*

[2] See Vol. III, No. 87.

Ch'è un grande aiuto,
E senza quest'ogn'aria è manco grata,
Ma il suon'e'l canto: *è gemma in or legata.*

(The first two numbers in the book are dedicated "alla M. Ill. Signora Laura Calori Cortese.") How charming this is: accompanied song is compared to a gem in a gold setting! How happily remote this is from the philology and archaeology of the Florentine Camerata! Like the Roman pieces collected in Verovio's publications (hence the call for "un' aria alla Romana"), these three-voiced canzonette can perfectly well be sung a cappella, but the two upper voices are always paired in the high register while the bass part stands at the opposite pole, like a basso continuo. There is also a musical letter (No. 8):

Al tremend'e potente Re del mondo,
Monarca de gl'amanti, il Dio d'Amore,
Patron mio colendissimo e signore.
   "Per questa mia t'aviso e ti dò nova
Com'infiniti si son ribellati
Dal regno tuo contra te congiurati.
   "Vogliono dar l'impero (ho inteso dire)
A una Leonora Pii, che di bellezza
Molto più di Ciprigna quì s'apprezza.
   "Non è più tempo di gir a la cieca;
Sciogliti pur la benda, e scocca i dardi
Contra costei ch'uccide altrui coi sguardi.
   "E sopra tutto s'à giornata vieni,
Non la mirare, ch'è sì bella e PIA,
Che preso rimaresti in sua balia.
   "E perche non ti colga à l'improviso,
Io t'hò avisato—hor dunque t'apparecchi,
Non altro:—il tuo fedele
                                      Horatio Vecchi."

Address, letter, and signature add up to a compliment to a lady: it is a game, but one would have to search a long time to find another one as graceful. As previously indicated (p. 182), there is no lack of coarse invective, and this too bears the stamp of Vecchi's lively personality. These pieces anticipate the new canzonetta or "arietta" of the seventeenth century. The "monodic" tendency is combined with the older style when Palestrina is quoted parodistically, as in Nos. 14 and 15, where Vecchi appropriates Palestrina's *Vestiva i colli* and *Io son ferito ahi lasso*. In reprinting these

I suppress the lute accompaniment.[3] Vecchi's mockery of the master of rarefied polyphony becomes a bit personal in the long melismas of the bass; here, of course, real three-part writing is required.

In dedicating the first of his four tendentious works, the *Selva di varia ricreatione*, to the brothers Jacob and Johann Fugger in Augsburg, Vecchi was perhaps recalling the dedication of the naïve miscellanies of Filippo Duc to the German students in Padua. Germany was less biased and more tolerant towards stylistic mixtures than the Italy of the *accademie*, the Florentine Camerata, or the *accademia* of Count Bevilacqua. Thus the whole purpose of the dedication is to justify and excuse this mixture (Vogel, II, 268): ". . . To the word 'Grove' I add 'of Recreation,' for just as in a grove the varieties of herbs and plants are seen to afford the beholder great delight, so the variety of the harmonies scattered among these my songs should seem like a grove. And having likewise combined in one the serious style with the familiar, the grave with the facetious and dance-like, there should arise from this combination that variety in which the world takes such delight. I am well aware that on first hearing some may perhaps think these my caprices base and trivial. Let them learn that it requires as much grace, art, and knowledge of nature to create a ridiculous character in a comedy as to create a prudent, wise old man. They have not learned that it sometimes becomes the musician to blend familiar music with grave, following the example of the poets. For although tragedy should remain within its own limits, not making use of the familiar speech of comedy, and vice versa, Horace says in his *Art of Poetry* that the comedian often raises his voice, while the tragedian sometimes speaks in a voice that is low and humble. . . ."

This makes things quite clear. In his own way, Vecchi is Shakespeare's contemporary, even though his mixture of the tragic and comic remains a mere juxtaposition and never becomes a "chemical process," and even though there can be no question with him of real tragedy or real comedy in the Shakespearean sense. Shakespeare creates unique characters, persons, and beings; Vecchi creates only figures from the *commedia dell' arte*. Shakespeare, a child of the Elizabethan age, sees things in their eternal aspect; Vecchi, in summing up the musical forms of his century, marks the end of an era and becomes a man without a future. He enumerates them in his title, these "varii soggetti"—*madrigali, capricci, balli, arie, giustiniane, canzonette, fantasie, serenate, dialoghi, un lotto amoroso, con una battaglia à diece nel fine.* By this time we know them all, these forms—with the exception of the *fantasia*, an instrumental form which is in this case identical with the *canzon francese*—and we can define them all. The list is not even complete: Vecchi does not mention his French chanson *J'ai vu le cerf du bois saillir* (reprinted by Weckerlin in his catalogue of the

[3] See Vol. III, No. 88.

Paris Conservatoire), or his villotta *O bella o bianca*. "Tragedy" is represented only in its sentimental and pastoral aspects by the madrigals for five and more voices. (Torchi, *Arte musicale in Italia*, II, 247, has reprinted one of those for five voices, *Se tra verdi arbuscelli*, a refined and graceful tribute to a certain Laura, quite in the style of Giovanni Gabrieli.) The emphasis is definitely on the comic and burlesque: the *Lotto amoroso*, an imitation of Striggio's *Primiera*, the quadripartite *Battaglia* between *Amor* (Love) and *Dispetto* (Contempt), the dialogue between Pantalone and his servant, of course in the Venetian dialect, the *giustiniane* for three voices, and above all the *capricci, arie*, and *canzonette* (the *capricci* for five voices, the *arie* for three, and the *canzonette* for four—one of the *arie* is likewise for four voices). Chilesotti (*Biblioteca di rarità musicali*, V, 1892) has reprinted some of these pieces because of his interest in the lute accompaniment, and he was justified in doing so. For this accompaniment is no mere doubling of the vocal parts but a real addition, sonorous and independent, richer and more exuberant than such similar attempts as those in Simone Verovio's Roman publications. There is little difference between the *arie* and the *canzonette*. For the *arie* too are *canzonette* in that they tend to fall into dance rhythms and to resemble the balletto with its fa-la refrain. Pure Gastoldi balletti are the *capricci*: a pavane, a saltarello, an allemande with text; another saltarello with the title "Trivella" is a purely instrumental piece. Everything is gay, light, and popular. In a few cases—especially in the serenata, of course—there is an obvious connection with the folk-song (cf. D'Ancona, *La poesia popolare italiana*, 2nd ed., pp. 120f.).

Seven years later, in 1597, Vecchi published two further works of this sort: on May 20 the *Amphiparnaso* and a few months later, on August 1, the *Convito musicale*. We shall take them up in reverse order: the *Convito*, already announced in the preface to the *Amphiparnaso*, was presumably the first to be written and is in any case the connecting link between the *Selva* and the *Amphiparnaso*. It too is dedicated to an "ultramontane," this time to a German prince, Archduke Ferdinand, the later Emperor Ferdinand II. In the dedication Vecchi says that he has learned from Don Pietro Antonio Bianchi, the Archduke's choirmaster, that from time to time Ferdinand takes pleasure in the songs of his *Selva*; if such wild fruits as those were to his taste, it is hoped that he will relish even more the dishes of this *Banquet*, "seasoned with the salt of urban harmony" (*queste vivande condite col sale della civile harmonia*). The foreword frankly preaches a "return to nature" and speaks out plainly enough against Gesualdo's sort of seasoning, for which Vecchi must have entertained a hearty dislike (Vogel, II, 271): "The proper spice for food is hunger, says Socrates; therefore let him who is about to sit down to this my Banquet bring a good appetite with him, so that each dish, however tasteless it may be, may seem to him sweet and savory. I say this because it would be no wonder (in view of the great abundance

of music going the rounds today) if the ears of many, grown satiated and through this satiety weak, were in the condition of the sick, who have no more than tasted one thing than they call fastidiously for another; thus it would be necessary to compose as many volumes of music as Didymus the Grammarian, who in the course of his life wrote four thousand books (as Seneca affirms), or to say still more, as Origen, who wrote seven thousand of them. But if the appetites of the guests are well disposed, it cannot be doubted that they will derive nourishment even from the slightest dish. And on the other hand, if the appetites of some should be so badly adjusted that they have need of some allurement in the way of an appetizer, let them not give it a thought. For here there will be prepared a pie of a banished ass from which they may perhaps derive the same appetite that jaded women do from charcoal, spleen, gypsum, and other things of the sort. And if this bait is not enough to captivate their ears, they will find to their taste a little ragout of canzonette, villotte, giustiniane, and other ingredients that will whet their sluggish appetites for them. Thus they will be able to apply themselves the more readily to the more substantial dishes, for let all be advised that although this is all one banquet, many tables are set, of which some are served with three, four, and five plates and others with six, seven, and eight. And every place is furnished with whatever is needed. And since Ceres and Bacchus are as it were near relatives, after the aforesaid dishes have been properly consumed, my gardener will serve the guests the sweet liquor of Agannippe to drink. With all this, if it should seem to some glutton, overly greedy for musical spices, that this banquet is sparingly provided with dishes, let him learn now that when the stomach receives food in moderation, it digests it the more readily. In a word, let these preparations be measured, not by their multitude or by the sweetness of the foods, but by the liberality of the host, who is lavishly spending what he finds in the purse of his feeble wit. For men of discretion praise a simple, familiar banquet as much more apt to call for serenity of spirit than one that by an excessive number of dishes fills the stomach of the ears to overflowing without satisfying it. But it is enough to have talked so much, for I see that the tables are now set and the dishes prepared."

There follows a musical invitation—for five voices—to sit down at the table, in an animated style that swings back and forth between the madrigalesque and the canzonetta-like. Only towards the end does the cheerful politeness take on a certain solemnity:

> Voi che già stanchi sete
> Di mirar l'alto Abete,
> Il verdeggiante allor, l'ombroso faggio,
> Ed altre piante nel fiorito Maggio:
> Per la selv'oggimai non v'aggirate,

S'altro piacer bramate,
Mentre vi chiam'e invito
Per ristorarvi al Musical Convito.

What follows really reflects the informal order and traditional arrangement of a Renaissance banquet. No musical dish is lacking that had met with approval in the course of the century. The most dignified and solemn is Petrarch's *Chi è fermato di menar sua vita*, the sestina that occupies the central position; Vecchi sets this for four voices, an archaic combination, and in an archaic style, somewhat in the manner of the early Andrea Gabrieli. At the beginning and end are complimentary pieces—one for five voices, bipartite, in honor of a Cinthia, and a wedding song for eight voices in honor of a Nichea or Vittoria, both of them lively and without especial solemnity. Another group of madrigals seem to be addressed to another lady (Clori) —*Ti diè natura*. A bipartite piece in the form of a cantata changes the scene to Mantua:

"Io ardo, e'l celo a lei,
Da cui forse pietade haver potrei;
Io pero e me n'aveggio,
Ne fuggo, ò al feritor aita chieggio.
Io son, ahimè, nel foco,
Ne vuò chiamar che'l tempri ò molto ò poco.
Hor che farem, mio core,
Fra spem'e tema involt'in tal dolore?"
Così dicea un pastor presso le sponde
Del chiaro Mincio c'ha d'argento l'onde,
Quando voce s'udì cantar: Ragiona,
Ch'Amor'a nullo amato amar perdona.

Vecchi takes these pastoral effusions as lightly and naturally as he can without becoming commonplace and without abandoning the graceful tone of the madrigal for that of the canzonetta. Everything pathetic is rigorously excluded. Once he seems intent on writing a madrigal in the style of Ingegneri or of Giaches Wert in his middle period:

Lunghi danni e tormenti,
Stratij, affanni, dolor, pen'e martiri,
E lagrime e sospiri,
E mille notti e dì, gridi e lamenti
Diami fortuna, e morte l'arco scocchi,
Pur ch'una volta baci que'begli occhi!

But this is parody, and the music leaves no doubt about it when it shifts from the

prescribed *misura di breve* to four-four and triple time for the last two lines, falling from the most old-fashioned into the most modern style. The madrigal becomes self-conscious and amuses itself at its own expense. It is an end, a cheerful, ironic end, a sort of euthanasia. Another of the madrigals for five voices (10) is a setting of a wholly unnecessary parody of the sestet from Petrarch's sonnet *In qual parte del ciel*:

> Veder beltà divina indarno spera
> Ch'il viso e gli occhi di costei non vide
> Come gli ferma dolcement'e gira,
>   Ne sa com'amor sani e a un tempo fera,
> Chi non sa come dolc'ella sospira,
>   E come dolce parla, e dolce ride.

In much the same spirit, the music has exchanged its tender sentimentality for an easy grace that avoids every deeper emotion. The book contains several other pieces of this sort, pieces that one might call "Horatian" in a twofold sense: *Augellin che la voce al canto spieghi* (8); *Fummo felici un tempo* (11), a particularly delicate and natural piece; and *Angioletta fugace* (26). Pieces that describe are written in the style of the *canzon francese* as a matter of course: *Corre la nave mia colma di gioia* (5); and the six-voiced *Vanne la nave mia pront'e sicura*, the octet of a sonnet. Here Vecchi is not content with simple means and begins at once with the augmentation and inversion of the motif:

After fifteen numbers Vecchi is tired of sentimentality. He greets the ladies with a mascherata, *Felice schiera di leggiadre e belle*, a cheery little piece in Gastoldi's manner; then follows a musical preamble to the gay part of the banquet:

> Non più pene e tormenti,
> Ma dolcezz'e contenti!
> Su tutti amanti, a l'allegrezz' uniamci,
> Tutti la fede diamci
> Che la gioia e'l contento e'l piacere
> La vita fa parere
> Lunga felice festosa e ripiena
> Di gaudio e di dolcezza.
> Dunque cantiamo: allegrezza, allegrezza.

And this summons is eagerly obeyed. These gay pieces are equally interesting as literary and social history and as music—perhaps one might even say that their purely musical side is by no means the most important, for they are naturally simple, homophonic, and largely dependent on their forceful rhythms. Rarely are we granted such insight into the way in which polite Italian society amused itself at the expense of its own and other classes. First of all, the peasant—the *bifolco* or *villanzone* —is once more the butt of the joke. The scene is a village wedding (18):

(The bride)
> "Non mi toccare,
> Non t'accostare,
> Lasciami stare,
> O Barba Ton!
> Che la Comare
> Me vuol provare
> La mia stanella,
> Pulita e bella:

> Se l'è curta
> Se l'è lunga
> Se l'è stretta
> Se l'è larga
> Fa lala lo o do
> Fa la la la."

(The bridesmaids)
> Monna Riccia orlata l'ha
> Di grognano e taffetà.

(Tutti)   Hor venga a nozze tutta la brigata
                           Della parentà della nostra vallata

(Solo voices)   V'è la Ianna de Zanon,
                           E la Togna de Piron,
                           La sorella di Pedrazz,
                           E la Menghe de Buttazz,
                           La Tadea de Manganel,
                           E l'Agnesa dal Sivel

(Tutti)   Che sta sera havrò l'annello
                           Havrò il gioello
                           Che non s'è vist'il piu bello.

Then comes a song in praise of a peasant lass (19):

> "Sapete voi, Bifolci, a cui somiglia
> La bella Manza mia?
> Somiglia ai gesti al viso,
> Se ben m'aviso,
> A una ridente Agnella,
> Quando gioisce,
> Quando saltella."
> O come è bella,
> Leggiadr'e snella!
> Se tesse, se fila, se innaspa, se miete,
> Se canta, se balla, se va alla festa.
> O come è presta,
> Gentil modesta,
> Se fa di testa,
> O come è onesta!
>
> "Ma dica ognun, qual parte habbia costei,
> Che sia più bella in lei."

(Spoken)   Il collo—Il naso—La bocca—Le poppe—Gli occhi—La
                             panza.

(Sung)   E viva il naso, il collo, la bocca, gli occhi, le poppe e la
                             panza
                                Della mia Manza!
                                O che bellezze,
                                O che fatezze,

O che diletto
D'un tal soggetto—
Ma vi manca Giandon
Col suo dirindon,
Cioè col suo pivon!

With Vecchi the Neapolitan *moresca* has found an original North Italian counterpart at last, and as in the *moresca* the aim is not "drama" or representation, but entertainment—the entertainment of the entertainers themselves—and it ends in roars
of laughter. The effect is irresistible. Somewhat less boisterous is the number that
follows, the *Giardiniero*, a dialogue whose text—more than appropriate in this
context—has also a certain scientific interest. A traveler looks over a wall, and the
following conversation takes place in "unaccompanied monody":

In the scene that follows, the musical treatment is constantly changing: some sections
are sung by the six-voiced tutti, others by half-choirs; the writing is sometimes in-
cisively homophonic and rhythmic, at other times imitatively animated:

"Ben venga, entra a tua posta,
Che nulla costa!
    Hor d'ogn' intorno mira,
L'uve dorate e l'uve purpurine
Vagheggia i vaghi frutti
E fanne se ti par saggio di tutti!"
    O bel vedere,
    O che piacere,
    O bel giardino,
    Ch' ha del divino—
    Mira, mira quel grappolino,
    Se non sembra rubino,
    Vedi, vedi quella rossetta
    Che spesso trà da gli occhi

Più d'una lagrimetta;
Vè vè che tra le fronde
Quelle che là s'asconde!
Ch'esposta al sole ardente
Somiglia oro lucente!
"Deh gusta un poc'o amico
Questa via più del mel dolc'e del fico!"
O com'è dolce,
O com'altrui diletta,
Com'è odorosa,
Com'è mustosa,
Come rinfranca
La vita stanca!
De i vini che tu premi
Da sì dolci racemi,
Fa ch'un sorso di tutt'almen n'accoglia
Di gratia volentier di buona voglia.
"Hor prend'e fanne il saggio,
Che men noioso ti parrà il viaggio.
Bevilo allegramente,
Ch'io vengo col secondo e più possente."
O ponderoso vino
O nettare divino!
Gentil più del Claretto,
Ch' ha'l leggiero e lo scarico e' l tondetto!
Come si chiama?
"Quest'è Marzemino
Quel che tanto s'appretia
Ne l'inclita Venetia."
Felice ch'ivi è nato
E c' ha gustato
Sì buon licore,
Ch'allegra il mesto core!
"Bevi bevi—Quest'è la lagrima di Roma,
Ch' ogni Tantalea set'ammorz'e doma."
O come dolce inaffia
E vag'ispruzza,
Che l'appetito aguzza,
Salticchia e brilla,

Rid'e sfavilla,
Mord'e rimorde e bacia,
E trà di calci,
O benedetti tralci,
O pretiosa vite,
Ch'altrui col tuo licor dai mille vite!
"Hor t'apparecchia
Che quest' è vin polputo da una orecchia!"
Lascia ch'io prendi fiato,
Ch'al tuo cortes'invito io sarò grato.
Quest'è un'altra bevanda,
Che merita ghirlanda.
"Tien dritto ch'una goccia non si spanda!"
E come si dimanda?
"Si chiama il vin Roteglia,
Perche'l perduto gust'arruota e sveglia."
O bevanda gentil, mi da la vita,
O questa sì che merta la stampita.
Tant'è gradita
Senza difetto pur d'un picciol neo,
O Bacco, Bacco, o Bacco Lyeo,
Vieni festoso,
Vien solazzoso,
E sii presente a dì sì glorioso!
"Quest'ultimo è Trebbiano,
Licor almo e sovrano,
Ch'in pioggia d'oro piove,
Questo fa gire altero e Secchia ed Arno."
Porgilo quà, ch'a berlo i mi ci incarno.
"Bevi sì buon licor infin al fondo,
Che quest' è un dì giocondo."
O vin brillante,
O vin frizzante
O l'è galante—
Ohimè ch'io vengo meno
Di grilli gri-gri-gri ho colm'il seno . . .
"Compagno non temer ma ti conforte
Che'l buon vin non da mai morte."

Deh mostrami la strada,
Ch'è temp'omai ch'io vada.
"Camina sempre lungo questo rio
Ne ti torcere mai
Che tost' a la Città tu giungerai."
Ti lascio . . .
"Hor vanne"
o giardiniero,
"Addio."

This is the first representation of drunkenness in music, full of droll details, and I do not think that I am wrong in supposing that Vecchi has parodied the Prince of Venosa a little at the height of this representation, where the traveler's dizzy spells and hallucinations become confused with one another, even in the music. No. 22 is a shorter song in praise of Bacchus, while the *madrigale pastoreccio* (28) falls into the style of the villanella and has nothing to do with the familiar pastoral masquerade. It is pure fun, pure nonsense, and we are reminded of the childish humor of Mozart's "Bäsle" letters when a crazy jumble of the voices is set off at the end or when after each line the final vowel is repeated:

O bella primavera—a
Cinta di vari fiori—i . . .

In Rossini's *Cenerentola* this sort of thing crops up again.

We are reminded of other things, of things like the hunting-scene and bird-concert of Janequin, in Vecchi's *Bando dell' Asino* (21), a piece that became the point of departure for a whole literature involving the musical imitation of the cries of animals. But if Janequin's pieces showed real feeling for nature and for poetry, this is pure entertainment, a game to be played in company. Some friends have assembled in the open air (*fra l'erbett' e fiori*), and to while away the time they elect a "King," who begins by calling for *il gioco di stromenti*: each member of the company is to imitate a different instrument—*arpicordo, violone, lira, cornamusa, liuto*—and this succeeds to the satisfaction of everyone concerned. But this is not sufficient:

Ma chi di rider brama,
Facciamo un'altro gioco,
Che musica del diavolo si chiama. . . .

The king orders each participant to imitate the cry of two animals, one bird and one quadruped, and the six singers choose their roles:

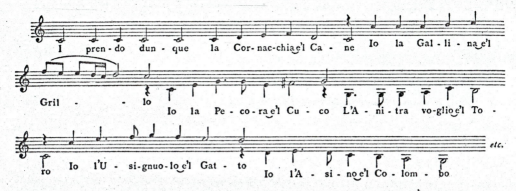

And now a crazy pandemonium breaks out, based on the C major triad, and this continues until the donkey breaks it up by descending to B, thus obliging the bass to ascend to E. He is promptly banished:

> ... si dia bando à l'Asino in eterno,
> Che non ha modo di cantar moderno!

The ceremony of his banishment is solemnly introduced by an imitation of trumpet blasts and the sentence is pronounced by three-voiced half-choirs with the higher one always repeating what the lower one proclaims:

> "Sia noto e manifesto
> A qualunque animal ch'alberga in terra,
> Da parte del Re nostro
> Re degli spensierati,
> Signor di Poco in testa,
> Conte di Bell'humore,
> Marchese di Buontempo, et cetera,
> Che nessun habbia ardire
> Mai più per l'avvenire
> In compagnia cantare
> Con l'Asino ostinato,
> Se non che ipso iure
> Sarà de la Giustitia castigato—"
> Vivan gli spensierati!

It may be that the shout of joy in the last line conceals an actual reference to the Accademia degli Spensierati. Very comical and addressed to the well-read is the quotation of the beginning of a sestina by Petrarch in the second line of the "manifesto."

As a sort of dessert to follow this musical banquet, the second part of Vecchi's book offers a number of lighter strophic pieces: canzonette; balletti (some of them with titles, for example No. 30, "Privilegi della Corte," and No. 33, "L'anno novo");

dialogues, among them a "Moresca de schiavi" (35), a genuine *mascherata*; a three-voiced canzonetta (37), "durchkomponiert"; and a "Mattinata" or serenade for six voices in the form of a dialogue (40), a highly realistic scene:

"Tibrina, bella Tibrina,
Destati homai, Tibrina, e scaccia il sonno,
O del mio cor Regina!"
        Chi è st'importun ch'a l'uscio s'avicina,
        Nell'ora ch'io m'assonno?
"Deh lasciati vedere!"
        Chi sei se t'è in piacere?
"Son'il tuo fido Aminta!"
        Hor son convinta.
        Che cerchi tu a quest'ore?
"Vò sfogando il dolore."
        Ah poverina, meschina, tapina che'l sonno mi piglia,
        Ne posso aprir le ciglia.
"Deh svegliati omai,
Ch'io sol vivo in virtù de tuoi bei rai!"
        Eccomi, guardami, toccami—Non più pene ne guai.

To the same class belong the *giustiniane* in the style of Andrea Gabrieli, some of them in the form of the *mascherata*, for example No. 42, *Semo tre Vecchinet' inamorai*. And as usual, Pantalone's indecent and abusive language is not precisely addressed to the flower of Venetian womanhood (41):

Non mi stornir pi el cao
O Dona del Postribulo,
Che mi te stimo tanto
Come le mie Pantofole—
Tira via co le to scrofole . . .
        Che voste? che zecchini?
No te darave un Tregolo,
Impara de soiare
E'l co za caro Tofano
        Va con dio, va con dio
        Volto di cofano!

We have seen that the madrigals of the *Convito* tend to become self-conscious and to amuse themselves at their own expense; this tendency now affects the *giustiniana* also, as may be seen from the following example (45), an exceptional one in that a naturalistic imitation of laughter takes the place of the usual stuttering:

No v'accorzè, Madona, che no femo
Tal'hora una Comedia vu e mi?
I nostri spettatori
Xe i Bamboletti amori—
Ah—Che de le risa mi no posso pi?
   Mi fazzo el Pantalon del naturale,
E vu la Ruffiana per amor;
La nostra prospettiva
Ae vù, cara mia Diva—
   Ah . . .
   Mi so inamorao, vu Inamorata,
Che fenzè de volermi tanto ben,
L'intermedi apparenti
Xe po i sospiri ardenti—
   Ah . . .
   Tal hor fazzo'e'l Spagnol quando che crio,
E vù se'l Zanni quando me soiè,
Monea no vadagnemo
Che per solazzo e'l femo—
   Ah . . .

Another piece, *E vorave saper* (46), is a long plea for mercy by Pantalone, not strophic but "durchkomponiert"; and in a "Dialogo in Echo" (48) the old man becomes involved in an abusive argument with his own echo and is at one point so beside himself with anger that he speaks instead of singing.

This brings us to the *Amphiparnaso*, which is not only the next work in chronological order but also a work that we are now in a position to understand quite well, both historically and musically.

There is no need for us to add to the oceans of ink that have already been spilled over the *Amphiparnaso*. Every ingredient of the work lay conveniently at hand, every one of its forms stood ready; all that is new is that Vecchi has personified the more or less ideal bearers of these musical forms, representative of an entire century, and has brought them together in a half-dramatic setting. His company includes the sentimental shepherds and shepherdesses, who are no longer called Aminta and Mopsus, Daphnis and Chloe, but Lucio and Isabella, Lelio and Nisa; it also includes all those figures that had long been shared in common by the *commedia dell' arte* and the villanella—Pantalone, Doctor Graziano, and the Spanish Captain, together with their entire train of shabby dependents, male and female—Ortensia, the *donna di bene*, and Pierulin, Francatrippa, and Zanni, the various servant-types. Only

Frulla, Lucio's servant, is not drawn in the comic vein. To speak of "drama" or "the beginnings of the opera buffa" is a grotesque misconception. Vecchi makes this quite clear in the prologue: "The place of this action is the great theater of the world, for everyone desires to hear [*sic*] it; know then that the spectacle of which I speak is seen through the mind, into which it enters through the ears, not through the eyes; be silent then, and instead of looking, listen."

> ... E la città dove si rappresenta
> Quest'opra, è'l gran teatro
> Del mondo, perch'ognun desia d'udirla:
> Ma voi sappiate intanto
> Che questo di cui parlo
> Spettacolo, si mira con la mente
> Dov'entra per l'orecchie e non per gl'occhi,
> Però silenzio fate,
> E'n vece di vedere, ora ascoltate.

From a "dramatic" point of view the action is rather sketchy and the development of the characters scarcely consistent. The central figure is Isabella, who believes her Lucio dead and is about to take her own life when she is prevented from doing so by Lucio's servant Frulla; there follows a reunion and a wedding. If Isabella is really intended as a serious character, her more than dubious love scene with the Spanish Captain is carried somewhat too far. The love affair of Lelio and Nisa remains sketchy and fragmentary; the comic scenes are mere episodes, especially the most famous one—the sabbath in the ghetto. This alleged "forerunner of the opera buffa" cannot be performed at all: there are unprepared changes of place within the scenes, so that even Palladio's famous ideal stage for the Teatro Olimpico in Vicenza would not have been wholly satisfactory.

From a musical point of view, the mixture of the sentimental and the gay, the cardinal point of Vecchi's aesthetic theory, is more intimate here than in the *Selva* or the *Convito*, but it is the same. On the one hand are the madrigalesque monologues and dialogues of the sentimental pairs of lovers, pure madrigals with little pseudo-monodic beginnings; on the other are the comic scenes which might simply be called an enormously expanded *giustiniana*. Thus all these scenes are in principle for three voices, for in the *giustiniana*, too, three-voiced writing is (or was) the normal thing. One asks oneself why Vecchi did not write his work for six voices, for this would have simplified the musical dialogue. The only possible answer is that he must have thought this too simple, too commonplace, and that he chose five voices in order to avoid this musical and dramatic banality. Thus he leaves open the possibility of returning to the madrigalesque at any moment. For particularly drastic purposes he sometimes resorts to "unaccompanied monody," for example at the beginning of act I, scene 2, where Pantalone is calling Pierulino. We have already seen this sort of thing in the scene of the gardener in *Convito*. Everything is calculated for performance by a merry company of noble dilettanti. For this reason everything is kept simple harmonically, though there are unusual intervals here and there and though the circle of fifths extends as far as B major. But the entire work does not contain a single A-flat or D-flat. Choral homophony assures incisive rhythm. We no longer understand all the melodic allusions with which the work is filled, but a few of the parodies are too obvious to be overlooked. The most obvious of all is of course Doctor Graziano's parody of Rore's *Ancor che col partire*, overwhelming in its comic effect. This is a variant of the parody to which Andrea Gabrieli gave the form of the *giustiniana* (cf. p. 374 above), the text put into the dialect of Bologna, the music elaborated. But apart from this, the work is full of parodistic details, textually and musically. Thus one asks oneself whether the representation of the word *precipizio* in Lucio's monologue (act II, sc. I) is not aimed at Marenzio, for it is an exact imitation of Marenzio's treatment of *per ogni pendice* in his first book for six voices (in the madrigal *Ben mi credetti già*):

col pre - ci - pi - tio mi - o Don - na cru - del   *etc.*

The madrigal and the lighter forms of sixteenth-century music have met as though by appointment and have made merry at one another's expense against what appears to be a dramatic background. It is an end. But Vecchi is so gay, so light, so impudent, so fascinating a companion, that we prefer to see his work as a golden sunset and not as foreshadowing the coming night. After Vecchi there is plenty of comedy in Italian music, but little gaiety that is as pure as his.

Vecchi amused himself with these forms for the last time in his *Veglie di Siena* of 1604. The subtitle gives in brief a full account of the contents: the various humors of modern music, composed for three, four, five, and six voices and divided into two parts: gay and grave. In the gay part are the facetious humors. And in the grave part are:

L'humor grave	L'humor gentile
L'humor allegro	L'humor affettuoso
L'humor universale	L'humor perfidioso
L'humor misto	L'humor sincero
L'humor licentioso	L'humor svegghiato
L'humor dolente	L'humor malinconico
L'humor lusinghiero	L'humor balzano.

This work too is dedicated to a northern, ultramontane prince, this time to a real Nordic, King Christian IV of Denmark, and the good king is advised, should the performance of this Italian music make difficulties, to apply to Melchior Borchgrevinck, his organist, who as a pupil of Giovanni Gabrieli will know just what to do.

Why the title *Veglie di Siena, Noctes ludicrae*? The *veglia*, or evening's entertainment, was the one form of amusement that was left to the Intronati of Siena, one of Italy's oldest and most distinguished *accademie*, after the subjugation of Siena by Cosimo I and the loss of the city's independence (1557). Mentioned as early as 1460, the Intronati were particularly interested in the cultivation of every sort of scenic representation, but this was interrupted during the year 1563 to 1603, presumably because all meetings—even those for this purpose—seemed suspect to the authorities. In 1600 the society divided, and a new *accademia*, that of the Filomati, resumed the theatrical performances. The *veglie* of the Intronati took the form of intellectual contests and games of wit, of caprices and merry-making—plays on words (*bisticci*), debates on the art of love, and riddles, all this blended with singing, the playing of instruments, and dancing. This sounds almost like a definition of any one of Vecchi's four larger works. Vecchi declines to explain the title himself, saying that its meaning is self-evident: "bastavi che'l Materiale Intronato, e'l Fratello n'hanno abondevolmente scritto, e con molto giuditio . . ."—"suffice it to say that the 'Materiale Intronato' and his brother have written about it at length and with great judgment..." The "Materiale Intronato" and his brother are the two Sienese academicians Girolamo (1537-1586) and Scipione Bargagli (1540-1612). The older, known for his comedy *La Pellegrina*, performed in Siena in 1589 on the occasion of the wedding of the Grand Duke Ferdinand and Christina of Lorraine, had written a *Dialogo de giuochi che nelle vegghie sanesi si usano di fare* (1572); the younger, whose verses found much favor with musicians, was the author of a *Trattenimenti, dove da vaghe donne e giovani uomini sono rappresentati onesti e dilettevoli giuochi, narrate novelle et cantate alcune amorose canzoni* (Venice, 1587). These are the literary models and forerunners of Vecchi's *Veglie di Siena*.

A certain irritation is clearly evident in Vecchi's foreword. After the appearance of the *Amphiparnaso* he had been accused, it seems, of debasing his art (*a rendere di poco grido, et di minore stima la professione*), very much as Joseph Haydn was by the Berlin critics 170 years later. He defends himself by appealing to the authority of the ancients—Castiglione's *Cortegiano* and Horace's "Aut prodesse volunt, aut delectari poetae" (*De arte poetica*, v, 333); how could a musician "profit" more than by being serious (*grave*), how could he "delight" more than by being ridiculous (*ridicolo*)? Poetry and music are one, for *poesis* means "imitation" (*imitazione*). "E però non ad altro effetto rappresento personaggi con poesia dramatica, che per poter meglio imitar le cose al vivo . . ."—"Thus I have no other purpose in representing persons with dramatic poetry than to be better able to imitate things to the life. . . ." Thus the first half of the *Veglie* is to be devoted to gaiety, the second to gravity, and in such a way that fourteen different characters shall be represented in all, not such as can be seen in Garzoni's house of fools, but well considered ones, such as might well figure also at a princely table.

I am sorry to say that I have not scored this work in the right time, myself, but from the description given by Vogel (II, 275) it may be concluded that the *Veglie* return once more to the principle of the *Convito*, except that the gay pieces now stand at the beginning, with the grave ones following. (J. C. Hol has recently devoted an excellent article to the *Veglie*; cf. *Rivista musicale italiana*, XLIII [1939], 17-34.) In form it is the *Bando dell'Asino* on a grand scale, but it is less extreme and more refined, in keeping with its more aristocratic setting. A "King" (*Prencipe*) is chosen, and he calls on the individual participants in the *veglia* to carry out specific musical tasks—to play "degli Imitati il gioco." Each scene is tripartite: first comes the announcement of the task (*Proposta, a 6*), then follows the *Imitazione* (*a 3!*), and the end takes the form of a favorable criticism (*Applauso overo Chiachiera della Veglia, a 6*). Ladies too are in the party: Laura is obliged to represent a coquettish peasant wench, Emilia a Frenchman desperately in love, Giulia a company of Jews, while of the gentlemen the "Stordito" represents a Sicilian, the "Frastagliato" a German in Italy, the "Sodo" a sentimental Spaniard, and the "Giocoso" a Pantalone. (The academic names seem to be fictitious.) Six choruses follow on the second evening: a fruitless hunt for Cupid, then a match of wits, and finally, as the moon rises, the dismissal by the *Prencipe*.

The fourteen *humori*, sung partly by six, partly by five voices, are introduced by five six-voiced choruses and concluded by the courteous words (*complimenti*) of the *Prencipe*. I keenly regret that I am unable to give any idea of Vecchi's wonderful art of characterization. For the "Licenzioso" he chooses a madrigal by Marino (*Di marmo sete voi*), which shows a good sense for the appropriate; for the "Dolente" he chooses Petrarch's sonnet *Or che'l ciel e la terra e'l vento tace*, a text often set to music. And we may be sure that he found the right expression for each of the various "moods." (In the meantime the work has been published in *Capolavori polifonici del secolo XVI*, II, ed. Bonaventura Somma, Rome, De Santis, 1940.)

GIOVANNI CROCE

VECCHI was a Modenese musician only in so far as he lived in Modena—this is a point that we have made before. By training and in spirit he was a real Venetian, a pupil of Andrea Gabrieli and a colleague of the Giovanni Gabrieli with whom he

stands on an equal footing. Perhaps it was only his duties as composer to the state and for solemn festivities at San Marco that prevented Giovanni Gabrieli from becoming, like Vecchi, a purveyor of light music for the entertainment of Venetian society. In his stead, another Venetian musician supplies this want—Giovanni Croce, a pupil of Zarlino's and like Zarlino a native of Chioggia, hence his nickname, "Il Chiozzotto." About eight or ten years younger than Vecchi, he was a priest at Santa Maria Formosa; Zarlino made him a member of the choir at San Marco, where in 1594 he became vice-choirmaster under the elderly Donati, whom he succeeded in 1603. He died as early as May 15, 1609, one of the most universal and most celebrated musicians of Venice and of all Italy.

Croce's work centers in his church music, and in this he goes even beyond Giovanni Gabrieli in that, besides works for divided choirs, he writes also in the *stile concertante*. But his secular work is likewise rich and many-sided; it ranges from canzonette for three and four voices (1601 and 1588), *mascherate* for four, five, six, seven, and eight voices (1590), and books of madrigals for five and six voices, to the *Sette Sonetti penitentiali* of 1596 (?), which became internationally famous both in the original version of F. Bembo and in a Latin adaptation, and deservedly so. They are dedicated to Cardinal Cinzio Aldobrandini, Marenzio's patron. For the rest, Croce's dedications center around Venice; he pays tribute to the great Venetian families—the Sanudos, Priuli, and Bembos, and the Morosini, to whom he dedicates his Opus 1 in 1585—and only once goes a little further afield by thanking the brothers Orazio and Curio Boldieri for their hospitality in Verona (1594).

Pierre Phalèse, who knew good music when he saw it, reprinted Croce's first book of six-voiced madrigals of 1590 in 1618, saying that among the various graceful madrigals printed in the famous city of Venice, he had until then found no book more beautiful and delightful than this one (*fra diversi leggiadrissimi madrigali nell'inclita Città di Venetia stampati non ho finora ritrovato Libro più vago e dilettevole che questo a Sei voci del Sig. Giovanni Croce Chiozzioto ...*). This judgment is characteristic of the northern taste, which patterned itself chiefly on that of Venice —not accidentally but because of an inner sympathy. For Venice was a conservative city and Croce is a very Venetian musician in that these eleven madrigals actually reflect the same harmonious blend of grace, opulence, and colorful brilliance that we admire in the paintings of Paolo Veronese. There is no change of tempo, no tendentious chromaticism (although short chromatic digressions are not avoided), no pathos, no extravagance—only grace, serenity, and art. Even in a piece as serious and as mournful as the lament by Tansillo with which the book begins, *Valli profunde al sol nemiche*, tranquillity and a certain "objectivity" prevail, so that the piece could not be more unlike what Marenzio, Monteverdi, or above all Gesualdo would have made of this text. Croce is given to breadth and goes in for text repetitions, recitative-like motifs, and melismas that are decorative and pleasing rather than expressive. The second and longest number in the book is a piece of festive choral music in six sections, for a wedding:

> Lieta spiegava un giorno
> Al sol d'invidia tinto
> Le chiome innannellate
> Clori . . .

The third, *Chiudea le luci Aminta*, is a scene worked out at some length and in the style of Guarini's *Tirsi morir volea*, a text that Croce adds at the end in a setting in four sections, equally opulent but by no means "sensuous." *Addio Filli mia cara* (No. 7), worked out as a dialogue, is a farewell written to order, as is evident from a reference to the Arno, while the number that follows is dedicated to a certain Graziosa. The whole is luxurious, animated, alive, full of artistic refinement, a reflection in music of social complaisance and elegance.

Among those works of Croce that are dedicated to merry-making, two can be recognized as sources for one of the numbers in Vecchi's *Convito* (the *Echo a 6*, No. 48, *O gramo Pantalon*)—the *Mascarate piacevoli e ridicolose per il Carnevale* of 1590 and the *Triaca musicale* of 1595. The first of these contains actual *mascherate*, presumably performed in the house of the Leonardo Sanudo to whom they were dedicated by the publisher, Giacomo Vincenti—beggar women, fishermen who cry their wares to the ladies ("Orae vecchie, sardelle grosse, e cievali da bon"), traders from Burano, peasants from Friuli, and finally the familiar *magnifici*, whose appearance is built around an echo scene, as in Vecchi; all this is extraordinarily lively and starkly realistic. In the *Triaca* we even find Vecchi's text. "Triaca" is the well-known medieval antidote known as theriac, an electuary of 64 ingredients, and Croce calls the musical equivalent of these ingredients *capricci*, a title that would also fit Vecchi's works. The contents of this *Triaca*, this musical theriac-casket, is like a recapitulation of the whole series from the entertainments of Vincenzo Ruffo and Giovanni Nasco for the Accademici Filarmonici of Verona (1554) to Vecchi. Besides Pantalone, there is a contest between a cuckoo and a nightingale (*Canzon del Cucco*), a musical nursery (*Canzonetta da Bambini*), a *mascherata* of Paduan rustics, the auctioning off of a slave girl (*Incanto della Schiava*), and a game of dice (*Gioco dell'Oca*). This last has been reprinted by Torchi (*Arte musicale in Italia*, II, 345-366). (The complete *Triaca* is now published in *Capolavori polifonici del secolo XVI*, III, ed. Achille Schinelli, Rome, De Santis, 1942.) It is the exact counterpart of Striggio's *Primiera* (cf. above, p. 768), although it stands closer to Vecchi in that real solos for the individual players detach themselves from the tutti of the six-voiced chorus. Experts in this sort of thing may judge for themselves just how

realistic this scene is. In the end, a lady wins all stakes—"Viva l'amore!" The music is as simple as possible: this is entertainment, not art.

Vecchi had very few imitators or successors. This is not surprising, for the form in which he wrote was an end in itself, a summary of forms that were already dying and that became absurd in dramatic performance, even though these performances were no more dramatic than the first performances of opera. One of these imitators is Gasparo Torelli, author of the *Fidi Amanti* (1600) reprinted by Luigi Torchi (*Arte musicale in Italia*, IV, 73-147).

We know very little about Torelli's life. He was a native of Borgo San Sepolcro (Lucca) and inherited his poetic gifts (for he was also a poet) from an uncle of the same name (the son of a Giovanni Francesco Torelli) who had written many sonnets in honor of contemporaries during the 'sixties (cf. Hugues Vaganay, "Un sonnet peu connu de B. Varchi," *Giornale storico della letteratura italiana*, XLIII [1904], 455). Some of his verses were set to music by his nephew as late as 1598. In 1607 our Torelli published in Padua a capitolo in praise and in defense of music. And in Padua he seems also to have spent his life, for in 1593 and 1594 the Paduan publisher Pietro Paolo Tozzi has Vincenti print some of Torelli's canzonette in Venice, and it is at Padua that the dedications of his madrigals (1598) and of a fourth book of canzonette (1608) are signed. From the dedication of the *Fidi Amanti* it also appears that since 1597 he had lived in Padua as a music teacher in the house of one Francesco Rosini.

Torelli's "Faithful Lovers" comes closer to the genuine drama, the later form of the pastoral opera, than any of the four works by Orazio Vecchi that mix "the grave and the gay." Torelli neatly separates the *grave* from the *piacevole*: a sentimental pastoral story is unfolded in three "acts" to a text by Ascanio Ordei of Milan while the two scenes of buffoonery have been relegated to the entr'actes as intermezzi. But alas, the whole is tedious and academic. Drawing heavily on his two most famous models, Guarini's *Pastor fido* and Tasso's *Aminta*, the poet has contrived a new *favola pastorale* in which there is not a single new motif: Clori and Tirinto, the enamored shepherdess and the cold-blooded huntsman, correspond exactly to Guarini's Dorinda and Silvio, while the main motif of the action is taken, without essential change, from the *Aminta*. On the musical side, Torelli is less indebted to Vecchi than to Simone Balsamino's *Aminta musicale* of 1594. The dialogue develops in choral responses with the four voices divided into half-choirs, now of three voices, now of two. As music, the whole is unbelievably poverty-stricken. At the beginning of act II, Clori's monologue is an attempt to combine a bit of pathos with the ever-popular and inevitable business of the echo, while the dialogue between the two fathers, Elpino and Silvano (I, 4), seeks to characterize the cautious old men by means of a somewhat more hesitant declamation. Strangely enough, all this is combined with an irresistible inclination to "eye-music": at every reference to *notte, ombra,* or *ombrose selve* Torelli shifts to the black notation, a detail naturally obscured in Torchi's reprint. The rapid chatter of the intermezzi is effective in its way, but for wit these scenes are not to be compared with Vecchi's pleasantries. The contemporaries were quite right in their judgment when they decided to let the first edition of the work remain the last.

ADRIANO BANCHIERI

ADRIANO BANCHIERI is Vecchi's real successor in so far as one can speak at all of a succession in this case, for Banchieri seems more like a small-scale Vecchi or a caricature of him. They were neighbors, so to speak, and it is hardly credible that they should not have known one another. The bibliographies list a book of canzonette by Banchieri—*Il Studio dilettevole, a tre voci nuovamente con vaghi argomenti e spassevoli intermedii fiorito dal Amfiparnasso comedia musicale dell'Horatio Vecchi* (Milan, G. F. Besozzi, 1600; Cologne, G. Grevenbruch, 1603), a work that can scarcely have been published without Vecchi's consent. If Vecchi was a Modenese, Banchieri was a Bolognese, and a Bolognese *pur sang.* Thus he is the author of a booklet on the advantages of the dialect of Bologna as compared with Tuscan in the form of a dialogue between a tradesman from Bologna and a nobleman from Siena; in reality, it is a sort of guide-book, an attempt to acquaint the visitor with the sights and celebrities of Bologna (*Discorso per fuggire l'otio estivo . . . di Camillo Scaliggeri dalla Fratta,* 1622). It contains a droll dedication in the form of a sonnet to Bologna's chief landmark, the taller and more slender of her two leaning towers— "in lode dell'Altezza Sublimissima la Torre de gli Asinelli." It was in Bologna that Banchieri was born in 1567. It is said that he was first a pupil of Lucio Barbieri, organist at San Petronio, and it is certain, on his own admission, that in 1598 he studied with Gioseffo Guami in Lucca, although by that time (after 1596) he was already organist at San Michele in Bosco, at the gates of Bologna on the northern slope of the Apennines, an Olivetan monastery to which he had belonged since 1587. There he spent his life, except for the years 1601 to 1607, when he was organist at Santa Maria in Regola in near-by Imola, and the two following years, during which he traveled in Upper Italy from Venice to Milan. Thus he spent twenty-five years in his monastery; in 1620 he became its abbot; he died in 1634. One can imagine him coming down from his heights and walking through what is today the Porta d'Azeglio, passing the Palazzo Bevilacqua and proceeding into the heart of the city to attend a session of the Accademia de'Floridi which he founded in 1615 and which was later to become the Accademia de'Filomusi and still later the Accademia Filarmonica. He is one of the patron saints of music in Bologna. His versatility is astound-

ing: he was a poet, a writer, a musician both in the old style and in the new *stile concertante*, a composer of church music, a composer of instrumental music (he hit upon the idea of using the form of the *canzon francese* for the motet), a theoretician and pedagogue, and above all a composer of secular music. As yet we have no complete view of his production, but in all probability his burlesque madrigal-comedies will be the works that will keep the name of this devout, delightful Olivetan monk alive.

The *Pazzia senile*, the first of Banchieri's madrigal comedies, first published in 1598 and reprinted at least five times, usually with slight changes in its contents, makes the stuttering Pantalone the very center of the "action" and accordingly uses the conventional three-voiced texture of the *giustiniana*; the whole might indeed be called a dramatized *giustiniana* in nineteen numbers. Vogel (I, 56ff.) has reprinted the argument and Banchieri's comments, and in Torchi's *Arte musicale in Italia* (IV, 281ff.) there is a complete reprint of the work on the basis of the 1607 edition, marred by a hundred mistakes. Thus we may be brief. The content is typical of the *commedia dell'arte*:

"In Rovigo, a region belonging to the illustrious Signoria of Venice, there lives an old man, Pantalone by name, a merchant from Murano. Talking one day with his servant Burattino dalla Vallada, he learns that Signor Fulvio has been singing serenades night after night to Doralice, his daughter, and that after Signor Fulvio has played and sung to the lute there follow many amorous conversations on either side. At this the good Pantalone, as a man zealous of his honor, is beside himself with rage, and seeking out Doctor Gratiano antico da Francolino, he promises him his aforesaid daughter to wife and agrees that the marriage shall take place that very evening. Doralice, who has heard all this from her window, sends for Signor Fulvio, her lover, and gives him a minute account of what has passed between her father and Doctor Gratiano. In the end they come to an agreement and marry without the old man's knowledge.

"For his part, the aforesaid Pantalone is in love with a courtesan from Mazorbo [?] called Lauretta, but on his revealing his love to her, she spurns him. Thus in the end the foolish old men are duped and left with their hands full of flies."

Banchieri's reduction of the forces to so small a combination and his adoption of the three-voiced texture endow his work with a new character. It is no longer designed for the entertainment of the singers alone; Banchieri has also an audience in mind. He directs that before the piece is sung one of the singers is to come before the audience and read the title, the argument, and everything else that is printed at the head of the single numbers in the part-books "acciò gli audienti sappiano ciò, che si canta" — "so that the listeners may know what is being sung." And the singers themselves are to have a look at the texts in dialect, "per esser lingue non molto toscane" — "the language not being particularly Tuscan." Finally, the better to distinguish the characters, the directions *piano* and *forte* are to be exactly observed. (This is probably the earliest occurrence of dynamic directions.)

The *Pazzia senile* is a madrigalesque, villanella-like imitation of a *commedia* with the most modest means. The three parts are continually changing their function. At one moment they represent the author, who explains in continuous homophony his reasons for writing the piece:

> L'altr'estate per bizzaria
> E passar maninconia
> Per fuggir i caldi estivi . . .
> Ho composto per piacere
> Con dolcissimi concenti
> Questi miei Ragionamenti.

At other moments the three voices are individualized, as in the *mascherate* (peddlers with "matches," chimney-sweeps, peasant girls) and the intermezzi (*Bando della Bertolina*). At still another moment they develop a forcefully dramatic dialogue in which two voices reply to one. Then there are the madrigals of the lovers, so short and sketchy that Banchieri has himself christened them *madrigaletti*. But the humor of the piece as a whole depends precisely on brevity and on its being only a sketch. It must move quickly to cover up the weak spots in the music. Vecchi is not only imitated; he is also parodied. Pantalone's dialogue with the courtesan begins deliberately, with rests after each question and each answer, but towards the end it moves faster and faster; when Burattin tells his master what is going on in the house at night, Pantalone interrupts his report with excited and highly naturalistic interjections. The most striking parody is the Doctor's serenade, with its strumming on the lute and its travesty of Palestrina's *Vestiva i colli*, a really comic piece in its text and in its music and one that has been aptly compared to Beckmesser's "Prize-Song." As music, the work is thin—mere suggestion, but it is as full of life as a sketch by a good painter. Gratiano's two pieces prescribe falsetto-singing quite needlessly, since the three singers are of course two altos and a bass, and since the writing of two soprano clefs is already a sufficient indication. To be sure, the work may also be sung by five voices, with two women and three men. Banchieri himself speaks of this possibility in his *Metamorfosi*: ". . . dove saranno mutationi di Chiavi mutisi la voce sempre in ottava, ò alta, ò basso, che ella sia, che il tutto farà discernere la voce Masculina dalla Feminina, et quando in tal canti fossero tanti cantori, che si facessero in dialogo, meglio riuscirebbe" — ". . . where there are changes of clef there is always an octave-transposition, either up or down as the case may be, so that the register of the whole body of voices will indicate whether men or women are being repre-

sented, and if for these pieces there are singers enough to permit their being sung as dialogues, the effect will be even better."

Banchieri's next work, *Il donativo* (1599) is unknown to me, and it is hardly necessary to discuss the one that follows, *Il metamorfosi musicale* (1600). It is likewise for three voices, and as will be evident from the argument alone, it is practically a duplicate of the *Pazzia senile* (Vogel, 1, 59): "Stefanello Bottarga of Chioggia, a seller of dried figs, promises his daughter Laura in marriage to the quondam doctor Michelino Partigiano antico da Francolino. When this comes to the ears of Florio, a Roman student in love with the aforesaid Laura, he plans to kill himself. But Zanni straightens out all the difficulties, and they are married by common consent, while the two old men are left looking foolish, duped and derided. Livio, a student from Siena, loves Flavia, and in the end they too are married together with the aforesaid. Stefanello loves Ninetta delle Papozze, a courtesan who spurns him to his great disgust." In a word, the action has simply been expanded by adding another sentimental couple, and instead of Pantalone himself, it is another "vecchio" who has bad luck. The whole is if anything even less dramatic than the *Pazzia senile*. This time the scene is Pisa; there are three servants—Trappolino from Val Camonegha, Pedrolin from Bergamo, and Zanni dalla Vallada. Pedrolin has the last word (*licenza*) "con un spassevole balletto"; the prologue is personified by "L'Humor cromatico." The two intermezzi are now called *Trattenimenti*. The first is a simple *Passo e mezzo con il liuto*, the second a *Villotta alla Contadinesca nel Chitarrino*, the third a *Mascherata de Soldati*. "L'Humor cromatico" may serve as an example of purely musical suggestion:

> Su, rallegrate i cuori,
> Benigni spettatori:
> Quì son venuto a voi,
> Per dirvela tra noi,
> Acciò voi stiate attenti
> A questi grati accenti!

A cadence on E was enough to suggest "chromaticism" to the sixteenth century singer. The most amusing piece in the work is perhaps No. 12, a parody on Marenzio's famous madrigal *Liquide perle amor*, here altered to *Liquide ferl' amor, ranocchi e spazzi* and introduced and followed by a burlesque imitation of a ritornello for lute. To understand the humor of this time, one ought to compare all these travesties with their models, beginning with the frottola and villanella and ending with the opera buffa, where Metastasio is the usual butt of the joke.

Banchieri's next work, the *Zabaione musicale*, was published by Besozzo and Lomazzo of Milan late in 1603 or early in 1604—two parts are dated 1603, three are dated 1604. It has two alternative titles—*Invenzione boscareccia* and *Primo libro di madrigali a cinque voci*. The meaning of the term "madrigal" has by now become so conventionalized that Banchieri classes a work as a book of madrigals simply because it is written for five voices and despite its having almost nothing to do with the madrigal proper. Having once settled on the category "madrigal," Banchieri sets the scene of his ideal comedy in "un prato amenissimo di primavera" — "a pleasant meadow in spring." Yet it is in the entr'actes that we find the actual madrigals—No. 6, Torquato Tasso's *Soavissimo ardore*, and No. 12, *Baci, sospir' e voci*. The three acts themselves contain the madrigalesque pastoral pieces—No. 8, "Un pastorello con un augellino uccisogli da un gatto" (*Augellin lascivetto*), No. 5, a dialogue between a shepherdess and a swallow (*Vago augellin*), No. 9, "Tirsi a Clori" (*Il cor non fu sanato*), No. 12, the dialogue or pseudo-cantata "Aminta, Dafne, e giudizii d'amore" (*Baciansi, pastorella*), and No. 13, "Ergasto appassionato" (*Il misero mio core*). But these are decidedly in the minority as compared with the gay pieces— the *mascherate*, balletti, and other caprices. They are also much less impressive. The "Passionate Ergasto" amuses itself with a slow tempo and chromaticism; the dialogue between Thyrsis and Cloris with double motifs: the narrative of Aminta and Daphne has near the end a step-wise bass that recalls Marenzio, and the other madrigals, too, seem like popularizations of Marenzio's mannerisms for the use of less demanding singers. It is almost like a card-game—one no longer plays for real money, but only for counters, and even so the stakes are low. Banchieri and his audience are not really at home until the fun begins, and for once it is for the most

part a pleasant sort of fun. The "Introduzione" itself is charming, with its musical distribution of the voices:

> Già che ridotti siamo,
> Tutti allegri cantiamo!
> Chi fà il Soprano?
> "Io che l'ho in mano."
> Questo Contr'alto—
> "Ecco de fuori salto."
> Ecco il Tenore!
> "Voi per nostr'amore."
> Chi canterà il Falsetto?
> "S'io il canto, havrò diletto."
> Ci resta il Basso.
> "Io'l canterò per spasso."
> Hor concertati per recreazione
> Gustiamo questo dolce Zabaione!

The scene is as lively as it is unpretentious. The best ingredients of this "musical egg-nog" are pieces like this one, for example the *Gioco della Passerina* which concludes the second act—the "Game of the Roast Hen Sparrow," with a somewhat dubious secondary meaning:

> Ecco la Passerina—
> Su, su, si mangi il capo!
> È poca robba.
> Ecco la Passerina—
> Su, su, si mangi il collo!
> È poca robba.
> Ecco la Passerina—
> Su, su, si mangi il becco!
> È poca robba.
> Ecco la Passerina—
> Su, su, si mangi il petto!
> È poca robba.
> Ecco la Passerina—
> Su, su, si mangi il resto!

(The number is reprinted in Fr. Vatielli's edition of Banchieri's *Musiche corali* for the *Classici della musica italiana*, vol. I, 23ff., which in vols. II and III also contains excerpts from the *Pazzia senile*, the *Saviezza giovenile*, and the *Festino*.) For the unfavorable judgment, in triple time, an additional voice is added each time, and at the end the whole chorus exclaims rapturously:

> O quanta robba, ma in conclusione
> Meglio è un Cappone, ò un Zabaione!

Equally graceful are the *mascherate*—a company of potters (*pignattazi*)—and the balletti—an *Intermedio di felici pastori*, a *Danza di ninfe e pastori*, and a *Danza di pastorelle* with an imitation of a hurdy-gurdy. A *Gara amorosa di pastori* (No. 15), the high point of the pastoral play, is a contest between the shepherds Silvio and Carino in imitation of Theocritus or Vergil; Sannazaro's *sdruccioli* are naturally much in evidence. It is introduced by a "Preparamento" with choral recitative. The real herald of this alleged madrigal book is "L'humor spensierato" ("Master Carefree"), who welcomes the company with a cheery greeting and dismisses it with the same music.

For his second madrigal book for five voices, the *Barca di Venezia per Padova* of 1605, Opus XII (!), Banchieri found an ideal alternative title—*La nuova mescolanza*. For it is a real mixture of every form that the century had called forth. The designation of these pieces as "madrigals" is as inappropriate as it was in the *Zabaione*. To be sure, four madrigals are actually included:

> Lasso perche mi fuggi? . . .
> Io disleale? . . .
> Hoggi nacqui, ben mio . . .
> Baci soavi e cari. . . .

They stand in the very center of the work. All four texts are by Guarini and had previously been set to music many times. But Banchieri is simply amusing himself at the madrigal's expense. The fourth of these madrigals, on a text already set by Marenzio and Gesualdo among others, is remarkable for a *mutazione*: the piece is in two "parts," of which the first begins in the *genus molle* (G minor) and ends in the *genus durum* (E major), while the second begins in F and ends in D. But this sort of thing is permissible in a *mescolanza a capriccio*, Banchieri tells us in his "argument":

> Stia a l'erta il buon cantor, ne questa usanza
> Gli parrà strana in tante mutazioni,
> Che ciò concede il nome: Mescolanza.

In the later edition of 1623, *Hoggi nacqui, ben mio* is described as having been written in the "stile del Marenzio, Romano": but it is not the expressive, bold, melancholy Marenzio, but the graceful, pastoral, flowing Marenzio of the effectively divided choirs and the parlando motifs. Immediately before this group stands a fifth

madrigal, *Lidia, per far morire,* in which the speaker is "Fulvio amante": in its affectation it is an obvious caricature.

Here again the charm of the work lies in the *capricci,* in the realistic fancies. And the setting of the whole is this time really delightful. It has to do with the night-trip of the market boat down the Brenta canal from Venice to Padua by way of Fusina and passing Dolo and Strà, a trip known to every Venetian and every visitor to Venice in former centuries; its incidents are sleeping, whispered conversation, singing and guitar-playing, love-making, and trifling adventures. The sleepers at the Banchina di Santa Marta are awakened by "L'humor Svegliato," who has come to Venice from the Marche:

> Neghittosi, che fate?
> A che sonno cercate?
> Svegliatevi dall'ozio, entrate in barca,
> E pigliate buon loco, mentre è scarca!
> Eccomi a voi mandato,
> Che son l'humor Svegliato,
> Sol per dirvi, ch'udrete belle botte,
> Solcando le paludi questa notte.

And now the musical gaiety begins: first a scene of fishermen *in lingua veneta antica* —*Pescaori nui semmo*—a *mascherata* in the midst of which a peddler roars out his wares:

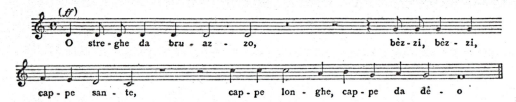

Then follows the departure of the boat, while the skipper takes leave of his Ninetta— and so delightfully that we must quote at least the text in full:

Dialogo: Parone e Ninetta

Par.	Cara Ninetta mia
	Collonna cara fia . . .
Nin.	Chi chiama la Ninetta
	Oimè con tanta fretta?
Par.	Me parto bella fia
	Ti xe la pì compia
	Che mai sia sta in Veniesia.
Nin.	Distù de senno, a mi?

Par. Certo che digo a ti!
Quel tò visetto d'oro
El' val'un Buccentoro.

Nin. Moia tasi ti me soij.

Par. Quel'ochio marioletto
Me fa andar in bruetto.

Nin. Ah can non me soiar!

Par. Quel labro inzucharao
E'l me passa e'l figao.

Nin. Tasi la, che me vergogno . . .

Par. Nò certo ben mio caro.

Nin. Car'moroso mi te lasso,
Son chiamada zo da basso.

Par. Duro me sa partir
Me sent'oime morir.
Su vogaori col vostro remo.
Chi dixe andemmo chi dixe andemmo an?
(Aggiunta il rumor de Gondole:)
Barche premi hò he hò va stagando.
(Risposta di tutta la compagnia:)
Tutti tutti sù andiamo allegramente
Senza timor di niente.

After this the stuttering pilot is heard inviting the company to while away the time on the trip, an invitation to which the glib Florentine bookseller at once responds. The next to be heard from is the singing-master from Lucca, with the famous solfeggio:

This leads to the assembling of the quintet: Giovanni Francesco of Naples for the soprano, Ceccho Bimbo of Florence for the falsetto, Greghetto of Chioggia for the contralto, Petronio of Bologna for the tenor, and a German for the bass; each singer introduces himself in his own dialect or jargon and in "unaccompanied monody," and all are enthusiastically acclaimed by the company. But before they begin, the German insists on quenching his thirst; bottle in hand, he sings a rollicking *brindisi* which he interrupts, just before his last solo, to take time for another gulp.

Now follows the group of madrigals already described. Their succession is broken up by the entrance of a new character, the merry Rizzolina. "Non più, di grazia, questi madrigali!" she objects, and with the approval of the entire company she introduces herself:

	Rizzolina son cortese—
Chorus:	"La più bella del paese"—
	Tutto il giorno fò l'amore—
Chorus:	"Poi la sera alle due ore"—
	Il mio caro (or: Horatio) Pellizzone
Tutti:	Fa sonar e cantar nel chitarrone.

The "allotria" or *capricci* that follow are amusing and as interesting to the student of social history as they are to the musician. Rizzolina and her Horatio begin with a burlesque dialogue whose characters recall the grotesque figures of Jacques Callot; after this they interpolate a duet of Jews ("La baruchaba"); and to conclude, Rizzolina sings to Horatio's vocally imitated lute-accompaniment an improvisation or strambotto ("parole all'improviso"):

> Io mi ricordo quand'ero bambina
> Che la mia mamma mi facea carezze,
> E mi diceva: bella Rizzolina,

Se non par d'or quelle tue bionde trezze!
Con le compagne poi sera e mattina
Facea con lor l'amor ch'erano avezze
E v'imparai sì ben a far l'amore
Ch'a mille amanti il dì rubbano il core.

Familiar as we are with the frottolistic strambotto and the origins of the *canzon alla villanesca,* we are not surprised when Rizzolina sings the same tune—one of the *arie veneziane*—four times over:

Does it recall the similar tune in Corteccia's madrigal of 1547 (*Io dico e diss'e dirò fin ch'io viva,* cf. above, p. 285)? No doubt it does, but with Corteccia the rise and fall of the tune went just the other way. The piece ends with the landing, the skipper and pilot demanding the fares, and the "applauso degli passaggieri, e tutta la compagnia":

Viva la mescolanza del Banchieri!

And to add a last touch of realism to the scene, a couple of beggars stand on the bank and represent themselves to be soldiers "tornati d'Ungheria": they are curtly turned down by the boatmen:

Va lavora, Guidon.

It is a curious coincidence that in the autumn of 1786, when Goethe traveled by boat from Padua to Venice, making the trip in the opposite direction, there were two "masks" on board—Catholic pilgrims from Westphalia—who received the same rough treatment from the rest of the party that the pretended veterans from Hungary received from Banchieri's troupe.

Banchieri's next work, the *Prudenza giovenile* of 1607, Opus xv, returns to the three-voiced texture of the *giustiniana*: on the title-page it is described as "il quinto libro de gli Terzetti." The later and somewhat altered edition of 1628 is called the *Saviezza giovenile* and contains a highly interesting preface with an attack on the "modern" opera. With its arias and *sinfonie* this is nothing but downright dilettantism, Banchieri says; the excellent musicians who laid down the rules would never have dreamed of this "istile moderno"; thus his own work, the *Saviezza giovenile,* belongs to the "scenico istile rappresentativo" and combines the old with the new.

There is no need for us to discuss this work. It is simply a duplicate of the *Pazzia*

senile, as will be evident from the "argomento": "Gratiano, a doctor from Franco-lino, has an only daughter, Isabella by name, whom he intends to marry to Panta-lone, a merchant from Chioggia. But just the opposite comes to pass, for Isabella marries her lover, Signor Leandro, without her father's consent. The aforesaid Doctor Gratiano is for his part in love with Signora Aurora, but she is loved by Signor Fortunato; thus this second marriage is also concluded, and the two old men are duped, while the young people enjoy the fruits of their love." This should suffice.

But we shall want to have a look at Banchieri's next work, the *Festino nella sera del Giovedì grasso avanti cena* of 1608 (Opus XVIII), already announced by Ricciardo Amadino, its printer, in the foreword to the *Barca di Venezia.* (I have not seen the reprint edited by Bonaventura Somma, Rome, A. de Sanctis, 1939.) It is also put forward as the third book of the composer's five-voiced madrigals. In the foreword, Banchieri now represents himself as a man of progress. The herald of the *commedia,* "Modern Delight," tells the readers, singers, and guests that on the stairs he ran across an old man who made himself known to him as "Ancient Rigor" and urged him to turn back. But he gave the old man an angry look and replied that he was indeed "Delight," but "Modern Delight," and that "Ancient Rigor" had best peddle his old trash somewhere else. It is not improbable that this was Banchieri's way of taking the side of the moderns in the quarrel between Artusi and Monteverdi. This foreword, which Vogel has reproduced with many gaps, is so characteristic of Banchieri that we shall quote it *in extenso:*

"Essend'io in obligo (gentilissimi Convitati) ritrovarmi con voi al godimento di questo *Festino,* in entrando all'antiporta per saglire le scale (udite stravaganza) mi s' è affacciato un Vecchio vestito in tal guisa: Beretta per bollire i verzi, barba ospi-zia, Giornea pedantesca, legato a traversa sotto la groppiera & sotto l'ala sinistra gran catasta di scartafazzi affumicati così favellandomi:

" 'Fermati ò Diletto ne saglire a atto alcuno atteso che l'Autore non havendo vol-suto me per suo osservante Maestro, che vengo da gli periti Theorici nominato *Ri-gore,* a fronte scoperta, posti in oblio, quei Generi Cromatici, & Enarmonici, che Ar-monica, & ragionevole, rendono la fondata Musica, si serve in vece, di proportioni, Dure rozze, & irragionevoli Diatonicamente conteste; Però (se tu sei il vero Diletto) ritorna a dietro, che in questo luoco, non havrai luoco.'

"Allo di costui impertinente cicalamento, con occhio biego gl'ho risposto (come usasi dire) a Coppe.

" 'Io in vero sono *Diletto* ma *Moderno,* pero sappi ò *Rigore* che se l'Autore (il quale per dirtelo sono io) non ha volsuto osservare ad unguem cotesti tuoi scartaf-fazzi pretende havere esequito ottimamente, vorresti pur con le tue soffestichezze, & cavillationi insinuar si gli Compositori moderni che praticassero le tue anticaglie; Mira il Pittore, leggi il Poeta, senti il Musico, non si scorge nelle di loro moderne invenzioni un gusto troppo grande? Dimmi un poco, chi veste, ò conversa più alla Filosofica come tù? Deh ti confonda, in scorgendo, che gl' intelletti al giorno d' oggi di cento, gli novanta si compiacciono di quella gran Massima che Omnia nova placent, & in particolare nel Compositore di Musiche havend'egli per scopo il Dilettare, si come l'Oratore il persuadere altrui; Però ti conseglio, o *Rigore Antico*, contratta cotesti tuoi scartafazzi con il pizzicaruolo, che questa futura settimana saranno eccellentissima Triaca per le Sardelle Tonina, Arringhe & Caviale.'

"S'accingeva egli di nuovo con sue importune repliche, ond'io assalito da un leggiadro tiro di Bastina gl' hò lasciata questa beneficiata di note nere, e letre da Speziali.

O (o o o o) che Na na na na nas O che Na - son

"Et frettolosamente correndo le scale eccomi a voi, Signori, per mantenere quanto fu promesso nella Barca di Venetia per Padova Secondo Libro de gli Madregali a cinque voci antecessori a questo stando quella trita sentenza, Omne promissum est debitum: Volevo arecarvi un Zerlino di ziambelle & Buzzolati, ma per non levarvi l'appetito l' hò ordinato per mentre si cena. Dirò per chiuso di questa mia Capricciosa Diciticcia, che in questa sera avanti cena udrete poca Theorica; cancaro vengha alle questioni & brighe, non hò potuto servirmi di Autori gravi, essendo eglino occupati per un stravagante occorso & è, In cucina il Cuoco & la fantesca accidentalmente sono entrati in disputa Vtrum se la ragghiata dell'Asino sia voce bastarda, overo consonanza mista, il Cuoco Platonicamente argumentando tiene sia voce bastarda, la Fantesca Pollicratescamente provando dice esser consonanza mista, la ziuffa, e attacata, & vi sarà che fare, (Come dice il Spagnolo) per todos, tutta via da gli speculativi moderni, si tiene che l'openione Platonica caverà le penne maestre alla Pollicratesca. Signori tenetevi ch'io vi lascio con questa cadenza finale, si canti allegramente leggendo gli tittoli posti sopra gli Canti, & pur che simile Compositione piaccia alla di voi maggior parte, del restante ogni rispetto stiasi in disparte; mò serrando gli registri concludo se vi fossero nel Festino qualche svogliato, ò Donna gravida gli quali havessero il gusto corrotto, si ritirino in cuccina a metter quiete tra il cuoco, & la Fantesca acciò la cena non vadi in maschera, ma in grazia mia faccino il ritornello mentre si cena al Fior Gradito quarto libro Madrigalesco seguente a questo, il quale sarà (senz'altro) appetitoso trattenimento per tutti."

"Being under an obligation (gentle guests) to join with you in the pleasures of this *Festino*, on entering by the outer gate to go up the stairs (mark now a strange tale!), I was accosted by an old man dressed in this fashion: a bonnet fit to boil

cabbages in, a moth-eaten beard, a pedantic gown tied crosswise under his crop, and under his left wing a great bundle of dingy folios; he addressed me as follows:

" 'Stay, O Delight, and by no means go upstairs, seeing that the author, having rejected me as his rightful master (I who am descended from the master theorists and am called Rigor) and having shamefully repudiated the chromatic and enharmonic genera that render the established music harmonious and rational, uses in their stead proportions, dissonances, and irrational things that are diatonically objectionable; wherefore (if thou art True Delight) turn back, for here there is no place for thee!'

"To the impertinent prattling of this person I replied, giving him an angry look and repaying him in his own coin (as the saying goes):

" 'I am indeed Delight, but I am Modern Delight; wherefore, O Rigor, hear what the author maintains (and to speak frankly, I am he): having refused to observe the rule of those folios of thine *ad unguem*, he has succeeded admirably, although with thy sophistries and cavilings thou hast sought to insinuate that the modern composers ought to put thy antiquated precepts into practice; observe the painter, read the poet, listen to the musician; dost thou not recognize great taste in their modern inventions? Tell me, who is a greater philosopher than thou in his dress and in his conversation? May it confound thee to recognize that the intellects of today, ninety out of a hundred, accommodate themselves to the great maxim *Omnia nova placent*, above all the composers of music, whose aim it is to delight others, as the orator's is to persuade them; wherefore I counsel thee, O Ancient Rigor, to peddle those folios of thine to the fish-monger, for the next week they will make an excellent catchall for sardines, tuna-fish, herrings, and caviar.'

"He was girding himself up anew with his inopportune replies, and so, spurred on my way, I left him with his benefice of black notes and druggists' prescriptions.

"And having run hastily up the stairs, here I am, gentlemen, to deliver what was promised in the *Barca di Venetia per Padova*, the second book of my madrigals for five voices and the predecessor of this one, remembering the trite saying *Omne promissum est debitum*. I had intended to bring you a little basket of cakes—*ciambelle* and *bozzolati*—but in order not to spoil your appetites I shall save this until we dine. To conclude this capricious dissertation of mine, I shall say that before dinner this evening you will hear but little theory (a plague take your questions and controversies!); I have been unable to use the serious authors, for they are already occupied by an extraordinary occurrence: the cook and the maid in the kitchen have fallen to disputing *utrum* the braying of the ass is a bastard sound or a mixed consonance; the cook, arguing Platonically, maintains that it is a bastard sound, while the maid, using a Polycratesque demonstration, says that it is a mixed consonance; the battle is joined, and there will be something to do *per todos* (as the Spaniards say), although the speculative thinkers among the moderns maintain that the Platonic opinion will pluck the feathers of the Polycratesque. Gentlemen, let me leave you with this final cadence: let your singing be merry, let the titles printed above the songs be read out loud, and as long as this sort of music pleases most of you, let all consideration for the rest be set aside; closing the accounts, I conclude by saying that if there be at this *Festino* any jaded men or pregnant women with corrupt tastes, let them retire to the kitchen to make peace between the cook and the maid so that the dinner may not turn into a brawl, but for my sake let them give us while we dine the ritornello to the *Fior gradito*, my fourth book of madrigals and the successor of this one, which shall (without fail) be an appetizing entertainment for us all."

The unusual thing about this work is that it is a social game in costume, and that it reproduces a real evening's entertainment, such as might precede a Shrove Tuesday banquet. The first to enter is the herald, who sings his jolly little stanza in triple time:

> Chi brama havere
> Spasso e piacere
> Per un tantino,
> Entri al Festino. . . .

He is followed by a group of five Pantaloni from Chioggia ("Giustiniana") who venture a dance and apostrophize one another in a most comical manner. Then— surely after a dramatic pause—comes a "Mascherata di villanelle," in several scenes. Two of the girls begin "una ottava rima bella," with an imitated *lira* accompaniment by the others:

> Ciascun mi dice che son tanto bella,
> Che sembro la figliuola d'un signore
> Chi mi somiglia alla Diana stella,
> Chi mi somiglia al pargoletto Amore
> Tutto il contado ogn'hor di me favella
> Che di bellezza port'in front'il fiore.
> Mi disse hier mattina un giovinetto:
> Perche non hò tal pulce nel mio letto?[4]

[4] Precisely this ottava is sung by Menghina in Carlo Goldoni's *Bertoldo, Bertoldino e Cacasenno* (1748):

> Ciascun mi dice, ch'io son tanto bella,
> Che sembro esser la figlia d'un signore,
> Chi m'assomiglia alla Diana stella,
> Chi m'assomiglia al faretrato Amore.
> Tutta la villa ognor di me favella,
> Che di bellezza porto in fronte il fiore.
> Mi disse l'altro giorno un giovinetto,
> Perchè non ho tal pulce nel mio letto?

Then all five continue *alla madrigalesca*:

> Chi cerca posseder sommo diletto,
> Segui Amor giovinetto . . .

To conclude, they sing a "Madrigale a un dolce Usignolo," a setting of Guarini's *Dolcissimo usignolo*, the opening of which recalls the three ladies of Ferrara.

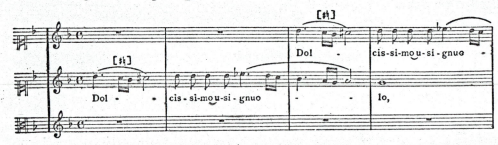

These peasant girls are obviously well-bred and well-educated.

A new group arrives: the *amanti*, the lovers. First they imitate a contest between *arpicordo* and lute, singing only the syllables *tronc toro tronc* and *diri din din din*; after this they dance a *moresca alla Gastoldi* entitled "Il Spagnoletto." It is now up to them to show their breeding and they sing a new setting, by Banchieri, of Guarini's ever-popular *Ardo sì, ma non t'amo*, after which they conclude with a burlesque farewell-scene between Bireno and Olimpia in the form of a canzonetta—two stanzas to the same music.

Now come the *capricci*, the *allotria*. "Aunt Bernardina tells a story" (*La zia Ber-*

nardina racconta una novella); this is the suggestive story of the talking magpie, and it is a lifelike scene that the singers perform. Then, after a *barzelletta* for three voices, follows the famous "Contrapponto bestiale a mente":

> Un cane, un cucco, un gatto, e un chiù per spasso
> Fan contraponto a mente sopra un basso.

The bass consists of a sort of Gregorian chant in whole notes and ligatures, with a nonsensical Latin text:

> Nulla fides gobbis
> Similiter est zoppis. . . .

The chief joke lies of course in the imitation of the animals' cries: the calls of the screech-owl and the cuckoo, the miaowing of cats, and the barking of dogs. Certain crude Italian caricatures engraved at this time (about 1600) might almost have been prompted by Banchieri's compositions of this sort.

As though to quiet the listeners after this "bestial capriccio naturale" there follows a "serio madrigale," very animated and pretty; then a fresh group of maskers appears, the spindle-makers, with a *mascherata* whose text and music would certainly bring about the removal from office and excommunication of any cleric today. Before they leave they sing a madrigal, Guarini's *Felice chi vi mira*. Next comes a new game, the "Gioco di conte," the "tongue-twister": the prize goes to the one who can sing these lines the fastest:

> Sopr'il ponte a fronte del fonte vi stava un Conte
> Cadd'il ponte nel fonte e il Conte si rupp'il fronte?

While the game is going on it strikes three o'clock: it is time for the banquet. They break up with an ottava and begin again with a *brindisi*, an archetype of Haydn's "Farewell" symphony: everyone who takes a drink must stop singing and wait until the "applauso." At the end there is still another *mascherata* with street cries in the dialect of Bergamo (*Strazz'e zavatt'*—a different text than in the *Pazzia senile*, despite an identical beginning) and the herald's *licenza*, a new text for the music of the *introduzione*.

Banchieri continued to publish works of this sort until 1630: a sixth (and last) book of three-voiced canzonette with the title *Tirsi, Filli, e Clori* (1614)—pastoral pieces, without Pantalone and Zanni or other *capricci*; the *Vivezze di Flora e Primavera* (1622), Opus 44, a book of five-voiced madrigals with the alternative title *Cantate recitate e concertate . . . nello Spinetto o Chitarrone*; a book of *Concerti musicali* (1626), Opus 49, for one, two, three, four, and five voices or instruments with the title *Il virtuoso ritrovo accademico del Dissonante*—"Dissonante" was Banchieri's academic name in the Accademia dei Filomusi; the *Sampogna musicale*,

performed (*rappresentata*) in the same *accademia* on November 14, 1625; and finally the *Trattenimenti da villa* (1630), "concertati . . . nel chitarrone," which Banchieri aptly calls a "vaga, e curiosa concatenazione drammatica." Nor does this exhaust the list; Banchieri even included burlesque musical pieces in his literary writings. It will have been noticed that he has gradually entered the camp of the *musica concertante*, of the basso continuo.

With Banchieri, the madrigal-comedy, the "concatenazione drammatica," is at an end. But burlesque composition for voices lives on. The quodlibet cannot die as long as there are jovial musicians to sing together. All that disappears is entertainment for the sake of the entertainers; even in the seventeenth century this sort of music requires an audience. An example has already been mentioned (cf. p. 768 above), a work from the second half of the seventeenth century by Carlo Grossi of Vicenza, a musician long in the service of the Estes at Reggio and Modena, later a singer at San Marco in Venice. He cultivates "all'uso delle Regie Corti" music "da camera, o per tavola"—madrigals, cantatas, canzonette, and dialogues. In 1681 he publishes a book of music for entertainment with the title *Il divertimento de'Grandi*, dedicated to Ferdinando Carlo II, Duke of Mantua, and containing among other things a "Gioco della morra" (a sort of guessing-game), a "Gioco della primiera" (a card-game), and a "Dialogo ebraico" (a Jewish scene)—subjects for the most part already familiar. The "Morra," a duet with basso continuo, is highly realistic; the three-voiced "Primiera," however, is shot through with moral reflections on the caprices of Fortune, in the form of arias:

> O come son fallaci
> Le tant'ingorde voglie
> O quanto son fugaci
> Di Fortuna le spoglie,
> Che se a vestir m'imparo
> Me ne priva talor destin'avaro!
> O carta maledetta,
> Ch'ammazza la Primiera
> Spada nò, ma saetta. . . .

The scene of the Jews, for four voices with solos, is by no means parodistic or burlesqued, unless one considers a solemn vigil in expectation of the Messiah—for this is the content of the text—and the mere use of Hebrew as in themselves a burlesque.

Grossi is by no means the last of the successors of Striggio, Vecchi, and Banchieri. There is also Benedetto Marcello with his burlesque pieces, especially his satire on the castrati, condemned to eternal damnation as "trees that bear no fruit"; in Southern

Germany, there is Valentin Rathgeber with his *Musikalischer Zeitvertreib* (a literal translation of the Italian *Divertimento* or *Fuggilozio*); then there is Bach with his "Peasant" and "Coffee" cantatas. Down to Haydn, Mozart, and Schubert this tradition remains alive: so venerable is the ancestry, so long the line of descendants, of which "Music as Entertainment in Company" can boast.

IN ERCOLE BOTTRIGARI'S dialogue *Il Desiderio* (1594, p. 8ff.) there is a half humorous discussion of the etymology of the word *concerto* or, in the Tuscan dialect, *conserto*, a discussion which arrives at the conclusion that for the harmonious union of musical instruments the right word would be *concento*, meaning "consonance." But the word *concerto* has a different meaning. Bottrigari defines it quite correctly: "... se voi verrete a cercare quello; che vuol significare concerto, trovarete ... che ... concerto significa *contentione, ò contrasto*. ..." — "If you will inquire into the meaning of the word *concerto*, you will find that it signifies 'contention' or 'contrast.'" Standing at the threshold of the new century, Bottrigari is as yet unable to bring the two concepts *concento* and *concerto* into their correct historical relationship. But for us they can throw a light on the changing relationships of the voices in the sixteenth and seventeenth centuries. In the madrigal, in the motet, the voices combine in a consonance, a *concento*. No voice stands out; each voice recognizes the rights of every other; there is a truly democratic spirit. But in the course of the century the tension of the voices with respect to one another undergoes a change: two or more voices stand out, begin to compete, and force the rest to accept a subordinate and menial role. We have made this point before (p. 151 above): even in the democratic musical community, the *concento*, the upper voice tends to lead, the bass tends to support, the inner voices tend to fill in. To all appearances there is peaceful collaboration on the common ground of equal rights: the conflict is as yet latent. But Josquin's example bears fruit, and when two pairs of voices begin to oppose one another in a four-voiced context, the first step towards the concerto-like treatment has already been taken. This situation becomes especially obvious in madrigals written *a voci pari* or *a voci mutate*—either for four low voices, as happens so frequently in the madrigal's first decade (between 1535 and 1545), or for four high voices, a relatively rare occurrence. Zarlino (*Istituzioni harmoniche*, III, cap. 65), in his chapter on the *Compositioni de quattro, ò de più voci*, already speaks of these various combinations of voices: one writes "con tre Tenori, et un Basso; overamente con tre Bassi et un Tenore: et alle volte con quattro Bassi ... si compone anche con due Soprani et un Contr'alto, over'un Tenore et il Basso; alle volte con tre Soprani et un Basso; et tal fiata con quattro Soprani..." — "for three tenors and a bass, or for three basses and a tenor, and sometimes for four basses ... ; one also writes for two sopranos and a contralto or tenor and a bass, sometimes for three sopranos and a bass, and sometimes for four sopranos. ..." An example—not for four sopranos, but at least for four high voices—is included in Maistre Ihan's madrigals of 1541. The pairing of the voices is reflected in the distribution of the clefs: the two voices in the mezzosoprano clef sing together, and the voice in the soprano clef (printed in the tenor part!) sings with the supporting voice in the tenor clef. Not only do the pairs enter into a concerto-like competition with one another, but this competition extends also to the single voices making up each pair:

Another example, even earlier, is Costanzo Festa's *Non s'incolpa la voglia* in Verdelot's *Madrigali a cinque* (ca. 1538), which opposes three high voices (two sopranos and an alto) to a tenor and a bass.

These are early and isolated examples but they are the forerunners of many others whose number grows as the century progresses. A historian of the changing vocal register would have to record that in the course of the century it rises higher and higher, just as the note-values become smaller and smaller. And while this is going on, the lady (*madonna* or *signora*) ceases to be the passive object of the madrigal and begins to assume a more and more active role. She is no longer sung to—she sings herself. And in the five-voiced madrigal, the classical norm from Rore on, the ratio of women's voices to men's is as two to three: two sopranos balance a falsetto alto, a tenor, and a bass. Thus the voices fall into two groups, and the group of women's voices develops a rivalry within its own ranks, for there can be no choosing between two ladies, even in music. They begin a concerto-like competition. One will find this already recorded in the contemporary *novella*, or rather in the connecting story that runs through it, for example in Giambattista Giraldi Cinthio's *Hecatommithi*. At the end of the third decade (I use the edition of 1565), after a *lagrimosa* or "tearful" sestina by one of the youths, there follows a gay (*di felice soggetto*) dialogue in song (*cantare a vicenda*) between Camilla and Cornelia, two of the girls; after this they declare themselves ready to go on singing "qualunque volta questi Giovani accompagnino le voci *suoi* col suon delle viuvole loro. I Giovani . . . pigliaron prontissimamente i loro stromenti, et, dopo una dolce ricercata, cominciarono a sonare, et le due Giovani, con soavissima voce, diedero principio al canto loro"— "whenever the youths accompany their voices with the sound of their viols. The

youths immediately take up their instruments, and after a soft prelude they begin to play; the two girls, singing most sweetly, then begin their song":

> Poscia che tu benigno
> A miei casti desiri . . .

And at the end of the third dialogue the girls even sing a quartet, *Quando il pensiero a contemplar m'induce*, accompanied by the youths on four viols which "gave forth the sweetest harmony" ("onde ne uscì una suavissima armonia"). We are by no means losing sight of the conventional, ideal character of such stories; in this case the history of the madrigal shows us that Giraldi is a realist. For further light on this change—this transition from men's to women's voices—one can turn to the connecting story in the *novelle* (London, 1793) of "Il Lasca" (A. F. Grazzini). The time is that of Paul III (1534-1549) and the scene is the house of a widow in Florence. One winter's night four youths were passing the time there with the widow's brother; ". . . era musico perfetto, e una camera teneva fornita di canzonieri scelti, e d'ogni sorte di strumenti lodevoli, sappiendo tutti que'giovani, chi più e chi meno, cantare e sonare" — "he was a perfect musician and occupied a room supplied with choice song-books and every sort of praiseworthy instrument, for all these youths were able to sing and play, one more and another less." While they were amusing themselves by singing and playing it began to snow and they turned to throwing snow-balls. . . . The mistress of the house then invited in four of her friends, all of them married ladies (*tutte maritate*), who took up the battle from the roof of the house. In the meantime the youths reassembled and began to sing certain five-voiced madrigals by Verdelot and Arcadelt (*si diedero a cantare certi madrigali a cinque voci di Verdelotto e d'Arcadelte*), and this brought the ladies back into the house: "e poi che essi ebbero cantati sei ad otto madrigali . . . si misero a sedere al fuoco . . ." — "and after they had sung six or eight madrigals . . . they sat down by the fireside. . . ."

We know the five-voiced madrigals of Verdelot and Arcadelt that were sung by the youths, and we also know the madrigals of a somewhat later period in which the Camillas and the Cornelias begin to take the upper hand. In the last third of the century, what might be called a "shifting" of the voices takes place in the five-voiced madrigal: the pair of voices having the same clef wanders from the lower register into the soprano. Earlier, whenever two voices detached themselves from the rest by singing in canonic imitation, they were as a rule two altos, or two tenors, or a soprano and a tenor; now they are two sopranos. Not even as conservative a master as Filippo di Monte can ignore this change. It affects his work quite suddenly: in his ninth book of madrigals (November 20, 1580) every voice has its own clef in every piece, but in the tenth book (June 26, 1581) the two sopranos are paired in most of the numbers. (The second number, *Quand'io tal'hor mi doglio*, is written for four sopranos and one alto.) This, too, belongs to the *variato stile*, the "changed style," that Monte announces in the dedication of his tenth book. And thus the conduct of the two sopranos comes more and more to approximate a duet, though without prejudice to the vocality of the whole, the uniformity of the melodic idiom. An example from Monte's thirteenth book (1588) will serve as illustration.[1] The two sopranos answer one another and come together, but as yet they do not completely detach themselves from the living body of the madrigal or degrade the three lower voices to the status of a mere accompaniment. What has happened? Just the year before (August 8, 1580) Luca Marenzio had come forward with his *Primo libro*, and in some of the madrigals of this epoch-making book the duet-like conduct of the two sopranos is as it were announced as a principle. The numbers in question are:

Liquide perle	(1)
Spuntavan già	(3)
Quando i vostri begl'occhi	(4)
Cantava la più vaga pastorella	(11)

It will suffice to quote the beginning of one of these pieces:

And this competition and reconciliation of the two sopranos continues from one end of these pieces to the other. It is a relationship or obligation that does not place itself in intentional and open opposition to the lower parts; it is hidden, but it is undeniably there. Within the framework of the *concento*, the *concerto* is born. Just as one can now distinguish between conservative and progressive madrigals on the basis of their time-signatures, one can also do so on the basis of their grouping of the voices. And the two distinctions run parallel: pieces in the older time-signature, with the breve as unit, prefer the old lower register with five different clefs; pieces in the *misura cromatica*, in four-four time, prefer the two competing sopranos. Here again the influence of the five-voiced villanella and canzonetta is undeniable, for in these, too, the sopranos tend to exchange roles when repeating groups of lines.

Hand in hand with this "shift" in the grouping of the voices goes a heightening

[1] See Vol. III, No. 89.

of demands on vocal technique, at least in so far as the preferred or upper voices are concerned. In the first two periods of the madrigal's development we find little trace of the qualities that the seventeenth century will expect of the singer—range, skill in making divisions, and delicacy of expression. Good vocal quality was perhaps not even required. Only the low basses were praised, and justly so, for their deep tones were essential if the upper voice was to sing falsetto. Anyone was supposed to be able to sing. The style of the early madrigal is vocal in the narrowest sense; it shrinks fearfully from any intrusion of the instrumental. Hence also the narrowness of the melodic formulas; every step, even the smallest, must be an event. In the *concento*, parity of the voices also implies parity of ability. Thus we shall not be surprised to find the two sopranos expressly mentioned on the title page of a collection of five part madrigals, the *Madrigali a cinque voci, Con duoi Soprani* (1598) of Gioseffo Biffi da Cesena, then choirmaster to Cardinal Andrea Bathory—a Milanese publication, dedicated to Duke Vincenzo Gonzaga.

The *concento* is forced to make the transition to the *concerto* when to the competition of the sopranos there is added the element of virtuosity. And this addition coincided with the appearance at the court of Ferrara under Alfonso II of those three celebrated ladies, so often praised in song—Lucrezia Bendidio, Laura Peperara, and Tarquinia Molza. It is the last flaring up of the musical life at the court of Ferrara, which had seen an uninterrupted succession of brilliant events since the times of Obrecht, Brumel, Ysaac, Josquin, and Willaert, thanks to such names as Maistre Ihan, Alfonso della Viola, Nicola Vicentino, Cipriano Rore, and Giulio Fiesco; which had attracted such guests as Lasso and Wert; which had included every sort of music—dramatic scenes and choruses, the pastoral drama, the tragedy, the madrigal, the budding instrumental music. In 1565, as though to challenge fate, Alfonso had caused two big halls—"del Pallone" and "dei Giganti"—to be built in his castle, the one for dramatic performances, the other for music (cf. A. Solerti, *Ferrara e la corte Estense*, Città di Castello, 1899, p. vii). This splendor ended for all time with the death of the childless Duke in 1597, when the duchy reverted to the Church as a papal fief and Pietro Aldobrandini entered Ferrara as Cardinal Legate. In 1601, when Luzzaschi dedicated his music for the three ladies to this very Cardinal, the grave-digger of Ferrara's splendor, it is hardly more than irony and a melancholy recollection of a happier time.

We shall need to introduce these three ladies, although Angelo Solerti devoted a brilliant chapter to them in his book on Ferrara and the court of the Estes (chapter IX). Lucrezia Bendidio, who was born in 1547, came to Padua in September 1561 in the train of Leonora d'Este and Cardinal Luigi d'Este, the sister and brother of the reigning Duke; here she was for a whole year the object of the Petrarchan passion of Torquato Tasso, then a seventeen- or eighteen-year old student—it was his first contact with music and with a beautiful voice. But Lucrezia kept him at a distance—doubtless because she had already accepted the Cardinal as the lover she later acknowledged him to be—and in the summer of 1562 or thereabouts, when she was married in Ferrara to Count Paolo (Baldassare?) Macchiavelli, she did not even permit the unhappy young poet to absent himself from the wedding. Later on, in 1570, she became the object of the persistent attentions and poetic rhapsodies of G. B. Pigna, the Duke's first minister. Her musical supremacy at the court remained uncontested until the Duke's third marriage, to Margherita Gonzaga, brought her a dangerous rival in Laura Peperara.

Laura Peperara was a native of Mantua and came from a well-to-do merchant family (the Peverari), originally of Cremona. She too was destined to be worshiped and extolled by Tasso, who visited Mantua about 1564; she too came to Ferrara, as a *damigella* or lady-in-waiting to Margherita Gonzaga, Duke Alfonso's bride; she too was married, in 1583. Laura was called "La Mantovana," and the ambassador Urbani speaks of her as singing duets with Giulio Cesare Brancaccio, in a report of February 1581 (Solerti, *ibid.*, p. 137). And on August 14, 1581, the same reporter offers us a lively description of a musical evening at the court: "Ier l'altro si ritornò da Belriguardo dove io sono stato due giorni invitato, come scrissi, dal signor Duca. ...La mattina si andava attorno in una carrozzina scoperta come si costumano quà, finche la Signora Duchessa era in ordine per udir messa, dopo la quale si desinava, e dopo il desinare immediate si giocava a primiera, dove interveniva il signor Duca, la signora Duchessa, la signora donna Marfisa, la moglie del Signor Cornelio, ed io: che si come seguiva per forza, così è pur forza dirlo, ed in un medesimo tempo si dava principio alla musica, a tal ch'ero io necessitato insieme giocare, udire, lodare e ammirare i passaggi, le cadenze, le tirate e si fatte cose, delle quali tutte, cominciando dal giuoco, poco m'intendo e manco mi diletto. Questa festa non durava punto meno di quattro ore, perche dopo aver cantato alcune altre dame, finalmente compariva la signora Peverara che è quella mantovana scritta altre volte, la quale sotto pretesto di far udire a me or una cosa ed or un'altra, e sola e accompagnata, e con uno e con più istrumenti, si faceva durare al più che si poteva. Poi si andava all'acqua, dopo la quale essendo già vicino a 23 ore si andava a sparviere, dove interveniva la signora Duchessa e tutta la corte. Questo è quanto è passato." — "The day before yesterday we returned from Belriguardo where I was for two days a guest of the Duke as I have already written. .... In the morning we drove about in a little open carriage, as is the custom there, until the Duchess was ready to hear mass, after which we had lunch, and immediately after lunch we played *primiera*; in this game the Duke, the Duchess, Donna Marfisa, who is the wife of Signor Cornelio, and I took part, and as I was forced to take part, so I am forced to admit it; at the same time the music began, so that I

had to play cards, listen to the music, and praise and admire the passages, the cadences, the *tirate*, and similar things, all of which, beginning with the card game, I know little about and enjoy still less. This festivity lasted no less than four hours because, after some other ladies had sung, there appeared Signora Peverara, the Mantuan whom I have mentioned in other letters; under the pretext of having me listen to one thing or another, either as a solo or accompanied by one or more instruments, she prolonged the session as long as possible. Then we went to the beach, after which, when it was already 23 o'clock, we went hawking, and in this the Duchess and the whole court participated. This is all that happened."

When Laura Peperara married Count Annibale Turco, in 1583, this was a great event for both courts—Mantua and Ferrara. The wedding festivities were unusually splendid: "con intervento di tutta la nobilità ... una bellissima giostra ... un bellissimo balletto della signora Duchessa con altre undici dame, vestite di concerto, parte d'oro e bianche, parte tanedo e oro; e dopo cena fu fatta una carriera, e la festa à durata quasi al giorno ..." — "With the whole nobility present ... a wonderful tournament ... a beautiful ballet danced by the Duchess and eleven other ladies, uniformly dressed, some in gold and white, some in tan and gold; and after dinner there was a horse-race, and the feast lasted until nearly day-break. ..."

A lasting monument of this wedding is the book of six-voiced madrigals which appeared in the same year (1583) under the title *Il lauro verde* and the imprint of the court printer Baldini, a present to the bride from the Accademia dei Rinnovati. The poems were supplied by Ferrara's poets, great and small, the music by the musicians of Ferrara and Europe, great and small—Luzzaschi, Macque, Marenzio, Vecchi, and Wert. Laura died on January 5, 1601, and was buried in the Jesuit church in Ferrara. Thus she barely survived the days of Ferrara's greatest musical splendor.

Tarquinia Molza was the eldest member of the trio, and also the most famous, for the eulogies of the poets have lent her name a certain added brilliance, and for this reason one may read about her in every history of Italian literature. In this book too her name has already come up. She was born in Modena in 1542, the niece of the poet Francesco Maria Molza, and on February 7, 1560, she married Paolo Porino, a nobleman from Modena whose widow she became after nine years of married life. In 1583 she came as a *dama d'onore* to the court of Ferrara, where she had already established "quel celebre concerto di Dame" while on a visit (cf. *Opuscoli inediti di Tarquinia Molza Modenese*, Bergamo, 1750, with a "vita" by Domenico Vandelli). "Da fanciulla cominciò Tarquinia ad imparare la Musica per trattenimento, e per divertirsi dai suoi studij più serj ..." — "As a child, Tarquinia began to study music as a relaxation, and as a distraction from her more serious studies. ..." "La condotta della voce, ch'ella aveva acquistata colle vere regole sui Libri, e non come per lo più si usa ponendosi a memoria ciò, che vien dettato da'Maestri nell'arte, di cui alcuni ebbero questa lodevole ambizione di poterle mostrare qualche cosa di raro in questa professione, come fecero fra gli altri Giaches d'Uberto, Lusasco Lusaschi, e Orazio detto della Viuola, col quale instrumento, oltre il Liuto, soleva musicalmente sonare una parte, e unendovene un'altra colla sua voce, e con tanta, e tale destrezza, e sapere, che non se ne poteva desiderare di vantaggio. . . ." — "Her manner of singing she acquired by applying herself to her books and not, as usually happens, by memorizing what was dictated by her singing-masters, some of whom had the laudable ambition to show her something new in this art, among others Giaches Wert, Luzzasco Luzzaschi, and Orazio surnamed della Viola, on which instrument, together with the lute, she used to play one part musically while she sang another, with such skill and understanding that one could desire nothing better. . . ." Tarquinia lived at the court of Ferrara for six years, and these years constitute the high point in the musical brilliance of that court. The tragic circumstances that led to her departure in 1589 have already been set forth in connection with the life of Giaches Wert (cf. p. 513). Tasso tells us in one of his sonnets (*Donna ben degna che per voi si cinga*) that Duke Alfonso himself once rode in her honor in a tournament. But this did not help her in her hour of trial.

It would be idle to ask whether the *concerto* of the three ladies was a result of the increasing concerto-like tendency in the madrigal, or whether, on the contrary, the tendency was brought about by the ladies. The fact is that the ladies did contribute to it all over Italy—for example, the Roman musician Giovanni Andrea Dragoni includes a few pieces for three sopranos and two lower voices in his fourth book of madrigals (1594)—but especially at the courts of Northern and Central Italy, in Mantua and Florence. Lasso too seems to have heard the trio when he visited Ferrara early in October 1585, and if, after Lasso's return to Munich, the Duke of Bavaria writes to Duke Alfonso that Lasso never tires of praising the rare music he has heard (*non si sazia di decantare la musica rarissima udita*) and of complaining that the ducal chapel in Munich no longer pleases him (*non può più lodare la musica mia*), this is surely more than a mere courtly compliment. Nowhere else could such music be heard (cf. Solerti, p. 119), and one can understand Lasso's amazement when one reads the description of one of the "mammoth concerts" (*concertoni*) by the Florentine ambassador Canigiani (August 14, 1571), who was anything but a eulogist of the Ferrarese court: ". . . de vespro a sera si festeggiò in corte . . . e si fece uno di quei concertoni di musica di circa sessanta fra voci e istrumenti, e dietro un gravicembalo tocco dal Luzzasco, cantorno la signora Lucrezia e la signora Isabella Bendidio a solo a solo, e tutt'e due, si bene e così gentilmente, che io non credo si possi sentir meglio" — ". . . from dusk till late at night there was feasting at court . . . and one of those great concerts, with about sixty voices and instruments, and behind a gravicembalo played by Luzzasco, the Signora Lucrezia and the Signora

Isabella Bendidio sang by turns and together, so well and so delightfully that I do not believe that I shall ever hear anything better." (*Ibid.*, p. 134.)

Ferrara was universally envied because of her "three ladies," and in our chapter on the beginnings of monody we shall see that there were attempts to spy upon their art and their repertory. The Duke was jealous, especially of Florence, and thus the repertory was kept secret; of the compositions written expressly for the three *cantatrici* little or nothing became available until Luzzaschi's publication of 1601. Yet the madrigal literature from 1580 on is full of pieces written with them in mind. Much to my regret I am unable to throw any new light on Paolo Virchi's three madrigal books of 1584, 1588, and 1591, the first two for five voices, the third for six (and not preserved complete), two of them dedicated to Duke Alfonso himself, one to Cardinal Alessandro d'Este. Virchi, born at Brescia about 1552, was an excellent *chitarra*-player and speaks of himself as an organist and musician in the service of the Duke, while his numerous settings of texts by Tasso show his relation to the court of Ferrara. But the influence of the three *cantatrici* extends far beyond the narrow confines of Ferrara. In Vienna and Prague, Filippo di Monte dedicates his fourteenth madrigal book (1590) to the Duke, and although he is unlikely to have been in Ferrara or even in Italy after his call to the Imperial court, his unusually long-winded dedication contains this passage: "la fama, che fra l'altre sue gran virtù celebra lo studio della Musica, la quale come con maravigliosa armonia risplende ne suoi Reali costumi, così vuole spesso udire, compartita *fra angeliche voci*, et cantata da così rari spiriti che vi si trova si crede haver certa caparra della beata vita . . ." — "Among your other great virtues, Fame celebrates your zeal for Music, and just as this art resounds with marvelous harmony in your royal bearing, so do you often desire to hear it, divided *among angelic voices* and sung by such rare spirits that he who listens believes himself to have a sure foretaste of the life of the blessed." And thus, besides being full of settings of texts by Tasso (*Amor l'alma m'allaccia, Gelo ha madonna in seno, Caro amoroso neo, Al vostro dolce azurro*) his book is also full of pieces in which there are episodes for two or three high voices: the old master has evidently tried to adapt himself to the tessitura of the three Ferrarese nightingales if not to their virtuosity, of which he can have known only from hearsay. But even before this there had been talk of the three ladies at the Imperial court, as we learn from a report of the Duke's ambassador in Vienna, on July 24, 1574 (cf. Solerti, p. 135). Naples too heard echoes of Tarquinia's fame, for in 1591 the Neapolitan composer Stefano Felis published a setting for five high voices of a madrigal written in Tarquinia's honor by Torquato Tasso:

> **Forsi** è cagion l'Aurora
> **Di** questo bel concento . . .

O con sì dolce modo
Il ciel Tarquinia honora . . .

One might perhaps also explore the work of Costanzo Porta for possible traces of his acquaintance with the *tre signore,* for the "fra Costanzo, musico eccellentissimo," who arrived at the court of Ferrara from Ravenna in April 1583 (Solerti, p. 138) can have been no one else.

Monteverdi also paid an early tribute to the three ladies. Later on he became the first great master of the *stile concertato,* the man who realized everything that the sixteenth century had dreamed about the virtuoso madrigal, the vocal concerto. But in his third book of madrigals (1592) there is a setting of *O come è gran martire,* a poem by Guarini—by Guarini the court secretary and court poet in Ferrara—that is already something halfway between the madrigal that gives prominence to a trio of women's voices (we might call it the five-voiced trio-madrigal) and the genuine *madrigale concertante.* The three ladies enter one by one to combine in three-voiced declamation:

The tutti does not enter until the twenty-second measure, and from here on it alternates with the more concerto-like episodes. The third soprano now becomes

more like an alto and the trio more like a duet; as a whole, the piece is not yet by any means a trio with two accompanying vocal parts. At the same time, it is no longer a madrigal in which the voices are equally privileged; it is a hybrid, as befits the restless 'nineties and a restless spirit like Monteverdi.

In this piece Monteverdi is an imitator of Giaches Wert, though still a rather timid imitator. Wert is already far more advanced. If anywhere, compositions for the three *cantatrici* must be sought in the work of Wert, particularly in view of his deep-seated and violent passion for Tarquinia Molza, the most mature and most important member of the trio. To be sure, his most radical pieces, which must have been at least as "progressive" as Luzzaschi's, are not preserved or were never printed —Duke Alfonso would never have permitted it. And by the time of Alfonso's death Wert was also dead, and no one seems to have been interested in his posthumous works—neither in Mantua nor at the rival court of Florence, neither Monteverdi nor Caccini, though one may be sure that both were deeply obligated to Wert artistically.

Apart from tendentious settings of texts from Tasso's *Gerusalemme liberata* and madrigals for the *tre cantatrici*, Wert's eighth book of five-voiced madrigals (1586) also contains certain pieces that point in the most positive way to a new trend that is beginning to affect the madrigal—the trend towards motivic working-out in general. Yet this motivic working-out is simply the other side of the competitive concerto-like conduct of the voices. The very first number furnishes the most striking example.[2] The first half of the text consists of four short lines, each of seven syllables:

> Io non son però morto,
> Donna, come pensate,
> Perche più non m'amate,
> Anzi ritorn'in vita . . .

Each line has its own characteristic motif and each motif is combined with every other, resulting in a motivic web of thirty-seven measures, as "discursive" as any development of Haydn's. By way of contrast, the second half is almost pure homophony, with two episodes for the trio of women's voices to which Wert expressly refers in his dedication to Duke Alfonso.

This dedication is too characteristic to omit: "Havrei commesso notabilissimo errore se dovend'io dar in luce questi miei componimenti di musica fatti per la maggior parte in Ferrara ad altro personaggio indirizzati gli havessi che a V.E.A. . . . . Et essi in qual parte del mondo potrebbon esser meglio cantati che nella Corte di V.A.? dove io non mi sò ben risolvere qual sia maggiore ò la maestria di chi canta ò'l giuditio di chi l'ascolta. Percioche lasciando stare di tanti altri

[2] See Vol. III, No. 90.

eccellenti et Musici, et Cantori che sono nella sua numerosissima e perfettissima Capella: à cui non sono hoggimai note le meraviglie et d'arte, et di natura, la voce,
la gratia, la dispositione, la memoria, et l'altre tante et sì rare qualità delle tre nobi-
lissime giovani Dame della Ser.ma Signora Duchessa di Ferrara? Il qual rispetto
per se solo bastar dovrebbe à indurre tutti i compositori del mondo, che le loro
opere indirizassero à V.A. perche da sì divine voci, et de sì nobil concerto riceves-
sero il vero, et naturale spirito della Musica. . . ."—"I should have committed a
noteworthy error if in publishing these musical compositions of mine, for the most
part written in Ferrara, I had dedicated them to any other personage than Your
Highness. . . . And in what part of the world could they be sung better than at
the court of Your Highness, where I cannot determine which is greater, the mastery
of the singers or the judgment of the listeners. For, leaving aside any number of
others among the excellent musicians and singers in your numerous and perfect
chapel, who is there today who has not heard of the marvels of art and nature, the
voice, the grace, the disposition, the memory, and all the other rare qualities of the
three young noblewomen of Her Ladyship the Duchess of Ferrara? This in itself
should be enough to induce every composer in the world to dedicate his works
to Your Highness so that these divine voices and this noble concert may endow
them with the true and natural spirit of Music. . . ."

Three numbers in this "Ferrarese" madrigal book reveal their destination for
the three *cantatrici* at first glance:

> Si come ai freschi matutini rai . . .
> Non è sì denso velo . . .
> Con voi giocando Amor. . . .

This destination is evident even in externals, for the three upper voices are written
in the same clef, either the soprano or the treble, and these voices alone carry the
complete text. The two lower parts are still vocal, but even when they combine with
the women's trio they do not always participate motivically in the musical conversation. They are not altogether eliminated, but they are at a disadvantage. We know
a singer who sang one of these lower parts—Giulio Cesare Brancaccio of Naples, a
soldier and adventurer, now an old man but familiar to us as the companion of the
young Lasso. Until 1583 Brancaccio lived at Alfonso's court, where his fine bass
voice was extolled by Tasso and by Guarini; his dismissal from Ferrara was due to
his having once refused to sing with the three ladies (cf. Solerti, p. 122). Two of
Wert's pieces begin with such extended trios that the entrance of the two lower
parts has the effect of a surprise, and such tone-painting as the text allows takes the
form of coloratura:

In the third of these pieces, *Con voi giocando Amor*, Wert combines a development on double motifs with his preferential handling of the trio, and the distinction between the three-voiced solo group and the tutti becomes somewhat blurred. Most characteristic despite its old-fashioned time-signature is the second piece, *Non è sì denso velo*, which we have included in our volume of illustrations.[3]

Benedetto Pallavicino, another Mantuan composer, Wert's successor and Monteverdi's forerunner as court choirmaster, seems not to have written directly for the three *cantatrici*, but even among his madrigals there are pieces in which the development of the *concerto* type has already been carried to a high point. I need only mention his setting of Guarini's *Tutt'eri foco, Amore* (*Quarto libro a cinque*, p. 6/7, 1588), in which the words *fuoco, soave, ardo, fiamma*, and *ardore* lead to extended roulades, not uniformly in all parts but chiefly in soprano and bass. An elder

[3] See Vol. III, No. 91.

compatriot of Monteverdi's, Pallavicino was at Sabbioneta in the service of Vespasiano Gonzaga (1531-1591) when he published his first book of five-voiced madrigals in 1581; after 1582 he was in Mantua, first as a singer, but later (1596-1601) as choirmaster; he spent the last years of his life as a Camaldulian monk. Neither his comprehensive work as a composer of madrigals (one book for four voices, one for six voices, and eight for five voices between 1579 and 1612) nor his historical position between Wert and Monteverdi have thus far attracted closer attention to him—Torchi (*Arte musicale in Italia*, II) is the only one to have published a piece of his. But how can one understand Monteverdi's development completely without knowing Wert and Pallavicino?

But let us return to Ferrara. The real composer in ordinary to the *concerto* of the three *cantatrici* is of course Luzzasco Luzzaschi. Traces of his work for them are already to be found in his polyphonic madrigals (cf. above, p. 701), but it is in his famous *Madrigali . . . per cantare, et sonare A vno e doi, e tre Soprani, fatti per la Musica del già Ser^mo Duca Alfonso d'Este* (1601) that a part of their actual repertory appears for the first time. It is a book of melancholy reminiscence and of pride, no longer turned out in Ferrara by Baldini, the court printer, but engraved by Simone Verovio in Rome. It contains three pieces for solo voice, four duets, and five trios with cembalo accompaniment. Six of the texts are by Guarini, but it should be noted that *O dolcezze amarissime*, despite its first line, has nothing to do with the *Pastor fido*, and that *Io mi son giovinetta* has nothing to do with the Decameron.

All three "monodies" and two of the duets have been reprinted—*Aura soave, Ch'io non t'ami,* and *Stral pungente* by Kinkeldey, who has the credit of having been the first to insist on Luzzaschi's importance; *O primavera,* by Schering, *Geschichte der Musik in Beispielen,* No. 166; *Cor mio, deh non languire* by J. Wolf, *Sing- und Spielmusik,* No. 48. But they are not as yet genuine monodies and hardly genuine duets. They are more like arrangements of four-voiced madrigals for the "agile throats" of the *signore* Peperara, Molza, and Bendidio and for the cembalo, in which the accompanying instrument simply takes over the lower parts of a composition that might easily be restored as a vocal quartet. There is as yet no new conception of the relationship between a vocal part and an accompaniment, no dualistic separation of opposing functions, no new declamation as with the "Florentines"—Caccini, Peri, Cavalieri, Marco da Gagliano, and Monteverdi. The old frottolists were already further along than Luzzasco. And with these pieces, Luzzasco is the last representative of an art-practice well known to us, the pseudo-monody of the sixteenth century, rather than the forerunner of the genuine monody of the seventeenth.

But he is certainly one of the originators of the genuine vocal concerto. Once more, it is most characteristic of the hitherto prevalent one-sided interest in everything connected with monody and opera that five of the seven pieces for one and two

voices have been reprinted, but not one of the trios, although Luzzaschi gives them the most prominent place of all, both in number and in scale. We shall try to make up for this. In our volume of illustrations[4] we have included the first of these trios (*O dolcezze amarissime d'amore*) and a facsimile of the first page of the last one. What Luzzaschi was driving at is perfectly clear. In conception these pieces are four-voiced madrigals of a conservative order, half homophonic, half imitative, but when two voices predominate, or one alone, the bass supplies the entire accompaniment and thus "releases" the virtuosity of the singers, which is most prominently displayed in the repetitions of the final sections. Here we have the actual beginnings of the *madrigale concertato*, which Monteverdi was to carry further.

[4] See Vol. III, No. 92.

FROM the very first, the equally privileged status of the several voices in the madrigal and motet was an illusion: this is a point to which we have already called attention in our account of the transition from the frottola to the madrigal, from the accompanied song to the a cappella form. The a cappella ideal bore within itself the germ of self-destruction, of internal discord: an upper voice cannot help but dominate, a bass must support and thus assume a subordinate function, inner parts must "fill in" and thus surrender a part of their independence. Zarlino already understands this very clearly when he compares the four voices with the four elements—the bass with earth, the tenor with water, the alto with fire, and the soprano with air (*Ist. harm.*, III, cap. 58); having made this comparison, he continues as follows: "Se . . . vorremo essaminar la proprietà di queste Parti, ritroveremo che'l soprano; come quello, ch'è più acuto d'ogn'altra parte, et più penetrativo all'Udito, farsi udire anco prima d'ogn'altra; . . . cosi il Compositore si sforzarà di far, che la parte più acuta della sua cantilena habbia bello, ornato et elegante procedere. . . ."—"If we were to examine the nature of these parts, we should find that the soprano, as the part that is higher and more penetrating for the ear than any other, makes itself heard above the others . . . thus the composer must see to it that the highest part of his composition has a beautiful, ornate, and elegant procedure. . . ." "Et si come la Terra è posta per fondamento de gli altri Elementi; cosi'l Basso ha tal proprietà, che sostiene, stabilisce, fortifica, et da accrescimento all'altre parti; conciosiache è posto per Basa et fondamento dell'Harmonia; onde è detto Basso, quasi Basa, et sostenimento dell'altre parti. . . ."—"And just as the earth has been constituted the foundation of the other elements, so the bass is of such a nature that it sustains, steadies, strengthens, and gives increase to the other parts, for it has been constituted the basis and foundation of the harmony; for this reason it is called 'bass,' as being the basis and support of the other parts. . . ." The tendency to self-dissolution, to a transformation of the democracy of the voices into an aristocracy on the one hand and a slave-state on the other, was innate in the madrigal as a work of art and is by no means confined to the madrigal. The frottola and the old frottola-like canzone had been forms of monody. Thus the trend towards the a cappella ideal seems like a deviation and the trend away from it like a return. But this is not the whole story, for even in the sixteenth century the flow of monody never ceased; it went underground, as it were, and continued to run parallel to the a cappella forms. It was essentially a form of improvisation.

Genuine monody was in existence long before the appearance of the Florentine reformers, in the form of a recitation over a *basso ostinato* or "ground." Too little attention is paid, I think, to that passage in Zarlino's chapter on the "effects" of the ·

ancient genera (*Ist. harm.*, II, 9—*In qual genere di Melodia siano stati operati i narrati effetti*) in which a sharp contrast is drawn between the moving effect of singing to the lute or viol and the neutral effect of the polyphonic "Canzonette dette Mandriali." Zarlino rejects the erroneous view of certain of his contemporaries who held that the famous "effects" of ancient music could only have been attained in the chromatic and enharmonic genera, for if the ancients had attained them in the diatonic genus, the genus used in modern times, the moderns would be able to attain them also. Zarlino holds that the moderns actually do attain them. "Laonde vediamo etiandio à i nostri giorni, ch'ella induce in noi varie passioni, nel modo che anticamente faceva; imperochè alle volte si vede, che recitandosi alcun bello, dotto et elegante Poema al suono d'alcuno Istrumento, gli ascoltanti sono grandemente commossi, et incitati à far diverse cose: come ridere, piangere, over'altre simili; et di ciò si è veduto l'esperienza delle belle et leggiadri compositioni dell'Ariosto; che recitandosi (oltra l'altre cose) la pietosa morte di Zerbino, et il lagrimoso lamento della sua Isabella; non meno piangevano gli ascoltanti mossi da compassione, di quello che faceva Ulisse udendo cantare Democodo [*sic*] musico et poeta eccellentissimo. Di maniera che se bene non si ode, che la Musica al di d'hoggi operi in diversi soggetti, nel modo che già operò in Alessandro; questo può essere, perche le cagioni sono diverse et non simili, come suppongono costoro; percioche se per la Musica anticamente erano operati tali effetti; era anco recitata nel modo, che di sopra hò mostrato; et non con una moltitudine de parti, et tanti Cantori et Istrumenti, nel modo ch'ella si usa al presente, ch'alle volte non si ode altro che un strepito et romor de voci mescolate con diversi suoni, et un cantar senz'alcun giuditio et senza discretione, con un disconcio proferir de parole; che non si ode altro che confusione; onde la Musica in tal modo essercitata non può fare in noi effetto alcuno, che sia degno di memoria: Ma quando ella è recitata con giudicio, et più s'accosta all'uso de gli Antichi; cioè, ad un semplice modo, cantando al suono della Lira, del Leuto, o d'altri simili Istrumenti alcune materie, che hanno del Comico, over del Tragico, et altre cose simili con lunghe narrationi; allora si vedono i suoi effetti; perche veramente possono muover poco l'animo quelle Canzoni, nelle quali si racconta con breve parole una materia breve; come si costuma hoggidi in alcune Canzonette, dette Mandriali; le quali benche molto dilettino, non hanno però la sopradetta forza."—"Thus we see that in our day music arouses various passions in us, just as it did in ancient times. For sometimes when a beautiful, learned, and elegant poem is recited to the sound of an instrument, the listeners are greatly moved and led to behave in various ways—laughing, weeping, and doing other similar things. And as to this, it has been our experience with the beautiful and graceful writings of Ariosto that when (among other things) the piteous death of Zerbino and the lamentable complaint of his Isabella are recited, the listeners are moved by compassion and weep not less than Ulysses did when he heard the singing of Demodocus, that excellent musician and poet. So if we do not hear that music affects people today as it once affected Alexander, this may be because the causes are different, and not similar as my opponents suppose. For if music had these effects in ancient times, it was being performed in the manner already described and not, as is usual at present, with a multitude of parts and with so many singers and instruments that one sometimes hears nothing but the noise and uproar of voices mixed with the sounds of various instruments, a singing without judgment or discretion and with the words pronounced in so disorderly a manner that nothing but confusion is heard. When music is performed in this manner it can have no effect on us worth remembering. But one will see its effects when it is performed with judgment and brought closer to the usage of the ancients—when to the sound of the *lira*, the lute, or some other similar instrument one sings in a simple style of matters that partake of the comic or tragic or of similar things that contain long narratives. For in truth the soul can be little moved by those songs that briefly recount a brief matter, as is customary today in those little songs called madrigals which, although they give much pleasure, do not have the power in question."

Zarlino as an advocate of monody! He goes on to clinch his argument by preferring choral recitation to the polyphonic treatment of narrative. And what are those "songs" and "little songs called madrigals" of which he speaks? Simply short pastoral narratives of the sort set to music by Nasco and Ruffo, simply madrigals on such texts as Tansillo's *A caso il giorno* or Guarini's *Tirsi morir volea*. It is Zarlino's opinion that the most affecting texts that can be sung to the lute are the impassioned laments of the *Orlando furioso*. He might also have mentioned the last words of Dido from the fourth book of Vergil's *Aeneid*. The settings of this text play their part—and it is an important one—in the early history of monody, and they continue to do so right down to 1638, when Domenico Mazzocchi pieces fragments of this book together in a genuine oratorio. (Oliver Strunk has given an account of the process in his admirable article "Vergil in Music," *Mus. Quarterly*, xvi [1930], 482f.) In Le Roy and Ballard's *Sixième livre de chansons* (1556), Arcadelt has a wholly homophonic four-voiced setting of the lines:

> At trepida et coeptis immanibus effera
> Dido . . .

This was surely designed as a monody with lute accompaniment in the first place; it must thus be counted among the incunabula of the cantata, for it already makes a clear distinction between the narrative introduction and the lyric-dramatic "aria."

As to the ottave rime from the *Orlando furioso* and the *Gerusalemme liberata*, we

can pretty well imagine how they were performed. This sort of "monody" begins with the appearance of Ariosto's poem and may very well be much older. Tromboncino's music (1517, reprinted 1520) for Orlando's lament, *Queste non son più lagrime che fuore* (XXIII, 126), can serve as a model for the recitation of entire scenes from the *Orlando furioso*. Need I add that in the same year (1520) the piece was at once arranged for voice and lute? Or would it not be more correct to say that the vocal version in Antico's print is the "arrangement"? I am reprinting this important piece after the copy at the Istituto Musicale in Florence (f. 45) in the version for the lute; I reduce the note-values and supply the alto in small notes after the vocal model, since the arrangement omits it.[1] But six years earlier, in the eleventh book of the *Frottole*, Tromboncino had found an even more striking solution of the problem, this one in triple time. In 1520 this too was arranged for lute, but I reprint it after the vocal model. I also figure the bass, for I am persuaded that in the last analysis the sixteenth-century lutenist played a simplified chordal version corresponding roughly to what such figures indicate.[2] We shall find similar melodies and basses a century later, almost unchanged—yet changed in so far as there is now the consciousness of the harmonic content of such a bass, of its chordal functions.

What is true of the ottava and strambotto is equally true of the canzone stanza and of the madrigal—indeed we already know (p. 113) that Michelangelo's *Come havrò dunque ardire* exists in two versions, in a "vocal" one for four voices, and in a "monodic" one for voice and lute. This is perhaps the place to introduce an index to the *Frottole de Misser Bortolomio Tromboncino et Misser Marcheto Carra con Tenori et Bassi tabulati et con soprano in canto figurato per cantar et sonar col lauto* (1520). I follow the copy at the Istituto Musicale in Florence (B. 3803), which is unfortunately very fragmentary: not only does it lack the last of its forty-seven leaves with Giunta's printer's mark but also leaves 14-19 and 30-34. The numbers which cannot be traced to a printed vocal model are marked with an asterisk; they presumably belong to the lost tenth book of Petrucci's *Frottole*:

*Almen vedesti el cor mio	p. 8 Tromboncino	Ecco colui che m arde		38 C.
Amor se d hora in hor	12 T. [Cara?]	*Facto son per affanni		29 C.
Aqua non e l humor	9 T.	Forsi e ver [!] forsi che no		39 T.
Ben mi credea passar	40 T.	Gli e pur cocente		37 T.
Cangia sperar mia voglia	18 C.	La non vol perche		14 C.
*Chi se po slegar d amore	2 T.	La speranza in tutto		17 [?]
Come haro donque ardire	5 T.	Longi dal mio bel sol		45 T.
Cum rides mihi	20 C.	Madonna la pietade		22 T.
De fussi almen si nota	43 T.	*Mia ventura ad venir		23 T.
Donna non me tenete	30 C.	*Movessi il vechiarel		28 T.
*Donna sol per voi	31 [?]	Muchos son d amor		40 T.
Dura passion che per amor	16 T.	Nel foco tremo		14 T.

[1] See Vol. III, No. 93.   [2] See Vol. III, No. 94.

*Ogni mal d amor procede .... 26 T.

*Per fugir la mia morte .... 7 C.

*Piangea la donna mia .... 46 C.

Piu volte fra me stesso .... 10 T.

*Quando i piango .... 27 T.

Queste lachrime mie .... 33 [?]

Queste non son piu .... 45 T.

Se alcun tempo da voi .... 10 C.

Se amor non e che adunque .... 13 C.

Se gliel dico che dira .... 13 C. [T?]

Se la lumacha .... 11 T.

Signora un che v adora .... 15 C.

*Voi gentil alme accese .... 35 T.

From this index it may be gathered that there was a demand for monodic versions of all the forms that occur in the books of frottole—frottole in the strict sense, strambotti, canzone stanzas, madrigals, even duets like *Gli e pur cocente il cor.* The one exception is the coarse villotta, whose effect depends on vocal performance. This changes as the madrigal develops. In 1536 (2nd ed. 1540) Willaert does not arrange all of Verdelot's madrigals for voice and lute, but only those pieces that have a self-contained, song-like cantilena with a simple "accompaniment." The little coda of the three lower voices is regularly used as an instrumental postlude: it is as though Verdelot had had monodic performance in mind from the first. And there are three lower voices, not two, for the alto is no longer omitted as it was in Petrucci's arrangements. The accompaniment has filled out. I am including one of these arrangements among the examples, although—or rather because—it is one already reprinted by Wilhelm Tappert (*Sang und Klang aus alter Zeit*) in a transposed and not altogether accurate form.[3]

This is the sort of "monody" that was cultivated by the lute-playing singers of the time and that was cultivated particularly in connection with dramatic performances. We take a few further examples from the *comedia* performed in 1539 on the occasion of the marriage of Cosimo de' Medici to Leonora of Toledo, the wealthy daughter of Don Pedro, the viceroy of Naples. The music was largely by Corteccia, though eight numbers are by Costanzo Festa, Baccio Moschini, Mattio Rampollini, and G. P. Masaconi. At the beginning of the *comedia* Aurora appears and, to the accompaniment of a "gravecimbalo con organetti et con varii registri," awakens the shepherds and nymphs:

> Vattene, almo riposo—ecco ch'io torno
> Et ne rimen'il giorno.
>   Levate herbette e fronde
> E vestitevi piagge et arboscelli
> Uscite o pastorelli
> Uscite o ninfe bionde
> Fuor del bel nido adorno
> Ognun si svegli e muova al mio ritorno!

[3] See Vol. III, No. 95.

I am reprinting the first two lines in the form intended—in the original the text is printed below each part.[4]

It was obviously not Corteccia's intention to simplify the cembalo or organ part in an instrumental style, in the spirit of an accompaniment, and to make it stand out from the vocal line. But I should say that his discreet coloratura makes the vocal line stand out, and as the piece goes on, the musical structure becomes still more chordal and the antithesis between the voice and the bass still more pronounced, until the concluding line again falls back into animated, almost restless imitation. All five parts attain the status of equally privileged voices when Day is driven off by Night, a low alto accompanied by four trombones:

> Vientene, almo riposo: ecco ch'io torno
> E ne discaccio il giorno.
>   Posate, herbette e fronde,
> E spogliatevi piagg'ed arboscelli:
> Entrate, o pastorelli,
> Entrate o ninfe bionde,
> Entr'il bel nido adorno
> Ogn'un s'adagi e dorma al mio ritorno.

Each voice preserves its independence; there is in this "monody" not one genuinely chordal, homophonic measure. As though in compensation, the song of Silenus at the end of the third act is relatively simple, "con un violone sonando tutte le parti, et cantando il soprano"; the chordal accompaniment is not really impracticable on a large viola da gamba. And thus "accompanied solo song" is not an invention of the Florentine Camerata: it is already in existence here. It is also to be found in the marvelous literature of the Spanish *villancicos* for voice and guitar (*vihuela*), beginning with Don Luys Milan's *El Maestro* (1535).

There is a similar piece, with the gamba accompaniment worked out in detail, in the treatise on the playing of the gamba by Silvestro Ganassi del Fontego, published in two parts in 1542 and 1543 under the title *Regola Rubertina* (reprinted in facsimile in the *Veröffentlichungen des Fürstlichen Instituts für musikwissenschaftliche Forschung zu Bückeburg*, II, 3 [1924], ed. Max Schneider; cf. also M. Schneider, "Zur Geschichte des begleiteten Sologesangs," *Kretzschmar-Festschrift*, pp. 138-140). It is found in the second part and is an arrangement of a three-voiced madrigal by Jacopo Fogliano; the vocal original had been printed in 1537 in the *Madrigali a tre voci* of Andrea Antico da Montona, a print of which only the bass-part has been preserved. We have reprinted the piece again,[5] but without the bowing and fingering for the gamba part, which are of no interest here. Perhaps it was

---

[4] See Vol. III, No. 96.　　　　　　　　　　[5] See Vol. III, No. 29.

Ganassi's preoccupation with his own instrument that led him to make the inspired and revealing statement (cap. x, p. 12) that of all the voices the bass is the most important: ". . . la più degna parte di tutte l'altre." And it is an early recognition of the function of the bass when he adds that it is the part "which gives shape to all the consonances" — "perche l'è quello che da la forma a tutte le consonantie." A few years later, in 1553, another player on the gamba, the Spaniard Diego Ortiz in Naples, gives the first examples of variations over a *basso ostinato*.

Ganassi's example teaches us what madrigals were thought most suitable for monodic recital. They were the ones which most faithfully preserved the poetic form. Such a madrigal tries to give rhymed couplets the same music; it repeats the two concluding lines; a musical poet might even have improvised music of this sort. One might also put it the other way around and say that in this "monodic" singing before the rise of monody, in the monodic improvisation of the sixteenth century, the poetic word always takes precedence over the music, and that the elaborate, polyphonically animated madrigal remains the special province of the a cappella singer. Thus Giovanni Bassano, a Venetian singer, in choosing an example of pseudo-monodic elaboration of a tenor part for his textbook on ornamentation (1598), takes a madrigal from Cipriano Rore's *Libro Quarto* (1563) which is laid out in a wholly homophonic and declamatory style; aside from this, it is the beginning of a sonnet lamenting the departure of a prince from Ferrara. But it would be naïve to conclude from the existence of arrangements that the whole madrigal literature is accompanied solo song. There is monody and there is pseudo-monody. The manuals on ornamentation become more and more numerous as the century progresses, but we ought not to allow them to mislead us and to persuade us that singers actually sang the monstrosities they illustrate. (We have manuals on ornamentation by the following authors: Gio. Camillo Maffei da Solofra [1562], Girolamo della Casa [1584], Richardo Rogniono [1592], Gio. Luca Conforto [about 1593], Giovanni Batt. Bovicelli [1594], Giov. Bassano [1598], Gio. Battista Spadi [2nd ed. 1609] etc. Cf. Max Kuhn, *Die Verzierungs-Kunst in der Gesangs-Musik des XVI. und XVII. Jahrhunderts*, 1902.) These arrangements of famous madrigals—Arcadelt's *Il bianco e dolce cigno*, Rore's *Ancor che col partire*, Palestrina's *Vestiva i colli*— are teaching examples and extreme cases, in which the possibilities of ornamentation, of the *gorgia*, are piled up to the point of barbarism and poor taste. This is a point that we have made before (p. 227): the virtuoso, the singer with a cunning throat and a flowing coloratura, is the deadly enemy of the creative musician whose chief concern is expression. Zarlino (*Istituzioni armoniche*, III, 46) already recognized this danger and insisted on the singer's obligation to adhere strictly to the text and to what the composer has written: "Primieramente dee con ogni diligenza proveder nel suo Cantare, di proferire la modulatione in quel modo, che è stata

composta dal Compositore; et non far come fanno alcuni poco aveduti, i quali per farsi tenere più valorosi et più sapienti de gli altri, fanno alle volte di suo capo alcune diminutioni tanto salvatiche (dirò cosi) et tanto fuori d'ogni proposito; che non solo fanno fastidio a chi loro ascolta, ma insieme commettono nel cantare mille errori. . . ." — "First of all, he must take the utmost care in singing to perform his part just as the composer has written it and not to imitate those of little understanding who, to make themselves thought worthier and wiser than the rest, sometimes invent divisions so inappropriate and wild (if I may say so) that they disgust the listener and at the same time commit errors in singing. . . ." To be sure, Zarlino certainly refers in this passage to part-singing, and there can be no doubt but that in "monody" and "pseudo-monody" the soloist had greater freedom. But there was not yet that abuse of freedom that characterized the beginning of the seventeenth century and whose correction required the century's untiring efforts.

Are there practical examples of pseudo-monody, of division-making in the madrigal—examples in which we may place our confidence? They are rare, but they exist, and I shall name one that takes us to Venice into the circle of the *cantatrici*—the two Bellamanos, Pecorina, Antonia Aragona da Napoli, Elena Veneziana, Isabella Bolognese, Irene di Spilimbergo, and the rest, singers whose praise fills the letters of Pietro Aretino, Antonfrancesco Doni, and Andrea Calmo to overflowing. It is the work of Baldisserra Donato, the favorite musician of these circles, and comes from his *Secondo libro a quattro* of 1568. This too I am reprinting in "monodic" form,[6] though all the voices are of course provided with text in my source. To be sure, this is not yet by any means the monodic ideal: thirty years later Caccini or Peri would have given the repetition of the concluding line an even more exaggerated coloratura and would have released the accompaniment entirely from any vocal obligation. But it was in this fashion that the noble courtesans of Venice sang in 1550 to the lute or *gravicembalo*, and we involuntarily recall a letter of Andrea Calmo to Signora Calandra (ed. V. Rossi, IV, 19, p. 295): "Ma del cantar può, mai ho aldio meio: ohimè che bela vose, che maniera, che gorza, che diminution, che suavitae da far indolcir cuori crudeli, severi e maligni al mondo! Mo le sorte de le parole, del sugieto, del significato tanto eccellente, tanto arguto, tanto doto, che la poesia istessa ghe perderave. . . ."—"And as for your singing, I have never heard better: oh, what a beautiful voice, what style, what runs and divisions, what sweetness, enough to soften the cruelest, hardest, most wicked heart in the world! How excellent the words, the subject, the meaning, so acute, so elegant that poetry itself lags behind. . . ."

That this sort of singing was not confined to Venice may be inferred from a

6 See Vol. III, No. 97.

madrigal by Torquato Tasso, which exactly describes the solo singing of this transitional period, the art of a tenor or of a falsetto singer:

> Mentre in voci canore
> I vaghi spirti scioglie
> Giulio, tempra in ciel l'aure, in noi le voglie:
> Si placa l'aura, e'l vento
> Placido mormorando,
> Risuona, e van tuoni, e procelle in bando:
> Un interno concento
> N'accorda anco ne'petti,
> E i membri acqueta da soverchi affetti:
> E se pur desta amore,
> Gli da misura, e norma
> *Col suon veloce, e tardo*, e quasi forma.

According to the headings in the old Tasso editions, for example those in the great six-volume Florentine edition of 1724, the individual in question is either a certain "Vincenzio Giusti Musico" or Giovanni Pietro de' Medici, the patron of the fine voice of "Brancazio." But it may well be that it is really Giulio Caccini, called Romano. Tasso had many opportunities to hear him in Florence and in Rome, and of all the Giulios of the time who were solo singers, Caccini is certainly the most famous.

Any mention of Tasso's name is bound to lead us to Ferrara, the home of the three famous *cantatrici*, Lucrezia Bendidio, Laura Peperara, and Tarquinia Molza, who one after another ruled his heart and his muse. From innumerable sonnets, madrigals, and canzoni we know that as a trio and as solo singers they were the delight of their aristocratic public at the court. From among many such poems I quote two by Livio Celiano (*Rime di diversi celebri poeti dell'età nostra*, Bergamo, Ventura, 1587, p. 117), one on Peperara, the other on Tarquinia Molza:

> "Canti LAVRA di Laura,
> Che sola può co'l canto addolcir l'aura,
> L'aura ne l'aria errante,
> Che ferma il volo, e le diviene amante.
> O Sirena felice,
> Cui l'aura di fermar ne l'aria lice."

> "Non è cor duro tanto,
> Che non si spetri al vostro dolce canto;
> Et al suon, che trahete

> Da le sonore corde,
> Molza gentil, mill'anime accendete;
> E sono i feminili fregi vostri
> Le dotte arti d'Atene, e i colti inchiostri."

(The second is sometimes attributed to the Abate Angelo Grillo, Tasso's devoted friend, but for a devout Benedictine it seems rather too worldly.)

In his remarkable publication of 1601, a book that seems almost to have been written as a memorial to the departed splendor of the court music in Ferrara, Luzzasco Luzzaschi has preserved for us a few specimens from the solo repertory of these three ladies. The pieces in question are the first three in the book—*Aura soave di segreti accenti,* Guarini's *O primavera gioventù dell' anno* (from the *Pastor fido*), and *Ch' io non t'ami,* likewise by Guarini. All three of them have already been reprinted, as mentioned above (p. 834). They are barely more advanced than Donato's madrigal and were in all probability not composed much later: Signora Bendidio was already at the court of Ferrara before 1562; Laura Peperara came in 1579, and Tarquinia Molza in 1580 or 1581. The setting of a text from the *Pastor fido* is the only one that cannot very well have been written before 1585. The three pieces are simply four-voiced madrigals in which the solo part doubles the upper voice in a more elaborate form. Performance without instruments, a cappella, presents no difficulty whatever; there are even some passages in imitation (*Svegliastila* in *Aura soave*), and it is easy to find purely vocal pieces with a far more "chordal" structure in Rore, Marenzio, and the early Monteverdi. *Aura soave* is written for an alto, *Ch'io non t'ami* for a fairly high soprano, *O primavera* for a soprano with a somewhat narrower range, and it seems that Luzzaschi must have intended to print a favorite piece of each of the three *virtuose.* Not one is particularly expressive; all swing back and forth in the somewhat neutral territory midway between *parlando* and the rambling mechanical coloratura of the virtuoso.

Yet they have real historical importance, and Florentine monody would scarcely have been possible without them. For from a realistic point of view, Florentine monody is a product of the rivalry between the hostile courts of the Este and the Medici, courts which were contending not only for political and ceremonial preeminence, but also for preeminence in culture, in art, and above all in music. Torquato Tasso loses the favor of Alfonso II chiefly because he makes advances to the Medici, but there is no objection whatever to his accepting any favor from the Gonzagas. It is most significant that the Florentine musicians—Malvezzi, Bati, Santi Orlandi, and even Marco da Gagliano—show the utmost reserve in selecting texts by Tasso: in Gagliano's whole production there is just one of his poems. Yet innumerable texts by Tasso are set to music by Wert, Marenzio, Gesualdo, and especially Monteverdi! Fortunately this rivalry is well covered by documents—invaluable letters written about 1584 by Alessandro Striggio from Ferrara to the Florentine court, namely to the Grand Duke Francesco and his secretary Belisario Vinta. (Cf. R. Gandolfi, "Lettere inedite scritte da musicisti," *Rivista musicale italiana*, xx, [1913], 527f.) Striggio, as a Mantuan nobleman in the service of the Medici and the Gonzagas, played a role in this that we today should call industrial espionage. For this role he was well fitted as a musician and a nobleman who had as such to be received courteously by the court in Ferrara. After listening to the ladies—"nay, angels from Paradise" (*queste signore dame, anzi angioli del paradiso*), as he calls them in his letter to Vinta of July 29, 1584—he begins by attempting to imitate one of the pieces from their repertory and sends a "dialogo con dua soprani diminuti e fugati per il concerto che mi ordinò V. S. Illma per ordine di sua Altezza," having already sent on a piece written in a different style—"un madrigale a quattro con tre soprani diminuito per il concerto." Striggio was a master of the "arciviolata lira," a bowed instrument with many strings that might almost have been made to order for the accompaniment of improvised songs; even before his visit at Ferrara he must already have composed *duetti concertanti* in Mantua. The same day he writes also to Grand Duke Francesco: "Qui ogni giorno il Signor Duca di Ferrara . . . per due hore continue mi favorisce di farmi sentire il suo concerto di donne il quale veramente è raro; e quelle signore cantano eccellentemente et nel lor conserto e a libro, al improviso son sicure. Il Sig. Duca mi favorisce di continuo di mostrarmi in scritto tutte le opere che cantano alla mente, con tutte le tirate e passaggi che fanno . . ." — "Here every day the Duke of Ferrara . . . is kind enough to let me listen for two hours on end to the music of his ladies, which is indeed extraordinary; these ladies sing excellently, both to accompaniment and from part-books; they are sure-footed in improvisation. The Duke is kind enough to be continually showing me in manuscript everything that they sing by heart, with all the runs and passages as they perform them. . . ." He promises to write something similar for the "concerto" of the Grand Duke on his return to Mantua. On August 24 he announces that he is sending on two monodies—*Cor mio mentr'io vi miro* and *Per voi, lasso, conviene*—"and I believe that they will go well when they have been learned by heart and when the words are well enunciated and sung to accompaniment by Master Giulio. . . ." ("e crederò che averanno a riuscire quando siano imparati a la mente, et che le parole siano ben proferite et consertati da messer Giulio. . . .") But Caccini demands greater virtuosity, and in November and December Striggio sends on four further attempts on texts received from Florence.

Two years later, in 1586, Alfonso d'Este considers the Florentine competition so harmless that he sends his three ladies to Florence to adorn the festivities in connection with the wedding of Cesare d'Este and Virginia Medici. On this occasion

Ottavio Rinuccini, later the librettist of the *Euridice*, writes five madrigals "fatti per le dame di Ferrara" which were presumably set to music by Striggio.

Ferrara's influence on Florence in the rise of monody is thoroughly obvious. The Florentine yearning for a variety of solo singing modeled on Ferrara, but with richer coloratura, is realized in the prologue of "Armonia" which opens the *Intermedii e concerti* for the wedding of Grand Duke Ferdinand and Cristina of Lorraine (1589). It is a piece conceived for four voices, with a richly ornamented vocal part, wholly decorative, wholly devoid of "expression," as lacking in taste as it is ornate. (The text is by Giovanni Bardi, the music by Emilio de'Cavalieri, and not by Cristofano Malvezzi or Antonio Archilei, the husband of the Vittoria Archilei who sang it. There are reprints by Kiesewetter, *Schicksale*, No. 41, and by Kinkeldey, *op. cit.*, p. 306.) Nowhere does the leveling, neutralizing effect of the *gorgia*, the coloratura, stand out more clearly than in these songs which, as so-called "pseudo-monody," clear the way for the genuine monody. And will genuine monody actually attain the ideal for which it is striving—the intelligibility and the power of the word, strengthened by and embodied in music? Only in very rare cases; far more often it goes astray—now in trying to comply with the theoretical insistence on the "intelligibility" of the word, as in Monteverdi's lean and sterile *Lettere amorose*, now in the "singer aria," as in Caccini's solo madrigals.

In the sixteenth century the problem of monody doubtless was best solved when the singer improvised over an unchanging and constantly repeated bass. To be sure, such improvisations were tied to specific poetic forms—the ottava, and perhaps also the sonnet, with the four statements of the bass familiar to us from the frottola. The historical development of this improvisation on a *basso ostinato* is strange, yet simple. Simple melodies for the recitation of strambotti and ottave, to be sung four times for each stanza, must have been available since the fifteenth century: we already know some of these from the madrigals of Corteccia and Hoste (cf. above, p. 285). But as this sort of improvisation developed and the singing of a great many stanzas became more and more usual—with the publication of the *Orlando furioso* it became almost a craze—there arose a need to vary the upper voice according to the expression, leaving the bass unchanged. Thus various basses come into being in various parts of Italy, the *Romanesca*, the *aria di Genova*, and the *aria di Firenze*. The most famous is the one called the *Ruggiero* or *Fedele*, after the stanza of the *Orlando furioso* that marks the superb, passionate climax of the poem:

Ruggier, qual sempre fui, tal esser voglio . . . (Cf. above p. 209.)

(In the first line, the name *Ruggiero* is sometimes replaced by *Fedel*—hence the name *Fedele* for the same bass.) One may read more about this question in my little study on the *Aria di Ruggiero* (*Zeitschrift der Internationalen Musik-Gesell-*

schaft, XIII, 444f.). This improvising of ottave stanze was one of the hidden sources of the monody that suddenly came out into the open at the beginning of the seventeenth century. Yet references to such melodies are by no means rare in the literature, for example in the austere Zarlino (*Istituzioni*, III, cap. 79), when he compares the ancient modes to the modern *arie*, which he says are simply "quei Modi, sopra i quali cantiamo i Sonetti, o Canzoni del Petrarca, overamente le Rime dell'Ariosto." They are the tunes that Michel de Montaigne heard "everywhere in Italy" in the course of his travels: when he goes to Empoli from Florence on Sunday, July 2, 1581, one of the things that surprises him is "di veder questi contadini il liuto in mano, e fin alle pastorelle l'Ariosto in bocca. *Questo si vede per tutta Italia. . . .*" (*Journal de voyage*, ed. Louis Lautrey, Paris 1909, p. 391)—"to see these peasants with lutes in their hands and even the shepherdesses with Ariosto on their lips. *But one sees this everywhere in Italy. . . .*" The peasants sing or recite Ariosto with the tune in the soprano, the courtly singers to the lute and viol with the tune in the bass. How else are we to suppose that Monteverdi improvised to the "viola" at the court of Mantua? How else are we to understand the hundreds of reports about the accomplishments of the singers to the lute and *lira*? And these reports are sometimes so clear that one is astonished to find that the correct interpretation has thus far been missed. Addressing himself on August 15, 1599, to Girolama Colonna, Duchess of Monteleone in Rome, Padre Giovenale Ancina has this to say in the dedication of his *Tempio armonico*, the most important work in the preliminary history of the oratorio: "potrà ancho V.E. . . . per sua più semplice et più domestica ricreatione sentirle cantar a suon di Lira dolce e soave, toccata dal gentilissimo Signor'Antonio Messia Musico eccellente, qual nuovo Orfeo de'nostri tempi: o pur (quel che sarà di tutto'l meglio) chiamarsi tal volta il Signor Giovan Lionardo dell' Arpa, il qual'in tal sua professione rarissimo et singolare, et in questa parte (senza adulatione) simile al Regio Salmista David leggiadramente cantando et suonando. . . . E per tal cagione à bello studio si sono lasciate alcune laudi nel fine dell' Opra schiette con le parole sole senza Musica, per serbarle à lui proprio, che accomodandoli divers'arie à suo modo, forsi più vaghe et più leggiadre . . ." (Bologna catalogue, III, 206).—"For your simpler and more private recreation . . . Your Excellency may have these [*laude*] sung to the soft sweet sound of the *lira*, played by the gentle Signor Antonio Messia, an excellent musician and the new Orpheus of our age, or (best of all) Your Excellency may send sometimes for Signor Giovan Leonardo dell' Arpa, who is unequaled in his profession and in this respect comparable (without adulation) to the royal psalmist David gracefully singing and playing. . . . And for this reason some *laude* at the end of the book are purposely left plain, with only the words and without the music; these are reserved for him alone, so that he may accommodate various *arie* [basses] to them in his fashion, perhaps more beautifully and more

gracefully. . . ." We know Giovan Leonardo as a composer of villanelle. The passage just quoted makes him one of the forerunners of monody. And we may be sure that we only half know the sixteenth century if we know its music solely from the printed sources.

We have reached the threshold of the seventeenth century. The composer is now subjected to an overwhelming demand to write music for the soloist—to write directly for the soloist who becomes his master. Up to now the composer has been his own master: he has written his music, leaving it to the virtuoso to arrange it to suit himself. Now the singer stands in the limelight, and the composer supplies him with ready-made goods; he sits at the clavier or organ, his basso continuo in front of him, and improvises the accompaniment.

Thus arises the problem of the new monodic form, and we witness the beginnings of a heroic struggle that the Italian musicians are left to fight out alone and without receiving the credit due them for it: it is the heroic age of Italian music. At the beginning stand Monteverdi and Gagliano and a hundred lesser masters; in the springtide of classicism, the masters of the "Roman School"—Mario Savioni, Luigi Rossi, Giacomo Carissimi; at the end, the baroque and decadent Alessandro Scarlatti. The aim is a fixed form, a form so fixed that it soon becomes rigid—the aria and the cantata. It is a fatal literary heritage that forces music into the confining limits of such a form and such a convention.

This literary heritage is a venerable one: it reaches back to Greek antiquity.

CHAPTER XIII · MONTEVERDI AND THE "MADRIGALE CONCERTATO"—THE END

IN HIS fifth book of madrigals, published in 1605 and again dedicated to the Duke of Mantua, Monteverdi openly takes the decisive step and embraces the *madrigale concertato*. In a foreword addressed to the reader he takes notice of Artusi's attack, calls his own way of writing the *Seconda Pratica over Perfettione della Moderna Musica,* and opposes it to the practice taught by Zarlino; he insists that he does not write his works at haphazard and speaks of a reply that lies ready in his desk and that will be published as soon as his exacting duties give him the necessary leisure.

Artusi's attack was not unfounded, but it was as one-sided as Monteverdi's reply would doubtless have been if he had published it—for he kept it in his desk. He left his defense to his brother, Giulio Cesare Monteverdi, who added to Claudio's *Scherzi musicali* of 1607 a *Dichiaratione della lettera stampata nel quinto libro de suoi Madregali* and who spoke, of course, with the authorization of his brother; we know, however, that even in his later years the composer still was occupied with the fuller justification of his case. Monteverdi's opponents and defenders fixed their eyes on a single point: his new harmonic style and his bold use of dissonance, a use that was simply the logical continuation of the experiments of a century. If this use was a *Seconda prattica,* then Willaert and Rore, Andrea Gabrieli, Marenzio, and Gesualdo were already representatives of the new practice, we may be certain. Particularly Marenzio—and he particularly in certain pieces in his ninth and last madrigal book—could have been a model for Monteverdi in the use of a bold, uncompromising, and thematically constructive harmony.

No, the real revolution in the history of the madrigal was set in motion by an impulse from quite a different quarter—the introduction of the basso continuo. If this revolution met with no opposition it was simply because it was general. To be sure, there were various kinds of basso continuo, just as there are bolder and more cautious advocates of its employment. A "basso seguente," a bass that merely duplicates the momentarily lowest voice of a polyphonic composition—and the writing of such basses is a custom that can be traced from about 1595 until far into the seventeenth century—is not a real basso continuo. A real basso continuo stands in relation to the upper voice or voices as an opposite pole; it is a firm instrumental foundation; it "releases" the upper voices and sets them free—free for expressive declamation, or for concerto-like rivalry, or for both. We shall not be surprised to find Monteverdi among the composers who belong to the "progressive party" and who stand, not on the side of the "basso seguente," but on that of the genuine basso continuo. But even in his work there are hesitations and relapses.

At first he is certainly hesitant, at least in this fifth book. The title reads: *Col basso continuo per il Clavicembano, Chittarone od altro simile istromento, fatto particolarmente per li sei ultimi, et per li altri a beneplacito.* But if in the last six numbers the basso continuo is indispensable, it is wholly unnecessary in the first seven—indeed it would even destroy their essential character. They still belong to the sixteenth century. To be sure, the homogeneity of the voices has been destroyed and their identity of function nullified; the part-writing itself has taken on the character of a dialogue, as in No. 6, *Che dar più vi posso io*, where the solo tenor is set off against the tutti:

But though the disintegration is already well advanced, these first seven numbers are still a cappella madrigals. Indeed they are so even more definitely than many a piece in the third and fourth books. One reason for this is that this fifth book must have been written in a sort of competition with Marenzio—perhaps at the request of the Duke, perhaps on Monteverdi's own initiative. The coincidences in the choice of texts are too striking: thus the text of the concluding piece (*Questi vaghi concenti*) had already been set by Marenzio, likewise in two sections (*Settimo libro*, 1595); in the same way *Amor, se giusto sei* (No. 10), which is wholly "unfashionable" and wholly unsuited to Monteverdi's taste, is drawn from Marenzio's *Sesto libro a cinque* (1594); again in the same way Monteverdi has chosen from Guarini's *Pastor fido* the very texts found in Marenzio's seventh book—Mirtillo's lament (1, 2), with its companion piece, Amaryllis' *O Mirtillo* (III, 4), and the great scene between Dorinda and Silvio (IV, 9), in five sections. Only in Mirtillo's declaration of love, *Ch'io t'ami* (III, 3), is Monteverdi really independent. But even here he is dependent in his musical style. It is the same controlled, frustrated, latent monody as in Marenzio, except that Marenzio is much simpler and more homophonic and that his lower voices are dominated to a far greater extent by the soprano. For Monteverdi too, choral recitative is the natural solution, but unlike Marenzio he leaves himself free to abandon it for the madrigalesque, for polyphony, combination, and the most austere expressive dissonance. Sometimes he even permits himself to relapse into Marenzio's sort of "eye-symbolism," for example in *Ch' io t'ami*, when he "paints" the steepness of the *alpestri monti*. Particularly in the first two numbers, the competition with Marenzio is so obvious that one may even speak of parody. But to recognize Monteverdi's independence and to determine how he differs from Marenzio in character and style, one need only compare the two beginnings:

Or one may compare the motifs worked out in combination in the two endings:

And to persuade oneself that Monteverdi was not the only one to use the unprepared dissonance, one need only look at the setting of the same text by Benedetto

Pallavicino, Monteverdi's superior and predecessor (*Sesto libro a cinque*, 1600):

But Monteverdi carries the procedures of his colleagues to such extremes that stylistic unity is threatened. The urge to outdo his predecessors sweeps him onward, just as it does Beethoven when he measures himself against Haydn and Mozart, except that Monteverdi lacks Beethoven's exuberance. There is something demonic in him, something bent on destruction; he is a man of destiny in the history of music, in an even more fatal sense than Beethoven is.

Is it not strange that Monteverdi uses the old a cappella style precisely for the "dramatic" texts, the monologues and dialogues from the *Pastor fido*? At all events the nineteenth and twentieth centuries have found it strange and have pointed with disapproval to the contradiction between the "monodic" text and its polyphonic treatment. But it is not that the sixteenth century overlooked this contradiction; it was not even conscious of it, and Monteverdi still looks on polyphony, and precisely on polyphony, as constituting a useful means for working out with especial sharpness the portrayal of a character or state of the affections. One might suppose that he would have used the *stile nuovo* and the basso continuo to make his music more "dramatic" and naturalistic than ever. But here just the opposite is the case. The six numbers with basso continuo are less dramatic and wholly in the *stile concertante*. In a purely musical sense they are dialogues. The first, Guarini's *Ahi come a un vago sol*, is a dialogue between two groups of voices, one of two voices, the other of three, with a concluding tutti. The basso continuo is strangely inactive and indifferent. But in the next number it becomes a genuine continuo that "releases" or liberates the alternation of solo and tutti, only to fall back into the role of a "basso seguente" in the polyphonic play of the epilogue, thus changing its character within the compass of a single piece. In *T'amo mia vita* (No. 11), likewise an epigram of Guarini's, the first soprano is for some time pitted against a choir of three low voices; a duet of the two sopranos above this choir is reserved for the end. A duet plus a trio—no longer a piece of real five-voiced writing! Again, in Guarini's *E così poco a poco* (No. 12), Monteverdi's first six-voiced piece, some time elapses before the dialogue-like arrangement of duets and trios is followed by a quartet and the tutti. *Questi vaghi concenti,* the nine-voiced final number, is a real *concento,* a real concerto, a real cantata, with an overture (*Sinfonia*) and a ritornello. With its division of the chorus into two half-choirs of five and four voices this is no longer Mantuan but Venetian. What a sacrifice it has cost! How little is left! A trivial game with triad motifs instead of expressive harmony! An exhibition of the singers' vanity in the solos and in the duets! The novelty of these pieces has been dearly bought, and the victory has entailed serious losses. But this is an end and a turning-point. Conceived as a form of music-making in company, and in this sense socially conditioned, the old madrigal is dead. The new *madrigale concertato* no longer can be sung by aristocratic dilettanti: it requires the services of the virtuoso, and it brings with it the applauding listener. It is significant that in his dedication Monteverdi reminds the Duke that he has repeatedly *heard* and applauded these madrigals: "et udendoli diede segno di singolarmente gradirle" — "and hearing them, [Your Highness] gave a sign of special approval." Guglielmo Gonzaga had been a composer and a singer; Vincenzo Gonzaga is a mere "appreciator."

By 1620 Monteverdi's fifth book had gone through eight editions in rapid succession (1606, 1608, 1610, 1611, 1613, 1615 [twice], and 1620). The effect was very curious, as is often the case with sudden manifestations of a revolutionary spirit for which the age is only half prepared. The effect was first seen in Rome.

In Rome, strange as it may seem, the soil had been prepared for certain stylistic characteristics of Monteverdi's art. There had been many changes since Marenzio had become a Roman musician and had unwittingly aroused the anger and aversion of the elderly Palestrina. We have an accurate picture of the circle of the "Roman" musicians of the 'sixties in a publication brought out in 1562 by the composer-publisher Antonio Barre, the *Terzo libro delle Muse a quattro . . . madrigali ariosi* (not known to Vogel); Barre seems to have picked up its contents from the by-ways, so to speak: ". . . questi belli parti di diversi autori (che quasi per negligentia de i padri perivano)" — ". . . these beautiful productions of various authors (which have been languishing, as it were, through the indifference of their fathers)." Here we have real Romans—Palestrina, Annibale Zoilo, Francesco Rosselli, and Barre himself, and with them Lasso and Monte, who in those days counted as Romans. Each

of these is represented by several pieces. We also have Rore—significantly enough at the very beginning of the book—Giovanni Domenico da Nola and Luigi Dentice of Naples, Vincenzo Ruffo of Verona, and Lodovico Agostino of Ferrara. In the 'eighties the picture looks distinctly different. In the *Dolci affetti*, a collection of five-voiced madrigals "de diversi eccellenti musici di Roma," published in 1582 by the heir of G. Scotto in Venice and dedicated to Monsignor Ottavio Bandini, the Apostolic Referendary, Palestrina and Zoilo are the only older names; among the newer ones are Marenzio, G. M. Nanino, Stabile, Soriano, Dragoni, Macque, and Moscaglia, not to mention those lesser names that have only a passing interest. To these we might add Ruggiero Giovanelli, Romolo Naldi, Asprilio Pacelli, Paolo Quagliati, G. B. Nanino, Felice Anerio, and G. F. Anerio. Some of these names are also to be found in the books of canzonette brought out by Simone Verovio, the Roman publisher and engraver (his real name seems to have been Werrewick), a native of Hertogenbosch (Holland) who had come to Rome in 1575, the year of the jubilee. Between 1586 and 1608, in the incunabula of music-engraving, he collected the secular and spiritual by-products and leavings of the Roman musicians—not masses and motets or madrigals, but little canzonette for three and four voices; these he offers in their original vocal form and in arrangements for clavier and lute. These canzonette are related to the *canzonette alla francese* that Monteverdi published in 1607 under the title *Scherzi musicali*. Both are anacreontic and both exhibit the same "polarity" of the two upper voices with respect to the bass. But unlike Monteverdi the Romans make no use of the new rhythms of Gabriello Chiabrera and Ansaldo Cebà, and although they may intend instrumental ritornelli, they do not write them down. Marenzio's villanelle anticipate these Roman trifles and Monteverdi's *Scherzi* as well. It was the Marenzio madrigal that influenced the Roman madrigalists, even those who sided with Palestrina and may be presumed to have regarded Marenzio as an intruder. And it was the Marenzio madrigal much more than the madrigals of the Venetians, Florentines, and Neapolitans that prepared the Romans for Monteverdi's influence. Not, to be sure, with respect to harmony: on this point the Romans remained conservative. But definitely so with respect to the principle of combination, which presupposes the *contrapposto* of strikingly formulated subjects or motifs. None of the Roman composers has the delicacy, the refinement, the sensitive taste of Marenzio, who also uses the combination of motifs to further his poetic intentions. But all of them understand the constructive side of this technique and they raise it almost to the status of a principle. The later works of Giovanni Maria Nanino (died 1607), as a church musician a member of Palestrina's intimate circle, already make use of combination, the musical equivalent of the poetic oxymoron; his younger brother Giovanni Bernardino (died 1623) is an apt pupil, as are others among his compatriots—Ruggiero Giovanelli (died 1625) and above all Giovanni Francesco Anerio, the younger brother of Felice Anerio. Giovanni Francesco is almost incapable of beginning a madrigal "monothematically"; his technique recalls the Gloria and Credo settings of the eighteenth century, in which various parts of the text are recited simultaneously with a view to saving time. No oxymoron justifies or necessitates his beginning Torquato Tasso's *Mentre nubi di sdegno* in this fashion:

The working-out of these four motifs consumes no less than twenty-six measures. There is an obvious relation between this technique and the similar procedures in Marenzio and Monteverdi. But with these masters its employment usually has a more compelling poetic justification.

The intrusion of the basso continuo coincides with this tendency to combine and to digress, and *combinazione* becomes *concerto*. At first this intrusion confuses the Roman musicians completely, just as it also confuses others. A classical example of this is the *Primo libro de' Madrigali a 4 voci* of Paolo Quagliati of Chioggia, at that time (1608) organist at Santa Maria Maggiore. He describes his madrigals as "concertati per cantar con l'instromento, con un libro separato dove stà il Basso seguito per sonarli," and one might assume that they were real "concert pieces" like the last six in Monteverdi's fifth book. But Quagliati leans in two directions at once and favors both styles, the old and the new. He explains himself at length in a letter to the reader: ". . . vedendo che nell'età d'hoggi alcuna parte hà gustato della Musica piena de più voci, se bene dalla maggior parte par che sia desiderata et applaudita la Musica vota, cioè di voci sole con l'instrumenti, et ciò forse per maggior intelligenza, et chiarezza delle parole, ò forse per maggior distintione, et godimento delle belle voci, et bei cantanti; mi risolsi per sodisfare all'una, et all'altra parte, procurare di pascer più gusti, et presi per espediente di comporre questi miei

madrigali in questa nuova foggia. . . ."—". . . seeing that nowadays one party takes pleasure in 'full' music with many voices, although it seems that the larger party desires and applauds 'empty' music for solo voices and instruments, perhaps because of the greater intelligibility and clarity of the words, perhaps of the greater distinctness and charm of beautiful voices and beautiful singers, to satisfy both the one party and the other I have made up my mind to cater to more than one taste and have deemed it expedient to compose these my madrigals in this new fashion. . . ."

What does this mean? It means that Quagliati has tried to side-step the distinction between the a cappella and the continuo madrigal, that he has sought a compromise between two epochs and two styles. Although Quagliati's title and foreword might lead us to think so, what is involved is not the permission to perform these madrigals either a cappella or as concertos with basso continuo; they are designed with a double purpose—for performance either as concert madrigals or as monodies. Quagliati wrote them about 1605 to the order of his employer, Cardinal Farnese, for the entertainment of Donna Serafina di Braganza, Marchioness of Vigliena, the Cardinal's cousin and momentary guest. The special title of the "basso seguito" tells the whole story; above the bass part we read: "un Soprano sopra, acciò non ritrovandosi tal' hora le quattro voci, possino esser cantati con una sola voce, cioè ò Soprano, overo Tenore all' Ottava bassa"—"with a soprano above, so that if four voices should happen not to be available, [the pieces] may be sung by a single voice, either a soprano, or a tenor singing an octave lower."

The nineteen numbers can no longer be performed as pure a cappella music. Such a performance would be altogether too much at variance with the character of the solo parts, which are constantly being made to stand out—a character entirely dependent on the ornamented parlando of the *stile recitativo*; apart from this, Quagliati expressly relies on his gracious singers to adorn his music with those graces and affections that it requires (*d'adornarli con quelle gratie, et affetti, che questa Musica richiede*) and calls for the support of the basso continuo. An a cappella performance would also be at variance with the overly informal texture (*tessitura*) of these pieces. No, Quagliati simply leaves the singers free to perform his music either as concerto-like quartets or as monodies. A few measures will be enough to make his procedure clear:

He reduces the melodic and motival content of a madrigal to a single line, a sort of common denominator. And he does the same with the bass when it is supported by the two lower parts; when this is not the case, it serves as an additional support. But his procedure is a compromise. His four-voiced version cannot attain the density and artistry of the full-blown madrigal, and his monodic version falls short of the freedom and expressive intensity essential to monody. He carried his experiment no further. During the carnival of 1606 he performed his *Carro di fedeltà d'amore*, a belated imitation of the Florentine *carri* and one of the most delightful examples of the early dramatic monody, with solo voices, chorus, and orchestra. In 1617, in his *Affetti amorosi spirituali*, he offers some early examples of the oratorio, and in 1623 in his *Sfera armoniosa*, he boldly invades the territory of the *musica concertante* with obbligato instrument.

Quagliati begins with a compromise, but he soon sides resolutely with the genuine *madrigale concertante*, with monody, which (as he says himself) has already found favor with the majority. During the first decade of the new century many composers still behave as though nothing had happened in Florence or Mantua, as though the whole realm of music had not changed, as though there were no *Seconda prattica*; these are not only provincial musicians but also musicians from the great musical centers like Venice, where the brilliant example of older masters, Croce for example, and the tradition of Zarlino were unfavorable to innovation. (We shall deal with Giovanni Gabrieli later on.) But in the long run everyone is forced to decide whether to change or to give up. And often enough, a musician accepts

the basso continuo without fully understanding its role as the foundation of the *stile concertante*. In 1609 Michel Angelo Nantermi, the organist at San Lorenzo Maggiore in Milan, published his first work, a book of five-voiced madrigals "co'l Basso continuo per il Clavicembalo, Chittarone, od altro simile istromento," the same formula that Monteverdi had used in his fifth book for the accompanying instrument. That Nantermi knows Monteverdi may also be inferred from his second number, a setting of a text (*Anima del cor mio*) found in Monteverdi's fourth book. But in his treatment of the basso continuo he is completely under the spell of the Milanese tradition; especially in church and instrumental music, this assumes the presence of an accompanying and supporting instrument at a very early date, perhaps earlier than anywhere else in Italy. Nantermi's basso continuo is simply a "basso seguente." Yet the use of this "basso seguente," conventional though it is, is in itself enough to loosen the texture and to bring the voices into a more concerto-like relationship, even if it does not endow them with the complete freedom of the voices of a concerto. Nantermi too is a "compromiser," though in a different sense than Quagliati: at the end of his book stands a sort of *trionfo* in which Cupid appears with his train:

> Son'io, donne, che rimirate,
> Forse sì cieche siete,
> Ch'Amor non conoscete?
> Amor son io
> Che nell'altrui martiro
> Ognor più crude vi conosco e miro. . . .

Cupid—or rather, the soprano—begins alone, but our illusion that a monodic drama like Quagliati's *Carro di fedeltà* will follow is promptly dispelled by the entrance of the chorus. Thus it is not surprising that Nantermi sets Mirtillo's concluding lines (*Pastor fido*, Act v, 3) *alla madrigalesca*, with a naturalistic pianissimo at the end.

Conflicting tendencies start to become reconciled in the work of Giovanni Priuli. One of the liveliest musicians of the first half of the seventeenth century, Priuli begins in 1604 in the neighborhood of Urbino and Ferrara with bold, colorful a cappella madrigals, and after having been as a young man in the Archducal service in Graz and after 1619 court choirmaster to the Emperor Ferdinand, he ends as one of the chief exponents of the showy *madrigale concertante*. The turning-point in his development is a madrigal book of 1612 (*Il terzo libro de Madrigali a cinque voci. Di due maniere, l'una per voci sole, l'altra per voce, et istromenti. Con Partitura*), and this despite its title, which seems to be connected with that of Monteverdi's fifth book. His "partitura" is an ordinary "basso seguente," and in nine pieces it runs along at the side of the momentarily lowest voice, although it is at the same time provided with a few scattered figures. In the last four pieces, which are described as "Madrigali per Concerto"—in the index and on the title-page they are called "Madrigali per voci et istromenti," but in this context "istromenti" can only mean the continuo—the "partitura" changes its function and is now more fully provided with figures; even a change of key is indicated here and there. But the movement of the voices is much less cantata-like than in Monteverdi, and the distinction between the solo voices and the tutti much less schematic. One does not know whether to call this progress or conservatism. It is an informal and lightly animated vocal game above an instrumental foundation. One could easily convert the a cappella madrigals into concert pieces by giving the "basso seguente" the genuine "polarity" of a basso continuo. But it must be admitted that one can no longer adapt the concerto-like numbers to the old style. Parlando, the long-drawn coloratura of the solos and duets, choral declamation, motival development—Priuli shifts from one to another in a flash; his style is one that exploits every advantage of the concerto principle without breaking with the madrigalesque. Yet it is not a compromise; it is a youthful art, forward-looking and "new."

Much the same thing might be said of Pietro Pace, who comes from the same environment; after many years in the service of Monsignore Giuliano della Rovere (Priuli dedicated his Opus 1 to a Rovere, Princess of Urbino) and a long career as organist at the principal church of Pesaro and Loreto, Pace wrote a festival opera for Urbino in 1621—the score is still extant. His Opus 1 (1597), a book of five-voiced madrigals, is naturally a work in the pure a cappella tradition. His second book of 1612, preserved only in a single part-book, also bears the stamp of the old style. His third book has completely disappeared. But his fourth book of 1614, for four voices and labeled "Opus VI," is devoted to concert music as a matter of principle and its bass part plays a stylistically decisive role; this is obvious even from the wording of the title-page: "con quattro madrigali sopra l'aria et istesse parole, A caso un giorno; con uno in ultimo a cinque sopra Ruggiero; avertendosi che sono fatti per concertare sopra il clavicimbalo ò simili instrumenti." Tansillo's pastoral canzone *A caso un giorno* seems to have been just as closely associated with a *basso ostinato* as Bernardo Tasso's stanza with the Ruggiero tune. The two numbers in several sections, a quadripartite pastoral *partenza* and the stanza by Tansillo, mark the exact point at which the canzone becomes a cantata. These madrigals of Pace's have broken so completely with the old madrigal style that the individual part now presents only fragments of the text. Yet with poets like Cesare Orsino, Giovanni Batista Leoni, Rinuccini, and Marino, these texts are important enough. The whole seems like a rapidly assembled mosaic, and its effect is due to its little tensions and points of emphasis and to its ingenious exploitation of the poetic

oxymora to produce contrasts of motif. Perhaps this unknown choirmaster of the Santa Casa will one day occupy his own place in history at the side of Monteverdi, just as Veronese does at the side of Tintoretto.

The decisive step to the cantata is taken by Monteverdi in his sixth book likewise published in 1614. None of his works unites such extreme antitheses as this one, none reveals more sharply the break in style between the old madrigal and the new, both in retreating and in advancing. The retreat, of course, is the polyphonic version of Monteverdi's most famous monody, the *Lamento d'Arianna* from the opera of 1608. Monteverdi undertook this arrangement in 1610 at the request of a Venetian patrician (*a richiesta di un nobil Veneziano*)—so we are told by Giovanni Battista Doni, the theorist of the new style, who seems almost to be apologizing for him. But is an apology really called for? In the opera, monody was the logical solution, the artistically legitimate medium of expression; in chamber music the analogous medium was the madrigal, in particular the five-voiced madrigal. This madrigal-esque *Lamento d'Arianna* is a link in the long chain of *lamenti*, chiefly from the *Pastor fido*—*lamenti* in madrigal form, "ideal" character portraits, richer in their sonority and more delicate in their elaboration than any monody could be. Monteverdi's monodic original seems poverty-stricken when compared with the rich complement of bold and yet most delicate passing harmonies that he provided for the choral version. That the work remains a hybrid despite all Monteverdi's resourcefulness and ingenuity is undeniable; with all the liberties that he permits himself in transforming the original, the polyphonic elaboration is still cramped.

As we know from a letter of the Mantuan diplomat Francesco Campagnolo to Cardinal Gonzaga, it was originally planned that this sixth book should contain three *lamenti*: in addition to the lament of Ariadne there was to be one by a shepherd on the death of his nymph, the words by Scipione Agnelli on the death of the singer Caterina Martinelli ("parole del figlio del Sig^r. Conte Lepido Agnelli in morte della Signora Martinelli"), and one by Hero over the body of her Leander, the words by Marini ("il pianto di Leandro ed Heroe del Marini"). This last piece is not included in Monteverdi's book and seems to be lost, but Agnelli's lament, the *Lacrime d'Amante al sepolcro dell'Amata*, proves to be the most comprehensive piece in the whole collection. For the first and last time in his life Monteverdi sets to music a sestina. And his setting is a strange mixture of old and new: he sees the mourning lover—the name "Glauco" is a literary pretense—as he stands at the open grave, like Tancred at Clorinda's tomb; with this picture in mind, he makes the tenor the dominant voice and gives the "chorus" the lugubrious responses that follow his lines, leaving the way open, however, for lyricism, the madrigalesque, and the *contrapposto*, especially in the *Terza parte*. Thus the piece shows the same spirit of compromise that sanctions the participation or omission of a "basso seguente" in those pieces that stand outside the *stile concertante*. (In his sixth book, and also in the fifth, an instrumental bass-part, more or less fully figured, is provided for every number, even for those that stand outside the *stile concertante*. That Malipiero's edition simply omits it is most misleading.)

This sixth book also contains other *lamenti*, all of them settings of texts in the most unexpected form—that of the sonnet, which Monteverdi has thus far avoided as much as possible. What is more, they are sonnets by a most unequal pair of poets— Petrarch and Giambattista Marini. Thus for the first time Monteverdi associates himself with the author of the *Adone*. It is natural that he should do so, for after all he is always for the latest thing, and as contemporaries Monteverdi and Marini, who is only two years younger, have much in common, however great the differences may be between the passion of the one and the sensuality of the other. But why has Monteverdi fallen back on Petrarch? Simply because he saw a favorable opportunity for a display of his "modernity" in the two sonnets *Zefiro torna, e'l bel tempo rimena* and *Oimè il bel viso! oimè il soave sguardo!* In its octave, *Zefiro torna* paints an enchanting picture of the return of spring; in its sestet, it contrasts with this the sadness of the poet, who has lost his beloved Laura forever. Monteverdi exploits this contrast for all it is worth through changes of rhythm, of mode, and of tempo: the first part is a choral dance-song in which the two quatrains have the same music, the second is an adagio with an episodic reminiscence of the first part at the words:

> ...E cantar augelletti e fiorir piaggie
> E'n belle donne onesti atti e soavi.

The whole is as baroque as possible—Monteverdi thinks always of the contrast and never of Petrarch, and it never occurs to him that the first part ought also to be understood and sung as though the poet himself were speaking. Still more baroque is the second of the two sonnets. In the first part he breaks up the five-voiced texture by setting six lines as a trio or as solos for the three lower voices; above this the sigh *oimè* (or *et oimè*) is repeated over and over again as a "hocket" or duet for the two sopranos. Not until the final couplet and the second part does Monteverdi remember that he is writing for five voices, and even here the texture is novel, conceived in terms of groups of voices, discursive, and no longer polyphonic. Yet how ingenious it all is! And at the same time how restless, how devoid of inner harmony, how unlike Marenzio's harmonious setting of the same poem (*Terzo libro*, 1582), written thirty years earlier!

If these pieces with a mere "basso seguente" are no longer genuine madrigals, those with a real basso continuo, the *madrigali concertanti*, are not yet full-fledged cantatas. It is noteworthy (though as yet unnoted) that these too are, except one, settings of sonnets. In 1610 Monteverdi did not yet have at his disposal any genuine

cantata texts, ready made for musical treatment; he accordingly falls back on sonnets with a connecting narrative, or to put it more precisely, on Marini's *Sonetti bosche-recci.* (The single exception, written to order in 1609, is a sonnet by a poet unknown to me, *Una donna fra l'altre onesta e bella,* a piece in which Monteverdi treats the single lines as solos, duets, and trios to close "discursively" with five voices. The piece stands midway between the two styles.) In setting Marini's texts, Monteverdi makes a real point of separating the narrative from what is dramatic or lyric. All narrative sections are composed as choral recitative, while the dialogue, everything that stands within quotation marks, is given to solo voices. These are the first attempts at a realistic or naturalistic cantata, the realization of an ideal that Monteverdi had sought to realize in his *Non si levava ancor* and that the many composers of *Tirsi morir volea* had sought to realize but that no one had yet attained—either because the time was not yet ripe, or because of a lack of courage, or perhaps because of an excess of good taste. For this mixture of naturalistic solos and stylized choral recitative is by no means tasteful. But to Monteverdi the need for texts was urgent, the difficulty of finding poetry suited to his intentions acute. He forces Marini's *Qui rise Tirsi* and makes a poetic monstrosity of it in order to be able to construct a vocal concerto on the plan of a Venetian concerto grosso: the final line is used as a choral refrain or tutti ritornello after each of the quatrains and to conclude the sestet, these parts of the stanza being treated as duets, solos, and trios. His baroque grandeur reveals itself in the sensuality with which he succeeds in endowing the purely instrumental or ornamental exuberance of these "concertini." In two of the other numbers marked "concertato"—*Misero Alceo dal caro albergo fore* and *Batto, qui pianse Ergasto, ecco la riva*—he respects the outward form of the sonnet only to destroy it by his contempt for its inner "proportions"; the neat division of the sonnet into quatrains and tercets leaves him completely indifferent. He composes the first two and last three lines of *Misero Alceo* as tutti, as narrative setting, while the heart of the text is treated as monody, as arioso, as an embryonic aria, for Marini was as yet incapable of providing him with a genuine aria text. The second sonnet is more madrigalesque, but filled as such with the wildest "madrigalesque" exaggerations. The last number in the book is a seven-voiced setting of Marini's *Presso un fiume tranquillo,* not a sonnet this time but a sort of canzone in the style of Chiabrera. Here Monteverdi as it were singles out from the tutti the roles of the shepherd and shepherdess, treats them as solos and as a duet, and calls the whole a "dialogo." But it is a naturalistic, dramatic dialogue, a far cry from the dialogue of the sixteenth century, that purely musical conception in which the dramatic tide could only flow along as a hidden undercurrent.

This is the last work of Monteverdi's with which this book will be concerned. For his *Libro settimo* of 1619 no longer recognizes even the nominal difference between the *madrigale a cappella* and the *madrigale concertato su l'istromento*. The madrigal has become the concerto. Very few of the twenty-nine numbers of the seventh book have even a tenuous connection with the sixteenth century; one that has is Marini's *A quest'olmo, a quest'ombra, e a quest'onde* (No. 3), but nothing could be more significant than the double title of this piece—*Madrigale a sei, concertato,* or *Concerto a sei, voci et istromenti.* Out of the six-voiced tutti (to which the entire first quatrain belongs) two altos and then a baritone are singled out as solo voices, while two violins or two flutes constitute a ritornello, accompanying or doubling. Guarini's madrigal *Con che soavità, labra adorate* becomes a monody accompanied by an orchestra of three choirs, and the representation of the *soave armonia*, which under the old dispensation would have been a matter for vocal suggestion, now becomes a realistic task for *nove stromenti.* To be sure, the title page still retains the old designation *madrigali*, but it speaks also of *altri generi de Canti*, doubtless in reference to the outright monodies—the *Lettera amorosa*, or the *Partenza amorosa* in the new style, "in genere rappresentativo." But the quartets, trios, and duets of this book seem even more worthy of the designation "other novel types." They are no longer madrigals. They belong to the new concerto-like chamber music. This applies particularly to the series of fifteen duets, which make up half the contents of the book. They begin the history of a new form, which ends only with the chamber duets of Agostino Steffani, Handel, Clari, and Padre Martini. They are the vocal counterpart of the trio sonata for two violins and basso continuo, the ideal combination in the Italian instrumental music of the seventeenth century, arrived at after a hundred artistic experiments. In contrast to the realistic sonnets of the sixth book, Monteverdi's duet is an "ideal" form, not a naturalistic dialogue but a "concerto" for two voices over a neutral bass. It is one of his greatest creations, but when he created it he had, inwardly, long since finished with the madrigal, to which he may be said to have dealt the death blow. As to Monteverdi's eighth madrigal book of 1638, the *Madrigali guerrieri, et amorosi*, in which he follows the Platonists and Aristoxenians in establishing three forms of expression (τρόποι μελοποιίας), the *concitato*, the *molle*, and the *temperato* (diastaltic, systaltic, and hesychastic), we shall not be surprised to find that this many-sided work of the composer's old age has almost nothing to do with the madrigal. The most madrigalesque pieces, indeed the only ones that are purely vocal (with basso continuo), are the two numbers "alla francese"—*Dolcissimo usignuolo* and *Chi vuol haver felice*; in these Monteverdi follows the musicians of the Pléiade, especially Pierre Guédron, and essays a straightforward homophonic declamation of the lines of Guarini's madrigals, with occasional changes in the number of voices. They are real *Airs de cour*, but with Italian texts. How far we are from the spirit of the madrigal can be seen from Monteverdi's two settings of sonnets by Petrarch—*Hor*

che'l ciel e la terra e'l vento tace (complete) and *Vago augelletto che cantando vai* (the octave only). The first is one of his most grandiose compositions. The contrast between the peace and quiet of nature and the conflict and turmoil in the poet's heart is painted with such realism and animated with such ingenuity that all objection to its baroque opulence and orgiastic description grows mute. The modernity of this setting is overpowering, and the coloristic treatment of the chorus and orchestra (two violins and continuo) has an immediate appeal for the nineteenth century and still more so for the twentieth. Petrarch is simply a purveyor of texts and the reverence with which he was once regarded has disappeared. The octave of *Vago augelletto* is simply an excuse for an experiment in form; the *laceramento della poesia* could not be carried further. Petrarch's *Hor che'l ciel e la terra* had been set to music by Tromboncino in his day (1516), and we may number Rore (1542), Monte (1576), and Vecchi (1604) among his successors. But Monteverdi no more belongs to this line than Schubert, who happens also to have set this sonnet to music. We have reached the end.

One cannot help observing how closely the extremes approach one another—the beginning, about 1500, and the end, about 1620. It is as though Monteverdi had sought to prove that from first to last the splendid development of the madrigal was nothing but a detour, a deviation from the natural course. A strange bond connects Monteverdi's *Scherzi musicali* of 1607 with the frottole of Tromboncino and Cara: both have the same rhythmic animation, both have the same metrical peculiarity— the neutral time-signature C conceals an ambiguous triple time that is sometimes a 3/4, sometimes a 6/8—and this metrical peculiarity has led insensitive interpreters into the same misunderstandings in the one case as in the other. To be sure, Monteverdi no longer writes for four voices, like the frottolists, but for three, for he has the development of the villanella behind him; he is familiar with the experiments of the French musicians in the service of the Pléiade; he is more explicit in his separation of the vocal from the instrumental. But his affinity with the frottola is undeniable; through improvisation, the tradition of the frottola must have reached him, for his *scherzi* are much more Italian than French. The same applies to his treatment of the sonnet. This too is a return, a return to the practice of improvising variations over an unchanging bass that is stated four times for a sonnet or an ottava, a *basso ostinato*. Thus are united, in one strange personality, the most extreme antitheses—the very old and the very new, tradition and revolution, preservation and destruction, reaction and progress.

As early as 1608 Paolo Quagliati had already observed that most music-lovers preferred the *musica vota*, the *musica concertante* over a basso continuo, to the a cappella madrigal, or rather to the old madrigal of the sixteenth century, and he was quite right. The old madrigal has fulfilled its mission and is about to die. To be sure, there are still musicians—especially provincial musicians—who maintain the fiction that it is still alive. But it is at the same time symptomatic that the reprints, even of the most successful works of as great a master as Marenzio, do not go much beyond 1610. In 1627 when Monteverdi republished Arcadelt's madrigals for four voices in a "corrected" version, he had a purely pedagogical purpose in mind, for it was from Arcadelt that beginners learned the rudiments of pure four-part writing. The conflict or lack of direction evident in Monteverdi's work as a madrigalist are characteristic of the time as a whole: it is simply that Monteverdi is the most brilliant representative of the conflict. He is not even a leader of the revolution, for despite his passionate nature, he is by temperament saturnine, given to introspection, inspired and impeded by nebulous Platonic doctrines, and thus slower to side with the new movement than other masters of smaller stature. Salamone Rossi, the most important among the Jewish musicians of Mantua, and incidentally also the most amiable and most spontaneous, deeply influenced by Monteverdi but unaffected by the many problems that stirred his great colleague, published between 1600 and 1622 five books of five-voiced madrigals (among other things), and the very first of these, some years before Monteverdi, is divided into a cappella pieces and pieces "per cantar nel Chittarone, con la loro intavolatura posta nel soprano." In the second book of 1602 the theorbo becomes an indefinite "basso continuo per sonare in Concerto" to be used in every number, and from the third book (1603) on it is a "basso continuo per stromenti da corpo"—for all harmonic instruments such as clavier, lute, and harp. All these pieces in the *stile concertante* are written with an easy grace that finds its purest expression in Rossi's *Madrigaletti a due* of 1628, the most enchanting *duettini*, and the most perfect in form, until the little masterpieces of Carissimi and Luigi Rossi.

Nor is Salamone Rossi the only musician to anticipate Monteverdi in siding wholeheartedly with the "modern" movement. Another member of the advance is Antonio Cifra, a Roman master or at least one brought up in Rome, where he was for a short time the choirmaster at the Collegio Germanico; from 1609 to 1629, with a brief interruption, he is connected with the music at the Santa Casa in Loreto. He too publishes six books of five-voiced madrigals between 1605 and 1623, and although only the last two books are expressly *concertati* with basso continuo, his heart is in the new style, in the *scherzi* and *arie*, of which he wrote six books of secular ones and two of spiritual (*scherzi sacri*). The sixth book, dedicated to the Grand Duke Cosimo II, is preserved only in manuscript. In monodies and duets Cifra is the Ariosto and Tasso composer par excellence, but even when he writes trios and quartets, and he does not do so very often, they no longer have anything to do with the madrigalesque spirit: they are discursive and in the *stile concertante* throughout

—sometimes openly in the manner of the dialogue or cantata. Much the same might be said of the work of two masters who were closely associated with Monteverdi in their professional duties and in their writing—Alessandro Grandi and Giovanni Rovetta. In 1615, while still choirmaster at the cathedral in Ferrara, Grandi publishes his *Madrigali concertati a due, tre, e quattro voci*, which are no longer madrigals but duets, trios, and quartets, purer in form, but also more commonplace and tiresome than anything that Monteverdi ever wrote. In 1617 Grandi came to Venice as a singer at San Marco, where he served for three years as assistant choirmaster under Monteverdi: he was one of the first to use the term "cantada" to describe his monodies in several movements (1620). And where he breaks off, Rovetta takes up the thread—both biographically and stylistically. Both musicians may be regarded as having lived off Monteverdi's patrimony: untroubled by his scruples, they are less imposing and less interesting but at the same time more progressive and more versatile than their great contemporary, who had by this time become a sort of patriarch. One can only conclude that there must have been a Venetian school and a Venetian literature of the "concerto," independent of Mantua, Florence, and Rome, and one thinks involuntarily of Giovanni Gabrieli, whose later work in the secular field we know so little about. The madrigal production of such northern pupils as Heinrich Schütz (1611) and Johann Grabbe (1609)—a discussion of which would not be relevant here—suggests that this teacher must have written madrigals unknown to us; is it likely that the master who wrote the *Sonata con tre violini* should not also have tried his skill in the field of the *musica concertante* for voices?

Let us repeat: No musician who lived beyond the year 1600 could evade the issue. Each one had to decide whether to stand still or go forward. Few stood still. With amazing rapidity the madrigal takes the form of the concerto, closely or loosely knit. Those that are close-knit stand nearer to the old ideal, the loose-knit ones nearer to the cantata. And the close-knit ones become less and less frequent as time goes on, for the character of music-making in company has changed, and the virtuoso, as the central figure of the new music-making, is demanding his due.

In 1638 there appears a work that might be considered the last milestone on the road over which the madrigal has traveled—the *Madrigali a cinque voci ed altri varii Concerti* by Domenico Mazzocchi, dedicated to Cardinal Francesco or Antonio Barberini, which one we do not know. Mazzocchi published these pieces simultaneously in score and in parts—in score "because they can be sung more readily in this form" ("perche con questa potranno più francamente cantarsi"). Domenico Mazzocchi has thus far attracted little attention except as a composer of operas and as one of the representatives of the Roman oratorio, including the secular oratorio; we do not even have a complete bibliography of his works. Born at Città Castellana near Rome on November 8, 1592, he was a pupil of G. B. Nanino and spent his long life (he died as late as 1665) as a priest in the service of the Aldobrandini and Borghese families. As a musician he is the most important intermediary between the circle of G. F. Anerio and that of Carissimi, who created the great classical cantata and the classical oratorio and who was the first to gain a clear and complete insight into the nature of modern tonality. The lexicons also credit Mazzocchi with having made use of explicit signs for the finest shades of dynamics, from forte to pianissimo, for crescendo and decrescendo, and for the "messa di voce." Domenico Mazzocchi divides the twenty-four numbers of his work into three groups (he counts the *seconde parti* separately—actually there are only nineteen numbers): (1) *Madrigali che si concertano su l'istromento*, (2) *che si cantano senza istromento*, and (3) *variamente concertati*. The score, he says, may be used for study and also to accompany the second of the three groups, the a cappella pieces, although this would be against his intention, for he has left these pieces "naked and plain, just as he would have them sung" (*nudi, e schietti, si come desidero, che si cantino*). His concern extends to every detail of the interpretation, and he is also concerned for his poets, whose names he never omits and who, with the exception of Tasso, Guarini, and Marini, were all Roman contemporaries—Pier Francesco Paoli, Ludovico Adimari, Ottavio Tronsarelli, Francesco Balducci, and Giovanni Ciampoli. Tronsarelli, in particular, is the author of *Dolci godete*, a homage to the Barberini family. In his dedication he regretfully admits that "the most artistic study known to music is that of the madrigal; but few are being composed today and fewer sung, they being to their misfortune all but banished from the *accademie*" (*Il più ingegnoso studio, che habbia la Musica, è quello de' Madrigali; mà pochi hoggi dì se ne compongono, e meno se ne cantano, vedendosi per loro dissaventura dall' Accademie poco men che banditi.*) From this it may be inferred that his madrigals are somewhat retrospective, above all the seven a cappella pieces. They derive from none other than Gesualdo, whom Mazzocchi praises, in his dedication, as a model of exact notation. But it is a clarified and purer Gesualdo whom we meet here: the extreme contrasts of vivace and largo are still present, as is the flexibility of tempo, but there is also a synthesis, a fusion of the contrasts through the combination of motifs. To show this, I need only quote the beginning of Marini's *Di marmo siete voi* (see opposite page). In the intricate play of his motifs, Mazzocchi sometimes resembles the Prince of Venosa even more closely. But it will have been evident at once that he surpasses his model in the complete clarification of his harmonic writing. His chromaticism obeys a natural law, even when it is extreme—and it is never so without poetic justification;

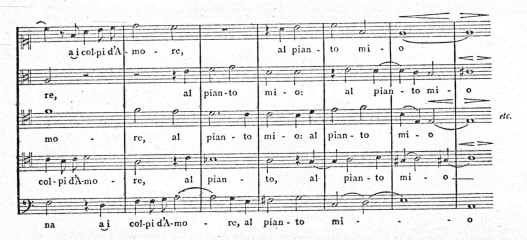

this wonderful passage from the last number of the first group, *Pian piano, aure tranquillo*, is a case in point (see below and p. 871).

This example will also serve as an illustration from the first group, the group "con istromenti." It is characteristic of these pieces that the solos that detach themselves are always short; despite the *stile concertante*, the unity of the whole is preserved intact. When Mazzocchi sets a sonnet the divisions may be more sharply marked: thus in No. 5, *Oh, se poteste mai, luci adorate*, he gives the first quatrain to the tutti, the second to the solo tenor, and the first tercet to the solo first soprano; the second is *a cinque concertante*. Other pieces, for example No. 4, *Poi che a molti fai parte*, are laid out as chains of responses: the tenor or soprano sings one or more

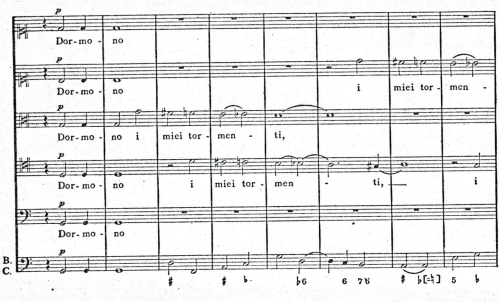

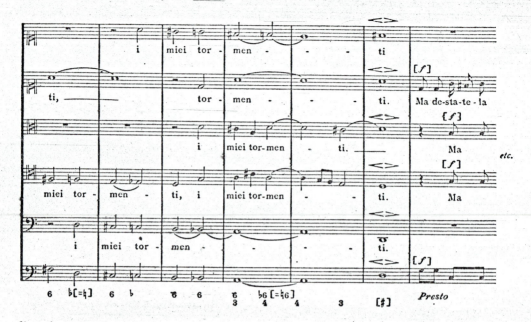

lines by way of announcement; the choir follows with intricately divided imitations.

The third group, with the pieces that are "variamente concertati," is the freest and the most varied, even in the number of voices, which ranges from four to eight. Two pieces are described as "arias"—No. 15, *Hor che gli armati*, and No. 16, *Dolci godete*; they are short, lively, festive, but still somewhat madrigalesque. Another is drawn from the *Gerusalemme liberata* (XVI, 61)—No. 17, *Chiudeste i lumi Armida*; it is Armida's lament, and Mazzocchi has accordingly written it over four statements— free repetitions—of the "Ruggiero" bass as a set of five-voiced variations. Since the piece is headed "per le viole," it presumably belongs among those of which Mazzocchi says in his dedication that they were sung in the Palazzo Barberini to the accompaniment of the Cardinal's own chamber-musicians (*sopra il conserto delle sue viole*). The remainder consists of *concerti*, a canzone with echoes, the ritornello sung by a five-voiced choir, or in another instance (No. 19, *Verginelle*) by a quartet of sopranos. It is a new, Roman art, and it will be further developed and refined by Carissimi, Luigi Rossi, and Mario Savioni.

It is a fitting conclusion. Mazzocchi is a master in the full sense of the word, a master of plastic and expressive invention in whose work the harmonic and con- trapuntal factors are balanced with the utmost refinement, the first musician who resolutely abandoned the church modes for modern tonality. Thanks to him the Roman school—in vocal music Carissimi, in instrumental music Corelli—is the preeminently modern and classic school and in this a leader for the rest of Italy.

But despite his conscious modernity, Mazzocchi has still another Roman quality— the sense of tradition. He retains a certain connection with the great period, with the ideals of the sixteenth-century madrigal; in taking leave of it, he pays it a tribute.

What follows comes more and more to assume the character of archaism. There is a protracted late-flowering, an "Indian summer," and it was perhaps richer than we know, for in the seventeenth century the printing of music becomes less usual and many manuscripts have been lost or have remained uncatalogued. Some landmarks are the *Madrigali morali e spirituali* of Mario Savioni (Rome 1668), or the *Madrigali a cinque voci* of Giovanni Maria Bononcini (Bologna 1678), or perhaps the *Concerto madrigalesco a tre voci diverse* of Ercole Bernabei (Rome 1669), which avoids all cantata-like solos. As late as 1672 Savioni is still distinguishing between *madrigali a tre voci differenti* and *concerti*—the one tightly woven, the other with solos after the manner of the cantata. And as late as 1705 Antonio Lotti publishes a first work that attained a certain historical notoriety as a result of Benedetto Marcello's criticisms: in it he distinguishes between his twelve "duets" and his four "madrigals" for three voices, which are followed by one for four voices and one for five. With this, even archaism is at an end. In 1774 Padre Giambattista Martini of Bologna publishes his *Saggio fondamentale*, in which for the first time the madrigal becomes an object of sympathetic and penetrating historical interest. But the living development had ceased long before the writing of its history began.

INDEX OF NAMES

Accolti, Bernardo, 453
Accoramboni, Vittoria, 500
Achillino, G. P., 41
Adimari, L., 868
Agazzari, A., 116
Agnelli, Lepido, 861
Agnelli, Scipione, 861
Agostini, Lodovico, 769, 855
Agricola, A., 10, 20, 21f., 31, 40, 54, 125
Alamanni, Luigi, 95, 280f., 474, 628, 697
Alauro, Girolamo, see Lauro
Albani, Francesco, 675
Albert, Duke of Prussia, 226, 439
Albert IV, Duke, 53
Albert VI, Duke, 498, 762, 828
Alberti, Filippo, 721f.
Alberti, Innocentio, 390, 424, 471, 472
Alberti, L. B., 18, 54
Alberto, Nicolo, 163
Albrecht V, of Bavaria, 385f., 480, 498, 522, 762, 828
Aldobrandini, Cinzio, 611, 612, 614, 669, 799
Aldobrandini family, 685, 868
Aldobrandini, Pietro, 211, 614, 755, 825
Aldoviti, Antonio, 479, 481
Aldoviti, Bindo, 429, 479, 481
Aleotti, G. B. detto d'Argenta, 726
Alessandro d'Este, Cardinal, 775, 829
Alessandro Farnese, 491, 501
Alessandro da Genova, 471, 472
Alessandro Mantovano, 41, 127
Alessandro de'Medici, see Medici
Alessandro de'Medici, Bishop of Pistoia, see Medici
Alessandro Organista, 31
Alexander VI, Pope, 7, 56, 78, 94
Alexander the Great, 837, 838
Alexandrino Venitiano, 761
Alfonso of Calabria, 37
Alfonso I d'Este, 46, 344
Alfonso II d'Este, 211, 301, 334, 386, 433, 478, 491, 502, 513, 535, 540, 555, 569, 573, 610, 618, 627, 628, 670, 675, 705, 723, 726, 754, 769, 825, 826, 828, 829, 831f., 832, 845, 846
Alfonso Gonzaga, see Gonzaga
Alfonso I di Nuvolara, 512, 513
Algarotti, G. Fr., 217
Allegretti, Antonio, 720
Altoviti, see Aldoviti

Alvise d'Este, Cardinal, 472
Amadino, Ricciardo, 653, 660, 813
Amanio, Nicolo, 200, 314, 394, 417
Ambra, Francesco d', 282, 284, 407, 763
Ammanati, 617
Ana, Francesco d', 40f., 85, 100, 768
Anacreon, 310, 666
Ancina, Giovenale, 848
Andreini, Isabella, 730
Anerio, Felice, 240, 548, 855, 856
Anerio, G. F., 855, 856, 868
Angelico, Fra, 75
Angelieri, Giorgio, 523
Angelo (Giovanni Angelo Venturi), 198
Anglia, see Robertus, Galfridus
Angosciola, Girolamo, 184
Angosciola, Ippolita B., 184
Anhalt, Rudolf von, 729
Animuccia, Giovanni, 188, 289f.
Animuccia, Paolo, 291f.
Anne de Guise-Lorraine, 628
Ansanus Senese, 41, 114, 352
Antico, Andrea da Montona, 41, 43, 52, 57, 58, 59, 66, 77, 91, 95, 99, 125, 126, 127, 128, 135, 138, 139, 140, 141, 143, 165, 166, 171, 206, 258, 297, 324, 325, 350, 402, 771, 839, 841
Antinori, Lorenzo, 21
Antonio da Cornetto, 197
Apuleius, 43
Aquila, Serafino dall', 40, 43f., 55, 61, 89, 108, 170, 200, 280, 355, 358
Aragon, dynasty of, 27
Aragona, Antonia, 843
Aragona, Tullia, see Tullia
Arborea, Cardinal, 94
Arcadelt, J., 20, 104, 110, 113, 114, 116, 125, 138, 150, 151, 153f., 159ff., 166, 171, 175, 176, 177, 178, 179, 186, 189, 192, 202, 207, 223, 246, 247, 254, 257, 258, 261, 262, 264ff., 278, 281, 290, 296, 297, 305, 306, 307, 308, 310, 311, 314, 315, 316, 317, 324, 327, 339, 344, 348, 360, 374, 375, 384, 393, 396, 399, 400, 415, 426, 430, 431, 433, 434, 435, 440, 447, 469, 481, 491, 517, 558, 559, 604, 620, 622, 624, 626, 643, 684, 732, 744, 750, 754, 779, 823, 838, 842, 866
Archilei, Antonio, 847
Archilei, Vittoria, 740
Arco, Count, 500

Aretino, Paolo, 293
Aretino, Pietro, 49, 94, 173, 174f., 184, 194, 195, 320, 322, 374, 444, 843
Argenti, Agostino, 301
Argentil, Charles, 157, 178, 262
Ariosto, Lodovico, 38, 42, 87, 91, 93, 128, 171, 172, 174, 205, 206ff., 209, 232, 244, 248, 257, 285, 295, 304, 333, 356f., 370, 390, 405, 410, 424, 426, 427, 433, 439, 442, 458, 462, 464, 466, 467, 468, 482, 495, 496, 500, 515, 517, 518, 545, 547, 549, 554, 564ff., 568, 573, 586, 600, 622, 641, 643, 661, 691, 719, 727, 732, 764, 765, 837, 839, 847, 848, 866
Aristotle, 112, 215, 220, 242
Aristoxenus, 864
Armonico, Giovanni, 529
Armonio, Frate, 528
Arnoldo, 262
Arnolfo da Pisa, see Pisano
Aron (Aaron), Pietro, 41, 54, 77, 158, 196, 226, 294, 319, 399
Arpa, Gio. Leonardo dell', 479, 582, 583, 718, 848, 849
Arrivabene, Andrea, 185
Artusa, Elena, 460
Artusi, G. M., 224, 410, 411, 671, 691, 728, 813, 850
Arundel, Henry, 472
Ascoli, Prince of, 581
Asola, F. M., 667
Asola, Matteo, 236
Atalante, see Migliorotti
Atanagi, Dionigi, 50, 190, 474, 613, 634, 635, 641, 644, 663, 720
Attaingnant, Pierre, 139, 154, 165, 166, 172, 264, 604
Augustine, Saint, 23
Avalos, Alfonso Marchese del Vasto, 186, 189, 210, 269, 270, 404, 779
Avalos, Donna Maria d', 689f., 690
Avalos family, 690
Avanzini, Roberto, 51
Ayolla, Francesco, 31
Ayolle, Francesco, see Layolle
Azzaiolo (Azzaiuolo), F., 348ff., 375, 380, 750
Azzia, G. B. d', 479

Baccino degli Organi, see Bartolomeo Organista
Baccusi, Ippolito, 459, 512
Bach, J. Christian, 706, 718

Bach, J. S., 79, 201, 275, 286, 336, 402, 475, 489, 496, 640, 705, 718, 729, 743, 820
Badoer, Federigo, 522
Baif, Antoine de, 311
Baini, Giuseppe, 20, 241, 639
Bajazet, Sultan, 56
Balbi, Lodovico, 203, 754
Balbo, Scaramuccia, 9
Baldini, Vittorio, 827, 834
Baldinucci, Francesco, 280
Balducci, Francesco, 868
Ballard, Robert, 141, 165, 268, 838. *See also* Le Roy
Balsamino, Simone, 681f., 801
Banchieri, Adriano, 373, 526, 605, 802ff., 819
Bandello, Matteo, 444
Bandini, Ottavio, 855
Barbadico, Girolamo, 107
Barbarino, Francesco da, 118
Barberini, Antonio, 867
Barberini, Francesco, 867
Barberini family, 868, 871
Bardi, Giovanni de', 63, 216, 423, 593, 763, 847
Bardi, Pandolfo, 731
Bardi, P. de', 204
Bargagli, Girolamo, 797
Bargagli, Scipione, 730, 797
Barges, Antonino, 322, 324
Bargo, 196f., 384, 462
Bargonio, Tomaso, 174
Barignano, Pietro, 109, 468
Barozza, 332
Barre, Antonio, 165, 208, 275, 369, 373, 422, 431, 437, 481, 492, 499, 545, 645, 854
Barre, Leonardo, 324, 326
Barre, Yvo, 306, 399
Bartoli, Cosimo, 21, 22, 47, 156f., 159, 762
Bartolomeo Fiorentino (organista), 31f., 78, 130, 259
Bartolucci, *see* Rufino
Bassano, Giovanni, 584, 842
Bastiano, Pre (Sebastiano del Piombo?), 48. *See also* Sebastiano and Piombo
Bastini, Vincentio, 181
Bathory, Andrea, Cardinal, 825
Bati, Luca, 669, 729, 732f., 734, 738, 739, 845
Battista Siciliano, 479
Baude, H., 30
Baumann, Georg, 451
Beatrice d'Este, 12, 38, 39, 43, 108
Beccari, Agostino, 301, 302, 551

Beccuti, Antonio, detto Coppetta, 495f.
Becker, K. F., 605
Beethoven, Ludwig van, 167, 200, 275, 401, 490, 743, 853
Bel, Firmin le, *see* Firmin
Beldemandis, Prosdocimo de, 7
Bellamano, Franceschina, 447, 843
Bellamano, Marietta, 447, 843
Bellasio, Paolo, 695
Bellère, Jean, 500
Bell'haver (Bel'haver), Vincenzo, 453, 522, 525, 526, 639, 773
Belli, Girolamo, 211, 721, 754ff.
Bellini, Giovanni, 155, 318
Bellini, Vincenzo, 302
Bembo, Bernardo, 110, 111
Bembo, Pietro, 94, 109ff., 112, 117, 118f., 126, 146, 153, 165, 173, 181, 190, 200, 202, 205, 208, 212, 214, 265, 272, 274, 279, 281, 290, 314, 377, 405, 436, 437, 439, 441, 452, 456, 458, 472, 506, 509, 511, 515, 545, 546, 582, 598, 719, 722, 723, 741, 755, 799
Bembo family, 799
Bendidio, Isabella, 539f., 829
Bendidio, Lucrezia, 539f., 648, 671, 675, 699, 723, 728, 825ff., 844
Bendidio, M. A., 366
Bene, Giovanni del, 461
Bennett, Sterndale, 624
Bentivoglio, Ercole, 722
Benvenuti, Lorenzo, 323
Beolco, Angelo, 340, 344
Berchem, Jachet, 20, 173, 183, 194, 206, 257, 275, 289, 290, 399, 431, 432, 434, 564f.
Berg, *see* Montanus
Bergoto, A. Fr., 198
Berlioz, Hector, 718
Bernabei, Ercole, 872
Bernardo da Pisa, *see* Pisano
Bernardo, Laura, 444
Berni, Francesco, 161
Bernini, Lorenzo, 708
Bertani, Lelio, 459
Bertrand, Anthoine de, 404
Besozzi, G. F., 802, 806
Besozzo, Benedetto da, 425
Bevilacqua, Bonifazio, 444
Bevilacqua, Mario, 193, 476, 482, 483, 491, 494, 502, 511, 602, 610, 630, 662, 684, 773, 776, 781
Bianchetti, Lodovico, 637
Bianchetti, Lorenzo, Cardinal, 637
Bianchi (Bianco), Pietro Antonio, 720, 782
Bianchino da Pisa, 78

Bicci, Antonio, 669, 733
Bidon, 107
Bifetto, Francesco, 293f.
Biffi, Gioseffo, 825
Billi, Lutio, 542
Binchois, Gilles, 5, 10
Biribis (Brebis), J. de, 8, 34
Bisan, Z., 41
Bizet, Georges, 168
Blado, Antonio, 429
Blessi, Manoli, *see* Molino
Boccaccio, Giovanni, 5, 12, 14, 30, 117, 146, 169, 189, 190, 196, 272, 308f., 314, 315, 444, 458, 466, 602, 749, 753, 755, 834
Boccamazzi, Fabio, 218
Boccherini, Luigi, 478
Bodeo, Joan, 560
Boiardo, Matteo Maria, 426, 428, 549
Boldieri, Orazio and Curio, 799
Bolognese, Isabella, 843
Bolognini, Bernardo, 698
Bona of Savoy, 11
Bonadies, J., 8
Bonagionta (Bonagiunta), Giulio, 385, 390, 418, 454, 492, 521, 548, 593, 766
Bonaldi, Francesco, 528
Bonarelli, Guidubaldo, 612, 726
Boncompagni (Buoncompagni), Giovanni, 593
Bononcini, G. M., 872
Bonzanini, Agostino, 192
Booth, Michele, 653
Borchgrevinck, Melchior, 797
Borghese family, 214, 868
Borgia, Cesare, 39, 42, 78
Borgia, Lucrezia, 46, 78, 109
Borromeo, Carlo, 692
Borso d'Este, 8
Bossinensis, Francesco, 49, 107
Bottegari, Cosimo, 597
Bottrigari, Ercole, 346, 403, 413, 626, 629, 705, 821
Bourgeois, Loys, 340
Bovicelli, G. B., 842
Bracci, R., 33
Bragadino family, 432
Braganza, D. Serafina di, 857
Brahms, Johannes, 168, 609
Brambiglia, 198
Brancaccio, G. C., 479, 480, 826, 832
Brancazio, 844
Brandolini, R., 8
Brantôme, Pierre de, 689
Brith, Giovanni, 34
Brixia, M. de, 5

Brocus (Brocco, Broch), J., 40, 68, 70, 78, 91

Brocus, Nicolo, 40, 93, 350, 380

Bruett, 157

Brumel, Antoine, 8, 21f., 135, 226, **825**

Brumen, Denis, 262

Brunelleschi, Filippo, 617

Bruni, G. Fr., 230

Bruno, Giordano, 353

Bruno, Giovanni Battista, 492, 498

Bruolo, B., 5

Brusasorzi, Domenico, 192, 455

Buglhat, Giovanni de, 165, 298

Buonarroti, *see* Michelangelo

Buonavita, Antonio, 705

Buonvicini, Agostino, 513

Burchiella, *see* Molino

Burgomozo, L., 319f.

Burney, Charles, 116, 415, 449, 605, 684, 691, 705, 706

Busnoys, Antoine, 5, 10, 18, 30, 38

Buus, J., 152, 324, 432, 438, 447

Byrd, William, 93, 103, 270, 499

Caccini, Francesca, 740

Caccini, Giulio, 99, 216, 423, 554, 729, 732, 740, 763, 766, 831, 834, 843, 844, 846, 847

Caesar, 516

Caffi, Francesco, 438, 439

Caimo, Gioseffo, 377, 542, 561f., 599f., 602, 695, 776, 777, 778

Calcagnini, Celio, 93

Calcar, J. St. van, 324

Caldara, Antonio, 768

Callepio, Rogerio, 294

Callot, Jacques, 811

Calmeta, Vincenzo, 44, 89, 108

Calmo, Andrea, 48, 322, 324, 439, 447, 497, 527, 769, 843

Calori Cortese, Laura, 780

Cambio, Perissone, 177, 189, 197, 381, 385, 390, 403, 438f., 446, 449, 455, 460, 461, 576

Camillo I di Nuvolara, 512

Camillo di Parma, 577

Campagnolo, Ev., 603

Campagnolo, Francesco, 861

Campo, Diego de, 675

Caneto, G. A. de, 113, 353

Canigiani, Bernardo, 289

Canigiani (Ambassador), 828

Canis, Cornelius, 22, 499

Canisius, 53

Cantone, Serafino, 683

Capello, Bianca, 234, 453, 610, 639, 646, 648, 731, 763, 773, 776

Capilupi, Geminiano, 774, 779

Capilupi, Ippolito, 212

Caponi (Capponi), Neri, 198f., 199, 322

Caporali, Cesare, 637

Cappuccio, Don G. P., 709

Capreoli (Caprioli) A., 40, 93, 112, 123, 341

Capua, Donna Vittoria da, 512

Capuano, Giovanni Francesco, 591

Cara, Marco (Marchetto), 21f., 40, 42, 44, 49, 51ff., 53, 54, 55, 61, 63, 64, 65, 66, 68, 77, 95, 101, 102, 105, 106, 107, 108, 110, 111, 112, 114, 120, 123f., 124, 126, 127, 128, 134, 139, 141, 143, 144, 145, 146, 149, 154, 172, 297, 325, 341, 342, 358, 380, 381, 683, 839f., 865

Carafa, Antonio, 479

Carafa, Fabrizio, 689

Carafa family, 690

Caravaggio, Michelangelo (Merisi), 768, 773

Cardona, Maria di, 512

Carducci, G., 195

Cariani, Giovanni, 448

Carissimi, Giacomo, 45, 697, 849, 866, 868, 871

Cariteo, 41, 89, 91, 108, 170, 355, 356, 358

Carlino, G. G., 701

Caro, Annibale, 280, 454, 669

Carpentras (Elzear Genet), 40, 54, 114, 126, 623

Carpi, Girolamo da, 385

Carretto, Galeotto del, 42, 43f., 45, 52, 61, 64, 108

Cartolari, Antonio dei, 472

Casa, Giovanni della, 200, 385, 417, 472, 509, 515, 641, 653, 663, 668, 734, 778

Casa, Girolamo della, 842

Cascia, Giovanni da, 13, 118

Casella, 216

Casio, Hieronimo, 47

Casone, Girolamo, 613, 647, 721

Cassola, Luigi, 53, 131, 149, 171, 172f., 174, 181, 184, 185, 186, 194, 209, 249, 253, 254, 259, 267, 275, 298, 300, 307, 332, 426, 430, 439, 442, 467, 517, 535, 540, 556, 584, 622, 643

Castellanus, Petrus, 56

Castellino, Alvise, 348, 378f., 769

Castiglione, Baldassare, 38, 52, 93, 99, 106, 107, 108, 109, 112f., 126, 153, 598, 797

Castiliono, G. A. de, 463

Castrioto, Constantino, 479

Castro, Jean de, 542

Casulana, Maddalena, 510, 529

Cataldo, Don Salvatore di, 206

Cataneo, Don Maurizio, 612

Catherine de'Medici, *see* Medici

Catullus, 311, 452

Cavalieri, B. dei, 8

Cavalieri, Emilio de', 730, 834, 847

Cavalieri, Paolo, 695

Cavalletta, Orsina, 219f.

Cavalliero, Tarquinia del, 640

Cebà, Ansaldo, 855

Cecchi, Giammaria, 282, 284

Celiano, Livio, 511, 670, 681f., 683, 688, 725, 735, 844

Cellini, Benvenuto, 28, 277, 280, 283, 429

Cellini, Giovanni, 277

Cerone, Pietro, 199, 229, 235, 236, 241, 243, 257, 271, 325, 335, 511

Cervantes, 205

Cervo, Barnaba, 388

Cesano, Bartolomeo, 463

Cesare d'Este, 690, 763, 775, 846

Cesare Gonzaga, *see* Gonzaga

Cesarini, Cleria, 618

Cesarini, Giuliano, 612, 618

Cesena, P., 41, 78

Chamaterò, Ippolito, 192

Chamisso, Adalbert von, 249

Charles, Archduke (Carl), 233, 522, 600, 757, 763

Charles V, Emperor, 94, 158, 256, 269, 372, 392f., 403, 425, 478, 744

Charles V of France, 9

Charles VIII of France, 28, 56, 264, 276

Charles IX of France, 480

Charles of Lorraine, Duke of Guise, 162

Charles d'Orléans, 30

Charles the Good, 9

Charles (Ciarles), *see* Argentil

Chechin, Cecchino, 197

Chiabrera, Gabriello, 81, 735, 736, 741, 855, 863

Chopin, Fr., 275, 692

Christian IV of Denmark, 797

Christiani, Francesco, 313

Christina (Cristina) of Lorraine (Medici), 611, 797

Ciampoli, Giovanni, 868

Cicogna, Girolamo, 475

Ciconia, Johannes, 6, 7

Ciera, Ippolito, 321

Cifra, Antonio, 866

Cimello, Lelio, 405

Cimello, Thomaso (Giovanni Tomaso), 382, 404f., 443

Cinciarino, Pietro, 433

Cingoli, B. da, 44

Cini, G. B., 234, 284, 763
Cino da Pistoia, 189, 190
Cinthio (Cintio, Cinzio), Giraldi, G. B., 187, 291, 301, 385, 407, 426, 822f.
Cirenza, Galeazzo, Duke of, 498
Civitato, A. de, 5
Clari, G. C. Maria, 864
Clarice Medici, *see* Medici
Clario, Benedetto, 768
Claude, 139
Claudin, *see* Sermisy
Clemens VII, Pope (Medici), 158, 176, 425
Clemens VIII, Pope (Aldobrandini), 211, 481, 611, 614, 675, 755
Clemens non Papa, 22, 226
Cleopatra, 516
Clusius (de l'Ecluse), Charles, 501
Coclico, Adrian Petit, 152, 223, 225ff., 229
Cocq, Jehan de, *see* Gallus
Collalto, Collaltino, 460
Collebaudi, Jacques (Giachetto da Mantua), 22, 49, 226, 258, 289, 322, 432, 435
Colleoni, Bartolomeo, 347
Colombo, Alessandro, 198
Colonia, Joannes de, 354
Colonna, Fabrizio, 406, 479
Colonna, Girolama, 848
Colonna, Giulio Cesare, 312
Colonna, Livia, 313
Colonna, M. A., 382
Colonna, Vittoria, 200, 404, 405, 406, 719
Colonna family, 313, 406, 503, 619
Columbus, Christopher, 3, 23
Commer, Franz, 415
Compagnacci, 277
Compère, Loyset, 10, 40, 85, 120, 121, 325, 341
Con, G., 8
Conforto, G. L., 842
Consilium, Jean, 140, 159, 226
Contarini, Alvise, 52
Contarini, Giacomo, 528
Contarini, Giovanni, 52
Contarini, Sebastiano, 191
Contile, Luca, 598
Contino, Giovanni, 455, 513, 609, 615
Conversi, Girolamo, 598f., 602
Coppetta, Antonio, *see* Beccuti
Coppetta, Francesco, 773
Coppini (Coppinus), Alessandro, 34, 277
Corboli, Francesco, 198
Cordier, B., 10, 277

Cordova, C. F. di, Duke of Sessa, 512, 518
Corelli, Arcangelo, 626, 871
Cornaro, Catarina, 110
Cornazano (Cornazzano), A., 6, 8
Cornelio, 157
Cornelius, Peter, 604
Cornetto, Antonio dal, 301, 407
Correggio, Nicolo da, 44, 45, 97, 100, 104, 105
Corsi, Jacopo, 729, 732, 735
Corteccia, Francesco, 129, 156, 161, 164, 176, 179, 192, 206, 229, 276ff., 289, 290, 291, 293, 294f., 300, 301, 306, 339, 378, 380, 381, 382, 399, 407, 565f., 684, 729, 730, 763, 812, 840, 841, 847
Cortellini, Camillo, 165
Cosimo de'Medici (the Elder), *see* Medici
Cosimo de'Medici (Duke, later Grand Duke), *see* Medici
Cosimo II, Grand Duke, *see* Medici
Cossa, Andrea, 89
Courtois, L., 22, 226, 462
Crecquillon, Thomas, 22, 226, 595
Crispinus, 68f.
Cristina of Lorraine, 730, 847
Croce, Giovanni, 373, 459, 542, 543, 550, 798ff., 858

Danckerts, Ghiselin, 413, 645
Dante, 5, 10, 12, 13, 14, 21, 23, 97, 111, 139, 169, 170, 201f., 216, 377, 418, 553, 613, 616, 684, 699
Dati, Leonardo, 95
Demophon, Alexander, 41
Dentice, Luigi, 479, 576, 855
Dentice, Scipione, 116, 612, 689
Deslouges, Philippe, *see* Verdelot
Didymus, 783
Diomedes, 41
Dionysius, 112
Dionysius, *see* Papin
Dolci (Dolce), Lodovico, 509, 528
Domenichi, Lodovico, 185, 194, 195, 197, 614, 649f., 660
"Dominus," 41f.
Donatello, 21, 424
Donato (Donati), Baldisserra, 370, 381, 390, 409, 422, 438, 443, 446, 448, 450f., 525, 582, 673, 773, 799, 843, 845
Donato, Francesco da, 46
Doni, Antonfrancesco, 47, 154, 157, 174, 184, 186, 193ff., 221, 245, 269, 270, 275, 290, 318, 327,

384, 385, 431, 432, 439, 440, 444, 447, 462, 463, 532, 770, 843
Doni, Giovanni Battista, 204, 423, 861
Dorati, Niccolo, 208
Dorico, Valerio, 141, 149, 165, 497
Dossi, Dosso, 213f.
Dowland, John, 611
Dragonetto (Dragonetti), Bonifazio, 177, 248, 326
Dragoni, G. A., 612, 828, 855
Duc, Filippo, 236, 757, 760, 781
Duccio, 40
Dürer, Albrecht, 215
Dueto, Antonio, 641
Dufay, Guillaume, 5, 6, 7, 10, 12, 16, 17, 18, 30, 75, 76, 105, 226, 241
Dunstable, John, 4, 5, 7
Dupré, E., 40

Eccard, Johann, 771f.
Effrem, Muzio, 689, 690, 691, 707, 742
Eleonora d'Aragona, 38
Eleonora d'Este, 690
Eleonora Gonzaga, *see* Gonzaga (*see also* Leonora)
Eleonora di Toledo (Medici), 156, 499
Elisabetta Gonzaga, *see* Gonzaga
Elisabetta di Urbino, 52, 99
Elizabeth, Elizabethan madrigalists, 245, 671, 677, 781
Encina, Juan del, 94
Enrico de Alemania, 34
Erasmus, 24
Erber, *see* Herber
Ercole III, Marchese d'Este, 34
Ercole I d'Este, Duke, 8, 20, 38, 43, 319, 320
Ercole II d'Este, Duke, 5, 192, 301, 306, 344, 345, 378f., 385, 386, 391, 393, 413
Erfordia, Joannes de, 8
Ernst (Ernest), Archduke, 502, 600
Escobedo, Bartolomeo, 413
Essenga, Salvatore, 773
Este family, 300f., 390, 391, 472, 476, 513, 554, 555, 573, 610, 628, 646, 667, 670, 698, 705, 724, 755, 762, 773, 774, 819, 825, 845
Eugene IV, Pope, 6
Eustachius D. M. R. Gallus, 40, 102, 112, 136, 138, 139
Eustachius D. M. Romanus, 41, 136, 138, 139
Eyck, Jan van, 17

INDEX

Falconieri, Andrea, 697
Farina, Francesco, 660
Farnese, 332, 389
Farnese, Alessandro, *see* Alessandro
Farnese, Cardinal, 195, 280, 857
Farnese, Ottavio *and* Pier Luigi, *see* Ottavio *and* Pier Luigi
Fatucci, G. Fr., 159
Faveretto, Paolo, 472
Federico d'Aragona, 35
Federico Gonzaga, *see* Gonzaga
Federico da Montefeltre, 213
Federico of Naples, 38
Felis, Stefano, 689, 829
Feltre, Vittorino da, 5
Fenaruolo, Girolamo, 321, 322
Ferabosco, Domenico, 189, 261, 307f., 644f. *See also* Ferrabosco
Ferdinand, King of Aragon, 8, 35
Ferdinand, Archduke (later Emperor), 782, 859
Ferdinando Carlo II of Mantua, 819
Ferdinando I de'Medici, *see* Medici
Ferentilli, Agostino, 548
Ferminot, 143, 147, 150, 348
Fernando of Spain, 36f.
Ferrabosco (Ferabosco), Domenico Maria, 308, 448, 466, 753
Ferrabosco, Alfonso, 474
Ferrari, Christofano, 586
Ferraria, de, *see* Paulus
Ferretti, Giovanni, 538, 548, 593f., 598, 601, 602, 604, 692, 717, 776, 779
Ferro, Giovanni, 593
Ferro, S. B. de, 41, 109
Festa, Costanzo, 116, 121, 125, 135, 136, 138, 141, 143, 144, 150, 151, 153f., 156, 157ff., 162, 166, 171, 172, 173, 181, 192, 246, 247, 248, 254, 257ff., 262, 264, 268, 269, 275, 277, 288, 297, 298, 305, 306, 307, 311, 314, 324, 325, 329, 339, 358, 360, 365, 374, 375, 384, 399, 432, 447, 483, 553, 822, 840
Festa, Sebastiano, 103f., 125, 135, 136, 138, 139, 141, 142, 143, 246, 259, 329
Fevin, Antoine de, 140
Fiamengo, Giovanni, 445
Fiamma, Carlo, 721
Fiamma, Gabriele, 200, 238, 491, 494, 495
Fiesco, Giulio, 509, 554f., 825
Fiorillo, Silvio, 527
Firmin le Bel, 348
Fogliano, Giacomo, 41, 81, 279, 297ff., 306, 841

Fogliano, Lodovico, 41, 83, 297, 342, 402, 488
Folengo, Teofilo, 158, 458f., 527f.
Fondaco, Battista dal, 197
Fonghetti, Paolo, 548
Fontana, Vincenzo, 353, 368, 369, 449, 496
Fontanelli, Count Alfonso, 703f.
Forkel, Johann Nikolaus, 116
Fornaci, Giacomo, 542
Fornari, Cristoforo, 479
Forsempruno, *see* Giovanni Battista da F.
Fortini, Pietro, 548
Foscari, Francesco, 6
Foscari family, 344
Fossis, P. de, 9, 320
Franc, Guillaume, 340
Francesca, Piero della, 416
Francesco, Frate (Franciscus F.), 40, 109
Francesco Gonzaga, *see* Gonzaga
Francesco Maria de'Medici, *see* Medici
Francesco da Milano, 114
Francesco II di Nuvolara, 512, 513
Francesco Maria delle Rovere, 293, 447, 535
Franchi, Ferrante, 586
France, Anatole, 688
Francis of Assisi, Saint, 5, 12, 23
Francis I of France, 140, 143, 264, 391, 393, 479, 744
Franco, Veronica, 201
Frangipane, Cornelio, 549
Fregoso, Ottaviano, 546
Frescobaldi, Girolamo, 334
Friedrich, Emperor, 53
Frigera (Frizera), Polissena, 175, 447
Frixa, R. de, 8
Fugger, Johann, 498, 774, 781
Fugger, Johann Jacob, 576, 774, 781
Fugger, Wolfgang, 388
Fugger family, 482, 522, 772
Furlano, *see* Leonardo
Fux, J. J., 416

Gabella, G. B., 542
Gabrieli, Andrea, 5, 29, 173, 208, 238, 239, 240, 243, 323, 324, 370, 373, 374, 390, 400, 422, 453, 454, 488, 502, 511, 518, 520ff., 542, 543, 550, 567, 576, 593, 607, 615, 617, 626, 631, 638, 639, 643, 644, 653, 660, 671, 721, 725, 732, 763, 773, 774, 784, 793, 796, 798, 850

Gabrieli, Giovanni, 5, 29, 238, 239, 400, 520f., 522, 523, 525, 550, 553, 597, 615, 619, 624, 639, 782, 797, 798, 799, 858, 867
Gabucci, Giulio Cesare, 542
Gafori (Gaffurius, Gaffori), Franchino, 8, 11ff., 425, 456
Gagliano, Marco da, 213, 671, 691, 706, 729ff., 766, 834, 845, 849
Galfridus de Anglia, 7
Galilei, Galileo, 731
Galilei, Vincenzo, 166, 204, 230, 233, 234, 235, 236, 241, 242, 243, 308, 404, 423, 424, 463, 695, 731f., 734
Gallus, Johannes, 307
Gambara, Veronica, 200, 467, 628, 687
Ganassi, Silvestro, 297, 322, 841f.
Gandago, G. de, 8, 41
Gardano (Gardane), Alessandro, 653
Gardano (Gardane), Angelo, 320, 403, 422, 510, 750f., 751
Gardano (Gardane), Antonio, 121, 158, 159, 163f., 165, 166, 206, 247, 248, 254, 256, 258, 259, 261, 262, 264, 281, 298, 306, 313, 325, 330, 353, 380, 384, 385, 390, 399, 400, 402, 425, 430, 431, 433, 435, 436, 480, 590, 743, 744, 748
Garzoni, Tommaso, 776
Gascogne, 135
Gastoldi, G. G., 269, 514, 594, 602ff., 606, 607, 645, 667, 782, 786, 817
Gattola, Annibale, 667
Gazza, 50
Genet, E., *see* Carpentras
Gent, Joos van, 213
George Frederic of Ansbach, 772
Gerbert, Martin, 118
Germi, 34
Gero, Jhan (Jehan), 158, 159, 258, 259, 262ff., 264, 307, 400, 447, 560
Gesualdo, Carlo, Principe di Venosa, 28, 42, 199, 210, 234, 512, 519, 542, 553, 576, 607, 608, 624, 674, 688ff., 721, 727, 738, 740, 761, 782, 791, 799, 808, 845, 850, 868
Gesualdo, Ettore, 706
Gesualdo, Fabrizio di, 688f., 697, 698
Gesualdo, G. A., 452
Gesualdo, Isabella di Venosa, 690
Gesualdo, Luigi, 689
Gherardesca, Camillo della, 739

Ghevara, Don Geronimo de, 498
Ghiselin, Jean, 56
Giachetto, da Mantua, *see* Colle-
baudi
Giacomini, Bernardo, 483, 500
Giamberti, Alessandro, 744
Giamberti, Francesco, 18
Giambullari, P. F., 156
Gianiccho, 197
Gianotti, Donato, 272
Gibbons, Orlando, 269
Gilbert, 343
Ginori, Alessandro, 741
Ginori, Gino, 732
Giolito, Gabriel, 173, 181, 444
Giordan, Fra, 147
Giorgione, 45, 49f., 57, 155, 318,
448, 549
Giotto, 40
Giovanelli, Ruggiero, 205, 592,
613f., 653, 855
Giovanna d'Austria, 284
Giovanni de'Medici, *see* Leo X
Giovanni delle (dalle) Bande nere,
see Medici
Giovanni de'Medici, *see* Medici
Giovanni Battista da Forsempruno,
171
Giovanni Pietro de'Medici, *see*
Medici
Giovio, Bishop, 194
Girolamo Sanese, 92
Giudeo, Giammaria, 114
Giulia Gonzaga, *see* Gonzaga
Giuliano de'Medici, *see* Medici
Giunta, Giacopo, 139, 141, 165, 554
Giunti, Filippo (il Giovane), 354,
598, 609
Giusti, Vincenzio, 844
Giustiniani, Leonardo, 5, 7, 83, 87f.,
189
Giustiniano, Orsatto, 549
Gluck, Christoph Willibald, 4, 200,
475, 570
Goes, H. van der, 17
Goethe, J. W., 65, 168, 170, 183,
343, 589, 715, 812
Goldoni, Carlo, 816
Gombert, Nicolas, 22, 140, 141, 226,
256, 322, 479, 481
Gonzaga, Alfonso, 208
Gonzaga, Cardinal, 861
Gonzaga, Cesare, 52, 99, 111
Gonzaga, Eleonora, 308
Gonzaga, Federico (Marchese), 35,
53, 344
Gonzaga, Federico (Duke), 39, 11,
120
Gonzaga, Ferdinando (Duke), 730,
741

Gonzaga, Ferrante (1507-1557),
195, 366, 478f.
Gonzaga, Ferrante (1550-1605),
611, 680
Gonzaga, Francesco (Marchese), 34,
38f., 51f., 110, 478
Gonzaga, Giulia, 42
Gonzaga, Guglielmo (Duke), 199,
211, 240, 512, 513, 518, 602, 609,
638, 662, 704, 721, 751, 755, 756,
762, 854
Gonzaga, Ippolita, 479
Gonzaga, Ippolito, 463
Gonzaga, Margaret, 53
Gonzaga, Margherita (Este), 513,
573, 627, 670, 826, 827
Gonzaga, Scipione, 472, 611, 646,
697
Gonzaga, Vespasiano, 834
Gonzaga, Vincenzo (Duke), 240,
513, 514, 540, 569, 573, 602, 611,
662, 683, 688, 721, 723, 774, 825,
850, 851, 854
Gonzaga family, 221, 233, 393, 512,
515, 602, 667, 729, 762, 845, 846
Gorla, G. B. de', 425
Goselini, Giuliano, 681
Gosswin, Antonio, 597
Gostena, G. B. della, 499
Gottifredi, B., 194, 650
Goudimel, Claude, 340
Gozzoli, Benozzo, 75
Grabbe, Johann, 240, 867
Gradenigo, Giovanni, 460
Gradenigo, Paolo, 577
Granacci, F., 33
Grandi, Alessandro, 867
Granvella, Cardinal, 598
Grassi, Giuseppe, 598
Grazzini, A. Fr. (Il Lasca), 33, 823
Greban, A., 30
Greco, el, 511, 694, 697, 703, 708
Gregor XIII, Pope, 312, 463, 637
Gregor XV, Pope, 690
Grevenbruch, G., 802
Grillo, Angelo, 602, 613, 681, 683,
688, 708, 845
Grimani, Marino, 550
Gritti, Andrea, 320, 325
Grossi, Carlo, 766, 768, 819
Grullone, 196
Gualtieri, Attilio, 586
Gualtieri, R., 96, 517
Guami, Gioseffo, 597, 802
Guargante, Oratio, 389, 422
Guarini, Anna, 539f.
Guarini, G. B., 177, 185, 209ff., 482,
509, 511, 518, 519, 522, 539ff.,
547, 548, 555, 556, 557, 602f.,
610, 612, 613, 617, 627, 642, 646,
652, 660, 663, 668, 669, 670, 676,

680, 681, 684, 688, 691, 709, 719,
720, 721, 724, 725, 726, 728, 730,
734, 735, 736, 755, 764, 775, 777,
800, 801, 808, 817, 818, 830, 832,
833, 834, 838, 845, 851, 853, 854,
859, 861, 864, 868
Guarnier, 8, 89
Guasca, Isabetta, 197
Guédron, Pierre, 864
Guerra, D. and G. B., 50
Guglielmo Gonzaga, *see* Gonzaga
Guicciardini, L., 22
Guidi, Benedetto, 637
Guidiccioni, Giovanni, 269, 275,
472, 509, 515, 598, 764, 775
Guidiccioni, Lelio, 698
Guidobuoni, G., 602
Guidubaldo, Duke of Urbino, 56,
293, 308
Guinati, 10
Guise, Cardinal de, 610
Guise, Henri de, 629
Guise, Louis de, 628
Guise-Lorraine, François de, 628
Gusnasco, L., 39, 52

Habsburg, House of, 774
Handel, G. Fr., 45, 275, 864
Hasler (Hassler), H. L., 116, 340,
592, 604, 607
Hawkins, John, 116, 404, 653
Haydn, Joseph, 153, 167, 168, 244,
275, 459, 743, 797, 818, 820, 831,
853
Heine, Heinrich, 200, 340
Hellingk, Lupus, 435
Henry III of France, 195, 453, 549,
550, 629
Herber, Heinrich, 439
Heremita (Eremita), Giulio, 542
Héritier, *see* L'Héritier
Hesdimois (Hedimontius), J., 40,
109
Heyse, Paul, 90
Hobrecht, *see* Obrecht
Homer, 168
Horace, 51, 92, 95, 168, 307, 350,
386, 411, 421, 474, 653, 697, 743,
781, 785, 797
Hoste (L'Hoste), 196f., 285f., 479,
847
Hostia, Frate Pietro da (de), 141,
143, 146, 147, 148, 150, 196, 346
Hothby, John, 7, 8
Hucher, Antonio, 165, 298

Ihan, *see* Maistre Ihan
India, Sigismondo d', 563, 717
Ingegneri, M. A., 234, 388f., 573,
615f., 617, 620, 625f., 698, 699,
717f., 720, 721, 784

Innocent VIII, Pope, 7
Ippolita Gonzaga, *see* Gonzaga
Ippolita de'Medici, *see* Medici
Ippolito d'Este, 42
Ippolito d'Este II, the Younger, 345, 366, 385, 411, 413, 472, 610
Ippolito Gonzaga, *see* Gonzaga
Ippolito de'Medici, *see* Medici
Isaac, *see* Ysaac
Isabel of Valois, 9
Isabella d'Aragona, 89
Isabella di Capua, 366
Isabella d'Este (Gonzaga), 12, 38ff., 42ff., 51, 52, 53f., 93f., 97, 104, 105, 108, 109, 110, 111, 174, 191, 308, 330, 344, 366, 478, 479, 548
Isabella of Spain, 36f.

Jachet da Mantua, *see* Collebaudi
Jachet (Jaquet), 143, 147, 248, 289, 325
Jacopo, 197
Jacopo da Bologna, 13
Jacotin, 10
Jacotin, *see* Arcadelt, 266
Janequin, Clement, 140, 143, 162, 233, 382, 744, 765, 766, 767, 791
Japart, J., 40, 56
Jardin, Du, 96
João IV, 554
Johannes de Florentia, 53
John XXII, Pope, 18
Jordan, Fra, 143
Josquin, *see* Prés
Juan d'Austria, Don, 523
Julius II, Pope, 39, 56f.
Junta, Jacopo, *see* Giunta

Kiesewetter, R. G., 193, 404, 605, 643, 691, 709, 847
Kisl, Johann Jacob *and* Karl, 757

Lafage, P. de, 135
Lago, Giovanni del, 48
Lambardi, Camillo, 308
Lambardi, Francesco, 697
Lambertini, G. T., 493
Lambertino, Alessandro, 446
Landi, Ottavio, 197
Landini (Landino), Francesco, 6, 12, 14ff., 17, 75, 90, 214, 278, 327, 583
Lando, Ortensio, 156
Lando, Stefano, 583
Lang, Matthew, Bishop of Gurk, 277
Lannoy, Colinet de, 7
Lantins, Hugo de, 6, 16
Lapicida, Erasmo, *see* Rasmo
Lappacino (Lupaccino), 40
Lasca, Il, *see* Grazzini

Lasso (Lassus), Orlando, 20, 21, 29, 100, 208, 228, 232, 238, 283, 292f., 314, 353, 366, 369, 370, 373, 381, 411, 414, 415, 416, 422, 424, 432, 440, 449, 477ff., 498, 500, 501, 502, 503, 509, 511, 512, 514, 522, 533, 534, 536, 551, 560, 577, 612, 613, 618, 620, 624, 633, 665, 671, 680, 684, 718, 726, 756, 772, 774, 775, 825, 828, 832, 854
Launay, Carlo di, 43, 53f.
Lauro (Alauro, de Lauro), G. a, 41, 109, 149
Laurus, 247, 262
Laurus, Patavus, 139, 147
Layolle, Alamanno, 281
Layolle, Francesco, 192, 279, 280f., 288, 301, 306, 399
Lazzarini, Benedetto de', 593
Le Bel, *see* Firmin
Lebrung, Jo., 139
Legrenzi, Giovanni, 626
Leo X, Pope (Medici), 7, 19, 34, 94, 107, 109, 126, 140, 156, 157, 191, 228, 277, 282, 319, 320
Leonardo detto il Furlano, 174
Leonico, Foscho, 472
Leonora d'Este, 472, 554, 825
Leonora de'Medici, *see* Medici
Leonora (Eleonora) di Toledo (Medici), 278, 283, 288, 291, 840
Leoni, G. B., 860
Leopardi, Giacomo, 67
Le Roy, 141, 268, 838. *See also* Ballard
Lesueur, J. Fr., 718
Leyva, Antonio de, 425
L'Héritier, Jean, 139, 140
L'Hoste, *see* Hoste
Limburgia, Joannes de, 6
Lisa, G. de, *see* Gandago
Liszt, Franz, 617
Liuto, Cavaliere del, 612
Lodi, Pietro da, 109
Lodovico da Milano, 41
Lodovico il Moro, 11ff., 28, 38, 56, 277
Lodovicus da Siena, 41
Lollio, Alberto, 301
Lomazzo, Filippo, 602, 806
Lombardo family, 296, 297
Londarit, Francesco, 446
Lorena, Jachetto di, 35
Lorenzino de'Medici, *see* Medici
Lorenzo, Duke of Urbino, 180
Lorenzo da Firenze, 189
Lorenzo de'Medici, *see* Medici
Lotti, Antonio, 872
Lotto, Lorenzo, 155
Louis XII of France, 56, 126, 391
Loyola, Ignazio da, 553

Lucan, 10
Lucian, 44
Luciani, Sebastiano, *see* Piombo, del
Lucrezia d'Este (della Rovere), 513, 535f., 554, 610
Ludbicus de Arimino, 6
Ludovisi, Nicolo, 690
Luigi (Alvise) d'Este, 472
Luigi d'Este (Cardinal), 610, 628, 638, 660, 825
Lulinus, J., 41, 97, 123, 434
Lulli (Lully), G. B., 606
Lunadoro, Scipione, 612
Lupacchino, B., 171, 188, 208, 455
Lupato, 320
Lupi, 22
Luppatus, G., 41
Luprano (Lurano), F. de, 40, 64, 65, 66, 78, 82, 93
Lusitano, Vincenzio, 413
Luther, Martin, 3, 23, 24
Luzzaschi, Luzzasco, 203, 220, 502, 515, 539, 540, 542, 610, 616, 663, 698ff., 710, 723, 740, 755, 769, 774, 825, 827, 829, 831, 834ff., 845f.

Macchiavelli, Niccolo, 66, 157, 250
Macchiavelli, Paolo, 539, 826
Machaut, G. de, 13, 53
Machgielz, Jean, 218
Macque, Giovanni de, 20, 474, 653, 689, 692, 695, 697f., 827, 855
Madruzz, Christoforo, Cardinal, 385, 609
Madruzz, Lodovico, Cardinal, 609
Maffei, G. C., 842
Magiello, D., 217
Magno, Celio, 549, 550
Maio, G. T. de, 41, 124, 353, 354, 355, 360, 361, 363, 364, 366, 367, 368, 382, 598, 599, 623
Maione, Ascanio, 697
Maistre Ihan, 20, 158, 173, 177, 183, 192, 226, 244, 254, 257, 301, 306ff., 744, 821, 825
Maistre, Mattheus le, 744
Malaspina, 731
Malatesta, Cleophe, 6
Malatesta family, 16
Malvezzi, Cristofano, 542, 729, 730, 845, 847
Malvicino, Annibale, 198
Manelli, Francesco, 698
Manenti, G. P., 189, 645, 730, 732
Mantegna, Andrea, 516
Marasechi, Giovanna de, 52
Maravila, J. de, 8
Marcellini, Valerio, 641
Marcello, Benedetto, 496, 819, 872
Marchetto da Mantova, *see* Cara

Marchettus of Padua, 13
Marcolini, Francesco, 114f., 154, 221, 324, 325
Marenzio, Luca, 29, 116, 190, 204, 205, 221, 237f., 239, 240, 241, 242, 243, 244, 264, 270, 275, 295, 375, 377f., 389, 415, 432, 470, 474, 491, 501, 502, 506, 511, 519, 534, 542, 553, 554, 560, 561, 562, 569, 574, 576, 585ff., 603, 608ff., 688, 689, 692, 694, 695, 696, 697, 698, 699, 707, 710, 721, 722, 723, 725, 726, 733, 734, 754, 763, 779, 796, 799, 806, 808, 824, 827, 845, 850, 851, 852, 854, 855, 856, 863, 866
Marescotti, C. & G., 165, 730
Margaret of Austria, 158
Margaret Gonzaga, *see* Gonzaga
Margareta of Parma, 386, 387
Margato, Andrea, 433
Margherita d'Este (Gonzaga), *see* Gonzaga
Maria of Portugal, 491f., 501
Maria Anna, Archduchess, 768
Maria Theresia, Archduchess, 768
Marini, Biagio, 103
Marini (Marino), Giambattista, 310, 312, 646, 736, 739, 776, 798, 860, 861, 862, 863, 864, 868
Marino, Alessandro, 473, 548
Marra, Don Ferrante della, 690
Marsi, Antonio, 100
Marsili, Luigi, 15
Martello, G. B., 382
Martial, 270
Martin, Thomas, 135
Martinelli, Caterina, 861
Martinengo, Ascanio, 473
Martinengo, Gabriele, 192
Martini, Giovanni, 10, 56
Martini, Padre G. B., 8, 116, 235, 244, 540, 623, 653, 659, 684, 709, 864, 872
Martoretta (La Martoretta), Giandomenico, 193, 208, 527, 625f., (*also* Il Martoretta)
Masaconi, G. P., 840
Maschera, Florenzio, 641
Masino, 39
Massaino, Tiburtio, 453, 512, 548, 773
Massenus (Maessens), P., 235
Matarazzo, Francesco, 27
Matthias (Fiamingo?), 306
Matthias (Mathias), Fiamingo, *see* Werrecore
Mauro, Mattia, 197, 730
Maximilian I, Emperor, 20, 57, 69

Maximilian II, Emperor, 218, 473, 500, 512, 563, 600
Mazza, Lotto di, 763
Mazzaferrata, G. B., 540
Mazzocchi, Domenico, 204, 514, 838, 867ff.
Mazzone, M. A., 223, 583f.
Mazzuoli, Giovanni, 78f., 221
Medici, Alessandro de', 158, 161
Medici, Alessandro de' (Bishop of Pistoia), 463
Medici, Catherina de', 180
Medici, Clarice, 180
Medici, Cosimo de' (the Elder), 6, 10
Medici, Cosimo de' (Duke, later Grand Duke), 78, 100, 129, 135, 156, 194, 197, 262, 276f., 278, 283, 288, 291, 479, 499, 761, 797, 840
Medici, Cosimo II (Grand Duke), 866
Medici, Ferdinando de', I (Grand Duke), 502, 540, 611, 666, 730, 797, 847
Medici, Francesco Maria de' (Grand Duke), 234, 284, 293, 645, 730, 763, 773, 846
Medici, Giovanni de' (son of Cosimo Pater Patriae), 6, 10
Medici, Giovanni de', *see* Leo X
Medici, Giovanni delle (dalle) Bande nere, 78
Medici, Giovanni Pietro de', 844
Medici, Giuliano de', 19
Medici, Ippolito, 42
Medici, Isabella (Orsini), 499f., 502, 506, 508, 611, 645
Medici, Leonora, 763
Medici, Lorenzo de' (il Magnifico), 5, 6, 11, 17, 18ff., 24, 31f., 105, 125, 130, 189, 276, 277, 278, 279, 343, 503
Medici, Lorenzino de', 161
Medici, Piero de', 19, 53f.
Medici, Virginia de', 763, 846
Medici family, 193f., 233, 246, 279, 280, 282, 283, 393, 429, 479, 611, 645, 646, 667, 729, 736, 762, 764, 845, 846
Megnier, I., 20
Meldert, Leonardo, 542
Melozzo da Forlì, 213
Memo family, 296, 297
Menchini, Girolamo, 141
Merkerich (Mercerich), Leonardo, 757
Merlin Coccai, *see* Folengo
Mermann, Dr. Thomas, 491, 495

Merulo, Claudio, 166, 204, 247, 259, 326, 327, 354, 422, 445, 446, 453, 522, 525, 528, 529, 546, 549, 550, 566, 609, 639, 695, 753, 773
Messia, Antonio, 848
Messibugo (Messisburgo), Cristoforo, 344, 444
Metastasio, Pietro, 4, 575, 736, 806
Michelangelo, 17, 21, 47, 113, 159, 161ff., 173, 214, 272, 393, 424, 480, 496, 551, 608, 715, 718, 839
Michele, *see* Novarese
Michele, Prete, 31
Micheli, Domenico, 191, 203, 525
Micheli, Parrasio, 447
Migliorotti, Atalante, 11, 42
Milan, Don Luys, 841
Milano, Francesco da, 154
Millet, François, 277
Milleville, Alessandro, 542
Milton, John, 45
Mira, Leandro, 502
Mocenigo, Luigi, 550
Mocenigo, Tommaso, 6
Moderne, Jacques, 135, 165, 264, 279, 281, 288
Molfetta, Princess of, 366
Molinaro, Simone, 695
Molinet, J., 30
Molino, Antonio, 323, 425, 453, 454, 502, 527ff.
Molino, Girolamo, 48
Molu, Pierre, 135, 149
Molza, Francesco Maria, 200, 393, 626, 650, 827
Molza, Tarquinia, 512f., 539, 540, 648, 671, 675, 699, 723, 728, 825ff., 844f.
Monferrato, Guglielmo del, 12
Montagna, Bart., 112, 472
Montaigne, Michel de, 95, 848
Montalto, Cardinal, 612
Montanari, G. B., 202
Montanus (Berg), Johannes, 226
Monte, Cola Nardo di, 598
Monte, Cristoforo de, 6
Monte, Filippo di, 20, 189, 218, 415, 422, 459, 477, 478, 482, 498ff., 511, 512, 534, 542, 612, 620, 630, 631, 633, 639, 655, 661, 685, 695, 697, 698, 718, 726, 727, 737, 753, 763, 775, 823, 824, 829, 854, 865
Montecucoli, Alvise, 775
Montella, Giovanni Domenico, 692, 697
Monteverdi, Claudio, 81, 93, 99, 199, 204, 209, 210, 213, 221, 224, 234, 237, 264, 270, 288, 400, 408, 410, 411, 490, 493, 502, 512, 514,

516, 519, 542, 553, 554, 563, 569, 575, 583, 599, 602, 608, 615, 627, 645, 647, 652, 670, 671, 678, 679, 691, 704, 706, 707, 717ff., 734, 762, 763, 764, 766, 799, 813, 830ff., 833, 834, 835, 845, 846, 847, 848, 849, 850ff., 855, 856, 859, 860, 861f., 866, 867

Monteverdi, Giulio Cesare, 223f., 410, 850
Montfort, Counts, 757
Montorio, Pier, 612
Montorsoli, G. A., 718
Morales, Cristobal, 226, 258, 399
Morari, Antonio, 597
More, Thomas, 224f.
Morley, Thomas, 604, 607
Morosini family, 799
Morto da Feltre, 155
Morton, 30
Moscaglia, G. B., 474, 653, 697, 855
Moscheni, Francesco & Simone, 57, 165, 425, 744
Moschini, Baccio, 197, 840
Mosto, Francesco, 598
Mosto, G. B., 203, 609
Mouton, Jean, 21f., 22, 135, 140, 149, 319, 325
Mozart, Leopold, 766
Mozart, W. A., 153, 167, 168, 205, 244, 275, 280, 478, 525, 617, 646, 743, 791, 820, 853
Mudarra, Alonso de, 99
Muelich, Hans, 386
Mula, Lorenzo da, 475
Muratori, Lodovico, 18
Muris, Jean de, 13

Nadal, 409, 448
Naich, Hubert, 157, 180, 306, 314f., 424, 429f., 481
Naldi, Paolo, 192, 458
Naldi, Romolo, 855
Nanino, G. B., 855, 868
Nanino, G. M., 240, 422, 474, 612, 653, 697, 855
Nantermi, M. A., 859
Napoleon, 318
Nardi, Jacopo, 24
Nardo, Ben. Serafico di, 567
Nasca, Giacoma C., 193
Nasco, Giovanni, 20, 182, 192ff., 239, 307, 310, 381, 390, 424, 432, 455ff., 462, 463, 464f., 466, 469, 470, 471, 473, 503, 576, 627, 749, 767, 800, 838
Navagero, Andrea, 452, 467
Negro Groppalo, Ag. di, 462
Negrona, Paretta, 467

Nenna, Pomponio, 689, 692, 694
Neri, San Filippo, 289, 291
Neri family, 291
Nero (Neri), Nicolo del, 289
Nicholas V, Pope, 7
Nicolao (Nicolo) da Perugia, 189, 613
Nicoletti, Filippo, 542, 548, 549
Nicolo de Raphael, 166
Nicolo Senese, 352
Nicolo Tedesco, 34
Nola, Giovan Domenico del Giovane da, 178, 259, 338, 353ff., 366ff., 370, 372, 373, 374, 377, 378, 381, 382, 383, 422, 443, 449, 479, 497, 527, 582ff., 584, 591, 598, 599, 600, 689, 697, 855
Nollet, 207, 257, 306
Novarese, Michele, 196f., 432, 462, 770
Novello, Lodovico, 345f., 348

Obrecht, Jacob, 8, 18, 22, 56, 155f., 226, 825
Obregón, Cristobal, 697
Occagna, Gottardo, 385
Ockeghem, Johannes, 5, 18, 21, 22, 30, 54, 85
Oefele, A. F., 53
Olimpo, Baldassarre da Sassoferrato, 60f., 63, 179, 356, 361
Ongaro, Antonio, 613, 670, 688
Onofrio Padoano, 41, 84
Ordei, Ascanio, 801
Organi, Alessandro dagli, 318
Origen, 783
Orio, Girolamo, 529
Orlandi, Santi, 669, 845
Orsi, Aurelio, 637
Orsini, Flavio, 500
Orsini, Leone, 163
Orsini, Paolo Giordano, 499f., 506, 645
Orsini, Virginio, 611, 667
Orsini family, 499, 500, 619
Orsino, Cesare, 860
Ortiz, Diego, 842
Orto, Mambriano de, 96f.
Ostiano, Vincenzo, 219
Ottavio Farnese, 387, 388, 515
Ovid, 28, 93, 444, 763

Pace, Pietro, 860f.
Pacelli, Asprilio, 855
Padovano, Annibale, 390, 422, 446
Palagio, G. T. del, 15
Palestrina, Pier Luigi da, 20, 29, 110, 188, 189, 202, 212, 235, 236, 237, 238, 240, 241, 257,

275, 289, 308, 310, 311ff., 348, 390, 402, 422, 424, 429, 432, 435f., 437, 452, 472, 478, 479, 488, 489, 498, 500, 506, 514, 545, 559, 590, 591, 592, 593, 610, 611, 612, 622, 623, 624, 633, 639, 643, 658, 659, 670, 694, 726, 755, 775, 780, 804, 842, 854, 855
Palladio, Andrea, 523, 549, 795
Pallavicino, Benedetto, 213, 542, 573, 602, 615, 726, 833f., 852f.
Pallavicino, Nicolo, 641
Pallazzo, P. J., 198
Pandola, Tiberio, 186
Panico, Gherardo da, 351
Paoli, P. F., 868
Papin da Mantua, 109
Parabosco, Girolamo, 181, 182, 184, 185, 197, 276, 279, 286, 324, 390, 438, 444f., 448, 460, 532, 541, 622, 719
Parabosco, Vincenzo, 445
Parixe, Don M. da, 8
Paruta, Domenico, 535
Pasoti, J. J., 141
Pasquali, Scipione, 612
Passereau, 140
Passetto, Giordano, 750
Patavus, see Laurus
Patricio, 612
Paul III, Pope, 110, 161, 389, 823
Paulus de Ferraria, 325
Paumann, Conrad, 53, 55
Pauson, 112
Pavesi, Cesare, 644
Payen, 226
Pazzi family, 277
Peacham, Henry, 685
Pearson, Martin, 228
Pecorina (Peccorina), Polissena, 164, 175, 198f., 320, 325, 327, 467, 843
Pedro, Don, di Toledo, 840
Pensabene, Z., 460
Peperara, Laura, 477, 648, 671, 675, 699, 723, 728, 769, 825ff., 844f.
Perabovi, F. M., 542
Pergolesi, G. B., 617
Peri, Jacopo, 704, 729, 733, 742, 766, 834, 843
Perino da Firenze, 479
Perissone, see Cambio
Perissone, Francesco Bonardi, 471
Perleone, Pier, 83
Perretti, Flavia (Orsini), 611, 667
Pesarese, Dominico, 412
Pesaro, Francesco, 529
Pescara, Marchese di, 404

Pescara, Marchese di (Governor of Naples), 516
Pescia, Fra Domenico da, 24f.
Pesenti, Martino, 705
Pesenti, Michele, 40, 55, 61f., 64, 65, 66, 75, 92, 108, 121, 123, 158, 170, 246, 259
Petrarch (Petrarca), Francesco, 5, 12, 13, 14, 24, 49, 60, 65f., 69, 100, 103, 104ff., 107, 108, 109, 110, 111, 116, 117, 125, 126, 128, 129, 131, 132, 134, 135, 139, 141, 143, 170, 171, 172, 173, 174, 181, 182, 185, 190, 191, 197, 200, 201, 202, 205, 212, 230f., 240, 249, 250, 258, 261, 262, 263, 264, 266, 272, 274, 275, 281, 287, 288, 289, 290, 291, 293, 294, 295, 296, 299, 300, 302, 308, 313, 317, 325, 326, 333, 334, 337, 355, 376, 377, 385, 393, 394, 396, 398, 399, 401, 402, 403, 405, 409, 410, 415, 418, 421, 426, 427, 430, 431, 432, 434, 436, 438, 439, 440, 441, 444, 447, 452, 453, 454, 455, 456, 458, 460, 467, 469, 482, 483, 484, 485, 486, 488, 489, 490, 492, 494, 495, 496, 500, 503, 506, 509, 511, 515, 516, 518, 521, 522, 531, 534, 535, 536, 540, 555, 557, 558, 560, 571, 573, 582, 584, 597, 598, 612, 613, 616, 619, 623, 624, 625, 627, 629, 633, 637, 642, 643, 645, 653, 654, 655, 656, 658, 663, 664, 665, 671, 684, 685, 686, 687, 691, 698, 699, 719, 721, 730, 731, 735, 736, 739, 741, 750, 755, 757, 764, 769, 775, 778, 784, 785, 792, 798, 848, 862, 864, 865
Petreius, Johann, 262, 744
Petrozzi, Fabio, 593
Petrucci, Ottaviano de', 12, 22, 40, 41, 42, 46, 50, 54, 55ff., 60, 61, 62, 64, 65, 77, 78, 80, 83, 85, 90, 91, 97, 98, 100f., 105, 106, 107, 108, 109, 110, 112, 113, 114, 120, 121, 122, 124, 125, 126, 128, 129, 130, 135, 139, 141, 147, 155, 165, 166, 169, 170, 171, 214, 216, 246, 297, 299, 341, 343, 346, 349, 381, 382, 400, 416, 425, 481, 554, 558, 749, 768, 839f.
Petrus Organista, 399
Phalèse, Pierre, 500, 799
Philip the Good, 7
Philip II of Spain, 480, 498
Philippus Mantuanus, 109
Phillips, Peter, 634
Phinot, Domenique, 257, 265, 311
Pia, Emilia, 546
Piccolomini, Alessandro, 214f.

Pic., Nicolo, Prete Senese, 41
Pier Luigi Farnese, 389
Piero da Lodi, 41
Piero di Cosimo, 18, 34
Piero de'Medici, *see* Medici
Pierobono, 6, 8
Pietrasanta, Plinio, 247, 249, 326
Pifaro, Nicolo, 41, 108, 342, 748
Piffero, Bernardino, 42f., 47
Piffero, Michele, 43
Pigna, G. B., 826
Pii, Leonora, 780
Pinelli, Cosimo, 498
Pinelli, G. B., 548
Pinelli, G. V., 498
Pintello, 32
Pinturicchio, B., 55
Piombo, Sebastiano del, 48(?), 154f., 156, 159
Pisani, Marquis of, 660. *See also* Vivonne
Pisano, Arnolfo, 129
Pisano, Bernardo, 31, 41, 60, 107, 115, 128ff., 132, 133, 134, 135, 139, 141, 143, 171, 172, 200, 201, 246, 256, 259, 279, 288f., 293, 324, 430, 435, 684
Pisano, Taddeo, 114f.
Pistrino, Giulio dal, 446
Pitagora, 322
Plato, 110, 215, 216, 218, 274, 279, 375, 483, 814, 815, 816, 864, 866
Plautus, 46, 160, 444
Plotinus, 217f.
Poccino, Paula, 46
Policreti, Giuseppe, 525
Poliziano, Angelo, 19, 20, 31f., 34f., 108, 297
Polo, Zuan, 344
Polo family, 641
Polybius, 614
Polyclet, 528
Polycrates, 814, 815, 816
Polygnotus, 112
Pontano, Giovanni, 96
Ponte, Giaches de, 110, 262, 438, 547
Pontormo, J. da, 34, 280
Ponzio, Pietro, 389
Porrino, Paolo, 513, 827
Porta, Costanzo, 188, 235, 324, 422, 512, 830
Porta, G. de la, 41, 198
Portinaro, Francesco, 390, 471ff., 757
Pozzo, Vincenzo dal, 542
Pozzobonello, G. St. da, 425
Praetorius, Michael, 615
Prato, Giovanni da, 12, 14f., 30

Prés (Prez), Josquin des, 7, 8, 10, 18, 20, 21, 22, 40, 55, 56, 114, 115, 121, 140, 141, 148, 156, 226, 228, 258, 260, 280, 289, 307, 319, 325, 337, 338, 341, 379, 390, 416, 553, 821, 825
Preti, Girolamo, 103
Prij, M. de, 8
Primartini, G. B. de, 113
Primavera, Gian Leonardo, 377, 576, 577ff., 581, 582, 689, 718
Printz, W. K., 116
Priuli, Gio., 762
Priuli family, 799
Proclus, 217
Propertius, 95
Prudenzani, Simone, 75
Pucci family, 277
Puliti, Gabriello, 404
Pythagoras, 629

Quagliati, Paolo, 690, 724, 855, 856f., 859, 865f.
Querengo, Antonio, 612
Quickelberg, Samuel, 386, 486
Quirini, Vincenzo, 22, 619, 641

Rabelais, François, 158, 162, 380
Raffaele (Raphael), 42, 109, 411, 429, 528, 694
Raimondi, G. B., 612
Ramis, Bartolomeo, 8
Rampazetto, Francesco, 348
Rampollini, M., 135, 288, 289, 840
Rangoni, Baldassarre, 773
Ranieri, 41, 77
Rasi, Francesco, 740
Rasmo, 41, 120, 341
Rathgeber, Valentin, 766, 820
Raval, Sebastiano, 612
Rayner (Ranieri?), 10, 11
Regnart, Jacob, 776
Reicha, Anton, 718
Reichardt, J. Fr., 624
Reinecke, Carl, 624
Rembrandt, 715
Renaldi, Giulio, 203
Renata of Lorraine (Renée), 301, 391f., 610
Renée of Lorraine (Bavaria), 577
Reni, Guido, 694
Resino, Ottavio, 412
Reulx, Ans. de, 372
Riario, Raffaele, 35
Ricchetti, Fabio, 774
Riccio, Luigi del, 161
Riccio, Prete Maria, 384
Riccio, Teodoro, 771
Richafort, Jean, 22, 135
Rigum, A., 41

Rinaldi, Cesare, 213
Rinuccini, Ottavio, 167, 191, 204, 727, 729, 741, 742, 847, 860
Robert, *see* Ballard, 165
Roberto, Don, 8
Robertus de Anglia, 7
Rodio, Rocco, 576, 583, 689
Rodolfo de Alemania, 34
Rogniono, R., 842
Romano, Alessandro, 324
Romano, Battista, 577
Romano, Matteo, 197
Romanus, A., 6
Romeo, Cesare, 463
Ronsard, Pierre de, 501, 644
Rore, Cipriano (de), 20, 21, 103, 179, 200, 208, 221, 224, 226, 227, 232, 238, 264, 267, 270, 284, 301, 306, 307, 314, 316, 324, 329, 330, 331, 333, 335, 374, 377, 384ff., 423, 424, 427, 429, 430, 431, 432, 433, 434, 435, 436, 438, 439, 440, 441, 447, 448, 452, 453, 454, 455, 458, 468, 469, 474, 477, 478, 480, 481, 482, 486, 491, 498, 503, 504, 506, 508, 509, 511, 512, 515, 518, 519, 520, 521, 522, 525, 529, 531, 532, 551, 553, 555, 559, 560, 562, 567, 592, 607, 609, 620, 623, 624, 664, 669, 683, 684, 691, 715, 718, 719, 720, 721, 722, 734, 754, 761, 763, 764, 766, 774, 796, 822, 825, 842, 845, 850, 855, 865
Rore, Lodovico, 388
Rosa, Salvator, 394
Rosini, Francesco, 801
Rosselli, Francesco, 313, 854
Rossello, Antonio, 6
Rosseter, Philip, 234
Rossetti, Biagio, 9
Rossetti, D. G., 635
Rossetti (Rossetto), Stefano, 208, 428, 500, 545, 645, 730
Rossetto, Domenico, 197
Rossetto da Verona, 41
Rossi, Giovanni, 165
Rossi, Luigi, 697, 849, 866, 871
Rossi, Salamone, 866
Rossini, Gioacchino, 791
Rossino of Mantua, 41, 121, 346
Rota, Andrea, 542
Rovere, Giuliano delle, 860
Rovetta, Giovanni, 762, 867
Rovigo, Francesco, 602, 603
Roy, Bartolomeo, 697
Rudolf II, Emperor, 500, 502, 510, 600 (then Archduke), 611
Rue, Pierre de la, 226
Ruffo, Vincenzo, 173, 192, 193, 221, 227, 244, 250, 275, 348, 384, 422,

424, 431, 455, 462ff., 473, 491, 520, 521, 522, 528, 627, 718, 749, 767, 800, 838, 855
Rufilo, Matteo, 479
Rufin, Fra, 135, 136, 141
Ruis, Girolamo, 638
Rutini, G. P., 93
Ruzzante, *see* Beolco

Sabino, Ippolito, 625f., 687
Sacchetti, Franco, 5, 14, 17, 117, 169, 170, 189, 190, 295, 613, 634f., 644
Sadeler, Jan, 501
Sagundino, Nicolo, 83
Saignand, R., 8
Salutati, Coluccio, 15, 214
Sambonetus, 58
Sances, G. F., 542
San Chirico, P. P., 768
Sandrart, Joachim v., 116
Sandrin, 604
Sandrino, 390, 761
Sanese, *see* Girolamo
Sangallo, Francesco, 155
Sannazaro, Jacopo, 37, 38, 99, 113, 204ff., 209, 240, 242, 264, 272, 274, 289, 290, 426, 431, 454, 467, 468, 473, 509, 555, 571, 581, 613f., 616, 626, 627, 637, 642, 645, 653, 654, 663, 664, 665, 666, 676, 698, 721, 730, 735, 777, 808
Sanseverino, Barbara, 518
Sansovino, 321, 528
Sanuto (Sanudo), Leonardo, 667, 762, 800
Sanuto (Sanudo), Marin, 46, 47, 52, 56, 85, 92, 191, 344
Sanuto (Sanudo) family, 296, 297, 669, 799
Sanvitale, Leonora, 518
Saraceni, Francesco, 726
Saraceno, Ambrosio, 261
Saraceno, G. C., 261
Saracini, Giovanni, 535
Sarto, Andrea del, 280
Sasso, Pamfilo, 200, 257, 334, 421
Savignana, Porzia, 460
Savioni, Mario, 698, 849, 871, 872
Savonarola, G., 17, 24ff., 34, 276f.
Scaffen, Enrico, 300
Scanderbeg, 596
Scarlatti, Alessandro, 540, 849
Schikaneder, E., 168
Schneider, K. E., 605
Schönberg, Arnold, 706
Schubert, Franz, 65, 74, 168, 275, 560, 624, 666, 820, 865
Schütz, Heinrich, 671, 867
Schumann, Robert, 168, 249

Scipione Gonzaga, *see* Gonzaga
Scorteccia, Biagio d'Andrea, 279
Scorteccia, Francesco, *see* Corteccia
Scotti, Paolo, 41, 62, 346
Scotto, Amadio, 166
Scotto, Brandino, 166
Scotto, Girolamo, 159, 166, 189, 194, 247, 259, 263, 264, 298, 325, 339, 348, 354, 372, 380, 385, 390, 399, 400, 401, 402, 403, 409, 418, 448, 453, 463, 532, 580, 584, 593, 597, 773, 855
Scotto, Ottaviano (senior), 135, 139, 149, 166
Scotto, Ottaviano (junior), 166
Scozzese, Agostino, 377
Scrivano, Joannes, 109
Sebastiano, Pre, 744. *See also* Bastiano
Sebastiano, 471
Seld, Dr., 5, 498, 501, 502
Selim, Sultan, 596
Sellaio, Jacopo, 468
Seneca, 242, 253, 783
Senfl, Ludwig, 226
Sera, Cosimo del, 741
Seraphin, Francesco, 139
Serbelloni, Count, 612
Serlupi, M. A., 653
Sermisy, Claude de (Claudin), 140, 162, 172, 325
Sforza, Ascanio, 40, 55
Sforza, Costanzo, 213
Sforza, Francesco, 9
Sforza, Francesco II, 425, 744
Sforza, Galeazzo Maria, 9, 85, 87
Sforza, Lodovico, 425
Sforza, Massimiliano, 51
Sforza family, 9f., 42, 88, 228
Shakespeare, William, 4, 87, 178, 200, 205, 747, 781
Shelley, Percy Bysshe, 200, 715
Sigismund, Emperor, 6
Sigismund III, Bathory, 611
Silva, Andrea da, 21f., 135, 248
Silver, Eucharius, 35
Silvestrino, Francesco, 381
Silvestro, Fra, 26
Simphosius, C. F., 386
Sirleto, Guglielmo, Cardinal, 382
Sixtus IV, Pope, 7, 10
Sixtus V, Pope, 618, 629, 637, 667
Smetana, B., 525
Smith, John Stafford, 455
Socrates, 782
Soderini, Piero, 20, 277
Sophocles, 549, 551
Soriano, Francesco, 202, 203, 206, 474, 614, 697, 855
Spaccini, G. B., 775

Spadi, G. B., 842
Spano, Donat'Antonio, 697
Spataro, Giovanni, 11, 54, 145, 319
Spengler, O., 17
Speranza da Genova, 472
Speroni, Sperone, 184, 473
Spilimbergo, Irene di, 50, 843
Spinola, 449
Spira, Fortunio, 489
Spontone, Bartolomeo, 422
Squarcialupi, Antonio, 5, 6, 10, 15, 16, 17, 18, 19, 58, 116, 634
Stabile, Annibale, 653, 855
Stampa, Gaspara, 200, 439, 441, 447, 460
Stampa, Massiminiano, 194
Stefani, Francesco, 197
Steffani, Agostino, 729, 864
Stella, Scipione, 612, 689, 695, 697
Stendhal (Henri Beyle), 688
Steynsel, W. de, 277
Stradino, see Mazzuoli
Straparola, 369, 770
Strauss, Richard, 768
Stravinsky, Igor, 706, 768
Striggio, Alessandro, 190, 199, 220, 232f., 284, 293, 390, 422, 502, 602, 610, 636, 663, 667, 704, 730, 733, 751, 760, 761ff., 769, 772, 774, 782, 819, 846, 847
Striggio, Alessandro, the Younger, 729, 762
Stringari, A., 41, 341
Strozzi, Filippo, 176, 180, 181, 277, 291
Strozzi, G. B., the Elder, 291
Strozzi, G. B., 185, 555, 662, 669, 670, 721, 731, 732
Strozzi, Lorenzo, 291
Strozzi, Pietro, 732, 735
Strozzi family, 161
Sullivan, A. S., 343
Susato, T., 414, 595
Sweelinck, J. P., 5, 240, 614
Sylva, A. de, see Silva

Taglia, Pietro, 390, 414, 424, 425f., 562, 563, 744
Tansillo, Luigi (Lodovico), 432, 477, 496, 511, 518, 545, 548, 582, 585, 596, 615, 616, 670, 673, 674f., 741, 764, 769, 799, 838, 860
Tarasconi, Alessandro, 423
Tasso, Bernardo, 39, 201, 209, 239, 464, 493, 511, 555, 661, 698, 732, 764, 765, 860
Tasso, Torquato, 39, 87, 185, 199, 201, 204, 209ff., 219f., 241, 386, 424, 472, 473, 476, 477, 482, 496, 502, 513, 514, 517, 518, 519, 522,

536, 539, 554, 556, 564, 567, 568ff., 574, 610, 611, 612, 613, 618, 630, 637, 639, 646, 648, 653, 661, 663, 668, 675, 680, 681, 690, 691, 695, 698, 708, 719, 720, 721, 722, 724, 725, 727, 735, 742, 755, 757, 764, 770, 775, 801, 806, 825, 826, 828, 829, 831, 832, 838, 844, 845, 856, 861, 866, 868, 871
Tebaldeo, A., 44, 46, 52, 109
Tedesco, Guglielmo, 423
Tempo, Antonio (da), 117, 118
Tenaglia, A. F., 697
Terence, 160, 444
Terrazza, Stefano, 300
Testagrossa, 114
Theocritus, 654, 808
Tiburtino, Giuliano, 333, 409
Tiepolo (Doge), 456
Timoteo, 41
Tinctoris, J., 8, 11, 18, 22, 60
Tini, Pietro, 599
Tintoretto, Jacopo, 511, 544, 697, 703, 861
Titian, 17, 38, 112, 182, 318, 324, 394, 511, 528, 549, 703
Tolomei, Claudio, 200
Tomitano, Bernardino, 473
Tonto (Macque), Isabella, 697
Torelli, Gasparo, 801f.
Torelli, Giovanni Francesco, 801
Torlion, Raffaelo, 192
Torre, G. B. della, 467
Toscanello, Orazio, 446
Tozzi, P. P., 801
Trabaci, G. M., 225, 692, 697
Trasentino, Vido, 705
Trissino, G. G., 111, 112, 116f., 474
Trivisano, Marco, 320
Trivulzio, Catelano, 195
Troia, G. da, 8
Troiani, Giovanni, 612
Troiano, Girolamo, 663, 667, 668
Troiano, Massimo, 28, 576f., 580f.
Trombetti, Girolamo, 213, 542
Tromboncino, Bartolomeo, 28, 40, 41, 42ff., 52, 53, 54, 55, 61, 64, 65, 66, 67, 69, 70, 72, 77, 80, 81, 88, 90, 91, 92, 93, 94, 95, 96, 99, 103, 104, 105, 107, 108, 109, 110, 113, 114, 120, 121, 122, 123, 128, 134, 135, 139, 141, 142, 143, 144, 154, 202, 206, 274, 285, 297, 325, 341, 346, 349, 351, 353, 358, 370, 374, 376, 402, 606, 683, 839f., 865
Tromboncino, Ippolito, 48
Trombone, Bartolomeo, 47, 197
Trombone, Francesco, 47
Trombone, Lucia, 47

Trombone, Luigi, 47
Trombone, Zaccaria, 47
Tronsarelli, Ottavio, 868
Tudor, Mary, 480, 498
Tudual, 193, 254, 306
Tullia d'Aragona, 175f., 257
Turco, Annibale, 827
Turco, Giovanni del, 704, 729, 735, 738f.
Turco, Lorenzo del, 738

Ubretto, see Obrecht
Ugolino, Baccio, 35
Ugone, Paolo, 195
Urbani, Ambassador, 826
Urbino, servant of Michelangelo, 161
Usque, Salamon, 582
Uttinger, Jheronimo, 385

Vaet, Jacobus, 500
Valderravano, E. de, 463
Valdicozzo, Celio, 472
Valentini, Giovanni, 762
Valenzola, Pietro, 192
Valesio, 612
Valgrisi, 209
Valle, Pietro della, 614, 698
Vandelli, Domenico, 827
Varchi, Benedetto, 113, 733, 801
Varoter, see Castellino
Varotto (Varotti), Michele, 770f.
Vasari, Giorgio, 33, 50, 116, 154, 281
Vasto, see Avalos
Vecchi, Girolamo, 775
Vecchi, Orazio, 28, 116, 138, 166, 177, 182, 237, 242, 269, 275, 373, 389, 425, 453, 526, 542, 592, 596, 599, 605, 636, 639, 667, 692, 704, 717, 742, 760, 761, 767, 769, 770, 772ff., 798, 799, 800, 801, 802, 804, 819, 827, 865
Vecchietti, Giovanni Battista, 612
Vecchietti, Girolamo, 612
Veggio, Claudio, 173, 186, 197, 198, 384, 399, 438, 532f.
Veneziana, Elena, 843
Venier (Veniero), Domenico, 446, 451, 474
Venosa, see Gesualdo
Vento, Ivo de, 225, 597
Ventura, Comin, 681, 844
Venturi, Pompilio, 618f.
Venturi, Stefano, 640, 669, 732, 733
Verardi, Carlo, 35, 37
Verbonnet, Jean, 43
Verdelot, Philippe, 20, 22, 114, 116, 125, 132, 138, 139, 150, 151, 153f., 154ff., 158, 159, 162, 166, 171, 172, 173, 176, 177, 181, 192, 200, 206, 207, 246ff., 257, 258,

259, 260, 262, 264, 268, 269, 275, 277, 278, 285, 288, 296, 297, 298, 305, 306, 307, 308, 311, 317, 324, 325, 326, 327, 328, 339, 348, 358, 374, 384, 396, 401, 408, 426, 432, 433, 447, 469, 478, 481, 483, 517, 532, 558, 643, 650, 754, 822, 823, 840

Verdi, Giuseppe, 168

Vergelli, Paolo, 197, 385, 528

Vergello (Vergelli), Giovanni Maria, 472

Vergil, 23, 27, 93f., 96f., 202, 219, 386, 517, 710, 808, 838

Verità, Marco, 721

Veronese, Paolo, 451, 523, 544, 799, 861

Verovio, Simone, 780, 782, 834, 855

Verrecore, Armanno (Alemanno?), 425

Vespasiano Gonzaga, *see* Gonzaga

Vicentino, Michele, 41, 126f., 135, 136, 138

Vicentino, Nicolo (Nicola), 221, 222, 224, 225, 228, 230, 324, 385, 411, 412f., 414, 678, 705, 825

Vicomanni, 542

Vicus, A., 150

Vigne, de, 56

Villano, Giuseppe, 198

Villon, François, 30

Vincenet, 7

Vincenti, Giacomo, 166, 653, 660, 800, 801

Vincenzo Gonzaga, *see* Gonzaga

Vinci, Leonardo da, 11, 18, 38, 42, 49, 112, 264

Vinci, Pietro, 203, 671, 687, 731, 773

Vinciguerra, Gaspare, 525

Vinta, Belisario, 846

Viola, Alfonso della, 206, 284, 300ff., 306, 307, 407, 481, 540, 551, 825

Viola, Andrea della, 301

Viola, Francesco, 324, 334, 386, 440

Viola, Giampietro della, 35, 42

Viola, Marc'Antonio dalla, 472

Viola, Orazio della, 828

Virchi, Paolo, 829

Virginia de'Medici, *see* Medici

Visconti, Cesare, 264

Visconti, Filippo Maria, 9

Visconti, Gasparo, 45

Visconti, Gian Galeazzo, 9, 10f.

Visconti, Valentine, 9

Visconti family, 9f.

Visdomini, Sisto, 774

Vitali, Bernardino de, 49

Vitali, Filippo, 729

Vitaliano, Mattio, 472

Vitry, Philippe de, 13

Vittorino, *see* Feltre

Vivonne, Jean de (Pisani), 660

Waelrant, Hubert, 324, 584

Wagner, Richard, 4, 167, 168, 203f., 280, 398, 424, 570, 609, 688, 714, 756, 764, 804

Weinlig, Chr. Th., 609

Wenceslaus, King, 9

Werbecke, Caspar van, 7, 10, 11, 121

Werrecore, Matthias (Mathias), 743ff., 750

Werrewick, *see* Verovio

Wert, Giaches (de), 20, 96, 208, 210, 220, 221, 238, 240, 243, 244, 275, 415, 422, 477, 479, 502, 511ff., 529, 542, 545, 553, 561, 567, 568ff., 602, 603, 610, 612, 639, 643, 644, 663, 671, 683, 684, 686, 698, 699, 723, 724, 725, 726, 730, 751, 761, 765, 769, 784, 825, 827, 828, 831f., 845

Wilhelm V of Bavaria, 495, 496, 577, 762, 774

Willaert, Adrian, 4, 20, 21, 22, 29, 114f., 138, 140, 149, 152, 154, 156, 166, 171, 179, 181, 198f., 200, 221, 224, 226, 228, 246, 247, 248, 249, 250, 252, 254, 257, 258,

262, 266, 270, 289, 298, 306, 310, 318ff., 351, 378, 380, 381f., 383, 384, 388, 390, 399, 403, 409, 411, 412, 415, 416, 418, 421, 423, 430, 433, 438, 439, 443, 445f., 446, 447, 448, 449, 450, 452, 453, 454, 461, 467, 478, 481, 486, 487, 491, 496, 503, 506, 511, 520, 522, 529, 532, 554, 568, 576, 584, 607, 612, 620, 715, 722, 825, 840, 850

Winterfeld, Carl von, 238, 619, 624, 653, 658, 709

Wolf, Hugo, 90, 167, 168, 170

Wytzel, Georg, 439

Ycaert, 8

Yonge, Nicholas, 615

Ysaac, Heinrich, 6, 19ff., 31ff., 54, 56, 75, 85, 125, 130, 226, 259, 283, 353, 451, 825

Yvo, *see* Barre

Zacconi, Lodovico, 312, 335, 410, 501, 512

Zambo del Val Brembana, 596

Zanluca, Ippolito, 476

Zanotti, Camillo, 542

Zantani, Antonio, 446

Zappasorgo, Giovanni, 584f.

Zarlino, Gioseffo, 5, 208, 227, 228, 229, 235, 242, 319, 322, 324, 335, 352, 388, 392, 412, 445, 448, 453f., 522, 549, 550, 568, 678, 705, 732, 799, 821, 836, 837, 838, 842, 843, 848, 850, 858

Zedler, J. H., 478

Zeferini, Ippolita, 731

Zeferini, P. L., 731

Zelter, Carl Friedrich, 170, 624

Zesso, G. B., 41, 341f.

Zocolo (Zocholo), P. de, 5

Zoilo, Annibale, 474, 697, 854, 855

Zuccarini, G. B., 323, 638f., 646, 776

Zuchello, Andrea, 458

INDEX OF PLACES

Agnadello, 318

Albany, 365

Alessandria, 194

Amalfi, 352

Amsterdam, 5

Ancona, 195, 593

Antwerp, 5, 7, 384, 386, 387, 414, 424, 432, 480, 485, 491, 496, 498, 499, 500, 501, 593

Apulia, 576, 598

Aquila, 387

Arcetri (near Florence), 291

Arezzo, 169, 279, 281, 293, 416

Argenta, 211, 754

Asolo, 109f.

Assisi, 136

Augsburg, 388, 498, 512, 522, 576, 772, 774, 781

Avignon, 7, 24, 240

Baiae, 255, 264

Bari, 591, 598, 689

Barletta, 576, 741

Benevento, 382

Berchem, 432

Bergamo, 11, 148, 199, 203, 293, 294, 296, 344, 346, 347, 351, 389,

527, 535, 731, 750, 768, 773, 805, 818, 827, 844
Berlin, 438f., 797
Bicocca, 744
Blois, 56, 629
Bohemia, 522
Bologna, 8, 11, 47, 54, 94, 140, 157, 165, 181, 203, 224, 230, 250, 257, 298, 307f., 319, 320, 325, 346, 348, 351, 360, 411, 413, 469, 472, 493, 526, 535, 645, 668, 730, 734, 735, 750, 757, 771, 773, 774, 796, 802f., 811, 848, 872
Borgo San Sepolcro, 801
Bosnia, 107
Bracciano, 499, 506, 611, 667
Brenner, 478
Brescia, 40, 123, 445, 447, 608, 609, 624, 626, 641, 772, 773, 829
Brussels, 387, 498
Burano, 800

Calabria, 527, 626
Camaldoli, 834
Cambrai, 57
Campania, 512, 614
Canareggio (Venice), 488, 521, 522
Candia (Crete), 528
Capri, 352
Capua, 366
Caravaggio, 602
Carpentras, 154
Casale, 43, 46
Caserta, 360
Castelfranco (Veneto), 155
Cerreto Guidi, Castello, 500
Cesena, 755, 825
Chioggia, 494, 550, 799, 805, 811, 813, 816, 856
Cittaducale, 387
Civita Castellana, 618, 868
Coccaglio, 608, 609
Cologne, 802
Copenhagen, 226
Corduba, 576
Corfu, 528
Correggio, 247, 598, 774
Cortona, 31
Cracow, 5, 600, 611, 675
Crema, 114f., 670
Cremona, 51, 393, 600, 615, 717, 826
Cyprus, 527

Dalmatia, 596
Denmark, 797
Dijon, 8
Dolo, 809
Dresden, 609

Empoli, 500, 848

England, 480, 499, 604, 607, 615, 671, 761
Erfurt, 451

Faenza, 8
Feltre, 155, 776
Ferrara, 5, 8, 20, 34, 39, 43, 44, 46, 47, 53, 82, 93, 94, 109, 140, 156, 165, 192, 195, 206, 213, 214, 228, 243, 284, 298, 300f., 318, 319, 325, 334, 344, 345, 378f., 380, 385f., 387, 391f., 393, 403, 407, 413, 414, 424, 433, 447, 476, 478, 479, 481, 512, 513, 515, 539, 540, 549, 554, 555, 556, 568, 569, 573, 603, 608, 610, 618, 626, 627, 639, 648, 663, 669, 670, 671, 675, 690, 695, 698, 703, 704, 705, 706, 721, 723, 724, 726, 728, 730, 754, 755, 762, 768, 769, 770, 773, 774, 775, 817, 825f., 842, 844f., 846, 855, 859, 867
Fiesole, 14
Flanders, 480, 488, 614, 757, 761
Florence, 5, 6, 12f., 17, 19ff., 24ff., 27, 30ff., 34, 38, 39, 40, 47, 53, 59, 77, 78, 79, 81, 95, 96, 99, 106, 107, 108, 109, 113, 127, 128, 129, 130, 135, 140, 141, 151, 155, 156, 157, 158, 159f., 161, 162, 164, 165, 169, 180, 187, 189, 192, 193f., 197, 198, 200, 201, 206, 216, 233, 246, 259, 262, 267, 271, 272, 273, 276ff., 289, 290, 291, 294f., 297, 300, 301, 306, 316, 318, 327, 341, 342, 344, 354, 378, 407, 423, 424, 428, 429, 447, 451, 458, 463, 479, 483, 499, 500, 508, 516, 531, 545, 550, 552, 565, 567, 603, 611, 626, 629, 634, 645, 653, 662, 666, 667, 669, 682, 683, 705, 718, 729, 730, 736, 761, 768, 775, 780, 781, 800, 810, 811, 823, 828, 831, 834, 836, 839, 841, 844, 845, 846, 847, 848, 855, 858, 867
Fontainebleau, 479
Forlì, 114, 213
Fossombrone, 55f., 171
France, 52, 215, 427, 450, 478, 499, 546, 565, 595, 604, 722, 744, 748, 761, 766, 781, 865
Frankfurt on the Oder, 225
Frascati, 593
Friuli, 800
Frosinone, 382
Fusina, 809

Gaëta, 352
Gagliano, 729
Garda, Lago di, 467

Genoa, 27, 34, 194, 197, 206, 424, 449, 463, 472, 479, 498, 499, 641, 695, 770, 847
Germany, 392f., 478, 499, 604, 607, 614, 744
Gesualdo, 689, 692
Ghent, 499
Graz, 522, 757, 763, 859
Guastalla, 479

Hainaut, 477
Hamburg, 609
Hampton Court, 516
Hertogenbosch, 855
Horn, County of, 512
Hungary, 319, 324, 812

Imola, 802
Innsbruck, 19

Königsberg, 5, 226

La Cava, 359
Lanciano, 626
Leipzig, 402, 475
Lepanto, 38, 195, 523, 549, 596f.
Levant, 527
Leyden, 501
Liége, 159
Lodi, 9, 41, 456
Lombardy, 140, 215, 365, 576, 604, 768, 770, 773, 788
London, 5, 78, 247, 498, 530, 593, 604
Loreto, 593, 775, 860, 866
Louvain, 500, 501
Lovrana, 40
Lucca, 8, 41, 730, 802, 810
Lübeck, 298
Lyons, 135, 165, 264, 268, 279, 280, 288, 311

Macerata, 593
Madrid, 182
Malines (Mecheln), 384, 498, 499, 500
Mandragone, 479
Mantova (Mantua), 5, 12, 17, 30, 34ff., 38ff., 44f., 49, 51f., 68, 79, 82, 93, 106, 107, 108, 109, 110, 114, 199, 211, 233, 240, 276, 318, 330, 344, 346, 352, 366, 458, 463, 478, 479, 512, 513, 514, 516, 518, 540, 548, 561, 569, 573, 600, 602, 603, 604, 608, 609, 610, 611, 626, 627, 638, 662, 671, 683, 721, 726, 729, 730, 741, 750f., 755, 761, 762, 768, 769, 774, 784, 819, 826, 827, 828, 831, 833, 834, 846, 848, 850, 854, 858, 861, 866, 867
Marche, 809

Marignano, 143, 744
Mazorbo (?), 803
Miglionico, 223, 583
Milan (Milano), 8, 9ff., 27, 34, 40,
    41, 51, 53, 57, 82, 85, 87f., 89,
    114, 120, 163, 166, 193, 194, 197,
    264, 277, 294, 316, 318, 338, 344,
    352, 411, 424, 425f., 427, 458,
    462, 463, 479, 480, 561, 599, 600,
    602, 637, 683, 743, 744, 750, 761,
    769, 770, 771, 801, 802, 806, 859
Modena, 41, 52, 89, 166, 182, 297,
    298, 319f., 342, 513, 690, 768,
    772ff., 774, 798, 802, 819, 827
Monferrato, 43, 44, 46
Mons, 477, 478
Monselice, 195
Montefeltre, 213
Monteleone, 382
Montepulciano, 404
Montesangiovanni, 382
Montona, *see* Antico, Andrea
Montpellier, 360
Monza, 166
Munich (München), 5, 53, 228, 386,
    422, 424, 479, 480, 481f., 486,
    491, 495, 500, 522, 577, 597, 600,
    762, 828
Murano (Venice), 577, 803

Naples, 4, 8, 27, 28, 34, 37, 39, 53,
    58, 89, 91, 100, 113, 114, 204,
    206, 215, 223, 225, 259, 338,
    352ff., 365, 366, 372, 373, 378,
    381, 382, 383, 405, 433, 449,
    477, 479, 480, 481, 497, 498,
    499, 500, 501, 503, 512, 516,
    527, 548, 567, 576, 577, 578,
    580f., 594, 598, 601, 608, 617,
    688, 689, 690, 697, 699, 701,
    717, 730, 750, 757, 770, 788, 811,
    829, 832, 840, 842, 843, 855
New York, 135, 258
Nice (Nizza), 428, 500, 545, 645,
    730
Nicosia, 731
Nola, 353f.
Novara, 770, 772
Noventa, 147
Noyon, 348
Nuremberg, 53, 159, 225, 262, 439,
    593, 604, 744
Nuvolara (Novellara), 208, 512f.

Orvieto, 75, 262

Padua (Padova), 7, 13, 40, 41, 56,
    57, 68f., 94, 108, 136, 184, 203,
    214, 340, 341, 344, 345, 346, 385,
    439, 447, 460, 471f., 472, 473,
    474, 475, 476, 577, 593, 750, 754,

757, 760, 781, 800, 801, 808f.,
    812, 825
Paestum, 352
Palermo, 479, 717
Palestina, 527, 626
Palestrina, 312, 313, 488
Paris, 5, 139, 162, 165, 195, 319,
    496, 497, 549, 604, 610, 629, 782
Parma, 332, 384, 386, 387, 388, 389,
    394, 423, 424, 475, 522, 577, 718
Pavia, 10, 39, 52, 89, 113, 194, 353,
    743, 744
Perugia, 27, 179, 189, 356, 613
Pesaro, 6, 16, 195, 308, 463, 860
Piacenza, 149, 172, 174, 194, 196,
    197, 198, 318, 445, 447, 600
Piedmont, 264, 479
Pinguiento, 165
Pisa, 19, 27, 39, 78, 129, 277, 288,
    705, 805
Pistoia, 27, 189, 288, 380, 462, 463
Po, 755
Poggio, 569
Pola, 165
Poland, 549, 611
Pontinian marshes, 352
Pordenone, 5
Portugal, 554
Prague, 482, 500, 501, 502, 775, 829
Provence, 280, 744
Prussia, 772

Ratisbon, 298, 501
Ravenna, 830
Reggio, 196, 285, 479, 774, 819
Rennes, 49
Rhine, Rhineland, 491, 522, 757
Rimini, 16, 18
Romagna, 56
Rome, 7, 27, 34, 35f., 37, 39, 40,
    79, 86, 89, 94, 109, 110, 114, 126,
    132, 139, 140, 149, 154, 156, 157,
    159f., 161, 165, 166, 175f., 180,
    181, 188, 194, 202, 205, 206, 208,
    213, 214, 226, 257, 262, 271, 275,
    276, 277, 289, 296, 297, 306, 308,
    314, 319, 320, 346, 353, 355, 365,
    366, 369, 373, 382, 385, 393, 413,
    414, 422, 424, 425, 429, 431, 436,
    463, 479f., 480, 481, 492, 494,
    497, 498, 499, 500, 503, 505, 506,
    507, 508, 514, 518, 549, 586, 592,
    593, 608, 609, 610, 611, 612, 613,
    618, 619, 623, 624, 626, 628, 629,
    637, 638, 639, 640, 645, 653, 667,
    669, 671, 689, 690, 692, 697, 730,
    761, 767, 768, 769, 775, 780, 782,
    789, 805, 808, 834, 844, 847, 848,
    849, 854, 855, 856, 866, 867, 868,
    871, 872

Ronciglione, 603
Rotterdam, 604
Roulers (Rosselaere), 319
Rovigo, 803

Sabbioneta, 834
Sacile, 463
Saint Didier, 478
Salerno, 209, 359, 512
Saluzzo, 746
Savoy, 16, 645
Schio (Veneto), 645
Schmalkalden, 393
Seville, 59, 130
Sicily, 4, 203, 478, 479, 717, 731,
    770
Siena, 27, 39, 41, 58, 81, 90, 97,
    141, 214, 242, 297, 344, 352, 618,
    731, 757, 761, 796f., 802, 805
Sorrento, 352
Spain, 215, 479, 564, 583, 600, 619,
    770, 841
Stettin, 226
Strà, 809
Switzerland, 744

Tagliacozzo, 479
Tarvis, 472
Terracina, 352
Thuringia, 489
Tivoli, 333, 472, 609, 612
Torresella, 51
Tournai, 481
Trent (Trento), 58, 382, 385, 393,
    414, 463, 600, 609
Treviso, 8, 41, 193, 219, 321, 456,
    458, 460, 525, 577, 584
Turin (Torino), 9, 157, 514, 603,
    770
Tuscany, 87, 90, 114, 169, 215, 277,
    343, 352, 453, 508, 610, 642, 767,
    802, 804, 821

Udine, 203
Uliveto, 277
Umbria, 169
Ungheria, *see* Hungary
Urbino, 34, 35, 42, 44, 82, 106, 107,
    108, 109, 110, 180, 195, 213, 293,
    313, 433, 447, 535, 546, 610, 612,
    681, 859, 860

Val Camonega (Camonegha), 805
Valenciennes, 689, 697
Venice (Venezia), 4, 6, 8, 9, 14, 17,
    27, 30, 34, 38, 39, 40, 47, 48, 49,
    52, 55, 56f., 69, 79, 82, 85, 87,
    88, 91, 92, 94, 97, 107, 109, 110,
    114, 123, 140, 154f., 157, 164,
    165, 166, 169, 173, 175, 176, 181,
    184, 192, 193, 195, 196, 197, 198,

INDEX

201, 206, 221, 224, 227, 249, 262,
276, 278, 279, 290, 294, 296, 297,
308, 314, 316, 318ff., 338, 340,
344, 346, 347, 348, 352, 354, 368,
369, 372, 373, 378, 380, 381, 384,
388, 400, 401, 407, 409, 411, 412,
413, 417, 424, 425, 432, 433, 436,
438, 439, 440, 442, 443, 444, 445,
446, 447, 448, 451, 453, 454, 456,
460, 461, 472, 473, 474, 480, 497,
498, 500, 502, 505, 511, 518,
520f., 546, 549, 550, 551, 567,
577, 578, 581, 582, 593, 596, 601,
604, 609, 610, 611, 615, 622, 626,
631, 638, 639, 650, 653, 660, 662,

667, 671, 681, 692, 695, 699, 705,
710, 721, 722, 730, 732, 736, 743,
744, 750, 754, 757, 763, 768, 769,
770, 773, 774, 775, 782, 789, 793,
797, 798f., 801, 802, 803, 808f.,
812, 819, 842, 843, 854, 855, 858,
861, 863, 867

Venosa, 548
Verona, 9, 13, 40, 41, 42, 51, 65,
110, 192ff., 244, 307, 320, 411,
432, 447, 455, 456, 461, 462, 463,
464, 467, 468, 471, 476, 482, 483,
491, 502, 511, 520, 521, 548, 609,
610, 627, 630, 662, 717, 718, 749,
773, 799, 800, 855

Vicenza, 40, 48, 111, 192, 432, 456,
458, 471, 523, 529, 549, 795, 819
Vienna (Wien), 5, 20, 78, 135, 193,
247, 424, 447, 500, 502, 509, 768,
775, 829
Vigorso (?), 598
Viterbo, 6
Vitre, 49
Vorarlberg, 757

Westphalia, 812
Wismar, 226
Wittenberg, 225
Wolfenbüttel, 135, 354

ADDENDA ET CORRIGENDA

VOLUME I

Page 41, line 29: page 91 *instead of* page 89

Page 59, line 22: Vokalmusik *instead of* Vokalmusick

Page 99, line 16: pastorale *instead of* postorale

Page 113, par. 2, lines 10 and 15: The collection of 1520 from which the name of the printer is missing is probably a publication of Giunta's and not of Petrucci's. See also p. 128, line 1f.

Page 140, line 31: "But this print also remains an isolated phenomenon." This refers only to the canonic form of Antico's print. There are, of course, numerous Venetian editions of French chansons, and Andrea Antico himself commissioned Ottaviano Scotto to print several between 1530 and 1540.

Page 150, last line and f.: "It is the first victory of music over the text." This seems to be a contradiction to the aesthetics of the sixteenth century that music is subordinated to the words. The motet-like style, however, as a transition from the song-style, establishes the supremacy of music just the same.

Page 163, lines 23ff.: The spurious first edition of Arcadelt's *Secondo libro* has been brought to light in the meantime: the cantus part of it is in the library of Mr. W. N. H. Harding in Chicago, Ill. The date is 1539; no printer given, but most probably Ottaviano Scotto commissioned by Andrea Antico da Montona. It contains twenty-five numbers of which only a few seem actually to be Arcadelt's compositions.

Page 192, line 2: Turrini *instead of* Turini

Page 238, par. 3, line 4: Winterfeld *instead of* Winterfield

Page 260, line 1: ". . . they were never collected in a single print devoted exclusively to him. . . ." This is not correct. Mr. W. N. H. Harding in Chicago owns the cantus of *Madrigale de M. Constantio Festa Libro Primo* . . . 1538 [probably Ottaviano Scotto], containing twenty-two numbers for four voices, two for five voices, and one for six, of which one of the two for five voices and the madrigal for six voices ("Cosi extrema è la doglia") are reprinted in other editions of Verdelot's (Vogel's Bibliography 1 and 6ᵃ). The greater part of the numbers for four voices are not to be found elsewhere.

Page 270, example, note 6 of the middle part: *add* punctum

Page 290, par. 3, line 9: campagne *instead of* campagni

Page 293, lines 6 and 7: delle Rovere *instead of* della Rovere

Page 293, last line of par. 2: S'i *instead of* Si

Page 295, line 14: Da poi *instead of* Da soi

Page 333, example, meas. 10, upper part: *add* punctum

Page 346, par. 2, line 13: Ai maroni *instead of* Al maroni

Page 392, example, meas. 6, alto: *add* punctum

Page 430, par. 2, line 12: *read* he shows us at times what . . .

Page 437, line 8: poneste *instead of* ponesti

ADDENDA ET CORRIGENDA
VOLUME II

Page 535, example, meas. 4, tenor: *add* punctum

Page 571, example, meas. 3, cantus: *add* punctum

Page 771, example: A chanson with the text and the melody of "A Paris sur [le] petit pont" is to be found as No. 12 in the *Canzoni francese di Messer Adriano, & de altri . . . Libro primo,* 1536.